William Massey

History of England

During the Reign of George the Third

William Massey

History of England
During the Reign of George the Third

ISBN/EAN: 9783741179082

Manufactured in Europe, USA, Canada, Australia, Japa

Cover: Foto ©ninafisch / pixelio.de

Manufactured and distributed by brebook publishing software (www.brebook.com)

William Massey

History of England

A

HISTORY OF ENGLAND

DURING THE

REIGN OF GEORGE THE THIRD.

BY

THE RIGHT HON.

WILLIAM MASSEY.

SECOND EDITION, REVISED AND CORRECTED.

IN FOUR VOLUMES.

VOL. III.

1782 — 1795.

LONDON:
LONGMANS, GREEN, AND CO.
1865.

CONTENTS
OF
THE THIRD VOLUME.

CHAPTER XXVII.

War with France and Spain—Rodney's Victory—Blockade of the Dutch Ports—Siege of Gibraltar—Negotiations for Peace—Provisional Treaty concluded—The Coalition—Shelburne's Resignation—Rockingham Party—Parliamentary Reform—Treaties of Peace.

	PAGE
Affairs in America	1
Washington's apprehensions as to relaxation	2
Siege of Gibraltar	3
Rodney's victory	4
Exultation in England	5
Whig dislike to Rodney	8
Public astonishment at Rodney's recall	9
Negotiations with France	10
Firmness of the garrison of Gibraltar	13
Floating batteries	14
Loss of the besiegers	15
Blockade a mere form	16
Negotiations for peace with the United States	16
Question of compensation	17
Claims of the Loyalists	18
Provisional treaty	19
Unfair treatment of the French	20
Pretensions of France and Spain	21
Defection of America	22
Concessions to France	23
Efforts of Spain to recover Gibraltar	23
Preliminaries of peace signed	24

	PAGE
Shelburne opposed by the Rockingham party	25
Intimidation of the Government	26
Virulence of Opposition	26
The treaties condemned	27
Amendment to the Address	27
Resignation of Lord Shelburne	28
Death of Rockingham	31
Virulence of Fox and Burke	31
The Coalition Ministry	32
Propositions of Fox and Pitt	32
Lord North's refusal of office	33
Formation of a new Ministry	33
Rupture in the Coalition	35
State of parties	36
Pitt's plan of reform	37
Opposition of Lord North	38
Irish courts of justice	38
Termination of the War of Independence	39
Unforeseen consequences of the struggle	40
Causes of the war	41
Supremacy of George the Third	42
English indifference to American affairs	42
Negligence of the royal troops	44
Institution of Congress	45
Vigour of its earlier conduct	46
Authority of Congress	47
Washington's difficulties	47
Washington as a general	48
Purity of Washington	49

CHAPTER XXVIII.

India and the India Bills—Dismissal of the Coalition Ministry—Pitt Prime Minister—Great Struggle in the House of Commons—Dissolution of Parliament.

Indian affairs	51
Sovereign power of the Company	52
Difficulties of governing India	52
Consequences of oppression	53
Regulating Act	54
Exposure of mal-practices	55
Proposition of Dundas	56
King's speech	57
Importance of India	57
Opening of the session	59
Proposed transfer of power to the Crown	61
Monopolies to be abolished	62

	PAGE
Provisions of the India Bill	62
Defects of the measure	63
Anomalous position of the Whigs	63
Burke's opinion of the proceedings in India	64
Unpopularity of the Coalition	65
The King's dislike of the Coalition	66
Pitt and Grenville	66
Fox and Burke's defence of the Bill	68
Burke's great speech	69
Erskine's failure	71
Conduct of the King	71
Baker's resolution as to the King's conduct	72
Opposition to Baker's resolution	73
Bold conduct of Fox	74
The King's imperious conduct	75
Nature of royal responsibility	76
The King's want of openness	76
Factious proceeding of the Whigs	78
Defeat of the India Bill	79
Factious proceedings of the Whigs	88
A dissolution of Parliament inevitable	89
Conduct of the Opposition	89
Fox obtains leave to bring in a fresh Bill	90
Agitation in the Commons	90
An attempt to form a new Coalition	91
Mr. Grosvenor's motion	92
Public meetings	93
Virulence of the Opposition	94
Determined conduct of the King	94
Votes as to want of confidence	94
Inflammatory language of Fox	95

CHAPTER XXIX.

Termination of the Struggle between the King and the Whig Party—General Elections—Pitt's Financial Measures—State of Ireland—India Bill—Sinking Fund—Reform Bill.

George the Third's determined opposition to the Whigs	97
The King's tortuous policy	98
Obloquy thrown upon the King	99
Weakness of George the First and George the Second	100
Unpopularity of Lord North	101
Whig want of unanimity	101
Case of Powell and Bembridge	103
Great popularity of Pitt	106
Wilberforce returned for Yorkshire	107

	PAGE
Meeting of the new Parliament	108
Westminster election	108
Pitt's impolitic conduct	109
Pitt's financial measures	109
Indian affairs	111
The India Bill probably prepared by Dundas	112
Civilization of India	113
Hindoos accustomed to despotic power	114
Close of the session	115
Pitt's letter to the Irish minister	115
The Irish volunteers	115
Prevalence of corruption	117
Distribution of parliamentary influence	118
Flood's measure	119
Ferocious conduct of the mob	120
Shop-keepers and priests implicated	120
Scene at a dinner-table	121
Critical state of Ireland	125
Pitt's plan of policy	125
Reasonableness of Pitt's plan	127
Opposition of the trading interest	129
Stormy debate	131
Propriety of Pitt's scheme	132
Want of interest in reform	134
Bill for regulating public offices	136
Pitt's measure carried	137
Attempt to reduce the national debt	138
The time favourable for the reduction of the debt	139
Plans for paying off the debt	140
Hastings' reception in England	143
Burke and Francis	144
Hastings heard at the bar of the House	144
The Rohilla war	145
Cheyte Sing	146
Reasons for Pitt's change of opinion	149
Commercial treaties with France	150
The new treaty signed	151
Consolidation of Customs and Excise	152
The Prince of Wales	153
The Prince reduces his establishment	156
The Prince Regent's affairs	160
Rolle's reply to Fox	161
Deception practised on Fox	162
Indignation of Fox	164
English dislike to Romanism	165
Duplicity of the Prince	167
Impeachment of Hastings	168
Impeachment of Impey	169
Opening of proceedings against Hastings	171
Burke's oration	171

	PAGE
Nature of State impeachments	173
The Benares charge	174
Prosecution of Stockdale	175

CHAPTER XXX.

The Slave Trade—King's Illness—Debates on the Regency—Claims of the Heir-apparent—Recovery of the King—Conduct of the Prince—Firmness and Prudence of Pitt—Pitt's Colleagues—Proceedings in Ireland—Thurlow—Divisions in the Royal Family—Wilberforce—Stamps on Newspapers—Addington chosen Speaker.

The slave trade	178
Wilberforce	179
Examination of delegates	179
Whitbread	180
The King's health	182
Prorogation of Parliament	182
Public excitement	183
Pitt's denunciation of Fox's proposal	184
Imprudence of Fox	185
Burke's attack on Pitt	186
Fox's attempt at explanation	187
Blunder of Fox	188
Real question to be considered	189
Pitt's resolutions	190
Modes of parliamentary delay	191
Lord North's motion	192
Effect of Pitt's speech	193
Speeches of the Royal Dukes	194
Thurlow's conduct	194
Hopes of the King's recovery	195
Dempster's amendment	196
Grenville elected Speaker	197
Proposed restrictions on the Regent	197
Names of physicians appointed	198
Confidence of the Queen and Pitt in Dr. Willis	199
Pitt's speech	201
Charge against the Queen	202
Second reading carried without a division	204
Bill passed in the Commons	205
Dr. Willis's opinion	206
Treatment of the King at Kew	208
Reception of Dr. Willis	209
Violent party spirit	212
Difficulties of Pitt's position	213

	PAGE
Dundas	219
The King's interview with Thurlow	220
General thanksgiving	221
Singular delusion of the King	222
Disagreements in the royal family	223
Wilberforce's speech on slavery	225
Tobacco duties	226
Grenville succeeds Lord Sidney	228
Addington's antecedents	229

CHAPTER XXXI.

French Revolution—Affair of Nootka Sound—The Test Act—A New Parliament—Abatement of Impeachment by Dissolution—The Slave Trade—The Russian Armament—Separation of Burke from the Whig Party—Progress of the French Revolution—Riots at Birmingham.

Russian policy	231
French policy	232
French National Assembly	235
Opinions in England	235
Burke's protest	237
Retractation of Fox	238
Rupture with Spain	241
Question of parliamentary reform	243
Parliament dissolved	245
Religious liberty	249
Right of juries in cases of libel	249
Wilberforce's motion	251
Case of Oczakow	251
Breaking-up of the Whig party	253
Canada Bill	254
Opposition of Fox	255
Quebec Bill	256
Fox's visit to Burke	256
Burke's violent speech on the Canada Bill	257
Lord Sheffield's motion	258
Burke's reply to Fox	259
Coolness between Burke and Fox	260
Fox's complaint against Burke	261
Severance of Burke from Fox's party	261
Fox inclined to retract	261
Close of the Session	263
Seditious publications	263
Sir James Macintosh's 'Vindiciæ Gallicæ'	264
Revolution Society	265
Dr. Priestley	266
Birmingham riots	268

CHAPTER XXXII.

Anticipation of Prolonged Peace—The 'Friends of the People'—Proclamation against Seditious Publications—The Slave Question—Invasion of France by the German Powers—Its Effects on the Revolution—Schism in the Whig Party—The Militia called out—The Alien Bill—Rupture with France—Declaration of War.

	PAGE
Surplus revenue	270
Movements of the Opposition	270
The Budget	272
Seditious publications	273
Conduct of the French minister	274
Address to the Crown	274
The Prince's speech	275
Exertions of the anti-slavery party	276
Motion to repeal the Test Acts	277
Negotiations with Austria and Prussia	279
Dilatory proceedings of the Allies	280
The Jacobins	280
First successes of the Allies	281
Effect of the war in England	282
Paine's 'Rights of Man'	283
Measures taken against sedition	284
The militia embodied	284
Dismissal of Thurlow	284
Failure of attempts to conciliate the Whigs	286
Pitt made Warden of the Cinque Ports	289
The King's speech	290
Windham	291
Attempts to intimidate Windham	293
Lord Grenville's Bill	294
The Alien Bill	296
Non-recognition of Chauvelin	298
Grenville's reply to Chauvelin	299
Declaration of war	300
Message from the Crown	301
Pitt's speech	301
French occupation of Belgium	302
French proposals	302
Final declaration of war	303

CHAPTER XXXIII.

The War with France—Misconduct of the Allies—State of France—Public Opinion in England—Prosecutions of the Press.

War with France	304
Disinclination of the Ministry for war	304
Admissions of Fox	307
Fox's amendment negatived	308
Fox's resolutions	308
Burke's reply to Fox	309
Alliance against France	310
The French in the Netherlands	310
Harsh conduct of the French	310
Plans of Dumourier	311
Defection of Dumourier	312
The Duke of York in Flanders	313
Liberation of the garrison	317
Defeat of Freytag	318
Surrender of Quesnoy	320
The Prussians at Mentz	320
Captures in the West Indies	323
End of the first campaign	324
The Rule of Terror	329
Conduct of the Whigs	330
Intemperate language of Fox	330
Moderate proceedings not to be expected in France	333
Conduct of Pitt	335
Seditious clubs	336
Exasperation of France	338
Repressive measures of Pitt	338
Petty State prosecutions	339
Severe sentences against inferior agents	340
Society for Constitutional Information	341
Prosecution of Winterbotham	343
Duffin and Lloyd's case	343
Proceedings against the press	346
London publishers	347
Ridgway's sentence	348
Subserviency of the judges	348
Movement for parliamentary reform	352
Thomas Muir	353
Palmer's case	355
Undue severity of the Scottish Courts	355
Traitorous Correspondence Bill	360

CHAPTER XXXIV.

Foreign Mercenaries and Volunteers—Trials for Treason—Hardy, Thelwall, Horne Tooke.

	PAGE
Public dislike to the Duke of York	359
Importation of foreign troops	361
Enrolment of volunteers	361
Sheridan's resolution	362
Defence of the Government	363
Raising of local battalions	363
Renewed proceedings against seditious writings	364
Vigilance of the Government	365
Corresponding Society	366
Impolitic measures	368
Provincial prosecutions	368
Prosecution of Walker and others	369
Case of Watt and Downie	371
Horne Tooke and others	371
La Motte, Lord George Gordon	372
Rash proceedings of the Government	373
Trial of Hardy	375
Partiality of the judges	377
Erskine's cross-examination of witnesses	378
John Horne Tooke	385
Effrontery of Tooke	387
Major Cartwright	389
Thelwall	391
Beneficial results of the trials	392

CHAPTER XXXV.

Progress of the War—Action of the First of June—Marriage of the Prince of Wales—Conclusion of Hastings' Trial.

French affairs	396
Escape of the Emperor	398
Check of Pichegru	399
Proclamation of the Emperor	400
Fall of the Belgian fortifications	401
Recapture of the Flemish fortresses	401
Dutch population in favour of the French	402
Corsica, Paoli	402
British expedition to the West Indies	403
Campaign on the Rhine	403
Austrians cross the Rhine	403
England successful at sea	405

	PAGE
Pressure of taxation	407
Determination to continue the war	409
Proceedings of the Opposition	412
Intemperate language of Pitt	413
Loan to Austria	414
Affairs of the Prince of Wales	414
Unwise conduct of Lord Malmesbury	415
Separation of the Prince and Princess	417
The Prince's establishment	418
Reception of the royal message	419
Pitt's proposal to relieve the Prince	420
Bribery and plunder attributed to Clive	427
Retirement of Hastings	428

A HISTORY OF ENGLAND

DURING THE

REIGN OF GEORGE THE THIRD.

CHAPTER XXVII.

WAR WITH FRANCE AND SPAIN—RODNEY'S VICTORY—BLOCKADE OF THE DUTCH PORTS—SIEGE OF GIBRALTAR—NEGOTIATIONS FOR PEACE—PROVISIONAL TREATY CONCLUDED—THE COALITION—SHELBURNE'S RESIGNATION—ROCKINGHAM PARTY—PARLIAMENTARY REFORM—TREATIES OF PEACE.

EARLY in the year, Sir Henry Clinton was informed of the determination of the Government to discontinue active operations on the continent of America; and that the military establishment in that country would be recruited only on a scale sufficient to maintain the posts and districts already in the occupation of British forces.

This determination, together with the inadequate provisions which had been made by the capitulation of York Town, for the protection of the Loyalists, spread great discontent and alarm among the adherents of British connection. The animosity between the two parties—those who were in arms for independence, and those who maintained their allegiance to the Crown—necessarily assumed all the virulence of civil warfare. The Loyalists, who fell into the hands

of their rebellious countrymen, were treated with
much greater severity than ordinary prisoners of war;
the Loyalists retaliated, and many irregularities were
doubtless committed. At length an incident occurred
which obliged the commanders on both sides to interpose for the purpose of putting an end to these
enormities. One White, a member of an armed
association of Loyalists at New York, having been
betrayed into the hands of the opposite party, and
put to death, the Loyalists retaliated upon Huddy,
an officer of Congress, whom they had made prisoner.
The American was hanged, under the direction of
Captain Lippincot, who assumed to act by the order
of the association. Sir Henry Clinton, resenting this
audacious invasion of his authority, and wishing to
check such barbarous proceedings, caused Lippincot
to be arrested and tried for murder. Washington, on
the other hand, incensed at such an outrage on a
prisoner of war, demanded that the perpetrator should
be given up; and on Clinton's refusal, he ordered that
an officer of equal rank with Huddy should be chosen
by lot, from among the prisoners of York Town, and
publicly executed. The lot fell upon Captain Asgill,
a young officer of the guards, only nineteen years of
age. The Congress urged that this cruel sentence
should be carried into effect; but Washington, with
that instinct of humanity which popular assemblies
rarely exhibit, still delayed execution, until the
generous intercession of the French Court afforded
him a sufficient excuse for releasing the English
officer.

When the resolution of the British Government to
desist from any further efforts to conquer
the territory of the United States was
promulgated in America, Washington, far
from welcoming the intelligence as the triumph of
his cause, became apprehensive, lest his countrymen,
who had shown so strong a disposition to devolve

upon their allies the vindication of their liberties, should now think themselves justified in suspending further exertions for independence, which seemed to be virtually conceded. Washington represented to Congress the fatal consequences which would probably follow a premature relaxation of their efforts; and, as he had now acquired an ascendency in that body, his counsels were implicitly followed. Votes of men and money were unanimously passed, as if the war was to be carried on with unabated vigour. But the authority of Congress was no longer what it had been. Supplies of money came in slowly, and but few recruits could be obtained. When Washington returned to the camp in April, he found his effective force under ten thousand men. So great, indeed, was the contempt into which Congress had fallen, that many of the officers at head-quarters urged Washington to put an end to the phantom of republican government, and to assume the supreme executive authority. But these overtures were rebuked in such a peremptory manner that no attempt was made to renew the proposal.

Meanwhile the war was actively prosecuted by France and Spain. The siege of Gibraltar was vigorously pressed by the Spaniards; *Siege of Gibraltar.* and the French Court, elated by their success in the West Indies, aimed at the entire conquest of the British possessions in the Carribbean Sea, and hoped to retrieve their position in the East Indies. The Count de Grasse, early in the year, sailed for Martinique, for the purpose of refitting, shipping troops, and effecting a junction with a Spanish squadron which lay off Cape François, preparatory to a grand attack on Jamaica. Rodney had returned to England in December, to urge upon the Government the expediency of fitting out a powerful fleet for service in the West Indies, early in the spring. His representations happily prevailed, notwithstanding the violent clamour of the Opposition, who would have had the fleet employed in the precarious and secondary object of intercepting supplies, instead of anticipating their arrival by proceeding at once to the scene of action, and striking a weighty blow at the unprepared enemy. The zeal and energy of the Admiral were adequately supported by the Government. On the 19th of February, Rodney reached Barbadoes with fourteen sail of the line, which, with the squadron under Hood, made the English fleet equal to the fleet which lay at Martinique, under the command of the Count de Grasse. The object of Rodney was to bring the Frenchman to an engagement before he could effect a junction with his ally. Between his anchorage at St. Lucie, and that of the French at Martinique, he established a line of frigates, by which every movement of the enemy was signalled to him with the utmost celerity. On the 8th of April, Rodney was informed that the French Admiral had put to sea.

<small>Rodney's victory.</small> Within two hours after this intelligence had reached him, the English fleet was under weigh. The next morning he was near enough to open a cannonade on the rear of the French fleet, but could not bring them to a general engagement. On the two following days, the enemy, favoured by the wind, had nearly effected his escape; but, through an incautious movement on the evening of the 11th, Rodney was enabled to get to windward. An action was now inevitable. The French had thirty sail of the line; the English had thirty-six. The firing commenced at half-past seven in the morning of the 12th of April, and raged until sunset. But the fortune of the day was decided by a celebrated manœuvre, called breaking the line, which, if not invented by Rodney, was certainly on this day for the first time attempted. By this daring movement, the enemy's line of battle was separated, and thrown

into confusion. The Count de Grasse, however, in the centre of the broken line, continued to fight his flag-ship, the renowned Ville de Paris, the largest man-of-war on the seas. She found her match in a British seventy-four. Shattered to a wreck by the broadsides of the Canada, the Ville de Paris still kept her colours flying, until Sir Samuel Hood, coming up with his ship, the Barfleur, which had not yet been engaged, in a few minutes compelled his brave antagonist to strike. Hood, who commanded the rearward division of six sail of the line, having been becalmed during the greater part of the day, this great battle was fought with a nearly equal number of ships on each side; but the French ships were more fully manned, and carried a greater weight of metal than the English. The victory was complete. Seven ships were taken; the loss of the enemy in killed and wounded was computed to exceed nine thousand, while that of the English was under a thousand; the French Commander-in-Chief was taken prisoner. The military chest, and all the artillery intended for the great expedition against Jamaica, fell into the hands of the British; and the shattered remnants of the French fleet which escaped were no longer available for active service.

The news of Rodney's victory was received in England with a burst of joy and exultation. The pride of the country had lately suffered severe mortification. The colonies, which she had ruled with so high a hand, had defied her power, and cast away her yoke. Her ancient enemies had wrested from her some of her richest possessions in the New World; and they had insulted her very shores with impunity. She was no longer the ruler of the seas; her commerce had been fain to seek the protection of a foreign flag; and the British waters swarmed with cruisers, which roamed the channel, intercepted the communication between England

Exultation in England.

and Ireland, and alarmed the ports and roadsteads of the British Isles.* Oppressed by this series of misfortunes, the spirit of the nation had sunk, and she was seeking, if not suing, for peace; while her insolent foes talked of insisting upon terms which should make England feel the humiliation and defeat which she had formerly inflicted upon them. The Government had fondly hoped, that the unqualified concession of the American claims would be accepted as a satisfactory basis of treaty by all the belligerents. But the ministers of the great powers at once declared, that the recognition of the independence of America would be no satisfaction to *them*; in vain did the British plenipotentiary represent the advantage which France and Spain would acquire in the diminution of the power of Great Britain by the loss of thirteen colonies; the cessions she was prepared to make in the East and West Indies, and the adjustment of the long-vexed question of the fisheries. The Count de Vergennes, on the part of France, plainly told Mr. Grenville, that such proposals as these would not be a sufficient basis for a treaty; intimating that Great Britain must submit to far more important and extensive sacrifices; and he hinted at the nature and extent of these sacrifices by an explicit allusion to the East Indies. 'Why not,' said he, 'content yourselves with Bengal? Your arms are grown too long for your body. We have experienced every kind of indignity from you in India, and that chiefly owing to the terms of the last peace—a peace which I cannot read without shuddering.' He added, 'that in making a new treaty, France must be relieved from every condition inconsistent with her dignity.' †

* M'Pherson's *Annals of Commerce*, vol. iii. p. 611.

† Abstract of State of Secret Negotiations, Paris, 10th May, 1782. From Mr. Grenville. This conversation is alluded to at the commencement of Fox's letter to Grenville, of 21st May.—*Courts*

Such was the state of affairs when the great event of the 12th of April was announced at Paris and at London. It produced almost as sensible an effect in the one capital as in the other. The French Government were bitterly disappointed. For the first time, after centuries of warfare, they had beheld the prospect of a peace which should redound to the glory of France and the humiliation of the haughty islanders. They hoped that the disgraceful terms of the last treaty, which had been dictated to France by her triumphant rival, would be annulled; that the rich possessions in the Western tropic, which had been taken from her, would be restored; and that she would be able to assert her right to an equal share in the vast empire in the East. But now that England had recovered her wonted ascendency upon the seas, these ambitious hopes must be moderated, if not abandoned. The high tone which De Vergennes and D'Aranda had adopted in the conference of the 10th of May was at once lowered; and, unless some unforeseen reverse should still befall the arms of Great Britain, there was every prospect of bringing the war to a speedy and honourable termination.*

It would be too much, perhaps, to say, that there was a party in England which shared the disappointment of the enemy; but it is certain, that the Whig Ministry, by a perverse and unjustifiable error, had excluded themselves from any share in the success and glory of the British arms. The expedition, which had been attended with such a great result,

and Cabinets of George the Third, vol. i. p. 28.

* When Mr. Oswald arrived, the French journalists, who published only what they were permitted, announced the event with this comment:—'It will not be an easy matter; we are sure of Gibraltar and Jamaica; and probably the English will not long retain any colony in the West Indies; nor are their prospects, to our certain knowledge, very brilliant in India.'—ADOLPHUS's *History*, vol. iii. p. 391.

had been planned by the former Government; and the admirable officer whom they had charged with the conduct of that expedition, in spite of the obloquy heaped upon him and them by their opponents, was superseded in his command only a few days before his victory was announced in London. In fact, the first despatch which Rodney received after the action, was a letter from the Secretary of the Admiralty, couched in the driest terms of official brevity, informing him that Admiral Pigot had been appointed his successor, and ordering him to proceed immediately to Barbadoes to relinquish his command. When the unlooked-for, if not unwelcome news of the 12th of April arrived, an express was despatched to stop the departure of the new Admiral, but it was too late; and while the West Indian fleet were eagerly anticipating what England would say to the 12th of April, they learned, to their astonishment and dismay, that their renowned commander had been ordered to strike his flag.

Had the Government, soon after their accession to power, asserted their right of appointing an officer in whom they had confidence to the important command in the West Indies, they would have had a fair pretext for gratifying their known dislike of Rodney. The factious clamour with which they had pursued the Admiral for his conduct in the affair of St. Eustatia, had not been without effect; and a large portion of the public regarded Rodney as a violent and arbitrary officer, who had confiscated British property, and wantonly interfered with the freedom of commerce. But it was not until several weeks had elapsed that the Ministry decided on recalling Rodney. Before his successor could reach the station, summer would have commenced. Rodney had left England to join his squadron in December. The Admiralty knew that Rodney's plan was to prevent the junction of the

French and Spanish fleets; and knowing this plan, knowing also the energetic character of the man, they ought to have calculated upon its failure or success before the month of June. If they continued, when in office, to disapprove of the plan, which they had so vehemently censured when in opposition, they might perhaps, by extraordinary despatch, have prevented the rash enterprise; but the recall of Rodney in the month of May, nothing having intervened to justify such a step, and the manner of his recall, seemed to spring more from private enmity than from regard to the public service.

Great was the astonishment of the people when it became known that the Admiral who had revived the fading glory of the British flag was suddenly disgraced: nor did it escape notice, that the hand which dictated this unparalleled insult was that of a rival chief, who had been tried and found wanting. The First Lord of the Admiralty was Keppel, who, in 1778, had been sent out to fight, and had sailed back hastily into port, on vague intelligence that the enemy numbered a few more sail than the fleet which he commanded; and who, when he afterwards met the French on equal terms, was content with holding his own, instead of winning, or striving to win, a glorious victory. It was not forgotten either how he had attempted to shift the blame of this failure upon his subordinate officer. This same Keppel, whom party spirit had for a time elevated into a hero, but who had long since sunk to his proper level, had lately, by the same party zeal, been raised to the peerage, and placed at the head of the service.

Public astonishment at Rodney's recall.

The members of the late administration did not neglect so fair an opportunity of retorting upon their old opponents. The removal of Rodney was made the subject of severe animadversion in both Houses. Lord Keppel, unable to justify the act, had the meanness and folly to evade even the admission of it. He said, that no evidence of any such act could be produced, and that it was to be treated only as a vague report, not fit for discussion in Parliament. This pettifogging quibble was followed by immediate exposure. The question was distinctly put to ministers in the House of Commons; and Fox, with the frankness which belonged to him, avowed that Rodney had been recalled, and gave the best reason which he could give for an act so ill-advised. He said, that Rodney had caused great offence and alarm to the planters by his conduct in the affair of St. Eustatia, and that, therefore, it had been thought expedient, before the recent intelligence had arrived, to remove him from the West India station. The real reason, no doubt, was, that Rodney had owed his appointment to the special favour of the King. A peerage and a pension were, of course, conferred upon the Admiral. Sir Samuel Hood, the second in command in the action of the 12th of April, was raised to the Irish peerage. Two other officers, Admiral Drake and Commodore Affleck, were made baronets.

The English Government hastened to assure the Court of Versailles, that, notwithstanding the success which had attended the British arms, their desire for peace was undiminished. Nevertheless, the negotiations lingered. The tone which the French minister had assumed in the conversation with Grenville on the 10th of May could hardly be maintained; but the propositions which he made were so vague and indeterminate, that his object was evidently to gain time. Spain, intent on the siege of Gibraltar, and limiting her views to the acquisition of that fortress, was unwilling to conclude a peace until her object could be secured. The fall of Gibraltar, which the Court of Madrid confidently expected as the result of the great efforts they had made, would compensate the allies for the failure of their designs upon Jamaica, and would enable them to obtain terms which, in the existing state of affairs, they could hardly advance with any prospect of success.

On the change of Ministry in July, Lord Shelburne, as the head of the new Government, renewed his pacific assurances to the two Courts; and Mr. Grenville having resigned his credentials, Mr. Fitzherbert was associated with Mr. Oswald in a commission to negotiate a treaty. On this occasion, Holland, which had hitherto taken no part in the conferences, was, at her own instance, admitted as a party to the negotiations. The Rockingham administration had made overtures to the Dutch through the mediation of the Czarina. Fox, with a view to propitiate the Court of Petersburg, as well as to detach Holland from the hostile alliance, offered to concede the main principle of the Armed Neutrality, namely, the freedom of the seas. The Dutch were willing to accept terms which would have redounded so much to their honour and advantage; but the intrigues of the French Court with a party at the Hague, opposed to the English alliance, prevailed against the dictates of good sense and moderation; and, instead of withdrawing from the contest, the prolongation of which could only serve the purposes of their allies, the States entered into an engagement with France not to conclude a separate treaty. The consequences were, the blockade of the Dutch ports by a British squadron, which effectually prevented an intended expedition to the Baltic; the loss of all their settlements on the island of Sumatra, together with Negapatam in the country of the Tanjore, and the capture of several of their East India ships; the final result being that after the Great Powers had signed a peace at the end of the year, the States were forced to conclude a separate treaty with Great Britain, on conditions far less favourable than those which they had rejected a few months before.

When Lord Howe, who commanded the home squadron, had completed the blockade of the coast of Holland, his services were required to protect the Channel, menaced by the combined French and Spanish fleets, amounting to twenty-five sail of the line. Howe left Portsmouth with only twelve ships of the same class; but with this force he found it an easy duty to cover the home-bound merchantmen, and to guard the Channel against any effort of the enemy.

The combined fleets having left the coast of England, Lord Howe was at liberty to proceed to the relief of Gibraltar, which had been closely invested for nearly three years. At first, the Spanish had endeavoured to starve the place; but their blockade having been on two occasions forced by the British fleet, they relinquished that plan, and commenced a regular siege. During the spring and summer of 1781, the fortress was bombarded, but with little success; in the month of November, the enemy were driven from their approaches, and the works themselves were almost destroyed by a sally from the garrison. Early in the year, however, the fall of Minorca enabled the Spanish to reform the siege of Gibraltar. De Crillon himself, the hero of Minorca, superseding Alvarez, assumed the chief command. He was joined by the two young French princes, the Count d'Artois and the Duke de Bourbon, sent to learn the art of war, and to grace the anticipated triumph of the French arms under such a renowned commander. Nor were their expectations presumptuous. The garrison of Gibraltar comprised no more than seven thousand men; while the force of the allied monarchies amounted to thirty-three thousand soldiers, with an immense train of artillery. De Crillon, however, who was well acquainted with the fortress, had little hope of taking it from the land side, but relied with confidence on the formidable preparations which he had made for bombarding it from the sea. Huge floating batteries, bomb-proof and shot-proof, were constructed; and it was calculated that the action of these tremendous engines alone would be sufficient to destroy the works. Besides the battering ships, of which ten were provided, a large armament of vessels of all rates was equipped; and a grand attack was to take place, both from sea and land, with four hundred pieces of artillery.

Six months were consumed in these formidable preparations; and it was not until September that they were completed. A partial cannonade took place on the 9th and three following days; but the great attack, which was to decide the fate of the beleaguered fortress, was commenced on the 13th of September. On that day, the combined fleets of France and Spain, consisting of forty-seven sail of the line, besides numerous ships of inferior rate, were drawn out in order of battle before Gibraltar. Numerous bomb ketches, gun and mortar boats, dropped their anchors within close range; while the ten floating batteries were moored with strong iron chains within half gun-shot of the walls. On the land, a hundred and seventy guns were prepared to open fire simultaneously with the ships; and forty thousand troops were held in readiness to rush in at the first practicable breach. The heights around the rock of Gibraltar were covered with spectators, assembled to behold the most tremendous conflict of arms that had taken place since the invention of artillery.

The garrison had witnessed the progress of the preparations for their destruction; and they awaited the event, not indeed with the arrogant confidence of their assailants, but without dismay. The natural strength of the rock was greater than that of any fortress in the world; and the art of the engineer had supplied every defect. The garrison were animated with that enduring courage, which

Firmness of the garrison.

never fails English soldiers who have confidence in their leader; and the Commandant, General Elliot, was one of those veterans whose experience, activity, and courage are calculated to inspire such confidence. Under his direction, every effort of the enemy had hitherto been repelled, and every damage had been promptly and effectually repaired. The well-directed sally of the 26th of November was not forgotten; and just before the completion of his arrangements, De Crillon beheld the best and strongest of his advanced works completely destroyed by an attack from the garrison.

The grand attack was commenced at ten o'clock in the forenoon, by the fire of four hundred pieces of artillery. The great floating batteries, securely anchored within six hundred yards of the walls, poured in an incessant storm from a hundred and forty-two heavy guns. Elliot had less than a hundred guns to reply to the cannonade both from sea and land; and of these he made the most judicious use. Disregarding the attack from every other quarter, he concentrated the whole of his ordnance on the floating batteries in front of him; for, unless these were silenced, their force would prove irresistible. But for a long time the thunder of eighty guns made no impression on the enormous masses of wood and iron. The largest shells glanced harmless from their sloping roofs; the heaviest shot could not penetrate their hulls, seven feet in thickness. Nevertheless, the artillery of the garrison was still unceasingly directed against these terrible engines of destruction. A storm of red-hot balls was poured down upon them; and about midday, it was observed that the combustion caused by these missiles, which had hitherto been promptly extinguished, was beginning to take effect. Soon after, the partial cessation of the guns from the battering ships, and the volumes of smoke which issued from their decks, made it

Floating batteries.

manifest they were on fire, and that all the efforts of the crews were required to subdue the conflagration. Towards evening, their guns became silent; and before midnight, the flames burst forth from the principal floating battery, which carried the Admiral's flag, illumining the whole scene of carnage, and enabling the garrison to complete the confusion of the enemy by a steady and well-directed cannonade. Eight of the ten floating batteries were on fire during the night; and the only care of the besieged was to save from the flames and from the waters, the wretched survivors of that terrible flotilla, which had so recently menaced them with annihilation. This duty, it is needless to say, was undertaken with no less alacrity and zeal than that which had been so nobly discharged during the whole of this memorable day.

The loss of the enemy was computed at two thousand; that of the garrison, in killed and wounded, amounted to no more than eighty-four. *Loss of the besiegers.* The labour of a few hours sufficed to repair the damage sustained by the works.

The French and Spanish fleets remained in the Straits, expecting the appearance of the British squadron under Lord Howe; and, relying on their superiority in ships and weight of metal, they still hoped that the result of an action at sea might enable them to resume the siege of Gibraltar. Howe, having been delayed by contrary winds, did not reach the Straits until the 9th of October; and, notwithstanding the superior array which the enemy presented, he was prepared to risk an engagement. But at this juncture, a storm having scattered the combined fleet, the British Admiral was enabled to land his stores and reinforcements without opposition. Having performed this duty, he set sail for England; nor did the Spanish Admiral, though still superior by eight sail of the line, venture to dispute his passage.

Such was the close of the great siege of Gibraltar; an undertaking which had been regarded by Spain as the chief object of the war, which she had prosecuted for three years, and which, at the last, had been pressed by the whole force of the allied monarchies.* After this event, the war itself was virtually at an end. The blockade of Gibraltar continued, as a matter of form, until the conclusion of peace; but the garrison, amply provisioned, sustained no privation from the presence of the combined fleets, and no further offensive operation was attempted. In the West Indies the power of the enemy had been effectually broken by Rodney's victory. The Bahama islands were surprised and taken by a small expedition, fitted out by the Governor of Cuba; and the English retaliated by capturing some Spanish forts on the Mosquito shore.

These events could not fail to facilitate the progress of negotiations at Paris. The Americans, their main object being attained by the recognition of their independence, had no desire to protract the war for French and Spanish purposes, in which they were nowise interested; and, as their treaty with the Court of Versailles precluded them only from *concluding* a separate peace, there was no obstacle to a separate negotiation with England up to the final point. Accordingly, the conduct of a treaty was entrusted to four commissioners on the part of the Americans, Dr. Franklin, Mr. Gay, Mr. Adams, and Mr. Sanders. The British plenipotentiaries were Mr. Oswald and Mr. Fitzherbert. The terms were adjusted without any serious difficulty. The principal point of difference arose with regard

---

* The Court of Madrid had been flattered with the certain hope of achieving this object, so important to their pride and power. Every morning the King enquired if Gibraltar was taken, and when answered in the negative, always replied, 'It soon will be.' — Coxe's *Kings of Spain*, vol. v. p. 121.

to the Royalists. The British Government felt bound to stipulate for the protection and indemnity of those faithful subjects of the Crown, who, throughout the various fortunes of the struggle, had maintained, and were still willing to adhere to, their allegiance.* But the Commissioners urged, with truth, that the Congress itself had no power to enter into any such engagement, and could do no more than recommend the several States which they represented to make restitution when it was practicable to Loyalists, who had been deprived of their property by the Provincial Governments. The British plenipotentiaries, however, were instructed to press for a more satisfactory adjustment of this point; and it was not until Franklin set up a counter claim on behalf of his countrymen, whose property had been destroyed by the Loyalists, that the English Cabinet consented to a considerable modification of their first proposal.

It was agreed, that Congress should *recommend* the several States to restore the property of British subjects, who had not borne arms against them during the war; and that other persons should be permitted to wind up their affairs, and to obtain restitution of their forfeited estates on payment of the sums for which they had been sold. On the other hand, the claim put forth on behalf of the Americans, whose property had been destroyed, was absolutely withdrawn, and no further mention was made of the proposition suggested by Franklin, at the commencement of the negotiation, that Canada should be ceded by way of indemnity. Provision

_{Question of compensation.}

---

* I have before me a paper drawn up by Mr. Galloway, of Pennsylvania, the member of Congress, who had joined the Royalists on the declaration of independence, and submitted to the Government so late as the 14th of August, 1782. This paper contained a detailed plan for the future prosecution of the war, and gives the most encouraging account of the Loyalists, both as regards their numbers and their ardour for the service of the Crown.—Bolton MSS.

was made for reviving the rights of British creditors of American citizens, which had been suspended since the commencement of the war. The boundaries of the new sovereignty were adjusted. The right of taking fish on the banks of Newfoundland was conceded by Great Britain; and the free navigation of the Mississippi was secured. The great point which had given rise to much controversy in the Cabinet of Lord Rockingham, namely, whether the independence should be immediately acknowledged, or should be ratified by express agreement between the contracting powers, was ultimately decided in the sense opposed to the opinion of the Rockingham Whigs. By the first article of the treaty the Thirteen Provinces were recognised as free, sovereign, and independent states.

These were the principal articles of the provisional treaty, which was signed at Paris on the 30th of November. The main point having been conceded without any reserve or qualification,* and in a manner which became the magnanimity of a great nation, the remaining terms were little more than matters of detail, and certainly contained nothing inconsistent either with the interest or the dignity of Great Britain.

Claims of the Loyalists. The only point contested by the Government of the King, though a point proper to be named, and even pressed to a certain extent, were it only from respect to the parties whom it concerned, was really untenable. The claims of the

---

* The King was extremely averse to the unqualified concession of the independence. The day after the Cabinet had decided upon unconditional acknowledgment, the Chancellor, who, above all the ministers, possessed the confidence of the King, wrote a private letter to Lord Shelburne, urging some modification of a term so humiliating to the country. But, though 'he cannot part with a persuasion he has so long entertained, that something more might be done upon this point,' Thurlow, true to the character in which Pitt afterwards described him, 'objecting to everything and proposing nothing,' suggests no modification of the offensive term. Bolton MSS.

Loyalists were undeniable; but they were claims upon Great Britain, not upon the American States. The Loyalists had taken part with the Crown against their countrymen, who were in arms for independence; and the cause of independence having prevailed, they must abide the fortune of war. If the issue of the struggle had been otherwise, and the Imperial Government had succeeded in asserting its authority, the Loyalists would have been justified in demanding the restitution of the property of which they had been deprived by rebels; but when the rebellion was successful, and the insurgent people had been recognised as an independent sovereignty, the advancement of any pretensions to indemnity by the inhabitants, whose proprietary rights had been confiscated for resistance to the new Government, became absurd. The American Loyalists had, in either event, a claim to indemnity from the parent state;* but they could not, at the same time, maintain a similar claim upon a Government to which they had never owed allegiance.

The provisional treaty was negotiated and signed by the American Commissioners without any concert with the French Government, [Provisional Treaty.] a proceeding which gave much disgust to the Court of St. Germains. The conduct of the Americans in this respect was at least ungracious. It was no sufficient justification that their ally had engaged in their quarrel from no interest in its object, but merely because it seemed to present a favourable opportunity for humbling the pride and power of his mighty rival. Great nations never take part in quarrels which do not immediately concern them, but from motives of policy and ambition; and if France took the part of the confederated States for

---

* This claim was, in fact, recognised before the negotiation of the treaty. The annual allowances, by way of indemnity, to the American Loyalists already amounted to upwards of thirty-eight thousand pounds.—*Treasury Paper.*

her own purposes, it certainly was not for them to excuse their discourtesy and ingratitude by any such plea. The Americans had supplicated the aid of France; they had accepted her money; they had even been willing to leave the conquest of their liberties to her fleets and armies; and now, the confederated States had made terms with the common enemy, not only without the concurrence of their illustrious ally, but without any acknowledgment of his services. Such conduct, if technically in accordance with the treaty of 1778, was certainly inconsistent with the spirit of that treaty. There had been nothing in the conduct of the French Government to justify such ungenerous treatment. The French had faithfully performed all their engagements. In the present year, and after it had become *Unfair treatment of the French.* known from the declaration of the British Government that the war in America was virtually at an end, the French King had nevertheless sent over six millions of livres (two hundred and fifty thousand pounds sterling) to Philadelphia, in continuation of his annual subsidy. The American minister at Paris had been admitted to the confidential counsels of the Court of St. Germains; nor does it appear that he had any sufficient ground for suspecting that the Government of the Most Christian King entertained views incompatible with the independence of his country, which had been expressly recognised by the treaty of 1778.* The truth appears to have been, that the Americans having obtained all they wanted, or could expect,

---

* It was said that the Americans entertained suspicions of the good faith of France; these suspicions, however, if they were really entertained at the time, have since been rejected as wholly gratuitous. The intercepted despatch of M. de Marbois, the French Secretary of Legation at Philadelphia, which discloses some jealousy of the new republic, could not have determined the separate negotiation, as it did not come to light until that negotiation was in progress.

were naturally apprehensive lest the conclusion of peace should be delayed or endangered, by the single point in which they were interested being complicated with European questions with which they had no concern.

Both France and Spain had taken up arms to aid the American people in the struggle for liberty; and though the pretence was sufficiently gross, it was nevertheless the avowed object of the war. But when Great Britain offered to concede this object, the European allies of the confederated States immediately set up pretensions of their own. The French minister 'could not allow the independence of America to be the only cause of war, because France had found, and not made, America independent;' and the Spanish minister declared 'that his master's griefs were totally distinct from the independence of America.'* The Americans, who were under no reciprocal engagement, either express or implied, to aid France and Spain in the prosecution of their separate claims upon Great Britain, might, therefore, after this intimation of the policy of the two Courts, have negotiated a separate treaty. And if they had justified their conduct on this ground, it would have been as much in accordance with good faith as it was with sound policy. But, instead of taking this plain course, the American Commissioners conducted the negotiations as if it were a clandestine correspondence, evaded the enquiries of the French minister, and answered him with representations at variance with the truth. Well might M. de Vergennes feel astonishment when he was informed by Franklin that the treaty between Great Britain and the United States had been virtually concluded.†

_{Pretensions of France and Spain.}

* *Secret Negotiations.* Paris, May 1782.
† De Vergennes to De la Luzerne, 19th December, 1782. Printed in FRANKLIN's *Works*, vol. ix.

The defection of America from the common cause, together with the failure of the great enterprise which had been undertaken by the allied monarchies, left not a motive or pretext for continuing the war. The French minister no longer mentioned the vague and exorbitant demands which he had put forward in the spring. The British Government had then offered to negotiate on terms consistent with the treaty of 1763; the Government of His Most Christian Majesty declared that the principles of that treaty must be wholly abandoned. It was in vain that Mr. Grenville had humbled his country so far as to urge the advantage which France would acquire by the severance of thirteen colonies from the sovereignty of Great Britain, and the full enjoyment of the fisheries on the banks of Newfoundland and in the Gulf of St. Lawrence, from the cession of the islands St. Pierre and Miquelon.[*] These overtures were put aside, in the month of May, almost with contempt, and the British plenipotentiary was informed that 'justice and dignity' were the objects which France would principally consult in the next treaty; and that, besides full satisfaction on these heads, she would require an ample admission of the demands of her allies, Spain and Holland. But in the month of December the tone was changed; for, in the meantime, Rodney had saved the British empire in the West Indies; Elliot had held the Rock of Gibraltar against the whole force of the united monarchies; America was satisfied. No more was said about the reparation due to France for the indignity she had suffered by the treaty of 1763; she was glad to take Miquelon and St. Pierre; she dropped her demand for a large cession of territory in the East Indies, and her allies were left to make their own terms.

[*] 'O pour la peche,' said De Vergennes; 'vous allons arranger cela bien d'une autre maniere.'— *Secret Negotiations.* May 1782.

The treaties with France and Spain were therefore ultimately concluded on the basis of the peace of 1763. France obtained some minor modifications of that obnoxious treaty, but nothing commensurate with her pretensions. The North American fisheries were restored, and confirmed in accordance with the former treaties, and the little islands of St. Pierre and Miquelon were ceded as fishing stations. In the West Indies, each Crown resumed its former possessions, with the exception of Tobago, which was ceded to France. In Africa, Great Britain gave up the Senegal River and Goree, which she had acquired by the treaty of Paris. In India, the French regained their commercial establishments, but were strictly excluded from any military occupation in the British presidencies. The articles in the treaty of Utrecht, relative to the demolition of the fortress of Dunkirk, which had long lost all political importance, but which were offensive to the pride and honour of France, were willingly abrogated by the English Government.

The recovery of Gibraltar had long been the dearest object of the Court of Madrid; and, making an effort to obtain by treaty what they could no longer hope to obtain by arms, they offered any concession, short of a dismemberment of the monarchy, in exchange for this fortress. The people of England have long prized this famous rock as highly as the nation to which it naturally belongs; Gibraltar, however, was at that time considered a fortress of secondary importance; and the British Government were not unwilling to listen to the proposals of the Spanish Court in this particular. But the glorious defence of Gibraltar had not yet ceased to be a topic of exultation throughout the country; and a strong repugnance having been expressed, both in Parliament and in public, to part with a possession, which, barren as it might be, was nevertheless associated with one of the most memorable achievements of British valour, the Court of Madrid was informed, that the project could not be entertained. A treaty was subsequently agreed to, containing terms, more advantageous on the whole than Spain had a right to expect. She retained her valuable conquest of Minorca; she remained in possession of West Florida; and East Florida was given up to her. It is true, that the Floridas were of little value to this country, but they were the only equivalent we had received, at the peace of 1763, for the restoration of the rich possessions in the West Indies, which the British arms had wrested from the Spanish Crown. On the other hand, the old claim of cutting logwood in the bay of Honduras was confirmed, and the Bahamas were restored. But, as these islands were recaptured by the British arms before the conclusion of the treaty, Spain had greatly the advantage in the adjustment of terms.

The preliminaries with France and Spain were signed on the 20th of January. Holland shared the usual fortune of a small state, which joins an offensive alliance with great powers, when there is no common interest in the war. The particular object of the Republic had been wholly disregarded in the negotiations at Paris. Holland, as a commercial nation, engrossing the greater part of the carrying trade of Europe, sought the freedom of the seas; and she had always resented the restrictions imposed by the English Navigation Act, as an impediment to her prosperity. The repeal or modification of that great law, which England considered as her maritime charter, was a leading principle of Dutch policy: and Fox, when Minister for Foreign Affairs, had, as we have seen, been willing to gratify the States in this particular. His overtures had been repelled; and now, when the other powers had withdrawn from the field of negotiation, Holland was eager to accept the terms which, a few months before, she had rudely rejected. But though England, when pressed by enemies on every side, might have thought it worth while to pay a high price for the purpose of detaching even one party from the hostile league, there was no longer any consideration for such a sacrifice as the British Government had, at that time, been prepared to make. The States-General were ultimately compelled to conclude a peace with Great Britain on the footing of a mutual restitution of all conquests, with the single exception of Negapatam in the Tanjore country, which was retained by England.

While the negotiations were in progress, the Government of Lord Shelburne was threatened with an opposition in Parliament of a most formidable character. The members of the Rockingham connection, who had retired from office on the death of their chief, had conceived the most violent animosity against their former colleagues, and were prepared to adopt any means, and any pretext, for overthrowing the administration. Intent upon this object, and blinded to every consideration of principle or consistency, Fox and his friends made overtures to Lord North, and the party of the ex-minister. The generous and placable character of the principals, wholly free from gall and malice, offered no obstacle, on personal grounds, to a reconciliation; they said, that their political differences having related chiefly to one great question of imperial policy now settled, there remained no valid reason why they should refuse to co-operate for the public welfare. And the public exigency, which seemed to these eminent persons to demand such a sacrifice of consistency, and such a sudden oblivion of recent differences, was the treaty of peace, which one of them had long thought

Shelburne opposed by the Rockingham party.

desirable, and which the other, up to the moment of the Coalition, had been engaged in negotiating as a minister of the Crown.

Intimidation of the Government. The Government, intimidated by the combination which had been formed against them, did not venture to put their case upon high ground. The question which they proposed to the House of Commons was whether such a peace as they had made was not preferable to the war in which they had found the country engaged? They urged the unparalleled increase of the public burdens, the interest of the debt more than doubled, the extreme difficulty of providing new resources, the want of ships and sailors, the failure of recruits for the army. We were engaged in war with two great military monarchies and three maritime powers. We had been worsted in the attempt to put down our insurgent colonies. We were without an ally in Europe. In these circumstances we had purchased peace by the cession of an island in the West Indies and the Floridas. We had submitted to the loss of Minorca; and had admitted the enemy to a participation in some fishing grounds, and to a share of our commerce in the East Indies. As to the Americans, we had done little more than recognise the independence which they had already conquered; and had made such arrangements with them, in respect of boundaries, as were calculated to prevent future dispute. And they fairly put it to the sense of Parliament, whether such terms were not preferable to a protracted war, the issue of which was doubtful, and which was carried on at an annual expenditure of nearly twenty millions.

Virulence of Opposition. But if the Ministry were too diffident in the defence of the treaty, the Opposition were grossly extravagant in their censure of it. A worse peace, according to them, could not have been concluded. It beggared all former treaties in infamy and disgrace; and exposed to the whole world the dismemberment and division of the British Empire. These assertions were supported by petty criticism and cavils, for which any measure, however just and wise, will afford scope to the ingenuity of faction. One of the objections urged may serve as a sample of the rest. It was admitted, that Dunkirk could no longer be considered of the same importance as it appeared to the framers of the peace of Utrecht; still, it was urged, the presence of an English commissioner on the territory of the enemy, for the purpose of preventing the erection of fortifications, was desirable, because it perpetuated the memory of former victories, exalted the dignity of Great Britain, and humbled the pride of France! It was Lord North who condescended to employ this silly and unworthy argument.

The treaties, though defended by the consummate skill and eloquence of Pitt, and though really open to no considerable objection, were, nevertheless, condemned by a majority of the House of Commons.* In other words, the combination of parties succeeded in their object of destroying the administration; for the very orators who were loudest in their invectives against the treaties, denouncing them as disgraceful and ruinous to the country, still cautiously disclaimed any intention of departing from the engagements which had been made, or even of desiring any modification of the terms. The sense of the House of Commons was, in the first instance, taken as an amendment to the Address, reserving to the House the power of disapproving the terms of the treaty, and expressing sympathy with the American Loyalists. This was followed up a few days after by certain resolutions, declaring the concessions

* The numbers were 224 to 208.

made to the enemy unnecessarily liberal. The resolutions were carried by a majority of seventeen.

Lord Shelburne immediately resigned; but the other members of the Government carried on the ordinary business of their respective offices until their successors were appointed. The Coalition did not find it so easy to profit by their victory as they had anticipated. Several weeks elapsed before the new arrangements were completed, the delay being caused by the repugnance of the King to submit to the dictation of the cabal. It seemed that his labour for the last twenty years had been thrown away, and that the capital object of his policy, which he had hoped to have seen securely effected, was doomed to disappointment and defeat. Little did His Majesty think that the means which had been taken to frustrate his purpose were exactly calculated to favour and confirm it. His kingcraft seemed to be altogether baffled. His policy had been brought into universal disrepute by the American war. The Economical Reform Acts had struck a blow at the foundation of his system. He had lost in Lord North an agent such as he could not hope to replace — pliant, yet able; eloquent and ingenious, yet of popular manner, and, amidst the corruption with which he was surrounded, of spotless integrity. To complete the discomfiture of the Court, a demand for responsible Government and honest representation had arisen, and was rapidly spreading through the country. An upright consistent conduct on the part of those public men, who, for a series of years, had opposed the measures of the Court, was alone wanting to consolidate public opinion, and to restrain the undue influence of the Crown. But at this critical moment, the Whigs, instead of being united in the common cause, no sooner found themselves in power, than they resumed those petty struggles for the ascendency in which they had

wasted their energies when they had no competitor
for power. When North's administration was driven
from office, the jealousy of the great Whig leaders
rendered the formation of a new Cabinet a work of
much difficulty. The Marquis of Rockingham and
the Earl of Shelburne were statesmen of long standing and great authority. They agreed upon every
important question of public policy, and differed no
more than men of independent judgment must differ,
as to the conduct of public affairs. They shared the
responsibility of the votes which removed the late
Ministry from office. But each of these powerful
noblemen was the head of a faction; neither would
yield precedence to the other; and, as every administration must have a chief, it was difficult to see how
a point of so much nicety could be adjusted. At
length the King, with whom the decision rested, hit
upon a mode of preferment which should have the
effect of mortifying the object of his choice. He
named Rockingham Prime Minister, but refused to
admit him to an audience during the progress of the
arrangements of the new administration, which His
Majesty chose to conduct through the medium of
Shelburne. The principal offices were equally divided
between the partisans of the rival leaders; and the
administration being constructed upon this principle,
discord was introduced into its councils at the
moment of its formation. The Cabinet was a constant
scene of intrigue and strife for the three months of its
existence. At a time when united and vigorous counsels
should have guided the executive government, either
in the prosecution of the war against the allied
enemies of the country, or in the negotiation of a safe
and honourable peace, the Whig administration, distracted by party division, made foreign policy the
battle-ground of their internecine conflict. If the
Cabinet had been composed of logicians and wranglers,
a question whether the independence of America

should be acknowledged by a preliminary declaration, or by an article in the treaty, might have been discussed with much subtlety of argument; but that men of vigorous understanding and practised in affairs, like Fox and Shelburne, should have attached any real intrinsic importance to such a point would seem absolutely incredible. Yet Fox and his friends maintained one side of this question, while Shelburne and his followers maintained the other, as if the difference, which, as far as it is intelligible, seems one of metaphysical nicety, was of the highest practical importance. The rival Secretaries of State appointed different emissaries to the seat of negotiation; while the ministers of the great belligerents, puzzled by the conflicting pretensions of these diplomatists, withheld their confidence from both, and assumed a tone of insolence and dictation which the weakness and distraction of the British counsels seemed to warrant. When the Rockingham party were in the ascendant, the foreign ministers were informed that the sovereignty of the American States would be unconditionally recognised; when the Shelburne faction prevailed, the recognition was to form an article in the treaty. Shelburne's agent at Paris privately discusses with the American minister a plan for the cession of Canada; and insinuates that he is about to be accredited with full powers. The Plenipotentiary of the Foreign Office, on discovering this intrigue, reports it in high indignation to his friend and patron.* Fox immediately instructed Grenville to furnish him with the evidence of this transaction, for the purpose of ruining his colleague. It was happy for England that this tangled skein of diplomacy and intrigue was at length severed by the sword of Rodney and of Elliot.

* Grenville to Fox, 10th June, 1782.—*Courts and Cabinets of George the Third* vol. i. p. 40. See also *Memoirs and Correspondence of Fox.*

The death of Rockingham broke up this ill-assorted administration, and broke up also the party which had been held together by the moderation and authority of its chief. Several members of the Rockingham connection saw no sufficient reason for abandoning the Government at such a critical period. Keppel, though agreeing with Fox and Cavendish, that remaining in office under such circumstances involved a sacrifice of party interests, had public spirit enough to feel that the circumstances of the country demanded such a sacrifice; and he retained his post at the head of the Admiralty until the war was virtually terminated by the progress of the negotiations at Paris.

Death of Rockingham.

No sooner had Fox and his friends quitted the Government, than they turned round upon their remaining colleagues, and attacked them with a ferocity which had not been exceeded during the many years that they had opposed the administration of their predecessors. Fox, from the impetuosity of his character, and Burke, from infirmity of temper, seemed alike incapable of employing the language of moderation, or even of decency. Both these eminent men had, by their previous conduct, disarmed themselves of any effective argument against the treaties; but Lord North laboured under no such disability. He had, indeed, for the last three years, been the unwilling agent of carrying on a war which he believed to be hopeless; but so far from thinking that the independence of the American states should be unconditionally recognised, he dissented expressly from this position. Lord North had declared, after his retirement from office, that the independence ought not to be conceded without an equivalent; that the country was not reduced to that abject state as to accept such terms as the enemy might offer, and that Parliament should be unanimous in demanding an honourable peace, or in prosecuting

Virulence of Fox and Burke.

a vigorous war. With these sentiments, it was competent to Lord North to object to the treaties, and to accept the alternative of their rejection; but the Whigs, who had openly espoused the cause of the insurgents, and bewailed the successes of the British arms, were in a very different situation.

The Coalition had been arranged chiefly through the agency of Lord John Townshend, Burke, George North, and Eden.* On the 14th of February, three days before the debate on the preliminaries, a meeting took place between Fox and North to complete this inauspicious compact. The terms were easily settled. Economical reform was to be pushed no further. Parliamentary reform was to be an open question. Fox stipulated, that, in the contemplated Ministry, the King should not be chief minister. To this Lord North replied, 'If you mean there should not be a government of departments, I agree with you; I think it a very bad system. There should be one man, or a Cabinet, to govern the whole and direct everything. Government by departments was not brought in by me. I found it so; and had not vigour and resolution to put an end to it. The King ought to be treated with all sort of respect and attention, but the appearance of power is all that a King of this country can have.'†

The Coalition Ministry.

Propositions of Fox and Pitt.

Lord Shelburne having retired, it was thought that his friends might be rallied under the lead of Mr. Pitt, that Fox might come back with the Rockingham party, that a dissolution of Parliament would disperse the old followers of Lord North, and that a new Parliament might be assembled in support of a united Government. But personal prejudices again interposed to prevent an arrangement so desirable. Pitt was unwilling to act without

---

* Lord J. Townshend to Lord Holland, 1830.—Fox's Correspondence, vol. ii. p. 21.

† Fox's Correspondence, vol. ii. p. 38.

Shelburne, and Fox refused to act with him. Fox was again committed to North, with whom Pitt declined to form a connection. Fox proposed to the Shelburne party to support an administration which should not include their chief; and Pitt made overtures to the friends of Lord North for a coalition, based on the exclusion of Lord North. It was easy to foresee the result of negotiations such as these. Every attempt to combine the existing elements of party proved fruitless. Still, the King left no effort untried rather than submit to the dictation of the Whigs; and, as usual, he threatened to go to Hanover, if he could not have his own way. A few days after the resignation of Shelburne, he offered the Government to Pitt; and the aspiring youth was even then willing to undertake the responsibility, but finding no encouragement from his friends in such a daring attempt, he was reluctantly obliged to withdraw the consent which he had given a few hours before. The King then successively offered the post of Minister to Lord Gower and to the Duke of Portland; but the former prudently declined, and the latter was no more than a passive instrument in the hands of the Whigs.

At last he sent for Lord North, and made a second appeal to his tried loyalty and fidelity to his Sovereign. But Lord North was resolved never again to be placed at the head of a government of King's friends. To His Majesty's entreaties he offered a firm refusal, and took the liberty of recommending the nominee of the Whigs, the Duke of Portland, as a proper person to be entrusted with His Majesty's commands. The King, vexed and disappointed at this reply, terminated the audience by wishing his old servant good evening.

Lord North's refusal of office.

Five days after this interview, the new arrangements were announced. The House of Commons had already voted an address to

Formation of a new Ministry.

the Crown, praying for the appointment of an united
administration; and another motion of a still more
pointed character was threatened. The King, finding
all his resources exhausted, at length reluctantly
yielded to a coalition, which, he thought, and not
without reason, would prove fatal to his power. The
Duke of Portland became First Lord of the Treasury;
Fox and North were Secretaries of State. Lord John
Cavendish, Lords Keppel, Stormont, and Carlisle were
the other members of the Cabinet. The Great Seal
was put in commission, the King having in vain
striven to keep Thurlow in office. The other offices
were divided between the principal adherents of Fox
and North. Burke resumed the office of Paymaster.
Though the Coalition Cabinet did not immediately
encounter any formidable opposition, its fate was
sealed in the hour of its birth. Both Whigs and
Tories agreed in reprobating a union which set all
political consistency at defiance, and which seemed to
be prompted only by a shameless appetite for place
and power. But the organisation of old-established
parties is not easily dissolved. The obligation of
party ties was, at that time, for the most part, scrupulously
respected. The effect of the close-borough
system was, to suppress the exercise of independent
judgment. The same kind of discipline, which now
precludes a member of the Government from voting
against any measure sanctioned by the First Minister,
then precluded any nominee of a borough proprietor
from voting against the wishes of his patron; and, as
the House of Commons was, to the extent at least of
two-fifths, composed of nominees, it followed, that
the King's Government was not subjected to those
sudden gusts of passion and prejudice which agitate
assemblies elected by popular suffrage, and which
render the action of modern administrations uncertain
and feeble, in proportion as their existence is
precarious.

The same seeds of disunion, which had, in due time, destroyed the administration of Lord Rockingham, were brought into the Cabinet of the Coalition, and would, without doubt, in the absence of any other cause, eventually have rent it asunder. The Whigs, with their usual arrogance, refused to allow Lord North a single nomination to the Cabinet, although the parliamentary contingent which he brought to its support far exceeded the following of all his coadjutors.* A few days before the Ministry was finally arranged, the Coalition had actually come to a rupture on this point. The Rockingham party were ultimately forced to give way; and Lord Stormont, the nominee of North, was reluctantly admitted to a seat in the Cabinet.†

Rupture in the Coalition.

Besides the disapprobation of their own supporters, the rising murmurs of public opinion, and their own internal divisions, the Coalition had to encounter the determined and almost avowed hostility of the King. At the levee on the 26th of March, when Lord Shelburne formally resigned, the retiring minister and his colleagues received ostentatious marks of the royal favour, while their triumphant rivals were treated with undisguised aversion. The King had often been in secret opposition to his ministers; but this opposition had been conducted through the medium of subordinate and irresponsible agents. On no former occasion had he committed himself as he now did by writing to an eminent statesman, and expressing his desire that support should be withheld from the ostensible advisers of the Crown.‡

---

* Of the majority of 224 against the peace, Lord North's share was from 160 to 170. Mr. W. Grenville to Lord Temple, 19th Feb. 1783.—*Courts and Cabinets of George the Third*, vol. i. p. 168.

† Grenville to Temple, 20th March.

‡ In a letter addressed to Lord Temple the day before the new ministers kissed hands, His Majesty uses this language: ' Judge of the uneasiness of my mind at having been thwarted in every attempt to keep the administration of public affairs out of

While the new Ministry rested on a foundation so unsound, beset with difficulties and dangers, it presented an outward appearance of strength and solidity. The great Rockingham party, which now comprehended the principal Whig families, led by an orator of unrivalled ability, was once more in power. The adherents of the old Ministry followed their chief, experienced in affairs far beyond any other member of the Cabinet, inferior only to his great colleague and former rival in debate, and equally strong in personal popularity. The country was relieved from the pressure of a lengthened and disastrous war, upon terms which, if not glorious, were less humiliating to the national pride than might reasonably have been expected. No great question of domestic policy seemed likely to perplex the counsels of the Cabinet; and it might be hoped, that, after a long term of anxiety and excitement, the nation would willingly repose for some time under an able and united administration. The Opposition was almost confined to the party of Lord Shelburne, which consisted mainly of the old personal followers of Chatham, a party insignificant in numbers and family influence. The leader of this party, however, was a host in himself, the young aspiring son of Chatham, qualified to fulfil the sanguine expectations which his great name and early promise had inspired. But it seemed much more probable that Pitt would eventually join the Government, than that he should engage in opposition to a combination of powerful parties under the guidance of leaders in the full maturity of abilities not inferior to his own.

---

the hands of the most unprincipled coalition the annals of this, or any other country, can equal. I have withstood it till not a single man is willing to come to my assistance, and till the House of Commons has taken every step but insisting on this faction being by name elected ministers.'—*Courts and Cabinets*, vol. ii. p. 4.

The first question of importance brought before the House of Commons after the new ministers had taken their seats, was Pitt's motion on the subject of Parliamentary Reform. *[margin: Pitt's plan of reform.]* But if the aim was to embarrass an administration divided upon this important question, it would have been difficult to shape the motion in a form less calculated for such a purpose. In the former year, following in the footsteps of his father, Mr. Pitt had proposed to transfer the franchise from decayed and corrupt boroughs to more considerable places, where freedom of election might be obtained. It is obvious, that a provision of this kind was the first point to be considered in any real plan for placing the representation of the people on a fair and equal basis. But in the plan which Mr. Pitt brought forward in 1783 this capital point almost disappeared. The whole of the *close* boroughs were left untouched; and to compensate the influence of nomination, it was proposed to add a hundred members to the counties, with the exception of a certain number, who were to be added to the representation of the metropolis. *Corrupt* boroughs were to be disfranchised when a majority of the electors should be convicted of corruption. It would have been difficult to devise a worse plan than this. The arbitrary nomination of members to the House of Commons is indefensible in theory, and had been found pernicious in practice. But by Pitt's plan, nomination was recognised as a permanent part of the constitution of the House of Commons. The remedy for corrupt practices was utterly futile. It is no easy matter to bring home a charge of corruption to a single elector, however notorious his malpractices may have been. To convict a majority of the electors in any constituency of corruption would have been simply impossible: nor is it necessary for the purposes of corruption that the majority of the electors should be corrupt.

The motion was opposed by Lord North and others, mainly on the ground, that there was no demand for parliamentary reform on the part of the people. No desire for direct representation had been expressed by the principal manufacturing towns, Manchester, Birmingham, Sheffield, Leeds, and Halifax. The few petitions on the table of the House, and which comprised no more than twenty thousand names, prayed for universal suffrage and annual Parliaments; revolutionary proposals, which could not be satisfied by a partial and moderate measure of reform. Burke, who had always opposed, with his usual vehemency, any and every scheme for the amendment of the representation, started up to denounce the bill; but his rising, as had frequently happened, was the signal for the House to disperse; and the mortified orator resumed his seat in silence.* Lord North, on the contrary, was heard with fixed attention, while he combated the arguments of the reformers in a lengthened speech; and the interest which the question created was manifested by the unusually large attendance of members. The motion was rejected by a majority of one hundred and forty-four, in a House of four hundred and forty-two.

An act to recognise and confirm the independence of the Irish Courts of Justice, and a provision for the separate establishment of the Prince of Wales, who had attained his majority, were the only other measures of importance which engaged the attention of Parliament during the remainder of the session.

The great event of the recess was the conclusion of the treaties of peace with France, Spain, and America. These treaties were substantially a confirmation of the preliminaries which had been signed

---

* Romilly's *Memoirs*, p. 277. Burke's speeches frequently contain querulous allusions to the impatience of the House.

some months previously, and the principal provisions of which have been already explained. The Emperor and the Czarina were admitted, in the character of mediators or formal parties, to the definitive treaties which were signed on the 3rd of September.

Thus terminated the great struggle in which England had been engaged for nine years. But though her pride had been humbled and her empire rent in twain, England, so far from having received a fatal blow, as her enemies fondly hoped, was only entering on another epoch of prosperity and grandeur. The very contest which the shortsighted perverseness of her statesmen had provoked, and in which the misconduct of her commanders had suffered her to be worsted, proved eventually more conducive to her welfare than any scheme of aggrandisement which could have been devised by political ambition, and accomplished by military skill. A great writer had recently demonstrated, that the maintenance of colonies for commercial purposes was a rude expedient, adverse to all sound principles of political economy; that, so far from promoting trade, it checked commercial enterprise; that the expenses of contributing to the civil government of these dependencies, and of providing for their military defence, were, therefore so much money thrown away. And though the distinguished authority referred to* somewhat exaggerates the case, when he insists upon attributing the whole charges of the war of 1739 and of the succeeding war to colonial quarrels, which were rather the pretexts than the causes of these wars, it is certain, that, however useful the monopoly of colonial markets may be to a country in the infancy of its commerce, such artificial aids are altogether unnecessary to a matured state of mercantile development. But if it is true, as Adam

Marginal note: Termination of the War of Independence.

* Smith's *Wealth of Nations.* 'Colonial Policy.'

Smith asserts, that the cost of the war of 1753, amounting to ninety millions, ought justly to be stated to the account of the colonies; the cost of the War of Independence, amounting to one hundred and twenty millions, was, so far as the material interests of this country were concerned, the more profitable outlay. America, released from the trammels which the selfish policy of this country had imposed upon her, sprang forward at once upon her prosperous career; and, in proportion as she has advanced in wealth and power, our free commercial intercourse with her has increased likewise, while all expenditure on her account has ceased, and the Empire is no longer vulnerable at distant points, which no expenditure could adequately guard.

No statesman of the time foresaw these happy results of an event which appeared to be the most disastrous calamity that had yet befallen the British Empire. But, after making every allowance for the benefits which both countries derived from the emancipation of the American colonies, the marvellous prosperity which has sprung from the commercial intercourse of the two nations, and which commenced almost at the moment of their political disunion, belongs mainly to the development of those great inventions which were in their infancy at the commencement of the American war. During the twelve succeeding years, the spinning-jenny, the water-frame, the mule, and the power-loom were brought nearly to perfection; and these magnificent engines only wanted the raw material to create sources of wealth, exceeding the dreams of fiction, and to confer upon the great mass of the population a material prosperity, such as the people of no other age or country had as yet enjoyed. In 1786, the year before Cartwright patented his second great power-loom, the whole imports of cotton wool from the British West Indies, the French, Spanish,

Dutch, and Portuguese colonies, Turkey and Smyrna, were under twenty millions of pounds; at the commencement of the nineteenth century, the southern states of America, which had hitherto contributed a very small quantity, furnished nearly a third of the raw material consumed in the British manufacture; and, at the present time, three-fourths of the cotton wrought in this country* are supplied by the United States.

The War of Independence, judged as usual by the event, has received unqualified censure; <small>Causes of</small> and the case has been stated, on either side <small>the war.</small> the Atlantic, as if England had been justly rebuked in the assertion of wanton and arbitrary power. But, as regards the origin of the quarrel between the mother-country and the colony, I have already endeavoured to show that the assumption on the part of England to tax her dependencies was no violation of their laws, and was in pursuance of the right reserved expressly in their charters.† The real grievance was the vexatious enforcement of those customs' duties, the right to impose which had never been disputed by the colonies. A wise and generous policy, which should have avoided the agitation of speculative questions, and consulted the commercial interests of the colonies, would, no doubt, have postponed for an indefinite period the separation of Great Britain and America; but it does not follow that the rigorous assertion of her rights, by the parent state, and the strict execution of laws, which were in that age considered necessary for the protection of revenue and the prosperity of commerce, justified the colonies in throwing off their allegiance. Still less was the insurrection of the colonies a sufficient reason why the imperial state should at once

---

* In 1857, 1,428,670 bales.—ELLISON's *Handbook of the Cotton Trade.*   † Vol. i. p. 183.

concede their demands, or refrain from attempting to maintain her authority by arms. The abstract right of any member of a sovereign state to separate itself, and declare its independence, is a doctrine which no theoretical writer has ever broached, and which no practical statesman could for a moment recognise. Many an empire has been dismembered by the tyranny, folly, or weakness of the Central Government; but no government can tamely submit to the revolt of any of its subjects, and yet retain any security for its own existence.

Whatever, therefore, might have been the policy which provoked the quarrel, or which afterwards sought to heal the breach, England had no alternative, when her dependencies broke into open rebellion, than an appeal to the sword. George the Third was, at the commencement of the American war, the most powerful monarch that had reigned in this country since Elizabeth; his Parliament was obsequious, his people were loyal: but if, instead of defending the integrity of the Empire, he had proposed, in 1774, to surrender his American colonies, and to recognise them as independent United States, his throne had hardly withstood the shock of public indignation with which it would have been assailed. The sympathy with the American cause, which Chatham and other leaders of the Whig party so powerfully expressed, found little response in the nation. The colonists were generally regarded as selfish and insolent rebels, who, under the cloak of patriotism and independence, sought to evade the payment of their just contribution to the common defence of the realm.

Supremacy of George the Third.

It was not, indeed, until the conflict became a real struggle for empire, that the American war excited much interest in the country; for the first year, at least, it was considered of no more importance than an insurrection

English indifference to American affairs.

of Caffres, or a Chinese insult at the present day. It was merely a question of time and adequate military force. That a few scattered settlements of tobacco-growers, negro-dealers, and smugglers, should dare to defy the whole force of the British Crown was marvellous enough; but that such presumption would be successful was an idea too wild and extravagant to enter into the mind of any inhabitant of this island before the evacuation of Boston by His Majesty's forces. Nor was such a design originally entertained by those American patriots who afterwards pursued it with so much vigour and constancy. The great intellect of Franklin had formed no plan for the independence of his country. The public spirit of Washington would have been satisfied with the redress of actual grievances. Even the Boston agitators, who first kindled the flames of war, would have been content to stop far short of separation. The colonies, so far from being actuated by the spirit which has urged other subject states to conquer their freedom, were proud of their connection with this country; and it was only when the policy of England was aimed at their commercial interests, that their ancient loyalty received a check. Still the colonies, with the exceptions of Massachusetts and Virginia, showed every disposition to avoid a quarrel with the mother-country; the non-importation compact was at first only partially adopted; and it was not until the Home Government manifested a determination to carry their measures by force, that the provinces organised an active resistance. At the first General Congress of the States, in 1774, moderate counsels prevailed; and while the grievances of which they complained were fully stated, the importance of British connection was as fully recognised. That these were at the time the genuine sentiments of the great majority of the colonists there is abundant proof, although in the following year war was raging, and the provincial militia had encountered the King's troops in a pitched battle with a result almost doubtful.*

Negligence of the royal troops.

Even after the battle of Bunker's Hill, and the evacuation of Boston, the war was conducted by the royal army with a carelessness which argued a rash and unfounded contempt for the provincials. Famous regiments, which had encountered the legions of France and Spain, almost felt it an indignity to be sent against a raw colonial militia, led by farmers, shop-keepers, and publicans. It is true, that the half-clad, ill-fed, unpaid levies, which could with difficulty be kept to their standards, and hardly ever stood their ground in the open field against the disciplined troops of Europe, might not in themselves have been a very formidable force; but they were defending their own soil; they were animated by a cause more moving than military glory; they knew the country; they were favoured by their countrymen; they could disperse and re-unite; their habits peculiarly qualified them to act as sharpshooters;—an arm of the most harassing description to an invading army, which has to occupy an extensive and thinly-peopled country. It was the rifle which inflicted the first great disaster that befell the British arms, the destruction of Burgoyne's detachment. It was the same weapon, in the experienced hands of the 'minute' men, which cut off the stragglers and foraging parties of the enemy, rendering every forest a fortress, and every bush a redoubt. Nevertheless, had prompt and

---

* The Congress of 1774, in their address to the people of Great Britain, used this language: 'You have been told that we are seditious, impatient of government, and desirous of independence. Be assured that these are not facts, but calumnies.' Nearly all the leading men in the colonies believed, at this time, that proper representations to the English Government would ensure redress and accommodation upon fair and just terms.— ELLIOTT's *New England History*, vol. ii. p. 381.

efficient military measures been taken at the outset, the rebellion would have been suppressed; and even in 1782, had England put forth her strength, she might have scattered the armies of Congress, garrisoned the principal cities, and established a chain of posts throughout the states; but she could not have conquered the country. The spirit of freedom, which had impelled a rude and unwarlike people to take up arms, and had enabled them, without military equipment or foreign aid, to hold their own for nearly seven years against the armies and foreign mercenaries of Great Britain, was not to be finally subdued by any force, however overwhelming, which might be brought against them. Nor would England have persevered in such an unprofitable and ungrateful effort. The war had been popular with all classes in the mother-country, partly from that imperial spirit which could not brook the insolence of a revolted dependency, and partly, also, because it was believed that America might be made to bear her share of the public burdens. But when it was found that the public burdens had been nearly doubled in the vain attempt to coerce the colonies, the English nation were as ready to put an end to the struggle by yielding everything in dispute, as they had before been arrogant in demanding unconditional submission. George the Third, self-willed and obstinate as he was, could, nevertheless, discern the temper of his people; and when he reluctantly gave up the contest, he did so, assuredly not from a conviction that his military resources were exhausted, or that his arms were hopelessly worsted, but because he saw that the House of Commons represented the sense of the country in demanding peace.

The narration of this great event has been of necessity brief, and therefore imperfect; but a reference to more copious details *Institution of Congress.* of the American revolution, and the war by which it was consummated, sufficiently shows, that if the conduct of England throughout the transaction was neither wise nor magnanimous, the victorious colonists had exhibited few of the qualities by which the noblest efforts of patriotism have been achieved. The agitators of Boston, with whom the revolutionary movement originated, and by whom it was for the most part kept alive until the outbreak of hostilities, contributed little, either by their counsels or their valour, to the success of the cause. The Congress of Delegates, from the various provincial assemblies, was an idea worthy of a people united and determined to conquer their freedom. The earlier meetings of this great assembly were guided by prudent counsels, and animated by eloquence, not below the grandeur of its theme; nor did the delegates spend their energy in debate, nor waste the precious time for action in declamations about liberty. They hit, with happy precision, the moment for casting aside temporary measures, and committing their constituents, while still irresolute, to a final conflict with the power of Great Britain. The Declaration of Independence followed promptly the collision of arms. Up to this period, the Congress of the United States may bear comparison with the most renowned Senates and Parliaments of any age or country. But, after the Declaration, the vigour of the assembly seemed to be exhausted. It lost its control over the provinces; it became an arena for personal jealousies and selfish aims; its deliberations had no result, and its counsels sank into imbecility. After the action at Long Island, and while the English forces were rapidly extending their lines from the base of their operations at New York; the Congress, in answer to the urgent requisition of their General for a few battalions of regular troops, occupied itself in discussing the question of the danger of standing armies; and, even after this trifling had given way to the stress of circumstances, no adequate provision was made for the pay, the clothing, or the equipment of the regiments which were to be raised. The deterioration of this once famous assembly proceeded so far, that at last they placed more reliance on the efforts of France or Spain, or any other foreign power which would undertake the conquest of American freedom, than on their own exertions or those of their countrymen. The Congress, jealous of the General, gave him little support or en- *Authority of Congress.* couragement; and the Provincial Assemblies, jealous of the Congress, were slow in supplying the contingents of men and money that were assessed upon them. The soldiers themselves, impatient of the discipline and service which regular military operations rendered necessary, could with difficulty be kept to their standards, even when they could depend on their pay, clothing, and rations. The regimental officers murmured at the preferment bestowed on foreign military adventurers, who had taken service in the continental army; and there were not wanting orators in the assemblies, to express indignation, that Congress and the Commander-in-Chief should favour captains and colonels, who had learned the art of war under Ferdinand or Frederick the Great, before the patriotic blacksmiths, tailors, and bookbinders, who commanded the companies and battalions of the Federal army.

We have seen that the difficulty of keeping an army in the field was experienced in the first year of the war; and with a leader *Washington's difficulties.* of less virtue, prudence, and constancy, than the admirable person upon whom the fate of the revolution ultimately depended, the event would probably have been reversed. Washington knew his own importance; and it was this sober conviction which sustained his equanimity, and enabled him to carry on the great work which he had undertaken, amidst all the disheartening circumstances by which he was surrounded. He attained the success which commonly waits upon courage, fortitude, and constancy. And as his object was the highest which can be proposed to human ambition, so has his success placed him foremost among that illustrious band of heroes and statesmen who have achieved the independence or the salvation of their country.

It cannot be said that this proud pre-eminence has been assigned to superior genius or capacity. Unless we accept the affair of Trenton, which was probably planned by Arnold, no great military exploit signalised the command of Washington during this protracted war. But, if he displayed few of the qualities which form a great military Commander, no General was more cautious, or committed fewer mistakes. His encampment at Valley Forge, in the winter of 1777, without having made any provision for sheltering, clothing, or even feeding his scanty force, would seem to have been an act of great temerity; for if the royal army at Philadelphia had made the attack which he provoked, it is difficult to conceive how he could have escaped utter destruction; he was saved only by a degree of negligence and misconduct on the part of the English Commander, upon which, however mean his opinion of Howe might have been, he could hardly have ventured to calculate. Neither was it by political ability that Washington either acquired or maintained his power. He was appointed to lead the army of the Republic, in preference to the shining orators and vaunting patriots of the Congress and Provincial Assemblies, because he was a man of approved sense and character, who had espoused the cause of his countrymen, not lightly, but from deliberate conviction. His success was owing far more to moral than intellectual qualities; and the great

Washington as a General.

example of Washington may be added to the numerous instances, which prove that honesty, patience, firmness, and perseverance, will prevail in human affairs, before the most brilliant talents, unsupported by these qualifications.

Washington has obtained greater fame for the purity of his patriotism, than even for the conquest of his country's freedom. We are so much accustomed to see the profession of patriotism abused by vulgar and hypocritical pretenders, that any display of unsophisticated public spirit excites unbounded admiration; and it so rarely happens in the history of the world that an individual, born in a private station, has the opportunity of declining supreme power, that he who resists such a temptation is considered the most exalted of the human race. Such was the Cincinnatus of Old Rome and the Doria of Modern Italy. It is extremely doubtful whether several states associated temporarily for a common object, but tenacious each of its separate independence, and alien from the other in character, religion, and race, could be united in monarchical government; though, even had the federal crown been solemnly offered to him, we may safely conclude that Washington would have had the firmness to refuse the dazzling gift. We know that he rejected with prompt indignation a proposal to elevate him in the usual way, by means of the army; and no further movement was made in that direction. His disinterestedness as regards pecuniary reward is hardly worth mentioning after the greater act of self-denial which we have had to record. It is more remarkable, that a man of ample fortune and domestic habits, singularly free from ambition or enthusiasm, should, in middle life, quit a happy home to engage in a doubtful cause, and endure for seven years the most harassing anxiety and vexation, than that he should reject a pecuniary acknowledgment of his services. After having effected the liberation of his country, not by any dazzling feat or masterstroke of policy, but by slow and painful efforts, this admirable man was content to return to his home, and to draw from his own conscience that reward which could not be conferred by the plaudits of a multitude, or the glitter of a crown.

CHAPTER XXVIII.

INDIA AND THE INDIA BILLS—DISMISSAL OF THE COALITION MINISTRY—PITT PRIME MINISTER—GREAT STRUGGLE IN THE HOUSE OF COMMONS—DISSOLUTION OF PARLIAMENT.

THE great question, which had principally engaged the attention of the Government and the country for the last twelve years, having been settled by the treaty of 1783, other affairs, of scarcely inferior magnitude, called for the immediate action of the Government.

Among these the most prominent was the condition of India. Within the lifetime of a single generation, a joint-stock trading company had become the masters of ancient kingdoms and rich provinces, which Alexander, in the height of his ambition, had vainly sighed to possess, which Timour had invaded, and Aurungzebe had ruled—the inheritance of the Great Mogul. How this vast territory was won by the valour of a captain taken from the counting-house of a trading company at Madras, and how it was extended and consolidated by the policy of a statesman taken from a counting-house at Calcutta, has been often related. I shall not enter upon the exploits of Clive, or the administration of Hastings. This wonderful theme has been illustrated by the pen most worthy to commemorate such deeds; and the detailed history of our Indian Empire is to be found in works of established reputation and authenticity.

The East India Company became in reality, though
not in name, a sovereign power. From
her central seat of government in London,
she appointed vicegerents of her widely-extended and
increasing empire. She made treaties with the
princes of India, whose independence she still deigned
to tolerate. The patronage which she dispensed was
larger than that of the British Government. Young
Englishmen of the best families sought commissions
in her armies, and employment in her diplomatic
service. Thousands of persons, despising the slow
and uncertain competition of the professions and
trades of their native country, sought a more open
and rapid road to fortune in the dominions of the
Great Company; and in a few years the adventurers
returned, many of them able to vie with the wealthy
proprietors and old nobility of their native land in
the profusion of their hospitality, and the splendour
of their appointments. Some of these Nabobs, as
they were called, obtained peerages, others became
purchasers of seats in the House of Commons. The
Company itself was a large borough owner; and some
of its tributary princes even had their nominees in the
British Parliament.

The difficulty of administering the government of
distant dependencies by the central authority
has, in all ages, been sensibly felt,
even when the desire of consulting the
interests and welfare of the governed has guided the
imperial rule; but it is obvious that these difficulties
must be aggravated to an incalculable degree when
the managing Board of a trading company, without
any political vocation, and constituted for the sole
purpose of obtaining the best return for the capital
invested in the common stock, attempt to discharge
so grave a duty. The Directors in Leadenhall Street
hardly affected to recognise the higher responsibility
which had devolved upon them in their political

capacity; but it would be far too great a compliment to say, that their Asiatic possessions were governed merely on the narrow and selfish principles of commercial profit. The mercantile system, as it had hitherto prevailed, though narrow and selfish, was, on the whole, consistent with common honesty. The greed of gain, stimulated by the sudden development of resources which seemed inexhaustible, broke all bounds; and riches were followed in the distant regions of Asia, not by the rules of commercial enterprise, but by rapacity and plunder. The servants of the Company went out to India, in the first instance, to make their own fortunes, and then to swell the dividends of their employers. Territories were added to the dominions of the Company by fraud and violence. Money was obtained from the helpless natives by falsehood and fraud; and, when these means were exhausted, by tortures and indignities, the practice of which, in the worst of times, had not disgraced the English name.

These excesses at length reacted on the guilty authors. While the Company occupied only a few trading stations in the country, their transactions with the people were fairly conducted, and yielded an abundant profit to the shareholders. Their dividend had ranged from six to ten per cent.; and they had been able to conciliate the favour of the Government, and obtain a renewal of their charter, from time to time, by fines and loans of considerable magnitude. In 1767, twelve years after the commencement of the war with France, during which short period the greater part of their conquests had been acquired, the Company were at the height of prosperity. Their net revenue was upwards of two millions sterling; their debt was under seven millions, about twice the amount of their trading capital. The annual profits of their trade were half a million. They readily agreed to pay four hundred thousand pounds per annum to the State in respect of the territorial revenues of India, to which the State laid claim. They proposed at this time to raise their dividend to twelve and a half per cent., but were restrained by Acts of Parliament, which obliged them to apply a portion of their revenues towards the liquidation of their debt. A few years passed, and this prosperity was reversed. The exactions of the Indian Government, in process of time, necessarily diminished, and the ordinary revenue was insufficient to maintain the civil and military establishments, which their rapacious and arbitrary policy obliged them to keep on foot. In 1773 they were not only unable to pay the imperial tribute of four hundred thousand pounds, but were forced to borrow nearly a million and a quarter to save themselves from impending bankruptcy. Their dividend was reduced to six per cent. The British Government took alarm. A parliamentary inquiry was instituted; and an Act was passed, known by the name of the Regulating Act, which made a material change in the constitution of the Company.

The regulations of 1773 proved a very inadequate remedy for the gigantic evils which they were intended to control. The great and manifest evil was, that a trading partnership, whose chief business, and even duty, it was to extort the utmost profit from the territory which they occupied, should be suffered to exercise the functions of political government in any form. But if it was deemed expedient to delegate to the Company the exercise of imperial authority, it was surely of the first importance that careful provision should be made for the separation of the mercantile from the political office. More especially, the department of public revenue should have been kept distinct from that of trade, and the proceeds of the former applied wholly to the exigences of the Local Government, under the control of an imperial audit. These precautions, however, were for the most part neglected. The chief seat of government, indeed, was established at Calcutta, and consisted of a Governor-General and Council, appointed by the Crown for five years; but in every other respect, except that of peremptory dismissal, subject and responsible to the Company. A Supreme Court of Judicature, framed on the model of the Superior Courts of Common Law in this country, was constituted also at the principal residency; but the authority of this tribunal was so ill-defined and so irresponsible, that it became another engine of oppression, rather than a shield against injustice and violence. The House of Commons emulated instead of corrected the vices of the Company. Led away by the same fatal error which lost the American colonies, and flattered by the delusive idea that India was a source of inexhaustible wealth, the Commons passed resolutions, by which they fixed a limit of eight per cent. to the dividend of the Company, and appropriated the surplus revenues of India to the purposes of the State. The Company, in consideration of this arrangement, were relieved from the further payment of the four hundred thousand pounds a year, which, by the act of Lord Chatham's Government, had been assessed upon them; and as the collection of the revenue was left in their hands, not a shilling ever found its way into the coffers of the State.

A few years of such government as this sufficed to bring the affairs of India to a crisis. *Exposure of malpractices.* In 1781, the whole condition of British India, as well as the affairs of the Company, became the subject of parliamentary investigation by two committees, the one secret, the other open. These committees, severally, made elaborate reports, all condemnatory of the Company's government; and especially of their Governor, Warren Hastings, and the Chief Justice of the Supreme Court, Impey. The disclosures made by these reports, relating as they did to transactions of a character such as had not been associated with British rule for more than two centuries, and equalling in cruelty and oppression the worst excesses of Norman tyranny, created such horror and indignation, that resolutions were passed by the Commons for the immediate dismissal of the Governor and the Chief Justice. The latter was accordingly recalled by the authority of the Secretary of State; but the Directors in Leadenhall Street reminded the House, that the right of naming and removing the Governor-General was vested in themselves, by Act of Parliament. And as the Directors were more fully informed than the committees of the Commons, as to the merits as well as demerits of their great officer, Hastings continued in power until the end of his term of office in 1785.

I shall have occasion to review the transactions which distinguished the administration of the eminent person principally inculpated, when the course of this narrative brings me to that great penal inquiry into his conduct, instituted by the Commons of England, and carried on with a rigour and oppression which, in modern times, have been paralleled only by some of the proceedings charged against Hastings himself.

It was impossible, however, that the labours of these committees, which had investigated the strange and complex question of Indian politics, with so much skill and industry, could be allowed to pass unnoticed. Accordingly, in the spring of 1783, immediately after the formation of the Coalition Cabinet, Mr. Dundas, who had been Chairman of the Secret Committee, obtained leave to introduce a Bill for the better government of India. His motion, however, partook of a party character, and was intended as much to embarrass the Ministry as to benefit the people of Hindostan. He proposed to increase the power of the Governor-General, by making him independent of the Council; to add to his duties those of Commander-in-Chief, and to confer the united offices upon a person of high rank and public character, whose position would be a security against those abuses of power to which a person of inferior condition would be prone. The individual designated by Mr. Dundas was Lord Cornwallis, in opposition to Mr. Francis, the late Member of Council, who, as he had been the chief witness before the committees and the most rancorous enemy of Hastings, was supposed to be the candidate favoured by Burke, and the administration of which he was a member. But the advanced state of the session, as well as the general sense of Parliament, that a matter of such importance should be dealt with by the responsible government, prevented the further progress of Dundas's Bill; and the public were content to wait, though with much interest and expectation, for the measures which the King's Government would take, with regard to a state of affairs so novel and so momentous.

The state of India and the Company formed the prominent topic in the King's speech, on opening the autumnal session of 1783; *King's speech.* and in a few days Mr. Fox introduced a Bill for the better government of India.

If there ever were a question, which, regarding its nature, should have risen above the low *Importance of* element of party, and which in its acci- *India.* dents had little or nothing to provoke the conflict of Whig and Tory, it was that which His Majesty recommended to the calm consideration of Parliament. The American controversy had been peculiarly fitted for party purposes; it brought into direct collision the principles which had agitated public opinion in this country for a hundred and fifty years; but no theories derived from the British Constitution could affect a scheme for regulating the government or the revenues of India. Vast dominions, the seats of ancient dynasties, the abodes of commerce and the arts of civilisation, at a time when this island was a forest, peopled by painted savages, had, by a strange and sudden turn of fortune, become a part of the British empire. Measured indeed by the ideas of modern Europe, these distant regions, though still accounted rich beyond comparison in many natural products and artificial luxuries, could not be placed on an equal footing with civilised nations. Retaining their manners unimpaired probably, and unimproved, through a series of ages, the people of Asia, blind to the light of revelation, and ignorant of political science, had no higher pretensions than those of splendid barbarians. With a religion, which, in ceremonial observance, and every art calculated to subdue the senses, emulated the religion of Rome, and with a doctrine compared with which the doctrine of Rome, at the time when she most sorely tempted the credulity and patience of mankind, was sublime and rational, the Hindoos have ever been the most superstitious of the human race. Their political institutions were few and simple, forming indeed a part of their religious system. Like all the people of the East, they had no other idea of government than that of absolute monarchy; whether under the dominion of their native princes, or their Mahometan conquerors, who had from time to time invaded and occupied various parts of the territory of the Great Mogul.

Such were the nations, which, in the marvellous vicissitude of human affairs, had fallen under English rule. They had been obtained, partly by the fortune of war, which comprises some of the most brilliant passages in our military annals; partly by violence and fraud, such as can hardly be paralleled in the dark and bloody history of conquest since the world began. Neither the glory nor the infamy of these conquests belongs to the British Government. It had no part in the exploits of Clive, nor in the administration of Hastings. The task which the British Ministry and Parliament undertook, was to provide for the government of the rich provinces, which the valour and policy of the servants of the Company had won, but which the unaided efforts of the Company were confessedly unable to manage.

Such was the great question with which Parliament had to deal; a question which seemed calculated to test the capacity, rather than the stability, of the new administration. But the Indian policy of the coalition gave rise to the most memorable struggle that had taken place within the walls of the House of Commons since the days of the Long Parliament, determining the fate of parties, and what was of far more importance, the character and general policy of the British Government for nearly fifty years.

On the earliest possible day after the commencement of the session, Mr. Fox brought forward the India Bill. It was introduced in a speech equal to the gravity of the subject and the high reputation of the minister. The measure itself, whatever judgment may be passed upon it at this distance of time, was one conceived by the mind of a statesman. It was no peddling temporising evasion of a great difficulty, but a bold, a comprehensive, and vigorous project.

Opening of the session.

The principles on which a measure adequate to the subject, as well as to the actual exigency, which demanded imperial legislation, should be framed would seem to have been obvious. A territory, wider in extent, more thickly peopled, and estimated richer than all the dominions of the British Crown put together, was held in actual sovereignty by a company of merchant adventurers, trading under the protection of charters granted by the British Crown. This was an instance of the *imperium in imperio*, on a scale to which the history of the world could furnish no parallel. It was true, indeed, that the Company could acquire no independent right of sovereignty over the provinces which they had conquered. That right belonged unquestionably to the Crown to which the Company owed allegiance; but until defined and set in motion by Parliament, the right was merely theoretical and nominal. The first question, then, for Parliament to determine, was whether the Crown should assume the active exercise of its rights. The anomalous character of the existing government of British India might not be a sufficient reason for deposing it; but the burden of proof seemed to lie on those who argued for the maintenance of the Company's authority. If the dominions of the Nabobs and the Rajahs were to be retained, it was surely more decent that a people who knew no other form of government than that of monarchy, should recognise as their sovereign lord the King of Great Britain, rather than a trading corporation; and, if their affairs could be administered in London, a Secretary of State's office at Whitehall was more appropriate than a counting-house in the City. There was another consideration, and that the most material. The Company lay under accusation of having cruelly and scandalously abused the privileges of rulers. Their principal servants had been inculpated of gross malversation by a unanimous resolution of the House of Commons; and the Company had, nevertheless, upheld their officers in spite of the opinion of Parliament and of the ministers of the Crown. The administration of justice had been so notoriously and scandalously abused, that the chief judge had been dismissed, in spite of the Company, by the authority of the King's Government. Nor had the Company purchased material prosperity by the open violation of the principles on which civil government, nay, society itself, is based. Plunder and extortion had only relieved their immediate and temporary exigencies. The ordinary resources of India were unequal to satisfy the greedy adventurers who were spread over the land, and to maintain the military force which was necessary to support an arbitrary and iniquitous government. The Company, therefore, came before Parliament as delinquents, who had grossly abused their trust, and as bankrupts unable to perform their engagements.

The remedy for these evils appeared on the surface. An anomalous power had accidentally fallen into hands wholly incompetent to exercise it. Let the power be transferred to lawful authority; let the Crown assume the responsibility of governing those dominions which belonged to it in right of sovereignty. This, in effect, was what the minister proposed to do. His plan was to erect a great department which should be charged with the direction of the whole administration of India. All the power and authority exercised by the Company over the territory and people of India were to be vested in seven commissioners, nominated, in the first instance, by Parliament, for four years, and afterwards to be appointed by the Crown. All the real property, charters, and title-deeds of the Company were to be transferred to the commissioners, who were also to stand possessed, as trustees, for the benefit of the Company, of all their stocks, goods, and chattel interests. The property and commerce of the Great Corporation were to be placed under the superintendence of a subordinate Board of eight persons, nominated also, in the first instance, by Parliament, but afterwards to be appointed by the Court of Proprietors. The Board was to sit in London, their minutes and proceedings were to be regularly laid before both Houses, and they were to exercise their functions under the immediate control of Parliament.

Proposed transfer of power to the Crown.

By a separate Bill, provision was made for the reform of some of the principal abuses in the local administrations. Monopolies were to be abolished; the acceptance of presents from the natives by persons holding office was prohibited; the Supreme Council were interdicted from delegating their powers; the tenure of land was placed on a more secure and equitable footing; and many other beneficial regulations were proposed. To this Bill, so far as it went, no considerable objection could be urged; but the principal measure was opposed with a vehemence almost unparalleled, and denounced as the most flagitious proposal ever submitted to Parliament.

Monopolies to be abolished.

The Bill, however, simply provided for the transference of the government of British India from a body elected by the proprietors of Indian Stock, to a body nominated, in the first instance, by the Legislature, and afterwards by the Crown; and insomuch as it was intended to deprive the Company of political power, which it was agreed on all hands they had abused, and were unfit to exercise, the Bill went no farther than the justice and the exigency of the case demanded. But there was a plain distinction between the political and the commercial character of the Company. The former was, in a sense, usurped; the latter rightfully and properly belonged to them. Their commercial privileges had been conferred and ratified by Charters and Acts of Parliament. The most recent statute, the twenty-first of the present reign, while it continued their commercial charter for a further period of fourteen years, expressly reserved the question as to their claim to the territories they had conquered; a reservation which clearly implied that Parliament, during the period limited, might deal with the one subject though not with the other. There was a plain reason for this distinction. The Directors in

Provisions of the India Bill.

Leadenhall Street had been bad rulers; but their commercial enterprise and ability were unquestionable. They had opened up extensive and permanent channels for the commerce of these islands. They had, for many years, divided a large per-centage among their proprietary; and they had diffused riches throughout the length and breadth of the land. These results could hardly have been attained by the efforts of private enterprise. It was true that the financial affairs of the Company had become embarrassed; but those difficulties were caused by the incongruous union of imperial with mercantile concerns, and in nowise affected their solvency or credit as a great trading corporation.

The measure of the Government dealt with the Company, on the assumption that they were as incapable of conducting their commercial affairs as of discharging the political functions with which they were charged. In this sweeping and indiscriminate legislation, the minister was hurried into the very error which it was the object of his Bill to rectify; for even admitting (which there was no pretence to allege) that the commercial affairs of the Company were in such disorder as to justify a breach of the stipulations contained in the Act of 1780, and to call for immediate regulation, it is certain, that a more unfit superintendence than that of a parliamentary commission sitting in London over commercial transactions, of which they had no special knowledge, and in which they had no pecuniary interest, could hardly have been devised.

Defects of the measure.

The principal Bill was open to other objections of considerable weight. The peculiar constitution of the new department, which it was proposed to create, might well alarm the jealousy of those who thought it of importance to maintain constitutional usage, and the due distribution of power among the several orders of the State. It

Anomalous position of the Whigs.

was proposed by a minister of the Crown that Parliament should delegate to a body of its own choice, and virtually responsible only to itself, the whole government and patronage of a large portion of the empire. Such an encroachment on the functions of the executive had not been attempted since the days of the Long Parliament. But the party in power were in this difficulty. When in opposition, they had committed themselves to the famous resolution which they induced the House of Commons to adopt, that 'the influence of the Crown had increased, was increasing, and ought to be diminished'—a proposition which refuted itself; for if such had been the power of the Crown, it would have prevented the House of Commons from recording such a conclusion. But the dogma, however absurd, was so recent, that the party who proposed it were, in decency, precluded from augmenting the influence of the Crown by the rich patronage of India. To avoid the odium and ridicule which would attach to such a proceeding, the Whigs were driven to a breach of the constitution, and a direct invasion of prerogative.

It was generally admitted that the state of India was such as to require measures of extraordinary vigour. An opinion prevailed, sanctioned by Burke and other public men of high authority, that the Company's servants had been guilty of every excess of cruelty and rapine. Clive, the conqueror of India, whose exploits were those of a hero of romance, and whose conduct was that of a consummate commander, had lately gone down to his grave covered with obloquy. Hastings, the vicegerent of the Company, who had consolidated and extended the empire which Clive had won, lay under grievous imputations, and was already menaced with that great prosecution by which, a few years later, the foremost men in England sought to bring him to infamy and ruin. All parties in Parliament, except, of course, the party of the East India Company, were agreed as to the necessity of extensive and searching legislation; the Government of Lord North had taken up the subject; and the succeeding Government had proposed a Bill, which virtually transferred the whole government of India to the Crown.

Mr. Fox's India Bill was not, therefore, on account of the sweeping character of its provisions, calculated to excite public alarm or indignation. On the contrary, the measure was likely to be approved in proportion as it dealt most severely with the Company. But, much as the Company were in disrepute, there was another body of men still more unpopular, and this was His Majesty's Government.

Unpopularity of the Coalition.

The Coalition had given public opinion a shock, from which it could not readily recover. Parties which, for the last ten years, had been confronted in bitter hostility; statesmen, who had personally and unceasingly denounced each other with a license far exceeding the limits of free discussion, had suddenly combined to supplant the minister of the day. No man, who considers the vicissitudes to which politics, in common with all human affairs, are liable, will exact from public men either a rigid consistency, or an eternal perseverance in their party divisions; and there are emergencies when public spirit calls upon statesmen to forget their past animosities, and unite for the common good; but the alliance of North and Fox was merely a combination of two parties to obtain political power, and to deprive the Sovereign of all choice in the appointment of his ministers. If such a manœuvre was to be successful, the Government would thenceforth become the sport of faction; there could no longer be any confidence in public men; and ministers would practically cease to be responsible, either to the Crown or to the country.

Under these circumstances, the Ministry depended on a majority of the House of Commons, which, in the present temper of the nation, might, by the exercise of prerogative, be at any moment dispersed; and it was probable that the King would seize the first favourable opportunity which presented itself, of appealing to the sense of the people, against the coercion to which he had been subjected. That opportunity was afforded by the India Bill. The measure might easily be represented by the arts of adverse eloquence, and, as has been shown, not altogether without reason, as at once an attack upon the Crown, upon chartered rights and vested interests, and upon the independence of Parliament. The Bill was received with a storm of opposition. In front of the battle appeared William Pitt, already the rival of Fox, in the House of Commons, and aspiring to the highest office in the State. He was ably supported by his cousin, William Grenville, soon to become a statesman of high authority. These leaders had a long following; among the most conspicuous of whom may be noted John Scott, afterwards Lord Chancellor Eldon, and Henry Flood, the rival of Grattan in the Irish Parliament. Both of these eminent persons addressed the House, for the first time on the India Bill, and the speeches of both were signal failures. Scott made perhaps the most absurd speech that had ever been heard within the walls of the House of Commons. It is not often that a member of the learned profession has the good fortune to be heard with favour by that fastidious and jealous assembly; and a finer opportunity than this debate afforded to a legal candidate for parliamentary distinction rarely occurs. It was a question of high constitutional law, of chartered rights, and vested interests. But the eminent lawyer, instead of confining himself to these topics, on which he might have

spoken with authority, fancied the subject was one
to be treated with wit, raillery, and sarcasm, and
that his was the hand which could wield those dangerous weapons. He pulled a Bible out of his pocket,
and proceeded to show, by quoting long passages, that
the Bill was foreshadowed in the Book of Revelation—an illustration the like of which had not been
witnessed within those walls since the time of Bare-
bones. From the New Testament, Mr. Scott passed
to Thucydides and Shakespeare; he accused Mr.
Fox of attempting to smother the constitution, citing
Othello and the death of Desdemona, as a precedent
in point. The House was too much amazed to laugh;
and the orator resumed his seat amidst significant
silence. Flood likewise failed altogether to sustain
the high reputation which he had brought from the
other side of the channel. He spoke in the last stage
of the discussion, when the subject, as well as the
patience of the House, was nearly exhausted. He
began by saying that he was wholly unacquainted with
the question, that he had not read a line of the Reports which lay upon the table, but nevertheless that
he had come over from Ireland expressly for the
purpose of taking a part in the debate; a singular
mode of propitiating the attention of any audience,
and especially of an audience jealous, beyond every
other, of mere oratorical display. This exordium,
followed as it was by a vapid declamation, soon
thinned the benches, which had been crowded by
the announcement that the great Irish orator was on
his legs, and the profound silence which denotes the
eager expectation of the House subsided into the
buzz of conversation, significant of its fatal disappointment and indifference. Among the most violent in
denunciation of the Bill was Wilkes, who, finding
there was no longer any occupation for a demagogue,
had lately appeared as the champion of order, the opponent of political progress, and the stoutest stickler

for prerogative against the 'hungry and ravenous Coalition,' which held possession of the Government against His Majesty's will.

The Bill was defended against a torrent of invective, chiefly by the eloquence and ability of Fox and Burke; the former, regardless of the provocation he received, maintained the demeanour which accorded with the magnanimity of his character, the position which he held as Leader of the House of Commons, and the grave importance of the question. He calmly exposed the exaggerations with which the measure and its authors were assailed. He admitted, with a boldness which is sometimes the highest reach of art, the principal argument of the Opposition. The Bill *was* an invasion of chartered rights; and it was justified by the necessity, which, though often the pretext of tyranny, was sometimes the plea of freedom. The Revolution, to which the country owed its liberties, was a violation of chartered rights. The magnitude and extent of the evil with which they had to deal were acknowledged on all sides. The Company had grossly abused the trust committed to them, and the foundation of their Charter was consequently gone. They had proved wholly incompetent to rule, and their own principal functionary, Hastings himself, who had so long administered their affairs, attributed all the disasters of India to the system of government adopted and pursued by the Court of Directors. The late Ministry had proposed to set aside the Company, and to vest absolute power in a great nobleman, who should be placed at the head of the Local Government. That was the plan of Mr. Dundas. The Secretary of State then reviewed the different wars in which the Company had engaged, and showed that under the discretion they exercised, no security existed against this country being involved against its will, and without its knowledge, in a war

Fox and Burke's defence of the Bill.

with France. He went also into a variety of details of mismanagement and malversation in the financial department, which had repeatedly demanded, and at the instance of the Company itself, the aid and interposition of Parliament. He proved by examples of recent occurrence, that the authority of the Indian Government was rapidly diminishing throughout its extensive territory, and that unless a thorough change took place, our rich possessions in the East would be wrested from us, or would recover their independence. If India was to be ruled by absolute government, and no other form of government was practicable, he was unwilling to confide such enormous powers to the hands of a single individual, exercising his functions in a distant land, far beyond the constitutional control of the British nation. He had adopted therefore the only alternative which presented itself, for securing the moderate and just exercise of absolute power, by delegating it to a body of English gentlemen, appointed by the supreme authority at home, acting under the eye of the Government and the people of this country, and responsible to Parliament for the performance of their duties.

Burke, who as the reputed author of the Bill was more immediately concerned in its vindication, supported his great chief in one of those elaborate and masterly orations which transcend all the recorded eloquence of modern times, and emulate the noblest effusions of antiquity. His mind, amply informed on every subject of importance to which he addressed himself, was stored with knowledge on every point relating to the history, government, and manners of the people of India. His genius, akin to all that was elevated and grand, and prone to exaggerate every object of its contemplation, had long dwelt on the antiquity, the splendour, and the traditions of the East. He regarded India, the earliest seat of industry and commerce, whose products and manufactures had been sought by the great people of antiquity, and which had first taught the arts of civilisation to modern Europe, as now given up to a generation of sordid factors, and subjected to the vilest tyranny, insult, and rapine. He could make no allowance either for the difficulties with which the Company had to contend in establishing the authority of the British name over vast provinces, differing from each other in religion and race, but to all of whom the manners and principles of Europe were unknown; nor for the faults of a government, which bad as it might be, could hardly fail to be an improvement on that of the native rulers. His ardent imagination could dwell upon nothing but the awful spectacle of a once mighty empire in ruins, of the subverted thrones, and undone princes of India. Fox, in his opening speech, had desired that the Bill might be discussed without reference to the merits or demerits of Hastings. The character and conduct of the individual who administered the local government of the day ought not, he argued, to affect the consideration of the principles on which the permanent government of the country should be settled. Most of the speakers acquiesced in a suggestion so plainly just and convenient. But Burke could observe no limits, and a great part of his speech was an elaborate and detailed impeachment of the Governor-General. Like Fox, he admitted, with an amplitude indeed which bordered on exaggeration, the chartered rights of the Company; and justified their violation, on the same ground that had been taken by the leading minister. On this part of the subject, he gave a happy turn to an expression which had been used by Pitt. The leader of the Opposition had allowed 'that there were abuses in the Company's government.' 'If that were all,' said Burke, 'the Bill would be needless. There are and must be abuses in all governments. But the question was, whether the abuses of the East India Company's government were of importance sufficient to justify the measure and means of reform applied to it in the Bill.' And the affirmation of this proposition he undertook to establish, by a review of the history of the Company, in their political and commercial relations with the princes and people of India.

Among the eminent men who took part in this great discussion, was Erskine. He had lately been returned to Parliament, and spoke for the first time on the second reading of the Bill. His reputation, as incomparably the greatest orator ever heard on the other side of Westminster Hall, had raised an expectation in the House which had never been equalled by the anticipation of a first speech. But the famous advocate was a parliamentary failure. Pitt, who had come down prepared to find an antagonist who would call forth his highest powers, after listening for a few minutes, contemptuously flung away his notes, and listened no more. The disconcerted orator soon afterwards sat down, amidst the faint applause of his friends, and the hardly suppressed sneers of the Opposition. Erskine frequently took part in debate, but never fully succeeded in obtaining the ear of the House of Commons. *Erskine's failure.*

In vain however was the Bill assailed, either by argument or vituperation. A majority of more than two to one supported the minister in every division, and on the 9th of December the Bill was carried in triumph to the Lords. But there it met with a very different reception.

During the progress of the Bill through the Commons, the King and his secret counsellors were in anxious deliberation as to the course to be pursued. His Majesty, eager to get rid of his hated ministers, would have dismissed them in the full career of their triumph. But, though *Conduct of the King.*

dissuaded from this precipitate measure, the King was determined that the Bill should not become law. Its passage through the Commons was certain, and, unless it could be arrested in the Lords, he would be driven to the extremity of refusing his assent. It was doubtful how far it would be safe to revive a prerogative, which had fallen into disuse since the time of William the Third, and was supposed to be no longer consistent with the independence of Parliament. After an anxious deliberation of a fortnight, it was determined to take a step hardly less bold and hazardous than that which His Majesty, according to the letter of the constitution, might have been justified in adopting. Instead of waiting until the Bill was presented for the royal assent, the King thought fit to intercept it in an intermediate stage. Accordingly, Temple was authorised, by a paper dictated by the King, to signify to any lord who might be willing to receive such a communication, His Majesty's pleasure that he should vote against the Bill.* This paper was freely circulated, and produced the desired effect. Several peers who were wavering, and others who were prepared to support the Government, and had actually given the minister their proxies, were deterred from acting in direct opposition to the Crown. The consequence was,' that the motion for the commitment of the Bill was negatived by a majority of nineteen. A member of the Cabinet, Stormont, the Lord President, voted in the majority.

* On the 1st of December, a paper drawn up by Lord Temple, exposing the character and tendency of the India Bill, was formally presented to the King by Lord Thurlow.

This remarkable document is in the following terms:—'His Majesty allowed Earl Temple to say, that whoever voted for the India Bill was not only not his friend, but would be considered by him as an enemy; and, if these words were not strong enough, Earl Temple might use whatever words he deemed stronger and more to the purpose.'—*Courts and Cabinets of George the Third*, vol. i. p. 288.

The Bill was rejected on the 17th of December, forty-eight hours after the King's pleasure had been intimated. On the same day the Commons met, after a short adjournment, and a scene of great excitement took place. Mr. Baker, a member unconnected with the administration, rose to call the attention of the House to the alleged interference of the King, for the purpose of preventing the progress through the other House of Parliament of a Bill which had been carried up from the Commons; and he moved a resolution ' *that it was necessary to declare*, that to report any opinion, or pretended opinion, of His Majesty upon any Bill or other proceeding depending in either House of Parliament, with a view to influence the votes of the members, is a high crime and misdemeanour, derogatory to the honour of the Crown, a breach of the fundamental privileges of Parliament, and subversive of the constitution of this country.'

This resolution, which aimed at bringing the House into direct collision with the Crown, and was founded on a notable precedent in the Long Parliament,* was strenuously supported by His Majesty's Government, and as strenuously resisted by the party of the King's friends, who had, from their first appointment, been in open opposition to the confidential counsellors of the Crown. But neither Pitt, nor any of the speakers of the Opposition, ventured to defend the course which His Majesty had thought fit to take. They contended rather, that no proof was before the House of such a proceeding as rendered it necessary to make such an assertion of their privileges as would bring the Crown into

* *Comm. Journals*, 67 and 344. November 12th, 1040, and December 10th, 1641.

disrepute, and produce discord between the two
Houses. The statements which had been made in
support of the resolution rested on mere newspaper
reports, which it was beneath the dignity of the
House to notice. Pitt concluded by moving the
order of the day, a mode of evading a question upon
which it is not convenient to pronounce a positive
and direct decision. But Fox and his friends felt
that this was the crisis of their fate. The contest
which, for three and twenty years, had been maintained, with various fortune, between the Crown
and the Whig party, had at length arrived at a
decisive issue. All chance of an accommodation
between these potent rivals for power was at an end,
and it was plain that they must prepare for an immediate and final struggle. The Whigs eagerly
accepted the challenge which had been so insultingly
offered them; and they flattered themselves that
the rash precipitation of their great antagonist would
insure them a final victory.

Fox, therefore, secure in the immediate advantage which he possessed, insisted that the
resolution should be put to the vote. He
denied that it rested on rumour, or surmise, but on
a written record, which would be produced; and
with accents of indignant emphasis, he held up and
read a copy of the insolent language by which Lord
Temple, with the express sanction of the Sovereign,
had successfully intimidated his peers. He declared
that Parliament was robbed of its rights, and menaced with immediate destruction; that the secret
influence, the machinations of which had been unceasing during the whole of His Majesty's reign,
had now risen to an alarming height, and he designated Jenkinson as the notorious agent of this irresponsible power. He knew, he said, that his great
Bill was to be defeated by a majority of bedchamber
lords; and that he himself, whom the people of

England had called to power, was to be displaced by a vile intrigue. But he would not abandon the post in which they had generously placed him. He afterwards repeated, in a still more pointed manner, that, at such a juncture, ministers stood pledged to the public, and could not abandon the affairs of the State to anarchy and destruction. The resolution was carried by a majority of one hundred and fifty-three to eighty. A further resolution, moved by Erskine, pledging the House to reform the abuses in the Indian administration, and denouncing, as a public enemy, any person who should presume to advise His Majesty to prevent, or in any manner to interrupt, the discharge of this important duty, was debated with closed doors, but was carried by a majority of two to one.

While Fox and his colleagues were assuring the House of Commons that they would remain at their posts, the King had determined on the step which should follow the rejection of the India Bill. Twenty-four hours after the fate of the Bill had been decided, and before the menacing resolutions of the House of Commons had been recorded in their journals, North and Fox received His Majesty's commands to resign their seals of office; they were denied even an audience for that purpose, but were desired to send the seals by the Under-Secretaries of State.*

The King's imperious conduct.

It is impossible to defend the conduct of either

* The letters were not delivered until twelve at night, the King having waited all day in expectation that the ministers would resign. Lord North' received his dismissal with characteristic humour. He was in bed when the despatch arrived, and being informed that Sir E. Nepean, the Under-Secretary, desired to see him, he replied, that in that case Sir Evan must see Lady North too; and he positively refused to rise. Sir Evan was accordingly admitted to the bedroom, and, on informing Lord North that he came by His Majesty's commands to demand the seals of his office, Lord North gave him the key of the closet where they were kept, and turned round to sleep.—*Locker MSS.*

party in the transaction, which finally terminated the long struggle between the King and the Whig oligarchy. The rule, which prohibits the use of the King's name for the purpose of influencing the deliberations of either House, operates as much for the protection of the Crown as for the independence of Parliament. The constitution has provided no means by which the opinion of the Sovereign upon any question pending in the Legislature can be communicated either to the Legislature or to the country. If it were otherwise, an opinion of such importance could claim no immunity from that freedom of censure, which, in this country, attends the expression of any opinion calculated to influence public affairs. It is needless to point out the mischievous and unseemly consequences which would ensue. The King, if a man of energy and ability, might press the influence of the Crown to an undue extent; if a man of ordinary capacity, he might bring monarchy into contempt. But it does not follow, because the King is wisely secluded from active participation in public affairs, that he is thereby rendered a passive instrument in the hands of his political servants.* He has in his nobility a body of hereditary counsellors, either of whom may at any time tender him advice, upon which it is competent for him to act. This privilege, however, is plainly abused, when the Sovereign avails himself of it to cabal against his responsible minister, and to open a correspondence with his personal friends and dependants, for the purpose of

Nature of royal responsibility.

The King's want of openness.

---

* George the Third, though he exercised more personal influence over public affairs than any monarch since Elizabeth, thought himself unduly restrained whenever he was prevented having his own way. I have seen the following memorandum, copied from the papers of one of the King's confidential servants. ' He (the King) said, he thought the English constitution the finest system in the world. If it had a fault, it was that of its not being fit for a king. *He was the only slave.*'—*Locker* MSS.

defeating the measures which his ministers have recommended to Parliament. Yet this was the practice which the King had pursued since the commencement of his reign, though he had never before acted with such contempt of caution and reserve as marked his conduct on the India Bill. If he had been advised that the Bill was an encroachment on the just rights of the Crown, he should have summoned his Cabinet, and demanded that the obnoxious measure should be modified or withdrawn. The alternative of compliance would have been dismissal, or retirement from his service. His Majesty would then have been in a condition to appeal to his Parliament, and from the Parliament to his people. But, far from taking this course, the King never made any communication on the subject of his accredited servants. He had been informed by his late Chancellor of the character of the Bill before it had been submitted to the Commons for a second reading; yet he suffered it to pass through all its stages in the Lower House without any intimation of his pleasure: and it was only when the Bill was brought up to the Lords that he interposed in a clandestine and irregular manner to arrest its progress. But the defeat of the Bill was only a secondary object. His aim, and that of his coadjutors, the two peers, who, under pretence of offering their Sovereign constitutional advice, furnished him with a scheme* for betraying his ministers, was to get rid of those ministers; and the India Bill was made use of for that purpose.

But if the conduct of the King in this transaction was unconstitutional and treacherous, the way in which it was met by ministers was equally indefensible. Their course was clear. If they believed that the King had interfered to defeat their measures, they should have lost no time in laying before His

* Memorandum of 1st of December, laid before the King by Thurlow and Temple.

Majesty the information upon which that belief was founded; and if no sufficient explanation was given, they should forthwith have resigned the offices which they could no longer hold, consistently with their duty to Parliament, to the country, and to each other. But, instead of pursuing this plain, direct course, they adopted a policy of retaliation. The sum and substance of the affair was this; that the King had withdrawn his confidence from his ministers; a case for which the constitution has provided an adequate remedy; but the mere fact of the King's having taken the irregular and unworthy course of discrediting his official servants through the agency of the House of Lords, was no justification for resorting to the extreme measure of obtaining a vote of the House of Commons, which was all but in terms a censure on the Crown. Improper and indecent as it was, that the King should authorise a lord of Parliament to inform the peers that he should consider as his personal enemies those who voted for a measure recommended by his responsible advisers, it would be difficult to make out that such a proceeding, in any sense, affected the privileges or the independence of the House of Commons. But the conduct of the Whigs from the beginning to the end of this business was factious and perverse. If there is one rule better established than another by the constitution of this realm, it is this, that the sovereign has a right to choose his minister, subject only to the approval of Parliament. The party which acceded to power on the overthrow of Lord North's administration, assumed to direct and control the exercise of this prerogative. The appointment by the King of Lord Shelburne to succeed the Marquis of Rockingham, without consulting the Cabinet, afforded the first opportunity for this innovation. The Whigs resigned for the purpose of coercing the Crown, and immediately formed a coali-

Factious proceeding of the Whigs.

tion with their political adversaries to compel him to part with the minister of his choice. The King was forced to yield, and so rigorous were his dictators, that they refused, in the first instance, his urgent request to be allowed to name a single member of the new administration. That His Majesty should seek an opportunity to escape from this duress is not surprising; and if his reign had not been a series of intrigues, and contrivances to undermine and discredit his ostensible and responsible ministers, it would be hardly fair to criticise too keenly the means which he employed.

In this manner the great India Bill was crushed, and the famous Cabinet of the Coalition was dispersed. It would be as difficult to make a vindication of the Bill as of the Government which brought it forward. The charge against the Bill which weighed mostly with the public, the violation, namely, of chartered rights, was little regarded by men of knowledge and reflection.* That the charter of the Company had been modified by successive Acts of Parliament, was certainly no sufficient plea for its resumption, if it was one of those compacts, which are, under all circumstances, to be held inviolate; but with respect to a charter of this anomalous description, involving public interests to an indefinite degree, it would be too much to say that the supreme power of the State was absolutely precluded from altering its provisions. The charge against the Company was, that they had abused, or at least mismanaged, power which had been confided to them, not for their own benefit, but for the welfare of

<small>*Marginal note: Defeat of the Indian Bill.*</small>

<small>* Lord Cornwallis, a man of strong sense, an opponent of the Bill, and an adherent of the preceding administration, which would have sent him to India with plenary powers, had they remained in office, in one of his letters ridicules the pretence that the Bill was a 'during invasion of chartered rights.'—*Correspondence*, vol. i. p. 157. No man of any note in either House dwelt much on this point, with the exception of Grenville.</small>

the large portion of the human race subjected to their control. The very nature of such a gift imposed responsibility on the grantee, and implied a power of resumption in the grantor. So far, therefore, as the Bill deprived the Company of political functions, it was a question of expediency and not of right; but, in limiting the absolute dominion which they possessed over their commercial capital to an usufructuary right, the Bill was arbitrary, unnecessary, and unjust. The grand principle of the Bill, the transference of the imperial authority from the Company to the State, or rather the resumption by the State of the authority which properly belonged to it, and which it could not absolutely alienate, was a sound principle; but the manner in which it was proposed to apply it was so much at variance with our constitutional system, so strange, cumbrous, and inefficient, as to constitute a fatal objection to the measure. Thurlow said, with rhetorical exaggeration, that the Bill would take the crown from the King's head, and place it on that of Mr. Fox. The objection was pointed out with more precision by Jenkinson, who was chiefly concerned in looking at the effect which the Bill would have on the future fortunes of party. 'Suppose,' he said, 'the Commissioners to be appointed for four years, and that a change of Ministry should take place in the meantime. What would be the consequence? The Directors would probably be acting in direct opposition to His Majesty's Government.' A Bill which created patronage to the amount of three hundred thousand pounds[*] a year, which was to be placed in the hands

---

[*] Pitt, on Francis's motion for a Committee on East India Establishments, read a list of the offices of which the holders were to be removable at pleasure, proposed to be created by Fox's Bill. Besides the governors and councils, there was one place of 25,000l. per annum, one of 15,000l., five of 10,000l., five of 9,000l., one of 7,500l., three of 2,000l., and down to places of

of a body of men taken from the ranks of one political party, eligible to sit in Parliament, many of them probably leading members of both Houses, must be equally formidable to the just rights of the Crown and to the independence of Parliament. It was easy to say, that the duration of this formidable body was limited; but the whole plan of the Bill contemplated it as a permanent part of the scheme; and, practically, there could be little doubt that the commission would be renewed before the expiration of its term of office. A permanent body would have been far less objectionable than one constituted for a definite period; in the former case the members would have been connected with the party by whom they were nominated, by what experience has shown to be the frailest of all ties, that of political gratitude; but a Board, in expectation of the renewal of its term, has every motive to be subservient to the minister of the day. These were the arguments which weighed most with men of candour and reflection; yet no satisfactory defence of this part of the scheme was made, or much attempted throughout the debates.[*]

It suited the objects of party to pretend that the India Bill was merely a contrivance for securing political power to its authors; but it is hardly necessary at this day to vindicate the memory of the great men who were concerned in that memorable business from such an imputation. That party considerations

1,000*l*., which, in comparison with the others, he said, were hardly worth mentioning. — *Speeches*, May 5th, 1785.

[*] Lord John Russell, in his Life of Fox, makes light of this objection. 'There is no reason,' he says, 'to believe, that during the four years to which these powers were limited, Lord Fitzwilliam and his colleagues would have exercised an influence greater than that which Commissioners of Excise and Customs, appointed by one Ministry, apply during the sway of a succeeding administration.—*Life of Fox*, vol. ii. p. 48. But Commissioners of Excise and Customs are excluded from Parliament, and are not entrusted with the patronage of their departments. These Boards are, in fact, merely Boards of supervision.

were altogether excluded from the view of the statesmen of the Coalition, it would be folly to maintain; but the first aim of such men as Fox and Burke was, undoubtedly, the good government of India. Those generous minds were capable of rising to the greatness of the subject, and of seeking, in the highest effort of legislation, a fame and a reward far above the fleeting triumphs of faction. Burke, indeed, had long thought, with the vehemence of conviction characteristic of his mind, that the iniquity and incapacity of the Company's government demanded a fundamental change; and no person who is acquainted with the ingenuous nature of Fox, can doubt the sincerity of the declarations which he often made, both in public and private, during the progress of the affair, that he had never acted more fully on principle than he had done on that occasion, and that he felt bound to risk his power, and that of his friends, when the happiness of so many millions was at stake.* The leading ministers, indeed, so far from regarding the India Bill as a means of confirming and consolidating their power, were well aware that they put it to hazard by such a measure, and that, if they consulted their own ease and safety, the most prudent course would be to leave matters as they were, or to propose only some inconsiderable alteration. Lord North, while the Bill was in draught, warned his colleague, that the proposal to vest the government of India in a great parliamentary Board, would probably be fatal to the project and to its authors;† and Fox, in his private communications with his friends before the meeting of Parliament, speculates, with doubt and anxiety, on the fate of the 'vigorous and hazardous' measure he was about to bring forward.

But, though suddenly and strangely hurled from

* *Speeches and Correspondence*, passim.
† Fox's *Correspondence*, vol. ii. p. 218.

power, the Coalition were firmly persuaded that they should almost immediately recover their ascendancy. With a great majority in the House of Commons, and with an equal following in the country, increased, as they flattered themselves, by an unconstitutional invasion of the freedom of Parliament, unprecedented since the time of Charles the First,* they would return to power with the additional strength which proverbially accrues from the discomfiture of a hostile cabal. And it seemed as if their confident expectations would be fulfilled. The seals of office, which had been taken from North and Fox, were delivered by His Majesty to Lord Temple, who, accordingly, sent letters of dismissal to the other members of the Government. It is to be presumed, therefore, that Temple had undertaken the task of forming a new Administration; but, from some unexplained cause, two days after this event, he resigned his office, retired from Court, and took no farther part in the new arrangements. His excuse, or the excuse made for him, was, that he could with more propriety meet any charge which might be preferred against him as a private member of Parliament, than clothed with the influence of office. But he should have thought of this before he assumed the grave responsibility, which attached to a minister of the Crown at such a critical moment, and before he took upon himself, in his capacity as an hereditary counsellor of the Crown, to advise his sovereign that a measure of the first importance, which his constitutional advisers had thought fit to promote, was one which would deprive the Crown of half its power.† Nor was there any charge pending against him. The House of Commons, which adopted the resolutions of the 15th of December, had no thought of pursuing Earl Temple. The

* Fitzpatrick to Lord Ossory. —*Correspondence*, vol. ii. p. 220.
† Memorandum of 1st of December, presented to the King by Thurlow and Temple.

decent forms of the constitution assume that every act of the Sovereign is done in pursuance of advice; but it was notorious that the vote of the House of Commons was really meant as a vote of censure, not upon a meddlesome lord, but upon the Crown itself. Temple, in truth, was a man of wayward temper and slender capacity; and he soon found, or was convinced by others, that he had undertaken a task to which his ability and his authority were wholly unequal. By his youthful and aspiring kinsman, who intended himself to be minister, and none other, the pretensions of Temple were treated with contempt. The haughty chief of the Grenvilles retired to brood over his chagrin at Stowe, and William Pitt kissed hands as First Lord of the Treasury and Chancellor of the Exchequer.*

Pitt was twenty-four years of age when he became Prime Minister of England. He had already attained the highest reputation as a speaker in the House of Commons, and was, therefore, considered qualified for the highest offices in the State. Since the dissolution of Lord Shelburne's Ministry, he had assumed the post of Leader of the Opposition; and in that capacity was, of course, designated for a prominent place in the next administration. Nevertheless, it is hardly possible to conceive a concurrence of circumstances less favourable than those under which Pitt became First Minister. A Court intrigue had displaced a Ministry powerful almost beyond precedent in ability, in experience, and in parliamentary following. Fox, and North, and Burke, and Sheridan had been rudely expelled from power. Against this formidable band, Pitt could oppose little more than

---

* According to Wraxall, Temple resigned, because Pitt refused to consent to an *immediate* dissolution of Parliament. — *Memoirs*, vol. ii. p. 459. Wraxall's authority is not worth much; but it was not unlikely that Temple would urge such counsels, and resign in dudgeon if his advice was not adopted.

his own illustrious name and rising reputation. His cousin, William Grenville, and the ready Scotch lawyer, Dundas, were the only members of his Ministry to whom he could look for the least support in debate; and these men were not of sufficient mark to be included in his Cabinet.* Before him was an insulting majority, confident in their strength and in the tried ability of their leaders, unrivalled in eloquence, in knowledge, and in power. The state of the empire was critical. India must be dealt with by a policy hardly less vigorous and resolute than that which the leading members of the new administration had denounced. Ireland was in a condition which required all the authority, wisdom, and promptitude of the English Government. The revenues of the kingdom were in a state of disorder and embarrassment, resulting from the late war, which called for the highest talents of a financier. To meet these accumulated difficulties, the youthful minister could rely only on his own resources and the support of the Crown. He could hardly hope that these would avail; and he shared in the general opinion that his attempt was desperate. Such was the commencement of the most durable and most potent administration that has ever guided the fortunes of this country.

The day after the dismissal of the Secretaries of State, the writ for Mr. Pitt's borough of Appleby was moved, amidst the derisive laughter of the crowded

---

* The Cabinet consisted of Mr. Pitt, First Lord of the Treasury and Chancellor of the Exchequer; Lord Thurlow, Chancellor; Earl Gower, President of the Council; the Duke of Rutland, Privy Seal; Lord Carmarthen and Lord Sydney, Secretaries of State; and Lord Howe, First Lord of the Admiralty. The Duke of Richmond was Master of the Horse, but not in the Cabinet. Dundas and Grenville held the offices of Treasurer of the Navy and Paymaster. It is remarkable that Lord Shelburne was not included in these arrangements. It does not appear that he was even consulted, nor did he ever again fill any office in the administration.

benches on the left of the chair; and Mr. Fox intimated, with the applause of his supporters, that the uniform practice of postponing important business until the first minister should have resumed his seat, was not to be observed on this occasion. Even the ordinary courtesy of yielding preaudience to a minister of the Crown was denied. Mr. Dundas, the only representative of the new Government present, having risen simultaneously with Mr. Baker, a member of the Opposition, was not allowed to speak, though called upon by the Chair; and it was not until the Speaker remonstrated, that the minister was vouchsafed a hearing. His proposal, which was merely to facilitate the passing of a Money Bill, already advanced towards its last stage, was opposed with as much vehemence as if it implied a vote of confidence in the Government; and it was in vain that the practice of the House, and the exigencies of the public service, were urged in support of the motion, before a majority deaf to reason, and blind with party rage. This was an ominous commencement of an opposition, on the justice and fairness of which the country would soon have to decide.

At the next sitting of the House, Grenville announced the resignation of his brother, Lord Temple, and his readiness to meet any charge that might be brought against him. Fox, however, passed by this challenge, with a contemptuous observation that the noble Earl was the best judge whether he should remain in office or not, and proceeded to move the order of the day, that the House should resolve itself into a Committee on the state of the nation. The Opposition had been accused of shrinking from the consequences to which they had committed themselves by the resolution of the 17th of December, in not following up that resolution by a proceeding against Lord Temple. But it is difficult to conceive of any proceeding which could have been taken.

The charge against Lord Temple, even supposing it could have been established by legal proof, was hardly a ground for impeachment; and the attempt to influence the votes of peers of Parliament by an unconstitutional use of the King's name was certainly no breach of the privileges of the Commons.* It was Temple himself, who shrunk from his duty, far more than the House of Commons from theirs. Having taken upon himself to advise his sovereign against the measures of his ministers, as he had admitted in his place in Parliament that he had done, he should have been prepared to assume the responsibility which attached to him by his sovereign having acted on that advice; and so far from resigning, he ought to have retained his office,† and supported the Crown in the policy which he had recommended it to pursue. It would have been time enough to resign his office when any charge against him had assumed a tangible shape.

Before the House adjourned for the Christmas holidays, the Opposition carried an address to the Crown, against either a prorogation or dissolution of Parlia-

---

* Lord John Russell says, 'Had the House of Commons traced to Earl Temple advice given to the King against measures which his authorised ministers were pursuing, and had they asked the King to dismiss him from his presence and councils for ever, they would have pursued a bold, perhaps a dangerous, but assuredly a constitutional course.' —*Life of Fox*, vol. ii. p. 61. This appears to be not quite accurately stated. Lord Temple, as a peer of the realm, had a constitutional right to advise the King that his ministers were pursuing bad measures: his fault, I apprehend, was in privately communicating to certain peers the King's desire that they should vote against the measures of his authorised ministers.

† This is well put by Lord North in one of his speeches, 'Secret influence, which might formerly have been problematical, was now openly avowed. A peer of Parliament had given secret advice, and gloried in it. He would not say that a peer or a privy counsellor had not a right to advise the Crown; but he would contend, that the moment he gave such advice, he ought to take the seals, and become a minister, that advice and responsibility might go hand in hand.'—*Parliamentary History*, vol. xxiv. p. 291.

ment. An assenting answer was returned, in addition to which, the minister took the unusual course, of authorising Mr. Bankes, a member unconnected with the Government, to give the House a similar assurance.

<small>Factious proceedings of the Whigs.</small> The recess afforded the country opportunities of being informed more particularly as to the character of the extraordinary political proceedings of the last few months; but, while the tendency of public opinion was adverse to the party deprived of power, the latter seemed to be wholly ignorant that their conduct was undergoing unfavourable criticism out of doors,* or that their return to power was a question of anything beyond weeks or days. Accordingly, when Parliament reassembled in January, the war of faction was resumed, at the point where it had been left. Hardly had the Speaker taken the chair, when Fox, without waiting until Pitt and the other ministers, who were in attendance for that purpose, had taken the oaths, insisted on bringing forward his motion for a committee on the state of the nation; nor would he give way to the minister, notwithstanding he declared that he was charged with a message from the Crown. Having at length obtained a hearing, Pitt complained of the violent and unjustifiable proceedings which had taken place during his absence, and asked the House to

---

* It is still more strange, that the same infatuation should have possessed the Whigs with regard to the King. Soon after the settlement of the Prince of Wales's allowance, which had nearly resulted in a breach between the King and the Ministry, Fox writes to Lord Northington in these terms:—' I believe the King is neither pleased nor displeased with us; that he has no inclination to do anything to serve us or to hurt us, and that he has no view to any other administration which he means to substitute in lieu of us.'—*Correspondence*, vol. ii. p. 118. At this time, His Majesty was plotting with Thurlow and Temple how to get rid of a Ministry which had forced themselves upon him, and to which he never even pretended to give his confidence.

postpone the Committee—which, in fact, was nothing more than an engine for launching resolutions against the King and the ministers of his choice—in order that he might be enabled to bring in a Bill to regulate the affairs of India which, it was admitted on all hands, was of urgent importance. In answer to this not unreasonable request, he was met by a demand for an explicit assurance, that there should be no dissolution until the Indian question, and other matters recommended in the Royal Speech, at the commencement of the session, should be disposed of. But Pitt prudently declined answering the question.

Several resolutions were moved, and of course carried, in consequence of Pitt's refusal to enter into any positive engagement with regard to the duration of the Parliament. It was declared a high crime and misdemeanour to apply any public money to the services already voted, unless an Appropriation Act shall have passed before the prorogation. Another resolution reiterated the truism, that there should be an administration which had the confidence of the House and the public. The second reading of the Mutiny Bill was then put off for six weeks. Another resolution censured the Ministry for having obtained office by unconstitutional means. In this manner, the House was occupied all night, and until half-past seven in the morning. *A dissolution of Parliament inevitable.*

On the 14th of January, Mr. Pitt was allowed to bring forward his India Bill. The Opposition having insisted on the necessity of immediately settling the affairs of India, as a principal argument against the premature dissolution of Parliament, could not refuse the minister an opportunity of proposing his scheme, although its fate was decided beforehand. The Bill was substantially similar to the one which Pitt brought forward, and carried with a high hand the following year. The plan, which differed essentially from that propounded by the late *Conduct of the Opposition.*

Government, was denounced by Fox, as an attempt to set up the opinion of an individual against the declared sense of the House of Commons. He described the Bill itself as utterly devoid of merit, partial and incomplete, crude and undigested, founded on secret influence, and which, if adopted, must inevitably terminate in public ruin. The Bill was rejected on the second reading, but by so small a majority* that considerable uneasiness was visible in the ranks of the Opposition. It was plain that the contest rapidly approached its crisis, and that victory was not so certain. After the division on the ministerial measure, Fox immediately obtained leave to bring in a third

Fox obtains leave to bring in a fresh bill. India Bill, and in doing so, asked once more, whether Parliament was to be punished by dissolution for the spirit and firmness which they had displayed? And he called for a distinct answer to this question. Pitt, however, perceived the advantage which he had gained, and met the furious attacks of his opponents with passive resistance. He gave no answer to the peremptory demand of the leader of Opposition. The menaces and entreaties of other members were equally unavailing; and the significant silence of the minister was far more terrible to his adversaries, than the most pointed invective. The debate—if that can be called a debate which was no more than a series of wild and passionate reproaches from a discomfited party—was not brought to a close until two in the morning. It was Saturday, over which the House would according to usage have adjourned; but Fox insisted they should meet at noon, in order, as he said, that the minister might have an opportunity of atoning for the insult which he had offered them, in refusing any explanation of his purpose.

Agitation in the Commons. The House reassembled in great agitation; but the party leaders no longer persisted in the vain attempt to intimidate the undaunted

* The numbers were 222 and 214.

minister. The anxiety of members to know their fate hushed for the moment the angry voice of faction. Powys, a country gentleman of great estate, respected for his candour and moderation, and the disinterestedness of his public conduct, was the first to stand up on this occasion. Tears filled his eyes as he rose and asked, in broken accents, and a humble tone, if, without intruding on the secret counsels of the Crown, he might inquire whether they might expect to meet on Monday? Pitt drily replied, that it was not his intention to advise the Crown to prevent the House meeting on *Monday*; and with this assurance, they were content to separate.

At this period an attempt was made by a party of members of the House of Commons, not immediately connected with either of the contending factions, to put an end to the contest, with the view of forming a united administration. An address to this effect, with fifty-three signatures, was agreed to at a meeting at the St. Albans Tavern, and presented to the Duke of Portland, and to Mr. Pitt respectively. Both statesmen expressed their concurrence with the object of the requisitionists; but the Duke declared that an indispensable preliminary to such a negotiation was Mr. Pitt's retirement from office. To this condition, Pitt was not disposed to agree. It was understood also, that the King insisted on nominating four of his friends,* or about a half of the projected Cabinet.† A proposal based on such a stipulation could not be entertained for a moment; and ultimately, without making any express reservation, the King desired Pitt to open a communication with the Duke of Portland, with the view of forming a united administration, on a *fair and equal basis*. The Duke took exception to these terms. The word 'fair' was vague

An attempt to form a new Coalition.

* LORD JOHN RUSSELL's *Life of Fox*, vol. ii. p. 75.
† Ibid.

and general, but 'equal' was a phrase of a more
specific character, and seemed to imply a partition of
power. Pitt replied, that the language in which his
communication was couched might be explained at
an interview. But the Duke would not waive his
objection; and thus the attempt failed at its commencement. The country gentlemen at the St. Albans
Tavern expressed their regret that the negotiations
should have gone off upon the meaning of a word,
which either party might have given up. The worthy
mediators might have seen that this difficulty would
have been easily disposed of, if either party had been
willing to enter into negotiations; but that a word
was sufficient to frustrate it, when there was no such
disposition. The independent members got no thanks
from anybody, for their well meant but futile attempt
to compose this great quarrel of twenty years' standing, which had lately been revived with every circumstance of exasperation, and was now in the agony of
a final conflict; nevertheless, the meeting at the St.
Albans Tavern made an effort to accomplish their
benevolent object, through the medium of a vote of
the House of Commons. Their chairman,

Mr. Grosvenor's motion. Mr. Grosvenor, moved 'that the present
arduous and critical situation of public affairs required a firm, efficient, extended, and united administration, entitled to the confidence of the people, and
calculated to terminate the divisions and distractions
of the country.' To this resolution all parties could
readily assent, and, as it hardly afforded a convenient
text for the usual recriminations of the evening,
Mr. Coke of Norfolk proposed a more pointed vote,
that the continuance of the present ministers was an
obstacle to the formation of such an administration
as the House had declared to be desirable. Upon
this, Mr. Pitt assumed an attitude of defiance. He
said, the motion, if carried, would form an effectual
bar to the proposed union. Was he to cast off his

armour, and beg to be admitted as a volunteer in the army of the enemy? If the House wished to put an end to the Ministry, it might address the Crown, or impeach them for their crimes. The motion was carried by a majority of nineteen, and the challenge of the minister was accepted, by the House ordering that the two resolutions should be laid before His Majesty.

The Lords now, for the first time, took part in this memorable conflict. Resolutions were adopted by large majorities, censuring the proceedings of the Lower House, as tending to restrict the right of the Crown in the appointment of ministers. An address was carried in conformity with their resolutions.

Manifestations of public opinion also began to take place. Fox, with questionable prudence, had challenged the Court party to show Public meetings. that they were supported by the feelings of the country; and the challenge was readily accepted. The metropolis, which at all times must take the lead in demonstrations of this character, responded to the appeal made by the partisans on either side; and the result showed, that opinion was pretty equally divided on the great questions which agitated the House of Commons. The genial character and popular principles of Fox made him a favourite with the public; but the hearts of many, whose fathers had worshipped William Pitt, now yearned towards the inheritor of that illustrious name, and felt an English sympathy with the gallant youth, who so stoutly maintained an unequal struggle against a host of powerful foes. At a meeting of three thousand persons, held in the Court of Requests at Westminster, Fox, though member for the City, could not obtain a hearing, and, with his friends, was thrust out of the building. The old sentiment of loyalty, too, which had languished for more than a hundred years, was again awakened, and a cry rose through the length and breadth of the land against the shameless factions which had laid aside their long animosities for the purpose of uniting to coerce their Sovereign, and deprive him of his just rights.

The Opposition, nevertheless, proceeded unchecked in their career. They discussed at their private meetings the expediency of stopping the supplies, but many hesitated to go to this length; and when Fox tried the temper of the House so far as to move for a short adjournment, his majority dwindled to twelve. No further attempt, therefore, was made to obstruct the money votes. The parliamentary war, however, was still carried on with undiminished vigour. On the 20th of February, after the contest had lasted several weeks without intermission, an address to the Crown, in a sense similar to that of the resolutions and motions which had been daily recorded, was carried, after a debate protracted until five in the morning, by a majority of twenty-nine.

It was sufficiently manifest from the answer which the King was advised to return to this address, that all hope of compromise was at an end. His Majesty refused to dismiss his ministers, on the ground that no charge had been made against them, either collectively or individually; and he plainly told the Commons that his ministers had the confidence of the country. Such language as this could be preparatory only to that exercise of prerogative which the Opposition had so strongly deprecated. It was not necessary that the Commons should allege any particular misconduct as a reason, or, indeed, assign any reason whatever, for a vote of want of confidence in the ministers of the Crown. An opinion of their incapacity is a sufficient ground for such a vote. It would have been difficult to shape any specific charge against the Duke of Newcastle, or Lord Bute, or

Mr. Addington, or Mr. Perceval, who were all respectable and well-meaning ministers; yet the House of Commons would have been perfectly justified in declaring that they had no confidence in either of those statesmen. The wholesome control of Parliament over the Executive Government would be greatly impaired, if an address to the Crown for the removal of its ministers must be founded on a stated charge, of the sufficiency of which it follows, that the Sovereign must assume the dangerous responsibility of deciding. Such a rule would, in effect, preclude the House from ever proceeding in such a matter by way of address, and would force them to the less convenient and less direct mode of attaining their end by the obstruction of the public service. The royal answer, in referring to the state of public opinion out of doors, was likewise undignified and unconstitutional. An assertion on that subject was calculated to provoke retort. If there had been addresses to the King in approval of his ministers, there had been public meetings in a contrary sense. The only mode in which the Crown can with propriety appeal to public opinion, is by means of the undoubted prerogative of dissolution.

These topics were urged with exaggerated force, and with language of the most inflammatory character, by Fox and his adherents in the debate. They would address the Crown, they said, no more in the usual manner, but would embody their grievances and complaints in the menacing and ominous form of a *representation*. But the House was not prepared for this violent proceeding. Many of the Whigs became alarmed; the time-servers, in obedience to their instinct, went over to the winning side. The great chief of the Opposition saw, with dismay, the defection of his supporters; and the consciousness of approaching defeat was visible in the bitter invective which he hurled at the deserters. The representation was carried by a single vote.*

The struggle in the House of Commons was, therefore, virtually at an end; and the war must now be transferred to the constituencies.† The supplies were voted without further opposition; the Mutiny Bill was passed after some faint demonstrations of resistance; and on the 25th of March Parliament was dissolved.

---

* The numbers were 191 to 190.

† 'Our battle,' said one of the ablest adherents of the Coalition, 'is converted into a campaign.'— Sir Gilbert Elliot to Harris, 10th March. — *Malmesbury Papers*, vol. ii. p. 64.

CHAPTER XXIX.

TERMINATION OF THE STRUGGLE BETWEEN THE KING AND THE WHIG PARTY—GENERAL ELECTIONS—PITT'S FINANCIAL MEASURES—STATE OF IRELAND—INDIA BILL—SINKING FUND—REFORM BILL.

GEORGE THE THIRD ascended the throne with one leading principle of action; and by adhering to it with undeviating constancy, he at length attained the success which usually follows determined perseverance. To humble the Whig oligarchy, and to reclaim the full independent exercise of the prerogative which the arrogance of a domineering faction had almost rendered obsolete, were the objects to which he devoted all his energies. The Whigs, accustomed to consider themselves the heirs of the Revolution, and the rightful possessors of political power, had, for nearly fifty years before the King's accession, parcelled out among themselves the great offices of State, and distributed all the patronage of the empire. It was no very hopeful undertaking for a young prince, inexperienced in affairs, with no faithful and able counsellor at his side, and with no party in the nation, to enter upon a conflict with a great and powerful body, the hereditary pillars of his throne, and which the country had long been accustomed to consider as the natural guardian of their liberties. An open and direct attack on such a formidable connection must soon have ended in discomfiture; but the King had qualities which peculiarly fitted him to conduct with success the only kind of action which

[marginal note: George the Third's determined opposition to the Whigs.]

could be ventured upon, without peril to himself, in such peculiar circumstances. He was patient and longsuffering, reserved, vigilant, and cunning, attentive to every detail of business, and careful to encourage and reward those who were inclined to attach themselves to his service.

His first rash attempt to set up his mother's chamberlain as Prime Minister of England was never repeated. After the failure of Lord Bute, the King adopted a secret and tortuous policy as best adapted to his purpose. He fomented the jealousies which had long existed between the great Whig houses. He organised a small and select band of individuals, mostly too obscure and insignificant to have any dependence but on his favour, or any opinion but his will. These men he provided with seats in Parliament, with small offices and pensions. Their business was to collect information, to fetch and carry tales, to listen, to whisper aside, to act as spies on the ostensible minister, to counterplot his plans, to undermine his credit, and, when required by special order, to vote against him in Parliament. These people were flattered by the title of the King's Friends; a designation intended also to be significant of the thraldom in which His Majesty was held by those who pretended to call themselves his Public Servants. We have seen how Ministry after Ministry languished and sunk under the insidious operation of this system. It was in vain that one statesman after another struggled to get free from the toils which surrounded him. Remonstrances, menaces, stipulations, were employed in turn. As it was a necessary part of the plan that the cabal should be disavowed, every attempt to crush it was eluded. If the chief of His Majesty's Government complained that certain subordinate officials had intrigued or voted against his measures, the King would very decorously express his displeasure, and go through the form of reproving the delinquents. If the great man, on being summoned to the royal closet, made it a condition of his accepting the seals of office, that there should be no secret agency, the pledge was readily given; for the existence of secret agency had never been admitted. Whether it was Grenville who lectured, or Chatham who rated, or Rockingham who dictated to his royal master, His Majesty met every form of objurgation with the same passive resistance. At length, the King found a man of character, ability, and station, unconnected with any of the great political families, who was willing to undertake the Government under his direction. The services of the King's Friends were no longer required when public affairs were conducted by a minister who was the obsequious agent of the Court; and, therefore, during the long administration of Lord North, the Cabal was a disembodied corps, but ready, upon an emergency, to resume their organisation.* They were in full activity during the late Government, but after Pitt's accession to power, there is no further trace of the King's Friends as a separate and peculiar party; from that period they were absorbed among the regular supporters of the Government.

George the Third has been covered with a load of obloquy for the mode in which he sought to discredit his responsible ministers, and to assume a power which, according to the spirit of the constitution, and consistently with the freedom of Parliament, the Crown can exercise only by delegated authority. But a candid consideration of the circumstances in which he was placed

<small>Obloquy thrown upon the King.</small>

---

* During the Coalition, Jenkinson, the leader of the King's party, having been taunted in debate with having resumed his active duties, had the effrontery to appeal to Lord North, whether he, when Prime Minister, had ever experienced secret influence? North could of course conscientiously answer in the negative.—*Parliamentary History.*

will relieve the memory of this monarch from much of the censure which has been heaped upon it. When George the Third came to the throne, the English Government was, in practice, assuming the form of an exclusive oligarchy. The independence of Parliament was all but lost through the decay of the constituencies, the corruption of the electors, and the increase of nomination boroughs. The King, though his prerogative still existed in theory unimpaired, had no more real power than a Doge of Venice, or a Merovingian King in the hands of the Mayor of the Palace. Neither of the two immediate predecessors of George the Third was in a condition to assert the rights and privileges of the Crown. The Elector of Hanover succeeded to the throne in middle age, a stranger to the laws, the manners, the very language of the island, with a disputed title, and therefore not likely to attempt the revival of high prerogative maxims. The next German King, for nearly the first half of his reign, had to contend against the pretensions of a competitor who divided the allegiance of his subjects. From the time when the combined factions succeeded in overpowering the great minister, who had alike disappointed the reactionary schemes of the Tories, and repressed the selfish arrogance of the Whigs, the pressure of the oligarchy was most severe, and the King could only chafe with impotent rage under the cold relentless thraldom to which he was subjected. But George the Second died, and his grandson, 'born and bred a Briton,' in the vigour of his youth, ascended a throne now established on the firmest foundation; and if his first impulse was to throw off the ignoble yoke which had been imposed upon his predecessors, it was one surely deserving of sympathy. The first attempt, prompted by the generosity and rash confidence of youth, signally failed; and it is not to be forgotten, in favour of this

Weakness of George I. and George II.

prince, that he did not resort to indirect means until open resistance had proved impracticable.

The country, resentful of the petulant folly which had thrust an obscure Scotch lord into the place newly vacated by Pitt, and which, within the memory of the existing generation, had been filled by Walpole, took no part in the weary conflict which ensued between the young King and the great families, whose arrogance and ambition overshadowed the throne. The administration of North was not calculated to recommend to popular favour the new system of government by courtiers in preference to that of statesmen, who, whatever their faults might have been, dictated the policy for which they were responsible. When, therefore, the Whigs returned to power on the ignominious termination of the American War, which they had consistently and courageously opposed, notwithstanding the public prejudice in its favour, a great opportunity was before them; and there can be little doubt, that if they had acted with prudence and public spirit, they must have secured a long tenure of power. Their course lay plain before them. A measure of Parliamentary Reform was called for by the country; was demanded by the justice and reason of the case, and was suggested by political expediency as the only effectual means of putting an end for ever to the secret intrigues and cabals of the Court. An alliance with the son of Chatham, who, it was evident from his first appearance in the House of Commons, must soon rise to the head of affairs, was, above every other connection, to be cultivated. But instead of making Reform a capital measure, the Ministry of Lord Rockingham left it an open question; they were distracted by the same personal jealousies and rivalries which had formerly left them a prey to the Court, and had excluded them from any share in the Government during twelve eventful years. The members of the Cabinet intrigued and caballed against each other as actively as ever the King had intrigued and caballed against the Cabinet. The result was a schism. Half, and that the most important half, of the Ministry, headed by Fox and Burke, withdrew into avowed opposition; the remaining half obtained the aid of Pitt, by offering him the great post of Chancellor of the Exchequer. Fox and his friends, by an act which was at once a political crime and a blunder, sought to balance the advantage which Shelburne had gained by allying himself with the youthful hope of the nation. They thought they could do so by forming a connection with the man whom they had, for the last ten years, denounced as a public enemy, the worn-out tool of prerogative, the insolent contemner of popularity, the disgraced chief of an administration which had inflicted greater calamities on the country than had been endured since the days of the Cabal. It would have taken long years of wise and patriotic government to have effaced the memory of this outrage upon the decency and morality of public life, and to have confirmed the power obtained by such unworthy means. But the subsequent conduct of the Whigs was marked with the same infatuation which had led to the union with Lord North. The coalesced Ministry had to deal with a question of great magnitude and novelty. A happily-conceived plan for the government of India, which should have redeemed the national character from the reproach which had justly fallen upon it, and, at the same time, have opened up the sources of wealth and commerce which our Eastern Empire was capable of yielding, might have gone far to atone for the Coalition. But their India Bill was so unhappily framed as to afford to their opponents some plausible ground for asserting, that it was designed, not so much with a view to the good of the people of India and the prosperity of this country, as to consolidate and perpetuate their own possession of power.

Among the minor causes which aided in discrediting the late Government, and in raising the fortunes of their successors, there are two or three worthy of mention. *Case of Powell and Bembridge.* Colonel Barré, who had been paymaster in Shelburne's administration, had dismissed or suspended two clerks in the office, named Powell and Bembridge, for defalcations in their accounts. Burke, who succeeded Barré as paymaster, restored Powell and Bembridge to their situations. These men, at the time, were held to bail; and whatever might have been Burke's opinion as to their guilt or innocence, it was in the highest degree indecent to reinstate them in their employment before they were acquitted in course of law. But so far from being acquitted, one of these persons was convicted and sentenced; and the other committed suicide before trial. The conduct of Powell and Bembridge had been investigated by a Treasury Board, at which Pitt, as Chancellor of the Exchequer, presided; their report was of such a character as left the paymaster no discretion as to the course which he should pursue; and it was by the order of the Treasury that the case was laid before the Attorney-General, with a view to prosecution. The re-appointment of these delinquents was brought to notice of the House of Commons by Martin, a member of the Opposition, who described it in terms hardly too strong, as 'a gross and daring insult to the public.' Burke started up in a violent passion, and would have given Martin the lie, had not Sheridan pulled him back into his seat. On a subsequent day, when Burke undertook to justify his conduct, it was expected that he would be at least prepared to state his own conviction of the innocence of the inculpated clerks, and the grounds upon which he had arrived at that conclusion;

but, so far from making any such statement, he admitted that their conduct was exceedingly questionable, and to the astonishment of his hearers, he read his own letter to Powell on his reinstatement in office, in which he admonished that gentleman of the grave suspicions attached to his conduct, and that he would be again dismissed, if he should be found guilty of the felonies laid to his charge. In the meantime, Burke assured the House, that by the improved arrangements of the paymaster's office, sufficient precaution was taken against any risk from the employment of clerks, who lay under the imputation of fraud and embezzlement. Nobody who knew Burke attributed this strange proceeding to any discreditable motive, but rather to that singular lack of judgment and discretion in which he was as much below ordinary men, as he was raised above them in respect of the rarest endowments of the human mind. But the appointment of two half convicted cheats, to offices of trust and emolument, produced less impression on the public mind than a rash word which fell from the lips of the Attorney-General, in one of the debates on the India Bill. When the arguments as to the violation of chartered rights was pressed, he, instead of meeting it in the manner which the gravity of the objection demanded, affected to treat it with contempt. 'What was a charter,' said the first law officer, 'a skin of parchment, with a piece of wax dangling at the end of it, compared with the happiness of thirty millions of people, and the preservation of a mighty empire?' Such loose doctrine as this might be employed to cover any act of spoliation. Every corporate body in the kingdom took the alarm, and prepared to defend its property against this new principle of confiscation for the benefit of the human race. Every proprietor who held his tenements and hereditaments, by virtue of a parchment with a seal of wax dangling at the end of it, was disposed to resent such an insolent disparagement of his rights. Nothing tended more to the discredit of the India Bill and its authors, than this unlucky defence of its most questionable provision, by the head of the legal profession.

Among other causes which contributed to the downfall of the Coalition, was their apparent unwillingness to reform the abuses, and retrench the extravagance of the public expenditure. Lord North's administration had issued a commission of inquiry into the state of the public accounts and the public offices. The reports of the Commissioners had from time to time disclosed numerous frauds and irregularities; and the Shelburne Ministry, under the direction of Pitt as Chancellor of the Exchequer, had prepared a measure of reformation. This measure Pitt brought forward after he had quitted office, but his successor, on the pretence that the proposed alterations could be effected without the intervention of Parliament, prevailed, not indeed in the House of Commons, but in the Upper House, to defeat the Bill. Pitt, on his return to power, took an early opportunity to renew the measure, and, by carrying it with the weight and authority of his Government, earned the reputation of a consistent and upright minister. He greatly increased his reputation by an act of personal disinterestedness—almost of magnanimity—rare indeed, but which might have been expected from the son of Chatham. During the heat of the struggle with the ejected Coalition, a rich sinecure, the clerkship of the Pells, was vacated by the death of Sir Edward Walpole, a son of the great Sir Robert. This office, according to the precedents of those times, the minister would have been justified in appropriating to himself. Pitt was under a stronger temptation than had urged any of his predecessors, except his illustrious father, to follow the usual course. He had little or no private fortune;

and in the event of the unequal conflict in which he was engaged, ending as everybody, himself and his friends included, expected it would end, in the triumph of his opponents, he had no alternative but to seek his fortune at the bar. A sinecure of three thousand a year would have rendered him independent, and enabled him to devote his whole energies to those great aims of public life, for which he was so eminently fitted. But, instead of making his own fortune, Pitt gave the place to Colonel Barré, for the purpose of redeeming the pension of similar amount, which the administration of Lord Rockingham had so scandalously bestowed upon him. It cannot fail to be observed, however, that if Pitt had been actuated solely by motives of public duty, the simplest and most effectual course would have been, to abolish this rich sinecure altogether; but such a proceeding might have passed unnoticed, and certainly would not have had such an imposing effect as that which he adopted, and which, to many of his admirers, appeared as if he had paid off a public incumbrance at his private charge.

Great popularity of Pitt. The dissolution of Parliament found the country eager to respond to the appeal. Never since the reign of Anne, had so great an amount of public spirit been exhibited at a general election. Many of the large constituencies discarded their old members, men of great estate, in favour of adventurers, who promised to defend the Crown against an overbearing oligarchy and shameless factions. The great county of York, the head quarters of Whig agitation during the time of Lord North, the county of the Marquis of Rockingham, returned a young gentleman, who at that time had little pretension to so great an honour, beyond his being the personal friend of Pitt,* and the energetic

---

* 'The name of being Mr. Pitt's friend has carried several popular elections. His own success at Cambridge was amazing.

denouncer of the Coalition, which he described with
some point, as 'exhibiting the characteristic vices of
both its parents, the violence of the one, and the
corruption of the other.' Wilberforce owed
his election chiefly to the manufacturers, <small>Wilberforce returned for Yorkshire.</small>
who were staunch supporters of Church
and King, and uncompromising in their hostility to
the pernicious doctrines of free trade, with which
Burke was misleading the Whig party. Pitt himself
was returned for the University of Cambridge. The
incorporated boroughs, in which the elective franchise
was limited to the municipal bodies, returned the
candidates who were pledged to maintain inviolate
the sanctity of charters. In fact, there was no interest or fancied interest in the country, hardly any
passion or prejudice, to which the partisans of the
new administration could not make a plausible
appeal. Fox himself, though personally popular,
had the greatest difficulty in regaining his seat at
Westminster, at that time the most intelligent and
spirited constituency in the empire. The poll was
kept open for forty days, the utmost period allowed
by law. For twenty-three days he was in a minority,
but on the fortieth day, he headed the Tory by two
hundred and forty-six votes. Unparalleled exertions
had been made to secure this result. Women of
rank and beauty, the famous toasts of the day, condescended to take active parts in the election, and
by the employment of arts beyond those of the most
zealous partisans of the male sex, succeeded it is
said, in captivating many of the electors. On the
day of the declaration of the poll, although the re-

<small>He carried Lord Euston's election by the votes he gave him. Numbers refused to vote for Lord Euston, till it was clear that he would support Mr. Pitt in Parliament. Lord Compton had the same question asked him in Northampton, and he was sent by his constituents from his own election to vote for Mr. Pitt at Cambridge.'—Lord Sydney to the Right Hon. Thomas Orde, 6th April, 1784.—*Bolton MSS*.</small>

turning officer refused to declare the election, because a scrutiny had been demanded, Fox was carried in triumph to Devonshire House, where he was received by the Prince of Wales, the Duke and Duchess, and a large company. The Prince, indeed, went so far as to ride through the streets, wearing Fox's colours, and a sprig of laurel in his hat. Yet amidst all this exultation, it was well known that the verdict of the country had been pronounced against the Whigs, and that for the first time in the course of seventy years, they were the minority of the House of Commons. In fact, the Whig party was utterly routed, and the victory of the Court was complete. The young minister, whose appointment a few short months before had been greeted with shouts of derision, was now almost powerful enough to defy opposition.

Meeting of the New Parliament. The New Parliament met on the 18th May; the late Speaker resumed the chair without opposition, and though the Royal Speech avoided any topic calculated to provoke controversy, the Opposition were determined to force an immediate trial of strength. An amendment to the Address, censuring the late dissolution of Parliament, was moved by the Earl of Surrey, and, after a party debate of the usual character, was rejected by a majority of more than two to one, in a full House.

Westminster election. The refusal of the High Bailiff of Westminster to make a return in accordance with the poll, would have excluded Fox from the House of Commons at the commencement of the session, had he not taken the precaution of procuring his election for another place. The High Bailiff was clearly wrong, in refusing to make a return, according to the exigency of the writ; and in taking upon himself to conduct the scrutiny which had been demanded on behalf of the defeated candidate, he intruded on the province of the

* The numbers were 282 to 114.

House. The statute law,* though not explicit upon the precise point, was, upon fair and reasonable intendment, sufficient to warrant a return of the candidate who had the majority on the poll. There was no precedent either way; but on principle, the point was free from doubt. The duty of a returning officer is merely ministerial, and if he were to take upon himself to determine the validity of an election before he made a return, the privilege which the House of Commons has always maintained with jealousy, of itself determining the validity of controverted elections, would be virtually superseded; and the House might be kept incomplete for an indefinite period, by the caprice or insolence of a functionary over whom it has no control.

Pitt was so ill-advised as to support the arbitrary and illegal conduct of the High Bailiff; *Pitt's impolitic conduct.* and he succeeded for a time in gratifying an unworthy resentment against his distinguished rival. For a whole session, Westminster was wantonly deprived of its representatives; but at length the better sense of the House prevailed against the petulance of the minister, and the petty vindictiveness of his followers. In the following session, a motion, ordering the High Bailiff to make an immediate return in accordance with the poll was lost by a majority of nine only; and a few days after, Mr. Pitt's attempt to defeat a similar motion by an evasive amendment, left him in a minority of thirty-eight. The members for Westminster immediately took their seats; and a Court of Justice ultimately awarded Fox two thousand pounds as damages in an action against the High Bailiff.

Pitt's first operations in finance were received with favour, even by the Opposition. The late *Pitt's financial measures.* war had left a floating debt of fourteen millions. Of this amount, he proposed to fund

* 10 and 11 W. 3, c. 7.

about a half, and to raise nine hundred thousand pounds a year by new and increased taxation. The additional imposts were, on the whole, fairly distributed. The rich were made to contribute to the revenue in respect of horses, licenses to kill game, gold and silver plate, hats, ribbons, and gauzes. Taxes on luxuries seem, at first sight, the least exceptionable of all imposts; yet they are hardly consistent with sound fiscal principles, and only to a very limited extent can they be relied on as a source of revenue. A tax laid on an article, the use of which may be limited, or altogether dispensed with, is really favourable to the rich man; it enables him, to the extent to which it is imposed, to assess the amount of his contributions to the State, and therefore, to diminish the proportion of the public burdens which it was intended he should bear; thus giving him an advantage over the general taxpayer, whose burdens are, for the most part, so exactly adjusted, that he cannot relieve himself from any considerable part of them. The reduction in the demand for articles of luxury, which are subjected to special taxation, the consequent diminution of trade, and of the demand for labour, are sufficient arguments for a very cautious and sparing application of imposts of this character. It was also proposed to derive a revenue from coals, candles, paper, bricks, and some other commodities. The tax on coals was subsequently abandoned; and a compensation for its estimated produce was sought in an augmentation of the assessed taxes, in an increase of the postage on letters, and in a retrenchment of abuses in the privilege of franking, which at that time, and up to a recent period, appertained to the members of both Houses. These proposals display no financial skill; they were merely of an occasional character, such as a clerk in the Treasury might have framed. The regulations as to franking were in accordance with a Report on the Post Office made to the Treasury in Shelburne's administration, when Pitt was Chancellor of the Exchequer.* A tax on houses and windows was also laid on, to indemnify the revenue for the losses which it had sustained by smuggling, which was carried on to a great extent, and almost in open defiance of the laws. Pitt did not venture to meet the evil in the only way by which it can be successfully encountered, namely, by a reduction of the customs duties. He contented himself with seizing a few smuggling boats at Deal, the principal emporium of the contraband trade, and in passing the Hovering Act, which prohibited small vessels laden with spirits, tea, or coffee, from approaching within four leagues of the coast. The Commutation Act, framed principally in the interest of the East India Company, had the same object indirectly in view.

A Bill to retrieve the immediate and pressing difficulties of the Company preceded the measure for the better government of India. Pitt, like his predecessor, took away substantially the political power of the Company; and his machinery, though not open to the same objection as that which the late Government had constructed, was not less clumsy and anomalous. The Government of India was still to be administered in the name of the Company; but a new ministerial department was to be erected, which should absolutely dictate the policy of the local Government, and control every act of the administration. The whole of the patronage, comprising all the appointments of the Civil and Military Service, with the exception of the Commander-in-Chief, and the higher functionaries, the nomination of whom was subjected to the veto of the Crown, was left in the hands of the

Indian affairs.

---

* *Bolton MSS.*—Mr. Orde was Secretary to the Treasury under Lord Shelburne.

Directors. In every other particular, the chartered rights of the Company were respected. They were even allowed such a participation in the higher privileges of Government as was contained in the right to examine the despatches, which they were directed to transmit; and the Board of Directors was to be the channel through which alone the Board of Control was to communicate its will to the Governor-General at Calcutta, the Commander of the Company's forces, and the Governors of the Presidencies. Some impracticable provisions for the administration of justice, and some vexatious enactments, for subjecting the property of persons coming from India to inquisitorial examinations, and for preventing persons returning to India, after a certain period of residence in this country, were subsequently abandoned, repealed, or never acted upon. The objections to the scheme were patent. The partition of power between the Crown and the Company, which was the main feature of the Bill, afforded the Opposition an abundant theme for censure. Nevertheless, the Bill passed the Commons by a great majority, only sixty members accompanying Fox into the lobby, while two hundred and seventy-one remained to support the Government. In the Lords, there were strong speeches against the measure, and a protest; but there was neither an amendment nor a division.

The India Bill in fact, like most other measures involving great principles or interests, resulted in a compromise. On the one hand, there was a loud demand for legislation, which should remedy the crying scandals and abuses of the Company's government. On the other hand, the Company were too strong to surrender at discretion. They knew they must make large concessions; but they knew likewise, the importance belonging to a body which can command a score or so of votes in the House of Commons. Pitt and the cautious col-

The Bill probably prepared by Dundas.

league who sat beside him, destined to be the first minister for India, under the new Bill, knew also the value of the Indian votes in a division, even when a majority of two thirds of the House supported the Government. Dundas, indeed, had probably prepared the draft of the Bill. But, besides those considerations, which in our system of Parliamentary Government, influence the action of the Legislature more than the merits of the case, there was another aspect in which the question might be viewed. It would have been easy to frame a measure, which should have commanded vulgar applause, as a work of statesmanship, at once grand and simple. The Government of Hindostan might have been administered by a Secretary of State in the name of the King, like the Government of Canada or Jamaica. But the dependencies of the British empire were, more or less, governed by local institutions and customs, administered by the native subjects of the Crown. In India there were no political institutions, and the customs of the country were chiefly matters of religion. The people, incapable of governing themselves, must be governed by the European race, which occupied their soil. But, barbarous as they might be, in the estimation of Europeans, the natives of Hindostan were associated by the bonds of a civilisation older than the civilisation of Europe; and the government of the stranger must be adapted to habits and manners, which for ages had undergone no material change. The servants of the Company had acquired a knowledge of the people, which experience only can confer. The conduct of these agents, many of them persons of mean education, and exercising a power greater than that which is possessed by the minor princes of Europe, had often been violent and corrupt. It was easy to denounce Anglo-Indian rapacity and oppression, and to adorn with accusing eloquence, the tales

Civilisation of ancient date in India.

which had been carried thirteen thousand miles from the land of perjury and chicane. Yet the government of the most arbitrary agent of the Company was probably a great improvement on that of the native ruler, whose licence he modified and restrained. It might have been practicable to break off at once all connection between the Imperial Government and the Company, and all connection between the Company and the Government of India; but, considering that all the information about India which this country possessed was derived through the Company, and that all the relations which subsisted between England and her Asiatic dominions were united by the same great connecting link, it would have been surely the extreme of rashness to undertake duties of which we knew nothing, and, at the same time, to reject the only hand which could guide us in our blind enterprise. Considering, likewise, that the millions of different races and religions which were united under our sway, by an opinion of the firm and unswerving hand which grasped the sceptre, it would have been hardly prudent, suddenly, and for no reason which could have been rendered intelligible to the people of the East, to change their Government, to depose the authority to which they had been accustomed to bow, and to substitute some other authority which should have no greater apparent claims to their respect. There was a domestic difficulty also attending the entire assumption by the Crown of its undoubted rights over this rich dominion. The patronage of India would have seriously disturbed the well-adjusted balance of power in the English Constitution. It would have been hardly possible at that time to have devised any mode by which this vast patronage could have been so dispensed as to avoid any undue increase in the influence of the Crown, or the overwhelming ascendancy of the House of Commons. Some such measure as that which was proposed by Pitt seems to have been dictated by a wise regard to expediency. The double government, however, was not designed for a permanent institution. The reasons which justified an arrangement so novel and anomalous, were of an occasional and temporary character. When these reasons should cease to exist, there could no longer be any pretence for perpetuating a system which had nothing but expediency to recommend it. Yet India continued to be governed under the Act of 1786, long after the foundations of that Act had crumbled away; and it was only yesterday that the sudden access of a terrible convulsion precipitated the change which would otherwise have been postponed for many a long year.

The session was brought to a close on the 20th of August, and the new Ministry had every reason to believe, as they did believe, that they were firmly established in power.* *Close of the Session.*

The Indian question was succeeded by another subject of still greater and more urgent interest. This was the state of Ireland, *Pitt's letter to the Irish minister.* which had engaged the anxious attention of the late Cabinet, and which had already occupied almost all the intervals of leisure which their successors could snatch from the immediate pressure of parliamentary business. On the very day that Parliament was prorogued, Pitt wrote a long letter to the Irish Minister on the various topics which entered into the consideration of Irish affairs.

The state of Ireland, contemplated at a distance, seemed to be one of imminent peril, and *The Irish Volunteers.* the dismemberment of the empire in its most vital part, as a matter depending merely on

---

* 'Our session has concluded most triumphantly, and nothing but very untoward events can give Opposition a chance to make a better figure in the next.'—Pitt to Secretary Orde, 20th August, 1784—*Bolton MSS.*

opportunity. But, on a closer examination, this danger appeared to be neither very near nor very probable. Irish grievances were, indeed, not easily intelligible to English politicians. The generous impulse which on the alarm of foreign invasion in 1779, had raised an army of a hundred thousand men, fully equipped, and officered by the leading gentry of the land, had been directed towards the redress of domestic grievances, when the danger from the common enemy had passed away. The legislation of 1782, dictated as it was at the point of the bayonet, having asserted the independence of Ireland, and extorted from the imperial pride of this country a substantial recognition of that independence, the volunteers began to disperse; in 1784 they were reduced to some sixteen thousand, and in the following year they disappeared altogether. This noble body, which, for purity and loftiness of purpose, may be advantageously compared with any patriotic association of ancient or modern times, seems to have exhausted for the time all that was wise, generous or true in the political character of their country. The decay of this patriotic corps dates indeed from the moment when political adventurers succeeded in turning them to account. It was not for the purpose of a brawling agitation, or to barter their country to a foreign power, that the bravest and noblest of the land, by a spontaneous impulse, sprang to arms. It was the defence of their country from foreign aggression; and her liberation from those fetters and badges of servitude which her imperious sister had imposed, that the volunteers of Ireland had resolved to effect. These great ends accomplished, their mission had been fulfilled. They could not lend themselves to minor details, or to questionable work.

Ireland was much disturbed during the whole period of the coalesced administration. Parliamentary

AGITATION FOR REFORM.

Reform was adopted by the popular leaders, as a convenient vehicle for their revolutionary purposes. A more plausible topic could hardly have been chosen; for the state of the representation in Ireland was so bad, that it would have been difficult even for native eloquence to exaggerate its condition. Corruption and decay had, to a great extent, impaired the ancient Parliament of Great Britain; but its noblest parts were still untouched; and when the occasion arose, it could still be worthy of its illustrious name. But the Irish Assembly had nearly lost what little resemblance it ever possessed to a representative chamber. The House consisted of three hundred members. In 1784, when Pitt was preparing his great plan for creating a unity of interests between the two countries by an equitable adjustment of the tariff, and had, at the same time, in contemplation a measure of Parliamentary Reform, he directed the Irish Government to furnish him with particular information as to the actual constitution of the House of Commons, and the parties and interests by which it was influenced. In accordance with these instructions, elaborate tables and digests were prepared, shewing not only the exact state of the representation, but containing likewise an account of the political position, character, connections, and private objects of each individual member.* One hundred

Prevalence of corruption.

---

* As specimens of this curious record, I take a few entries at random from the papers drawn up by Secretary Orde:

'H— H—, son-in-law to Lord A—, and brought into Parliament by him. Studies the law: wishes to be a Commissioner of Barracks, or in some similar place, would go into orders and take a living.

'H— D—, brother to Lord C—. Applied for office; but, as no specific promise could be made, has lately voted in opposition. Easy to be had, if thought expedient. A silent, gloomy man.

'L— M— refuses to accept £500 per annum; states very high pretensions from his skill in House of Commons management; expects £1,000 per annum. N.B. Be careful of him.

'T— N—, has been in the

and sixteen nomination seats were divided among some five and twenty proprietors. Lord Shannon returned no less than sixteen members; the great family of Ponsonby returned fourteen; Lord Hillsborough had nine seats; the Duke of Leinster seven; the Castle itself appropriated twelve. The whole reliable strength of Government in the House of Commons amounted to one hundred and eighty-six votes. These were distributed into five classes: 1. Eighty-six proprietary seats, the owners of which had let them out in consideration of titles, offices, and pensions, in possession or expectancy. 2. The twelve seats belonging to the Government. 3. Forty-four seats occupied by placemen. 4. Thirty-two votes of gentlemen who had promises, or who had avowed their expectations of favours and qualifications. Lastly, there were twelve members not registered in the secretary's book as demanding either peerages, places, or pensions, and, therefore, set down as supporting the Government on public grounds. Besides these, there was a party of twenty-nine, who, though willing to cultivate private intercourse with the Ministers, affected, and sometimes asserted, an independent position in the House. The regular Opposition appears to have been limited to eighty-two. Of these, thirty were the nominees of Whig proprietors, and fifty-two represented the popular party.*

Under the auspices of the Convention of Delegates

Distribution of Parliamentary Influence.

---

army, and is now on half-pay; wishes a troop of dragoons on full-pay. States his pretensions to be fifteen years' service in Parliament. N.B. Would prefer office to military promotion; but already has, and has long had, a pension. Character, especially on the side of truth, not favourable.

'B— P—, independent, but well disposed to Government. His four sisters have pensions; and his object is a living for his brother.

'T— P—, brother to Lord L—, and brought in by him, a captain in the navy; wishes for some sinecure employment.'— *Bolton MSS.*

* *Ibid.*

sitting in Dublin, a measure of sweeping Reform was introduced in the House of Commons by Mr. Flood, a popular leader of great eloquence, but one of the most factious and unprincipled members of that factious and corrupt assembly. Envy of Grattan, who, as a benefactor of his country, had been raised to an eminence which no aspirant to the honours and emoluments of patriotism had yet approached, seems to have determined Flood to extreme popular courses. His arts had already succeeded, to some extent, in depreciating the services and diminishing the influence of his great rival; and he now aimed, by means of the popular question of Reform, to supplant him altogether. Flood's motion, which directly affected the property and personal interests of three-fourths of the members, gave rise to a scene of violence and tumult unexampled even in that assembly, where an important debate usually resulted in an appeal to the pistol. The popular members took their seats attired in the uniform of the volunteers. Infuriated menaces were retorted on either side. The authority of the Chair, the rules of the House, the order of a deliberative assembly, were alike disregarded amidst the raging passions which prevailed. The Bill was, of course, rejected; but, early in the following session, Flood renewed his attempt in a modified form, with a view to conciliate the favour of that part of the Opposition which had always professed to be favourable to Parliamentary Reform. And thus even Grattan was forced, though much against his will, to give a qualified support to the proposal. The consequence was, that the Bill was discussed with some degree of moderation; and the minority, instead of being only fifty, as on the former occasion, amounted to eighty-five, which, as has been shewn, nearly represented the effective strength of the Opposition.

The rejection of this Reform Bill was the signal

for an outbreak of popular fury. The mob forced their way into the House, and put most of the members to flight. A series of outrages followed; and the savage populace gave a sample of the malice and ferocity of which the Celtic race are capable, when their blood is warmed. The odious practice of tarring and feathering they adopted from the Americans, whom they had been lately taught to imitate. The cruel and dastardly act of houghing was likewise resorted to, in revenge for the denial of the elective franchise; but instead of inflicting it upon animals, the Irish populace perpetrated this inhuman torture on their fellow-creatures. Many poor soldiers, who gave no other offence than that of wearing the red coat, and other persons from mere wantonness, were maimed in this manner. Under pretence of carrying into effect the orders of the Convention, and of supporting its authority, private grudges were avenged; creditors were deterred from enforcing their demands by threats of tarring and feathering, and, if the demand was considerable, with loss of their ears. The principal persons in authority were threatened with personal violence, if any attempt should be made to enforce the laws; and so formidable were these menaces considered, that it was not thought prudent for the Lord Lieutenant to go abroad without a guard.*

These disorders were, however, mainly confined to the capital; and, from the excesses by which they were characterised, it need hardly be added, were confined also, in a great measure, to the ignorant and needy population. The Roman Catholics and the lower order of priests were largely implicated in these proceedings; many of the Dublin shopkeepers were active instigators of sedition; and even some of the merchants and higher class of traders were well pleased that some pressure

* Correspondence of the Irish Government.—*Bolton* MSS.

should be put upon the Government, with the view of extorting those commercial concessions which it was so much their interest to obtain. The demagogues who swayed this promiscuous multitude were men of desperate fortunes, none of them occupying any social position, and most of them Roman Catholics.* Two or three briefless barristers and broken attorneys, a strolling player, a billiard marker, a journeyman saddler, and one or two small tradesmen, comprised the working staff of sedition in the city of Dublin. These men acted chiefly under the direction of James Napper Tandy, who fled from the gallows in the rebellion of 1798. He had narrowly escaped a similar fate before he took part in political affairs, having been tried for shooting a butcher. At that time he carried on the business of an ironmonger. By his superior energy and intelligence, Tandy soon obtained the ascendant among the popular leaders. There were only two individuals of station who openly countenanced the seditious proceedings in the capital. These were the Earl of Bristol (Bishop of Derry), and Sir Edward Newenham. The first appears to have been bordering on insanity, if not actually of unsound mind. As a peer of England and a prelate of the Irish Church, having a great stake in the welfare of both islands, it is difficult to conceive any rational motive which could have urged him to promote separation; a measure which many Irishmen were deluded enough to advocate as beneficial to their own country, but which none was found so absurd as to deny must be fraught with danger and difficulty to the sister kingdom.

An account of what took place at the table of the prelate-peer on a particular occasion, will *scene at a dinner table.* convey a more lively idea of this singular patriot than any description could afford. In the mouth of August, 1784, two young officers of a regi-

* Report to the Irish Government.—*Bolton MSS.*

ment quartered at Coleraine, visited the Bishop's palace in the vicinity, for the purpose of seeing the paintings and other objects of interest, for which the palace was famed. The gentlemen were received by the Bishop himself with the utmost politeness; and, after showing them every attention, he induced them to honour him with their company at dinner. Among the guests, which consisted principally of military men, were the Bishop's son, Colonel Hervey, who commanded the battalion in the district, three other field-officers, two of them in command of regiments, and the two subalterns from Coleraine. During dinner, nothing could exceed the good breeding and amenity of their dignified host; but no sooner was the cloth removed than the scene changed. The Bishop began by drinking the health of his son, who was present. 'Gentlemen,' said he, 'this is Colonel Hervey of the Coleraine battalion; he is your superior officer, and will shortly try the stuff you are made of; I hope that ere long we shall meet in the field.' One of the company, somewhat disconcerted at this unexpected intimation, said he hoped they should meet as friends. 'Never, sir,' answered the bishop; 'I am happy to see you under this roof as gentlemen, but in a military sense I shall never look on you as friends.' Upon this, one of the subalterns interposed a hope that his lordship, as a divine missionary, would appear in the field with his book of prayer to preach peace. '*Pax queretur bello*,' was the reply. The Bishop went on to contend with eagerness, that the time was now arrived when Ireland should erect herself into an independent state. A gentleman present could not restrain himself from declaring that he gloried in the name of Englishman; and the *Earl of Bristol* being an Englishman also, he was surprised at the difference in their sentiments. The Earl replied, that he was at one time an Englishman; but it was no longer his boast. He hoped to see the union of England and Ireland dissolved; he was of opinion, that no country could be better prepared for a revolution than Ireland was at that time; and he looked forward to the day when Ireland should be as independent of England as America was. The whole company was at this time in a flame with wine and indignation, 'for,' says one of the narrators of this scene, 'we were all drunk, he (the Bishop) likewise. I left the room unable to contain myself any longer, trembling with passion.' Other guests followed the example of this gentleman; and the party soon afterwards broke up.* Of the Bishop of Derry's lay coadjutor, Sir Edward Newenham, little is known; for the Baronet was as close and cautious as the Bishop was rash and undisguised. Newenham never committed himself by taking an active part; but maintained an intimate correspondence with Napper Tandy. He was also supposed to be principally in communication with the foreign agents, who had been sent or invited to' Ireland, for the purpose of watching or aiding the revolutionary movement. France, Spain, and America had, each of them, numerous spies and half accredited emissaries in the country; and the agents, at the first, had gone such lengths, as to make it a question whether the British Government should not make a representation to the Court of Versailles.†

The course of domestic treason was not, however, sufficiently prosperous for the foreign enemy to hazard any step, which he could not readily retrace. The revolutionary movements, in fact, had not spread far beyond the capital; the efforts to establish seditious associations in the country towns, being, for the

* A memorandum of this conversation was furnished by Lieut.-Colonel Dundas, one of the officers present, to the Irish Government. Another account is that of the subaltern, contained in a letter to a friend, which found its way to the Castle. —*Bolton* MSS.

† Correspondence between Mr. Pitt and Irish Government.— *Ibid.*

most part, kept down by the influence of the local
gentry and clergy, of both denominations. The higher
orders of the Roman Catholic clergy and laity were
all but unanimous in discountenancing any attempt
to obtain redress of their grievances, other than by
legal and constitutional means. It was difficult, indeed,
to see how the success of such a movement as that
which was going on in the capital could better their
condition. The popular leaders had never proposed
the emancipation of their Catholic fellow-countrymen
from civil disabilities as a part of their plan of political regeneration. On the contrary, Flood had denied
the suffrage to the Catholics, in his wide measure
of Parliamentary Reform. Sir Edward Newenham
departed from his habitual reserve, so far as to declare
his hostility to the pretensions of the Catholics to an
equality of civil rights. Even Napper Tandy de-
spaired of effecting such a union of the Irish people
as would enable them to achieve their independence,
unless the Catholics could be induced to forego their
claim to a participation in the elective franchise.*
The Catholic body plainly saw that they had nothing
to hope and everything to fear, from a Parliament
elected under a suffrage which was to include everybody but themselves.† Nor was there anything
inviting in the prospect of the erection of Ireland
into a Protestant republic, or even of her annexation,

---

* *Intercepted Correspondence.
—Bolton* MSS.

† One of the Catholic newspapers of the day alludes to the
rejection of Flood's second Reform Bill in these terms:—'Never
was the interposition of heaven
more visible than in the rejection
of the plans of Reform adjusted
at the National Convention; and
one would be almost tempted to
think that a certain assembly
acted from motives of virtue
when they rejected it, which, had
it been adopted, might have
proved fatal to Ireland; fatal,
because it tended to disunite, and
must have effectually alienated
the affection of the Catholics.'—
Herald, September 14th, 1784.
Immediately after the rejection
of Flood's Bill, the Roman Catholic Archbishop of Cashel, and
his suffragans of the Province of
Munster, thought proper to record their sentiments in a resolution expressive of loyalty and
confidence in the Government.

if such an event was possible, to the dominion of the Most Christian King.

Such was the state of Ireland, when the new Administration found themselves esta- *Critical state of Ireland.* blished in power. The critical condition of that vital part of the British empire had lately engaged the serious consideration of their predecessors in office. Mr. Fox, in his correspondence with Lord Northington, down to the day of his resignation, had expressed a decided opinion, as to the policy which ought to be pursued. He thought that concession and conciliation had gone far enough; according to his phrase, the account between England and Ireland was closed in 1782. He regarded the continued existence of the volunteers, as incompatible with all regular government, and he urged upon the Irish Government, the expediency of refusing all demands, which were supported by that body, and a resolute determination not to be swayed, in any way, by their movements. His opinion was, that the Irish were a nation of jobbers, and that, next to a job for himself, the Irish patriot looked to a job for his country.*

Mr. Pitt's views were widely different; and, whatever may be thought of their practical *Pitt's plan of policy.* tendency, they were certainly of a more enlarged character than those of the Whig statesman. Pitt was of opinion, that Ireland had still grievances to complain of, and that, until these were redressed, it was hopeless to expect tranquillity, or good government in that country. His plan of policy comprehended Parliamentary Reform, and the adjustment of the commercial relations of the two countries on an equitable footing. Although aware of the complicated difficulties which beset any attempt at reform in the representation—difficulties far greater than any which have prevented the settle-

* *Correspondence*, vol. ii. p. 170.

ment of the question in this country—Mr. Pitt still strongly urged upon the Irish Government the propriety and expediency of devising some means by which the scandals and iniquities of the House of Commons should be redressed.* The idea of a complete union between the two kingdoms, which he carried into effect sixteen years afterwards, in the only manner in which such a scheme was practicable, was, at this time, present to his mind;† and he indulged the hope, that it might be worked out through the agency of a Reformed Parliament, and a free trade. The first was soon given up as impracticable. The ingenuity of man could not contrive a scheme by which a proud, slothful and needy aristocracy should be induced to part with the means of obtaining peerages, places, and pensions for themselves, or their dependents; by which the popular party should be persuaded to abandon revolutionary projects for moderate reform; by which Protestants should be satisfied to share political privileges with Catholics; or by which Catholics should consent to Protestant ascendancy. It was on his commercial policy, therefore, that Pitt was forced to rely, for establishing the relations of the twin islands on a friendly footing. He was of opinion, that the internal poverty and distress were the cause of all the discontent that pre-

---

* 'Let me beseech you to recollect, that both your character and mine for consistency are at stake, unless there are unanswerable proofs that the case of Ireland and England is different, and to recollect also, that, however it is our duty to oppose the most determined spirit and firmness to unfounded clamour or factious pretensions, it is a duty equally indispensable to take care not to struggle but in a right cause.'—Mr. Pitt to the Duke of Rutland, 7th October,
1784.—*Bolton MSS.*

† He wished to make England and Ireland one country in effect, though, for local concerns, under distinct legislatures. '*One*, in the communication of advantages, and of course in the participation of burdens. If their unity is broken or rendered absolutely precarious in either of these points, the system is defective, and there is no end of the whole.'—Mr. Pitt to the Duke of Rutland, 5th January, 1785.—*Ibid.*

vailed;* and he hastened to the conclusion, that commercial freedom would prove the remedy for these evils. But commerce was, in fact, emancipated by the Acts of 1780, which threw open the whole foreign and colonial trade to the Irish ports; yet the poverty and distress of 1783 had been greater than the property and distress of 1780. The fact was, that the Acts of 1780 were almost a dead letter; they had been demanded at the point of the bayonet, but, when obtained, they were left to work out the prosperity of trade by their own inherent virtue. There was little or no capital or enterprise in the country; no means had been provided for conducting commercial undertakings on a scale adequate to the facilities which had been opened to them. There was no system of credit† established, no foreign correspondence; there were no mercantile arrangements of any kind.

Pitt's plan was, on the face of it, simple, just, and reasonable. Ireland, by several acts of *Reasonableness* the Imperial Parliament, but, chiefly by *of Pitt's plan.* the legislation of 1780, was free to trade with Europe and the British colonies in the West Indies. The proposal was, that the American and African trade should be, in like manner, opened to her, and that colonial produce, which could already be conveyed in Irish bottoms to British ports, might be re-shipped from Ireland to any part of Great Britain. By way of equivalent for these concessions, the surplus of the hereditary revenues of the Crown in Ireland, was to be appropriated to the common defence of the realm. And, as the hereditary revenue was derived, principally, from imposts on commodities, the contribution

* Letter to Secretary Orde, 19th September, 1784.—*Bolton* MSS.
† One significant fact is mentioned by the Irish Chancellor of the Exchequer: 'The Bank of Ireland, which was to do the business of the whole kingdom, have *never subscribed any capital*, and began with £60,000 only, which they borrowed at the same interest they are themselves allowed to take.'—Mr. Foster to Secretary Orde, 30th October, 1784.—*Ibid.*

demanded from the sister kingdom, would, according
to this arrangement, be adjusted in proportion to the
benefits which she obtained from the removal of
restrictions upon her trade and commerce. Resolutions, embodying these provisions, were proposed to
the Irish House of Commons, in February. They
were, on the whole, well received, and, though Mr.
Brownlow, a leading member of the popular party,
denounced them as an insidious attack on the independence of the Irish Parliament, they were com-
mended by Grattan, as just and beneficial to the
country; and were unanimously adopted by both
Houses. In a few days, Pitt laid them on the table
of the English House, and explained their purport
in a speech which expounded the enlarged principles
of a sound commercial policy. Such views, however,
were far in advance of the bigoted and selfish notions
which then generally prevailed, and especially
among merchants and manufactures. The Opposition quickly perceived the opportunity afforded
them, by this bold innovation on established maxims,
and they hoped, by an appeal to popular ignorance
and sordid prejudice, to ruin the growing reputation
of the youthful statesman. They demanded time,
which Pitt, with generous confidence in the force of
truth and reason,* readily granted. A distant day
was named. In the interval, petitions came pouring
in from Lancashire, and the great seats of commerce
and manufactures. A committee of merchants sat
in London. A cry was raised, that the great Charter
of Commerce, the Navigation Act, was endangered;
the British markets would be undersold, and the English operatives would be thrown out of employment,

* 'The more the subject is discussed, the more our cause will be benefited. . . . There are melancholy prophets here (as is always the case), who are not without their fears; but I do not myself entertain a doubt of complete success.'—Pitt to the Lord Lieutenant, 4th April. —*Bolton MSS.*

by the competition of cheap Irish labour. Witnesses were examined, and counsel were heard at the bar of the House, in support of their propositions. In this manner, several weeks were wasted. Pitt sought, by a modification of his scheme, to remove these objections. The eleven resolutions, which had been accepted by the Irish Parliament, received material alterations and additions; and ultimately, twenty resolutions were submitted to the consideration of the British House of Commons, on the 12th of May. The second and most important of the original resolutions, by which Ireland was to be admitted to a participation, on equal terms with Great Britain, in the commerce of the world, was now qualified, by excepting the trade with India; a restriction which would deprive Ireland of at least half the benefit she might derive from the proposed treaty, when the monopoly of the Company should be determined. There were several amendments of a minor character; but one of the interpolated resolutions, the fourth in the amended draft, introduced a new term into the compact; it provided, that the laws for regulating trade and navigation should be the same in both kingdoms; and that such laws and regulations should be framed by the Parliament of Great Britain, and be ratified by the Parliament of Ireland.

These concessions were of little avail in abating the opposition to the measure. The commercial interest was not to be propitiated by any modification of a scheme which was to lay them open to competition. The provision for giving legislative supremacy to Great Britain in matters of trade and commerce, the merchants and manufacturers regarded merely as a circuitous attempt to evade what they justly pointed out as the real remedy—*a union with Ireland under one legislature.* The leading opponents of the measure in the House of Commons were more vehement

Opposition of the trading interest.

against the resolutions in their amended form than
in their original state. Fox and North, in opposing
any further concession to the Irish people, acted consistently with the policy they had pursued in office.
Ignorant of the laws of political economy,* Fox regarded the commercial question between England
and Ireland as a question of bargain or extortion, in
which the one sought to obtain from the other something which could not be conceded without a proportionate loss. In this spirit, he denounced the scheme
as 'a tame surrender of the commerce and manufactures of our country,' and exerted the utmost power
of eloquence to give effect to the vulgar and selfish
prejudice with which the measure was assailed. Lord
North, indeed, roundly asserted, that Ireland had no
right to a share in the British markets, which ought
to belong exclusively to the British manufacturer;
and that until both countries were united under one
Parliament, it was neither just nor equitable that the
one should be enriched at the expense of the other.
He went still further, and denied that Ireland had
ever demanded the concessions which this country
was about to yield; they were erroneously called
Irish propositions, being the spontaneous offering of
England. In the last stage of the Bill the Opposition took new ground. Having in vain endeavoured
to obstruct its progress through their own Parliament, they sought to defeat the measure on Irish
ground, by inflaming the too susceptible jealousy of
the sister kingdom. Sheridan took the lead in this
unfair and factious warfare. He said the Irish Parliament would not dare to pass these resolutions;
and, should they hesitate, he appealed to the people
to assert their independence. Fox followed in a like
incendiary strain; and Burke, who had not the excuse of ignorance on such matters, which might be

* He admitted that he had never read Adam Smith, and that the science of Political Economy was above his comprehension.—BUTLER's *Reminiscences*.

urged on behalf of Fox and Sheridan, belied, for the sake of party, those principles which he had so nobly vindicated in 1780 at the cost of his seat. He did not, indeed, venture openly to attack the policy of free-trade; but, after endeavouring to disparage the scheme in the strain of coarse and clumsy ridicule, which he so often affected in debate, he took the course which, of all others, was calculated to excite a fatal prejudice against it in the sister country. He drew an invidious comparison between the two kingdoms, describing England as the great ruling power which must ever sway the sceptre, and Ireland as necessarily occupying a subordinate and subservient position: an inevitable truth indeed, and the force of which was most acutely felt by the keen-witted islanders themselves, when they most passionately asserted their freedom and independence. These sensitive people were now told by British statesmen of the highest authority, that the project of the British Government was a badge of their inferiority; that it annihilated their new-born liberties, and made them tributaries to the superior power.

These acts of a desperate and unscrupulous faction had the desired effect. Long before the *Stormy debate.* Bill had left the English Parliament, ominous murmurs from the other side of the Channel indicated the reception which it would find in the country for whose benefit it was designed. The Bill embodying the resolutions did not arrive in Ireland before the end of July; and on the 2nd of August it was introduced in the Irish House of Commons. Mr. Orde proposed an adjournment of ten days, in order that the Bill might be promulgated through the country before it was discussed; but the leaders of the popular party insisted that the Bill ought to be immediately rejected; and Flood gave notice of a motion declaratory of the independence of the Irish Parliament. On the motion for the first reading, the Bill was assailed with the whole force of Irish eloquence. Grattan, Flood, and Curran vied with each other in raising a storm of patriotic oratory, such as had hardly ever been heard even in the Irish Parliament. In vain did the English Secretary, in a clear and comprehensive speech, explain the provisions and bearings of the measure. It was not often that the voice of reason and moderation was heard in that chamber; and on this occasion it was drowned in the tumult and excitement which prevailed. No independent member of an assembly, in which almost every man was a speaker, ventured to rise in support of Mr. Orde. The Attorney General, Fitz-Gibbon, a man remarkable for his courage and contempt of popular professions, came to the rescue of his colleague, and addressed himself to the congenial task of exposing the exaggerations and absurdities of the patriots. The Chancellor of the Exchequer and another minister faintly attempted to sustain the debate. On the division, the Government prevailed only by the narrow majority of nineteen. This was equivalent to a defeat; and the Minister announced that the Bill would not be pressed further during the present session. Public rejoicings took place, Dublin was illuminated; and throughout the island the event was celebrated as a deliverance from a great calamity.

Such was the termination of Pitt's first attempt to deal with an Irish question; a branch of domestic policy which has perplexed and baffled every leading English statesman from that time to the present. The commercial propositions had been elaborated with the greatest pains. Pitt had been in communication with the principal members of the Irish Government, both personally and by correspondence, for several months. The English Board of Trade, under his direction, had investigated the subject in all its bearings; and every information which could elucidate the subject, and lead to sound conclusions, had been exhausted. That the measure would have to encounter prejudice and misconstruction on either side of the Channel, the Minister was fully aware; but he was as fully persuaded, that the more it was discussed, the more it would recommend itself to the approbation both of those classes in this country against whose interests it seemed to militate, and of the Irish people, for whose welfare it was more especially designed. This faith he retained unshaken up to the last hour; and, so far as England was concerned, his confidence was justified. Before the Bill had reached its final stage in the British Parliament, public opinion had come round, groundless alarm was dissipated, and the Bill was passed with a general acquiescence,* if not with a hearty assent. But in the sister island little reliance could be placed on that sober sense and candour, for the action of which in this country a public man, however adverse his fortune for the time may be, seldom waits in vain. It must be admitted, however, that the course which Pitt pursued was calculated to alarm the sensitive jealousy of the Irish nation. If he had thought fit, in the first instance, to submit his policy in the shape of definite propositions for the approval of the Irish Legislature, it became the more incumbent on him to take the sense of the Irish Legislature upon those propositions

---

* 'This business grows to be relished more and more in this country, as the different facts of it come to be understood; it meets with general approbation, and unless Opposition meets with encouragement from what may pass in Ireland, all their hopes are at an end. I do assure you, that I do not represent the state of things in too favourable a light. .... Many persons startle at some things that are entirely new, and do not at first see the necessity of them; but great numbers have changed their opinions here, and have of late warmly supported what they were first alarmed at.'—Jenkinson to Secretary Orde, 1st August, 1785.—*Bolton* MSS. There was no better judge on such a point than Jenkinson.

after they had been modified to meet the objections of the more powerful country. But this course was not taken; and the Parliament of Ireland had a right to complain, as they did complain, that they were asked to adopt a measure founded on terms materially varying from those to which their assent had been asked and given. The only answer which could have been made to such a complaint was, that the propositions had not been altered in a sense adverse to the interests of Ireland. The fact, however, was unfortunately otherwise. The second of the original propositions, which admitted Ireland on an equality with Great Britain to the commerce of the world, came back with one exception, which seemed intended to exclude her from any share in the most lucrative branch of that commerce. But there was one of the English clauses, which of itself was sufficient to decide the fate of the measure in Ireland. It was impossible to deny, that the fourth resolution, which denied to the Parliament of Ireland the initiative of any laws and regulations affecting commerce, did materially compromise its independence, and would have justified it, on the precedents and practice of the British House of Commons, in the indignant rejection of a Bill which contained such an offensive provision.

The moral of this transaction was that the existence of independent Legislatures in England and Ireland was incompatible with the union of the two countries, and to prepare the way for the great measure of union which was accomplished a few years later.

In this session, Pitt redeemed his promise to
<small>Want of interest in Reform.</small> bring forward a measure of Parliamentary Reform. But the moment at which this subject was revived, and the new form in which it was introduced, seemed to imply, that the Minister was more intent on getting rid of a troublesome pledge, to which he had committed himself under

other circumstances, than desirous of bringing the question to a happy conclusion. The demand for Reform, which had been excited by the pressure of the American War, and the miserable Government of Lord North, had subsided with the return of more prosperous times, and a confidence in the administration of public affairs, which had not been felt since the commencement of the reign. The plan itself was the weakest and the least practicable of any which had been proposed. Yet it is certain, that Pitt felt a sincere interest in the subject, that he believed it to be one of prime importance, and that his measure was framed with the view of removing the practical difficulties which stood in the way of substantial reform.* His idea was simple and sound; but the machinery by which he proposed to carry it into effect was so futile and absurd, as to cast a doubt upon the good faith of its able author. The principle was the one which Chatham had always maintained, namely, the increase of the county representation by the extinction of the small and decayed boroughs. Seventy-two additional members were thus to be given to the counties, and the constituency was to be enlarged by the enfranchisement of copyholders. A fund was to be raised to indemnify the patrons of the boroughs which were to be deprived of representatives; but, as the transaction was to be placed on the footing of a bargain between the borough-monger and the State, it rested entirely with the former, whether the plan should be carried into effect, or remain a dead letter. To meet this objection, it was intended that the unused fund should accumulate at compound interest, so as to reach a point which would tempt the cupidity of the

* Mr. Pitt pressed his plan with enthusiasm, not only in the House of Commons, but in private, with such friends as he thought he could influence.— *Diaries and Correspondence of the Right Honourable George Rose* vol. iv. p. 35.

man least disposed to part with his borough. A more childish or ridiculous scheme it would be difficult to conceive. If this kind of bastard ownership in boroughs was to be recognised as legitimate property, it should only have been for the purpose of presently attaining a great public object; the borough might have been disfranchised forthwith, and compensation awarded on the well-established principle, by which private property is arbitrarily taken under the authority of Parliament for public purposes; but to lay out a plan for the constitution of the House of Commons, and to leave the adoption of that plan, either wholly or in part, either to-day or to-morrow, dependent on the will of a few individuals, was not only trifling with a great question, but setting the authority of Parliament at nought. The Bill underwent a full debate, and was rejected by a majority of seventy-four. Pitt made no further attempt during his long administration to stir this question.

The only measure of importance which Pitt was enabled to carry during this session, was a Bill for the regulation of public offices, for retrenching wasteful extravagance and peculation in the several departments, and for providing an efficient audit of the public accounts. A Commission had been appointed, when Lord North was Minister, for the investigation of these matters; and the result had been a voluminous report, upon which the Bill brought in by the Government was, in fact, founded. The subject had engaged the special attention of Pitt, when he held the office of Chancellor of the Exchequer, under Lord Shelburne, and he had drawn the attention of Parliament to the subject after he had quitted office. He showed that the nation had lost immense sums, by leaving balances for a succession of years in the hands of clerks and accountants; that many public servants, though amply paid by salaries, were deriving large

Bill for regulating public offices.

emoluments from fees and perquisites; and that, in some cases, they received a percentage upon amounts which it was their duty to control and check. The habitual abuse of privileges by public officers frequently amounted to malversation. Secretaries and clerks had been known to furnish their houses and maintain their domestic establishments at the public expense. Under the head of stationery, the most impudent frauds had been perpetrated; and Pitt instanced a charge in a single year of more than three hundred pounds to Lord North, the Prime Minister, for pack-thread. The mention of these cases by a man who had held high office was quite sufficient to prove the necessity for some stringent measure; but the Coalition Ministry treated the matter as merely one of administrative detail, and though they could not prevent Pitt's Bill from passing the Commons, they took care that it should be defeated in the Upper House. This ill-judged opposition to a measure so plainly reasonable, was regarded out of doors as an attempt to screen scandalous abuses, and contributed not a little to the unpopularity of the Coalition.

The measure which the former Administration had with difficulty defeated, being now brought forward with the authority of a more powerful Administration, was passed without a division in either House. Sheridan and Burke distinguished themselves among the Opposition, by the perverse violence with which they still resisted this most just and necessary Reform. The plan was to be carried into effect by separate Acts; one for the regulation and audit of the accounts in the Navy and Ordnance Departments; and the other for a commission of inquiry into the fees, emoluments and perquisites, received by public officers. When the latter Bill was in its final stage, Sheridan, in a style of ribaldry, to which he often descended, affected to sneer at Pitt, as a hunter of small vermin. Burke rose and demanded, in solemn tones, that Magna Charta should be read by the clerk at the table. The House, accustomed to the eccentric flights of the great orator, had come to regard them with indifference; but this portentous opening caused a laugh. Burke, whose irritable temper gave way at the slightest provocation, broke into a fury, railed at the House, as caring no more for the great Charter than for Chevy Chase, and vociferated, that the Bill—the object of which was to prevent small frauds and peculations in the public services—was a gross violation of the Charter, and of the common law of the land. Fox, probably from good nature, said a few words in support of his friend's extravagance; but Pitt treated the Opposition with a silent contempt, which was often more galling than his keenest sarcasm. The Bill was read a third time, and passed without further observation.

Notwithstanding his signal failure in the two great measures of Free Trade and Parliamentary Reform, on which he had entered with the most assured confidence of success, public confidence in the young Minister continued without abatement; and when, in the third year of his administration, he undertook a great experiment in finance, the country was disposed to echo the boast of his admirers, that he was about to exhibit a new proof of the commanding genius which qualified him, above every other statesman, to direct the fortunes of the Commonwealth. In the last ten years, the public debt had been nearly doubled, and in 1786, it amounted in round numbers, to two hundred and fifty millions. Some effort towards the reduction, if not the ultimate liquidation of this prodigious charge, was justly expected; and when it was known that Pitt had undertaken this arduous duty, public expectation was raised to the height.

Attempt to reduce the National Debt.

There never was a time more favourable to an important fiscal operation. It has commonly happened, that the resources of a financier have been tried by the actual pressure of public burdens; but it was the singular fortune of Pitt, that he had to deal with a revenue oppressed, indeed, with debt, but with a debt, which, enormous and rapid as had been its accumulation, had not increased in proportion with the wealth and prosperity of the country. At the end of the second financial year of his administration, Pitt was enabled to announce that the public income exceeded the expenditure by one million, or about eight per cent. This surplus he proposed to appropriate towards the reduction of capital charge. It is now well understood that the only mode of making a surplus available to the reduction of funded debt, is by the extinction of an equivalent amount of stock. But instead of adopting this simple plan, Pitt was led astray by one of the most specious and shallow delusions that ever took possession of the human mind. He was persuaded that this million might be made the deposit of a Sinking Fund, which, in an ascertained number of years, by the operation of the law of compound interest, would infallibly absorb the whole debt of two hundred and fifty millions. There was no novelty in this idea. It had been started so early as 1716, and adopted by Sir Robert Walpole. It is not very likely, however, that the great sense and sagacity of that minister were ever beguiled by the extravagant doctrine which imposed on the youthful credulity of Pitt. Walpole would be willing enough to encourage any idea which would give him the command of a resource, that might be available in case of need. And accordingly, on the first occasion when he wanted money, he resorted to the Sinking Fund; and in a very few years, he mortgaged or anticipated the whole of its produce.

Half a century had elapsed since the extinction of the Sinking Fund, under the hands of Walpole; but though several millions of debt had been paid off in various ways during this interval, no attempt had been made to reconstruct this marvellous engine of finance. The magnitude which the debt had attained in consequence of the American War, had alarmed the nation; and men were disposed to consider with favour any project for getting rid of a burden which seemed beyond ordinary means of removal. At this juncture, an enthusiast, named Price, reproduced the scheme of a Sinking Fund, and undertook to demonstrate that, by the spontaneous action of this system, the debt of the nation would be wholly extinguished. The doctrine of a Sinking Fund, as it was laid down by Price, and implicitly adopted by Pitt, has been long since exploded; and a few words will suffice to show the utter fallacy of the principle upon which it was based.

Inventors of plans for the payment of the National Debt have long been classed among incorrigible visionaries or impudent impostors; but of all the plans that have ever been proposed, there was none more absurd than that which was deliberately adopted by the Government in 1786, with the general acquiescence of men of business; and which, for twenty years, regulated the fiscal system of this country. That the annual appropriation of a certain sum, suffered to accumulate at compound interest, will, in a given number of years, reach a given amount, is a mere matter of calculation, about which there can be no dispute. The only question is, whether this is the best mode of liquidating debt. By applying the amount annually contributed to the Sinking Fund, to the extinction of stock, the country is relieved from taxation to the extent of the interest of the

Plans for paying off the Debt.

stock so extinguished; but if the stock redeemed instead of being extinguished is capitalised, it follows, that the interest must still be paid; and, therefore, the amount of this interest, which, according to the ordinary process of liquidating debts, would be remitted, is just so much added to the principal sum annually contributed to the Fund. The only result is, that a heavier burden is borne for the purpose of abridging the period, within which the whole debt is to be discharged. The extent to which this plan could be carried, is obviously limited only by the endurance of the tax-payer.

It is not to be supposed, that the project altogether escaped criticism. Its fallacy was, indeed, fully exposed by unknown authors,* at the very time when the project was at the height of popularity; but these remonstrances appear to have attracted no attention, and accordingly, in the session of 1786, an Act of Parliament was passed, providing for the payment of two hundred and fifty thousand pounds, quarterly, to a Board of Commissioners, who should invest these sums in the purchase of stock, either at or below par, the dividend of the stock so purchased, being placed to the credit of the Commissioners, and to go on accumulating until the Fund should amount to four millions.

This notable scheme for paying off the National Debt, by means of a fund which was supposed to possess the faculty of multiplying itself, but which was really worth no more than the proceeds of taxation contributed to it, received the sanction of Parliament, without any dissent from an Opposition, eager to seize any pretence for discrediting the measures of Administration, and not scrupulous in the

---

* In two pamphlets, *The Challenge; or, Patriotism put to the Test, in a Letter to Dr. Price,* by Jos. WIMPEY; and *Considerations on the Annual Million Bill.*—Lord OVERSTONE's *Collection of Tracts on National Debt.*

means which they employed. The most that can be said for the plan is, that in times when the expenditure of the country was not in excess of ordinary revenue, it afforded some security for the application of a certain amount of income to the reduction of debt, and was only less advantageous than the ordinary mode of payment by the cost of management. But the author of the plan maintained that it was absolutely essential to its success, that the regular supply of the fund should not be dependent on surplus revenue; and that when extraordinary services required the aid of loans, the contribution to the fund should not be intermitted; in other words, that money should be borrowed to pay debt: and this was actually done when the surplus revenue was exhausted by the exigencies of the revolutionary war. Price's system was virtually abandoned in 1807; but the delusion was not dissipated until the publication of Dr. Hamilton's work on the National Debt in 1813; and Parliament did not formally recant its error until 1829, when it was enacted that the sum to be applied to the reduction of the National Debt should be the actual annual surplus revenue over the expenditure.*

In this session, a proposition was made, on the part of the Government, to provide for the permanent defence of the two great naval arsenals, Ports-

---

* 10 Geo. IV. c. 27. Even the term 'surplus revenue' conveys a fallacious idea. An individual, who must live within his income, may be said to have a surplus when his expenditure is less than his receipts. But the State, which adapts its means to its wants, and not its wants to its means, has no income but what it derives from taxation, assessed as nearly as possible to meet the actual exigencies of the public service. Any surplus, therefore, which may exist, is merely the productiveness of taxation in excess of the estimate of the Finance Minister, and should, properly, be carried to the credit of the service of the ensuing year. Debt should form a regular head of charge so long as the supplies are provided within the year, and not be left dependent on a casual surplus.

mouth and Plymouth. This design had originated with the Duke of Richmond, who was at the head of the Ordnance Department; and had been keenly discussed already, both in the House of Commons and by the public press. The project had been referred to a Commission of military and naval officers, whose report was, upon the whole, unfavourable. Assuming that the Channel was left open to the enemy by the absence or discomfiture of the British fleet, it might be necessary to provide for the protection of the great arsenals; and the Commissioners recommended a chain of detached forts, as the best mode of fortification that could be adopted; but they intimated their opinion, that an invasion under such circumstances was such a bare possibility, as hardly to justify an undertaking of such magnitude. The House of Commons inclined to the same opinion. Pitt himself did not give a very earnest support to the project of his colleague, and Parliament refused to sanction it. The division on Pitt's resolution was equal, and the casting vote of the Speaker was declared in the negative.

For some years past, when the affairs of India were the subject of discussion in the Commons, Burke seldom omitted the opportunity of holding up the Governor-General as the scourge and oppressor of that country. In the previous year, Hastings had resigned the Government on the expiration of his term of office, and returned to England. His reception by the Court of Directors had been marked by a due sense of the great services he had rendered to the Company. He was honoured by royal favour, and the Queen condescended to accept presents from his wife. It was fully expected that the late vicegerent of India would be summoned to take his place in the peerage of England, and that still further honours and dignities awaited the great proconsul. But, instead of receiving honours and rewards, Hastings soon found, that he had to defend his fortune and his freedom, if not his life, against the most powerful combination of foes that ever sought the ruin of a public man.

For some time before the storm broke, its approach was indicated by ominous murmurs. The year before Hastings quitted India, the distant thunder of Burke's accusing eloquence was heard. During the session of 1785, Burke and Francis were busily engaged in collecting materials for the grand indictment which was in contemplation. At length, early in the session of 1786, Burke came forward with a motion for papers, on the production of which he announced his intention to propose an impeachment of the late Governor-General.

Burke and Francis.

At first, the Ministry were disposed to discourage any proceedings against Hastings; but the question being taken up with great vigour by the Opposition, and Dundas, the President of the Board of Control, being reminded of the resolutions condemnatory of Hastings which he had moved in 1782, the difficulty was felt of a direct resistance to the movement. Burke proceeded, therefore, to reduce his charges into shape, and he exhibited them in twenty-two articles. The principal were the Rohilla War; the transactions in Benares; the treatment of the Oude princes; the Mahratta War; contracts, and acceptance of presents. Hastings desired to have copies of the articles of impeachment, and to be heard at the bar in his defence. After some opposition, the authority of Pitt, aided by a sense of justice and decency, inclined the House to comply with this demand. Accordingly, for two days Hastings was heard in reply to those charges, and to the statements of his accusers. The House immediately afterwards proceeded to take evidence in support of the several allegations; and when a suffi-

Hastings heard at the bar of the House.

cient ground was thus laid, the prosecutors of the impeachment began to open the several charges in detail. The first charge, which related to the conduct of the late Governor-General in the Rohilla War, was opened by Burke. A clearer case was never submitted to any tribunal. Hastings, on assuming the Government of Bengal, had been instructed to improve the revenues of the province for the benefit of his employers, so far as was consistent with justice and a due regard to the interest of the inhabitants. It was natural, perhaps, that a body of traders, exercising sovereign power, should consider it their first object to obtain a dividend from the resources of the country over which they ruled. In Hastings they found a servant devoted to their interest, able, prompt, and unscrupulous. The Company wanted money, and money he was determined they should have. The Nabob of Oude desired to seize upon a neighbouring territory, called Rohilcund; but such was the warlike character of the people, that he dared not invade them, notwithstanding the numerical superiority of his forces. If he could by any means obtain the aid of European troops, his object might be accomplished. The Governor of Bengal had a small but well-appointed army, lying unemployed in and around Calcutta. The Nabob was on good terms with the Governor, and he proposed to hire the British soldiers for the subjugation of the Rohillas. The proposal was accepted; and it was agreed, that, for the consideration of four hundred thousand pounds, an adequate force should be placed at the disposal of the Nabob for this particular service. It can add little to the infamy of this transaction, that the Company had no quarrel with the people against whom they undertook to prosecute a war of extermination, or that the despot who sought their destruction had no other quarrel with them than that which their superiority in arms, in manners, and government, was calculated to provoke. An English ruler who could bargain away the blood and valour of English soldiers for money was not likely to be deterred by the consideration, that they were to be sold to a cause more vile and cruel than any in which mercenaries had ever yet been engaged. No such scruple, indeed, appears to have troubled the mind of Hastings. It was enough for him, that he had got four hundred thousand pounds. He performed his contract with punctuality. The noble people, whom the military rabble of Oude dared not attack, struggled in vain against European skill and discipline; and the country of the Rohillas was safely occupied by the cowardly conquerors.

If the minister could defend this transaction, and persuade a majority of the House of Commons to agree with him, Hastings and his friends might well suppose that the impeachment was at an end. The Rohilla charge was supported by the leading members of Opposition, Burke, North, Fox, and Francis. Pitt took no part in the debate; but he suffered his subordinates to oppose the motion; and it was rejected by a large majority. The case against Hastings was now considered hopeless; but, before it was formally abandoned, it was determined to justify the course which his accusers had pursued, by placing the facts upon which the principal charges had been founded before Parliament and the country. Accordingly, Fox, to whom, in the distribution of the articles of impeachment, the next head of charge had been assigned, brought forward the case of Cheyte Sing, commonly called the Benares charge.

<small>Cheyte Sing.</small> The transcendent infamy of the Rohilla War casts a shade over the many other iniquities of Hastings, glaring as they were. The four hundred thousand pounds of blood-money, which had been received from the Nabob of Oude, had been exhausted; and the exigencies of war, together with

the incessant demands of his employers, taxed the ingenuity of the Governor to find new resources. Some years before, the Nabob of Oude, who was himself, in theory at least, no more than the vicegerent of the Mogul, had relinquished to the Company a doubtful claim to the sovereignty of the rich and populous city of Benares. The Rajah, or reigning prince of Benares, had, from that time, been a tributary of the Company, and his tribute had been assessed at a fixed sum. When war with France was declared, in 1778, Cheyte Sing was required to pay an extraordinary aid of fifty thousand pounds. The same amount was demanded in the following year. The requisition having been repeated in 1780, the Rajah offered a bribe of twenty thousand pounds to the Governor, with a view of being relieved from these exactions. Hastings took the money, intending, beyond a doubt, to keep it; but a fit of remorse, or a dread of detection, induced him, after some delay, to pay it over to the Company, and a fine of ten thousand pounds, in addition to the extraordinary tribute, was inflicted on Cheyte Sing for offering the bribe which had been accepted by his judge. But robbery by instalment was too slow a process for the rapacity of Hastings. He demanded half a million in one sum. The unhappy prince offered two hundred thousand pounds. Hastings entered his territory with an armed force, and seized his person. A revolution in Benares was the consequence; Cheyte Sing became a fugitive, his treasure was seized; and his deposition, which completed this series of iniquities, placed an annual revenue of two hundred thousand pounds at the disposal of Hastings.

An English statesman, who had failed to discover in the affairs of the Rohillas a sufficient ground for impeachment, might have been expected to find plausible arguments to palliate, if not to justify, the transactions with the Rajah of Benares. Pressed as he was by the emergencies of war, the Governor might perhaps be excused for having availed himself of the readiest resources for the defence of the rich dominions committed to his charge. The levying a war contribution on the tributaries of the Company might be regarded as a commutation for the military contingent, which they might fairly have been called upon to furnish towards the defence against the common enemy. It was probable, that this pecuniary impost would be unwillingly paid, and it was unfair to test by English modes of procedure, the strong measures which might be necessary to meet the duplicity and evasion of an Eastern potentate. Such an argument was plausible, and would have been readily accepted by a House which had negatived the Rohilla charge. But, to the astonishment of all men, Mr. Pitt, after justifying the conduct of the late Governor of Bengal up to a certain point, took offence, or pretended to take offence, at the exorbitancy of the demand made upon Cheyte Sing. The Government of Bengal, he said, were warranted in calling upon the Rajah for an extraordinary aid in time of war; the aid required was not excessive; the compulsion of payment by fine and invasion of his territory was justifiable; but the demand of half a million as a fine for the attempt to evade payment of fifty thousand pounds was out of all proportion to the offence. Mr. Pitt passed a high eulogium on Hastings, and denounced as illiberal and unjust the design imputed to him of ruining Cheyte Sing; Hastings was actuated only by zeal for the interest of his employers. Nevertheless, the minister arrived at the conclusion, that the charge of corruption and violence was so far made out, that he must vote for this article of the impeachment.

This sudden change in the counsels of administration give rise to many conjectures, and has never been satisfactorily explained.* The probability is, that Pitt had not given a serious attention to the subject, and had looked upon the impeachment as a movement of the Opposition. But when he came to examine the charge against Hastings, he must have seen that the more the case was investigated, the less defensible would it become. He could not but recollect also, that suspicions had been excited in the public mind, relative to the conduct of the Company's servants; and the obloquy which had been accumulated on the head of Clive, whose services had been far more conspicuous, if not more valuable, than those of Hastings, and whose conduct had never been subjected to the grave imputations which were deliberately fixed upon the late Governor-General, was a warning that the patience of the country might be tempted too far.

Pitt's authority over the House of Commons was, on this occasion, exemplified in a remarkable manner; the Robilla charge, unsupported by the minister, was rejected by a majority of fifty-two.† The Benares charge was voted in the following week by a majority of forty.‡ The promoters of the impeachment, content with this triumph, or unprepared for the prosecution of a cause, which, after the fate of

---

* Many ingenious speculations have been hazarded to account for the sudden change in Pitt's view of the impeachment; but, after all, the plain version of the affair contained in the following letter may be the true one.

'.... The only unpleasant circumstance is the impeachment of Hastings. Mr. Pitt and I have got great credit from the undeviating fairness and candour with which we have proceeded in it; but the proceeding is not pleasant to many of our friends; and, of course, from that and many other circumstances, not pleasing to us; but the truth is, when we examined the various articles of charges against him, with his defences, they were so strong, and the defences so perfectly unsupported, it was impossible not to concur, and some of the charges will unquestionably go to the Lords.'—Dundas to Earl Cornwallis, 21st March, 1787. — *Cornwallis Correspondence*, vol. i. p. 273.

† 119 to 67.
‡ 119 to 79.

the first count in the indictment, they considered as lost, made no farther progress in the matter during this session.

In the recess of Parliament, the Ministry were engaged in maturing two measures of great utility and importance. The one was a commercial treaty with France, and the other was a kindred project, the consolidation of various duties of customs and excise. An article in the late Treaty of Peace between France and England had provided for the negotiation of a commercial intercourse between the two countries. This was now happily effected by a Treaty based upon the most liberal terms, and conceived in a spirit which recognised the mutual interests of the great contracting parties. Prohibitory duties on the products of either country were to be repealed with some few exceptions. A moderate tariff, mostly for revenue purposes, was to be fixed on certain commodities. A great concession was made to France, by abolishing the differential duties in favour of the wines of Portugal, and thus abandoning the famous Methuen Treaty, which had been so long considered a masterpiece of British diplomacy. The Treaty was calculated to be highly beneficial to the trade, commerce, and manufactures of both nations; and to ruin the contraband traffic, which, in spite of repressive laws and a revenue fleet, had long infested the Channel.* But above all, it was valuable in its tendency to allay the barbarous animosities which had subsisted for centuries, and to introduce relations of a more humane and generous character between two great and enlightened communities.

The Treaty which had been signed at Versailles, on the 28th of September, was submitted to the appro-

---

* In his speech on the Treaty, Mr. Pitt stated the legal importation of French brandy was six hundred thousand gallons, while the smuggled article was estimated at four millions.

bation of Parliament on its re-assembly in 1787. The
wisdom of the policy which sought to The New Treaty signed.
open a market for our rapidly increasing
manufactures in a neighbouring country, with a population of twenty-four millions, was so striking, that
the Opposition, unable to urge any substantial objection
to the scheme, was forced to appeal to the jealousies
and animosities between the people of the two countries, as a reason for not contributing to the prosperity
of our ancient foe, even though we should by the
same act advance our own material interests in a far
greater proportion. Fox, while he laboured this
argument, seemed to feel that the exigencies of party
warfare compelled him to a course unworthy of a
statesman. He admitted—and the admission was
valuable as showing the improved state of public
opinion—that he might be charged with giving effect
to vulgar and illiberal prejudices; but he said, that
these prejudices had engaged us in war, which had
contributed more than any other circumstance to the
greatness and glory of the country. Burke, whose
penetrating intellect, when not obscured by passion
or prejudice, surveyed the whole field of politics,
though he could not quite bring himself to adopt the
doctrine of his leader, that war and glory were more
conducive to the prosperity of the nation than trade
and commerce, yet was scarcely more reasonable when
he denounced the narrowness of Pitt's mind in the
conception of this measure. The minister had unfolded his scheme in a speech, the singular perspicuity and intelligence of which had conveyed
information to those who had previously been little
acquainted with the subject, and conviction to many,
whose habitual opinions, though not hardened into
prejudices, had received a violent shock from a proposal so novel as that of amicable intercourse with
the ancient enemy of England. But Burke considered that the minister had treated the business as a

counting-house affair, a contention for custom between the Fleur-de-lis and the Red Lion! Such is a specimen of the taste and candour which too frequently gave pain and offence to the admirers of Burke's genius, and drew down upon him rebukes such as he received on this occasion. Wilberforce lamented over the decay of faculties which, in better days, had compelled the assent and admiration of the House. Pitt affected to remonstrate with his friend for taking notice of such silly and petulant animadversions, and, in his bitterest manner, spoke of the philosophic statesman and consummate orator as a man crazed by ill-temper and spleen, whose condition, though challenging compassion, was not free from disgust. The manufacturing and commercial interest, though somewhat uneasy at the innovating spirit displayed by Pitt on all subjects connected with trade, were so much under his influence, that they hesitated to offer that opposition to his measures, which a similar policy, if ventured upon by any of his predecessors, would probably have encountered. On this occasion, the General Chamber of Manufactures and Commerce presented a petition to Parliament, in which, while they admitted that they had not been able to arrive at any certain judgment on the subject, yet craved some little delay in coming to a final decision on the treaty, on account of its awful importance to the interests which they represented. A remonstrance so hesitating as this was not very likely to offer any impediment to the progress of the measure, which the House affirmed by a very large majority.

The other measure referred to, the plan for the consolidation of the Customs and Excise, was framed likewise with a timely recognition of the increasing importance of trade and commerce. A multiplicity of vexatious, uncertain, and unintelligible imposts were abolished, and in their place were substituted specific duties on every article; an arrangement which facilitated the transactions of commerce, simplified the collection of the revenue, and added considerably to its amount. The measure had been proposed by the administration of Lord North, but had been laid aside until it was revived and brought to maturity by the diligence and discrimination of Pitt. The Bill passed with general approbation.

A subject of far more popular interest, though of infinitely less importance, than the great measures which have just been described *The Prince of Wales.* occupied the attention of Parliament in the course of this session. The heir-apparent, though no more than twenty-five years of age, had long since acquired an evil reputation among all ranks of men. Following the example of his grandfather, Frederick, to whose character his own bore a strong family resemblance, he had, at the outset of his public life, connected himself in close political and private friendship with the dissolute leaders of the Whig party, who were engaged, not merely in opposition to the Court, but in personal hostility to the King. The Prince's education had been superintended by men of learning and piety; the manners and conduct of their Majesties in private life were exemplary. Nevertheless, the austerity of the domestic circle of the court was such, that a young man of spirit might be excused for some irregularities on being emancipated from its irksome restraint. The King, after the fashion of the age, maintained a strict discipline in his family, and a distant demeanour towards his children. He was far from wanting in paternal tenderness; but those who were nearest his person, and were impressed with the deepest sense of his virtuous and amiable qualities, have lamented the reserve which he habitually maintained towards every member of his family. The Queen herself had none of those endearing qualities of her sex, which often maintain harmony and happiness in a family. Bred up in the rigid formality of a petty German court, her manners were cold and punctilious; her understanding was dull, her temper jealous and petulant. It is not surprising, therefore, that the younger members of the family longed for the day when they should be emancipated from the sober state and grim decorum of the palace. The princes rushed into the brilliant world of pleasure and excitement which awaited them, with headlong impetuosity. But the less fortunate princesses were doomed to repine in their dreary captivity, longing for marriage as the only event which could release them.*

The Prince of Wales entered upon life with greater advantages than had attended his immediate predecessors. George the Third, kept in seclusion during the life of his grandfather, was hardly known to his people when he began to reign. His father had been too well known. George the Second was heir to a disputed inheritance, and had little in his personal character to conciliate popular favour. If we would seek a former example of the hopeful promise which attended the opening career of the heir-apparent, we must go back to the eldest son of James, that gallant Henry Stuart, whose early promise revived the memory of the Black Prince, and whose life, had it been spared, would probably have changed the fortunes of his house, and diverted the destinies of the country from the course they ran under the guidance of his successor. In respect of natural endowments, the Prince of Wales had the advantage over all his family. His parts were above mediocrity; and he excelled in those graces of person and deportment which so powerfully recommend men in exalted station to the affections of the multitude. The former princes of the House of Hanover had been dull and un-

---

* Throughout these volumes, I have availed myself of many curious and authentic particulars respecting the King and the royal family contained in Mr. Locker's Papers.

gainly, without being respectable. George the Third
was slow and awkward; but the homeliness of his manners
was redeemed by the decency of his private life.
A Prince in the bloom of youth, handsome, gay, and
gracious, was, nevertheless, a welcome contrast; and
he might have enjoyed unbounded popularity without
impairing the attachment of loyal subjects to a good
and worthy King. The faults of such an amiable
Prince would have been regarded from a favourable
point of view; and much license would have been
allowed to high place and youthful ardour. It was,
indeed, no ordinary misconduct which could have
effaced these favourable impressions. The manners
of the time permitted excesses, which are no longer
considered venial. So far as public opinion was
concerned, the Prince might have indulged with
impunity in the pleasures of the table, and in the
ordinary foibles of youth. The country would readily
have condoned his irregularities, and paid his debts.
But there is a point beyond which toleration is not
extended either to the high or to the low. Common
honesty and truth are exacted from every Englishman.
In these indispensable qualities the Prince of
Wales had been found deficient. It first became
whispered, and was afterwards the common talk,
that His Royal Highness was not a man of his word;
and many adventures in which he was engaged became
the subjects of public scandal.

In 1783, the Coalition Ministry, among the
numerous proceedings with which, during their short
career, they revolted public opinion, proposed that
the ample revenue of their ally, the Prince of Wales,
should be doubled. They insisted, that his fifty
thousand a year should be raised to one hundred
thousand. Considering that the establishment of the
Prince was maintained with little show of splendour,
and the notoriety of the fact, that his resources were
dissipated in gaming and debauchery of every kind,

a more indecent proposition could hardly have been made. The King positively refused to sanction it; and the Ministry were on the point of breaking up on this scandalous difference, when the Prince, seeing the case was hopeless, interposed to save his friends from the dilemma to which they were committed. In 1786, when Parliament was required to revise the former arrangements of the Civil List, some of the Prince's friends took the opportunity of again pressing his claims for an additional allowance; but Mr. Pitt declined to entertain the subject.

Having no hope from the Minister, and pressed by the urgency of his creditors, the Prince applied for assistance directly to the King; but His Majesty, after enquiry into his son's affairs, refused to take any part in relieving him from his difficulties. In these circumstances, His Royal Highness took a step which no man of sense or spirit could have advised. He dismissed his servants, sold his carriages and horses, shut up Carlton House, his town residence, and reduced himself to the level of a private gentleman of straitened means. But this proceeding failed of its intended effect. Instead of commanding public applause, as the impulse of a manly mind impatient of the humiliation of debt, it was regarded as an expedient for attracting sympathy to himself, and bringing odium upon the King. The time was gone by when an artifice so gross as the ostentatious parade of poverty by the heir-apparent would have had much chance of success. The Prince had long since lost the popularity which followed him at the outset of his career; and a recent transgression, which common fame laid to his charge, had caused a greater public scandal than any of the numerous offences against decency and morality of which he stood convicted. A beautiful and accomplished lady, named Fitzherbert, in her second widowhood, at the

age of twenty-five, had attracted the notice of the
Prince; and he sought to obtain her on those terms
which a man of his rank would propose to a woman
of her condition. But Mrs. Fitzherbert was a woman
of spirit and virtue, and she spurned the dis-
honouring advances of the first prince of the blood.
Inflamed by a resistance so unusual, if not unprecedented, and unaccustomed to be denied, or to deny
himself, any selfish gratification, His Royal Highness
gave vent to a paroxysm of passion. He wept, he
raved, he flung himself an the ground, he would renounce his heritage, he would fly the country. To
all these demonstrations the lady was insensible.
She was not obdurate; but her terms were the
highest; they were no less than marriage. Yet the
difficulties in the way of a legal union seemed in-
superable. Mrs. Fitzherbert was a Roman Catholic,
and the Act of Settlement declared, that any member
of the royal family intermarrying with a Papist forfeited his succession to the Crown. The Royal
Marriage Act pronounced any marriage contracted
without the consent of the reigning Sovereign, except under certain conditions, which were not appli-
cable to this case, absolutely null and void. Such
being the statute law, the Prince was advised that
the marriage ceremonies would be merely an idle
form. The lady, on the other hand, was assured by
the authorities of her religion, that, notwithstanding
the law of the land, a marriage could be lawfully
contracted in the face of the Church by a Roman
Catholic gentlewoman with the heir of the Crown.
These strange nuptials were accordingly solemnised
with the usual forms, though in strict privacy. The
parties subsequently cohabited; but no attempt was
made by the lady to assume the rank and privileges
which appertained to the consort of the Prince of
Wales. She retained the name of her late husband,
continued as before to live as became a person in a

private station, and, though the questionable engagement into which she had entered—if, indeed, it could be considered questionable—was well known, Mrs. Fitzherbert never, in the estimation of the most scrupulous, appears to have compromised her position in private society. The public, however, though they respected the character of Mrs. Fitzherbert, were loud in their reprobation of the insult which the Heir-apparent had offered to the law of the land, and to the feelings of the nation.

Such was the situation of the Prince, and such the estimation in which he was held, when he thought proper to appeal to Parliament against the refusal of the King and the Ministry to make any provision either for the discharge of his liabilities, or the increase of his income. His debts at this time amounted to nearly a quarter of a million. The Opposition, though bound to support the claims of their illustrious patron, yet thought it as well, probably on his account and their own, that the proposal to burden the nation with the payment of these debts, and to furnish his Royal Highness with the means for more profuse expenditure, should not directly emanate from Brookes's Club. Accordingly, a City alderman was induced to move the business in the House of Commons. Pitt intimated, that if the motion was persevered with, it would be his painful duty to meet it with a direct negative, and to justify that course by the disclosure of circumstances which he would willingly conceal. Rolle, member for Devonshire, a country gentleman of great estate, significantly observed that the question was one of even greater importance than it appeared, inasmuch as it affected the constitution in Church and State. This allusion to the Prince's alleged marriage with a Papist could not be passed over by his friends. Sheridan stood up, and affecting not to understand the language of the member for Devonshire, fastened upon the expressions used by Pitt, as carrying a weight and importance which did not belong to the other. The Minister could not venture to adopt the scandal which had been more than insinuated by the representative of the country gentlemen; therefore Sheridan might safely, on the part of the Prince, challenge any inquiry into his conduct, though he ventured too far, in seeking to deter the court by threatening to proceed in a hostile spirit. Sheridan's speech drew from Pitt the desired explanation, that the unpleasant circumstances to which he had referred were confined to the pecuniary embarrassment of the Prince, and the consequent correspondence with His Majesty; but he deprecated in his most solemn and imposing manner the agitation of a question which could not fail to be injurious to the honour of the royal family and the interests of the country. Other members, and especially Powis, joined in entreating Alderman Newenham to withdraw his motion, but without success.

It was evident, indeed, that the matter could not be suffered to rest here. The discussion referred to took place on Friday, the 27th of April. The subject was to be renewed on the following Monday. In the interim, Fox saw the Prince of Wales. Fox had not been in the House on the Friday; but as the chief political adherent and personal friend of the Prince, it was all but incumbent upon him to satisfy the public expectation by a statement in answer to the Minister, and, not less so, to notice the charge against the Prince, which a gentleman, unconnected with the Ministry, had more than insinuated in his place in Parliament. When public rumour had first assigned to the relation of the heir-apparent with Mrs. Fitzherbert, a more serious character than such a connection would ordinarily import, Fox had thought it his duty to address a letter to his Royal Highness, in which he pointed out, with the authority of a statesman and the earnestness of a friend, the grave consequences of such a step as he was supposed to have in contemplation. The Prince had replied * with an assurance that the report had no foundation. A few days after this assurance was given, the marriage took place. It now became necessary that the marriage should be denied in a more formal and positive manner; and the Prince did not hesitate to deny it in the most precise, comprehensive, and unequivocal terms. Whatever misgivings, from his knowledge of the Prince's character, and the notoriety of the rumour, Fox might have previously entertained, he appears now to have been satisfied. Had any doubt remained, he could not have taken the decisive course, which, on the Prince's repeated assertion, he immediately adopted. On the Monday, a crowded and excited House was assembled, in the full expectation of some extraordinary disclosures. It was known beforehand, that Rolle was to reiterate his allusion to the marriage, in terms more explicit than he had used on the former occasion; and that a contradiction was to be put forward by Fox. But the contradiction which was generally anticipated was a contradiction in law, a contradiction which would be quite compatible with the fact, that a ceremony of some sort had taken place. Alderman Newenham, having expressed his willingness to give up his motion for an address to the Crown, in favour of any other form of proceeding which the minister might consider more appropriate, and less likely to provoke opposition, directly challenged Rolle to explain what he meant by the allusions he had made on the former evening. Without waiting for Rolle's explanation, Fox rose, and declared that he was authorised to confirm the offer

---

* Fox's letter and the Prince's reply are published in Lord Holland's *Memoirs*, and in Lord John Russell's *Life of Fox*, vol. ii. p. 178.

which Sheridan had made on the previous day, of a full disclosure of all the circumstances which had led to the embarrassments of the Prince. His Royal Highness was prepared to render to the House a general statement of his affairs, and to the King or his ministers a particular explanation. Fox then proceeded to stigmatise the report alluded to by Rolle as a miserable calumny, a low malicious falsehood, fit only to impose on the lowest order of persons. It was a monstrous invention of a fact, not only destitute of the slightest foundation, but absolutely impossible to have happened; and he knew not, as there was no longer a Jacobite faction, what party could be interested in fabricating and circulating, with more than ordinary assiduity, a tale intended to injure the first subject in the kingdom, and the immediate heir to the Crown.

As this was exactly the sort of defence upon which the Tories had reckoned, Rolle was ready with his reply. He avowed that his allusion was pointed to the statement which had been the subject of comment in every newspaper in the kingdom, and had made a deep impression on the mind of every man who valued the constitution. Mr. Fox had said, it was impossible that such an event could have taken place. It was true that it could not have taken place with the formal sanction of the law; nevertheless, the law might have been evaded, and the mere fact of a marriage under the circumstances supposed would be productive of the most alarming consequences. Upon this Fox rejoined, that he had not denied the calumny merely with regard to the existence of certain laws; he denied it *in toto*, in fact as well as in law. The fact not only could never have happened legally, but never did happen in any way, and had, from the beginning, been a base and malicious falsehood. Rolle desired to be informed whether in what he

Rolle's reply to Fox.

said, Mr. Fox had spoken from *direct authority?*
Fox declared that he had. After this, there was no
more to be said. Rolle was silenced, but not convinced; though Sheridan and Grey insisted that he
was bound to retract the insinuations which he had
made, and to declare himself satisfied by the ample
contradiction which the slander had received. Pitt,
however, deprecated such a demand as an interference with the freedom of debate. But, though
he would not allow his party to make a formal admission of their error, he could not, in decency, avoid
expressing the satisfaction which so explicit a declaration, on such an interesting subject, must afford to
the House, as well as to the gentleman who had been
the means of eliciting it.

Though nobody doubted that Fox had received
the distinct authority of the Prince to
deny the fact of the marriage, few persons mingling in public life or in general society had
any doubt that a marriage had taken place. The
proofs of it, indeed, were notorious. Within four
and twenty hours after he had astonished the House
of Commons by his statement, Fox himself was undeceived.* The man who had slandered his wife,
and made his friend the instrument by which he
gave utterance to a deliberate falsehood, was not
likely to hesitate at the only act which was wanting
to complete the infamy of his conduct.

The falsehood had done its work, and was about
to recoil upon the author; there was but one mode
of averting such a deadly blow, and that mode was
adopted by His Royal Highness. He disavowed his

---

* 'On the day after Mr. Fox's declaration, a gentleman of his acquaintance went up to him at Brookes's, and said, ' I see by the papers, Mr. Fox, that you have denied the fact of the marriage of the Prince of Wales with Mrs. Fitzherbert. You have been misinformed; I was present at that marriage.'' — LORD JOHN RUSSELL's *Life of Fox*, vol. ii. p. 186.

friend. Mr. Fox, he said, had exceeded his instructions and mistaken his meaning. The Prince, of course, dared not to say this to Fox; neither dared he ask him to retract or qualify what he had uttered on instructions, which, there is reason to suppose, were reduced to writing;* but he sent for Grey, who had taken a prominent part in defending him against the insinuations of Rolle, and sought to make one of the most high-minded members of the Whig party an accomplice in his scheme of treachery and fraud. But Grey immediately replied, that if Fox had committed an error, Fox was the proper person to rectify it, and declined to interfere in the matter. The Prince, vexed and disappointed, then said he must get Sheridan to say something; but Sheridan, though less scrupulous than Grey, was equally shrewd; and he had no intention of impeaching the veracity of Fox, to be disavowed, in his turn, when required to produce his authority. It is not Sheridan's fault, therefore, that the manner in which he acquitted himself of his commission was so absurd as to make the matter worse,—so far as it was possible to do so. When the Prince's affairs were again brought under the notice of the House of Commons, and four hundred members were assembled in eager expectation of some further disclosures, Sheridan's rising was the signal for more than

* Lord Holland's *Memoirs of the Whig Party*, vol. ii. This statement first appeared in Moore's *Life of Sheridan*, published in 1825. On that occasion, George the Fourth, according to a writer in the *Quarterly Review*, 'deliberately and distinctly declared, that there was not a word of truth in it, and that he had never had any communication with Lord Grey on the subject.' But his Majesty proved too much; for, according to the reviewer, 'he went on to deny that absurd story of his supposed marriage.'—*Quarterly Review*, vol. xciv. p. 421. Lord Grey's account of what passed is given in a note to Fox's *Correspondence*, vol. ii. p. 228. His lordship concludes his memorandum of the conversation by these words, 'He [the Prince] confessed it [the marriage] in the interview which I have mentioned.'

ordinary excitement. But expectation was soon
turned into disappointment and derision. Referring
to the memorable allusions which had been made by
Rolle on the former evening, Sheridan seized the
opportunity of paying, what the Parliamentary com-
piler terms, 'a delicate and judicious compliment'
to the lady to whom those allusions were supposed
to point, and proceeded to affirm that ignorance and
folly alone could have persevered in attempting to
detruct from a character which was open to no just
reproach, and was in reality entitled to the truest and
most general respect. Now, whatever may be thought
of the judgment which the member for Devonshire
displayed in referring to a subject of such perilous
import as the marriage of the Heir-apparent with a
Papist, he had certainly avowed his meaning, and
had exacted and had obtained from Fox, as the
representative of the person inculpated, a direct and
positive answer. But Sheridan only paltered with
the question. If there was no connection between
the Prince and Mrs. Fitzherbert, the introduction of
her name was irrelevant. If the intimacy did exist,
it must have been of a character which could hardly
entitle the conduct of the lady to be termed irreproachable, unless the statement made by Fox was
absolutely false. The House had more delicacy and
humanity than the Prince or his agent, for they
suffered the subject to drop without further comment.

Fox felt all the indignation of a generous and
manly mind at the base and selfish fraud
which had been practised upon him. He
was placed, indeed, in a position extremely painful
and embarrassing. He had, in the opinion of unfriendly judges, stated that which he must have
known to be untrue; or, at least, he had shown a
credulous facility, of which few persons, who knew
the Prince of Wales as Fox knew him, would have

Indignation of Fox.

been capable. Many of his friends thought he was bound to undeceive the House of Commons and the public, who had been made to believe a falsehood on his authority. Self-defence is said to be the first law of nature, and the vindication of honour is assuredly the first maxim of self-defence. But in this case, there were considerations which a statesman and a lover of his country would hold paramount even to the vindication of his honour. The Bill of Rights expressly enacts, that any person who shall marry a Papist shall be excluded from, and be for ever incapable to possess or inherit the Crown and Government of this realm; and in every such case, the people of these realms shall be released from their allegiance, and the Crown shall descend to the next heir. That the heir-apparent had contracted marriage with a Papist was a fact capable of legal proof. A subsequent statute declared, that any marriage, or matrimonial contract, by members of the royal family under the age of twenty-five years, without consent of the Crown, should be null and void. Notwithstanding this enactment, grave doubts were entertained whether the penal provisions of the Bill of Rights did not attach. The question of the Prince's marriage under the circumstances contemplated by the Great Statute of the Revolution having been stirred in Parliament, had been happily set at rest by the solemn denial of the fact on the direct authority of the Prince himself. The revival of this question by the retractation of that denial would have been attended with most perplexing, if not perilous consequences. An Act to dissolve or nullify the pretended marriage, and an Act of Indemnity, were precautionary measures, which could neither have been safely neglected, nor safely proposed. Among a few strong prejudices which mark the character of the English people, there is one to which they have uniformly adhered with un-

shaken consistency. Their repugnance to the Roman
Catholic communion has undergone but little modification in three hundred years. The claims of the
Dissenters were favourably treated when the Church
of England was in the plenitude of power and arrogance. Independents, Baptists, Quakers, and even
Unitarians, have found no difficulty on account of
their religion in procuring the votes of the electors.
Within twelve months after the Jews were rendered
eligible, four members of the Hebrew persuasion
were returned to the House of Commons. But in
the thirty years which have elapsed since the Catholic Emancipation Act, no more than two or three
members of the Church of Rome have been sent to
Parliament by open constituencies. The repeal of
the clause in the Bill of Rights, which displaced a
Roman Catholic, or a person who had intermarried
with a Roman Catholic, from succession to the Crown,
was a proposal which no minister would have dared
to make; and it would have been hardly less difficult
for a minister to have come down to Parliament with
a Bill in his hand to remove any doubts which might
have arisen, whether the heir-apparent had not in-
curred the penalty imposed by the wilful breach of
one of the most sacred provisions of the great statute,
which constituted the final charter of English liberty.
It is possible, that such a Bill might pass both
Houses; but it is certain, that the disclosure of a
scandal so enormous, a violation so audacious of a
fundamental law of the realm, would have given the
principle of hereditary monarchy a shock, to which
no friend of the constitution would care to expose it.
Fox, therefore, held his peace; and, rather than exo-
nerate himself at such a price, he submitted to the
reproach of being accessory after the fact to a deliberate falsehood. *One* person believed that he was
the inventor as well as the propagator of the calumny.
Mrs. Fitzherbert was suffered to remain under this

impression, which was first suggested by the Prince, her husband;* and from that day forth she never admitted the supposed slanderer into her presence. Fox himself, on his part, refused to see the Prince for a twelvemonth.† His resentment certainly did not last much longer; for we find him, at the close of the following year, contending for the Prince's right to the Regency with unlimited power, eager to become his minister, and even speaking of him personally in the highest terms.‡ Such conduct, it must be owned, abates somewhat from the praise of magnanimity to which his behaviour on the question of the marriage seemed to entitle him. But his disposition was not implacable; his virtue was easy; the standard of morality in those days was low, and the exigencies of party were urgent. A loyal and high-minded man might have been content to save the honour of his Prince and the credit of the monarchy at the expense of his own. Such a man might even consistently remain in the service of the Prince who had wronged and betrayed him. There are injuries which leave no scar upon a generous mind after the wound has healed; but there are injuries also which no man, whose sense of honour has not been blunted, can forgive or forget.

The Prince of Wales was completely successful in this transaction. He betrayed both his wife and his friend, without losing the confidence of either; and, by this double treachery, he shook off a dangerous embarrassment, and obtained his immediate object, namely, money. After Fox's declaration in the House of Commons, the

Duplicity of the Prince.

---

* 'He (the Prince) went up to Mrs. Fitzherbert the day after Fox had made his statement, and, taking hold of both her hands and caressing her, said, 'Only conceive, Maria, what Fox did yesterday; he went down to the House, and denied that you and I were man and wife.'' — LANGDALE's *Memoirs of Mrs. Fitzherbert*. *Life of Fox.*

† *Life of Fox*, vol. ii. p. 187.

‡ *Correspondence of Fox.*

Minister thought it desirable to accommodate the differences which had so long subsisted between the Government and the Prince, relative to the discharge of his pecuniary liabilities. An interview took place between His Royal Highness and Mr. Dundas, on the part of the Administration. A short negotiation resulted in an engagement to add to the Prince's income ten thousand a year from the Civil List; and a message from the Crown to the House of Commons recommended the payment of the Prince's debts. Pitt named the sum of one hundred and sixty-one thousand pounds, together with twenty thousand more for the repairs of Carlton House. These sums were voted without opposition.

The impeachment of Hastings, which had received such an impulse from the sudden and unexpected support of the Ministers, was resumed this session with increased vigour. The third charge, relating to the plunder of the Begums of Oude, was brought forward by Sheridan in a speech, which, according to the concurrent testimony of all who heard it, was one of the most dazzling displays of oratory ever exhibited within the walls of Parliament. After holding the House for nearly six hours, he sat down amidst an excitement which burst forth, not merely in prolonged cheers, but in clapping of hands, a mode of applause which is justly considered disorderly and indecent, and has never since been tolerated. Pitt supported Sheridan's motion, which was carried by a majority of nearly three to one. The tide of public opinion was now turned against Hastings. His friends, who were neither eloquent nor judicious, could hardly obtain a hearing; and at length they almost gave up the contest in the Commons, reserving themselves for a more dispassionate and impartial tribunal. Twenty articles of impeachment were voted, and Burke was ordered to carry them up to the House of Lords,

Hastings was afterwards taken into custody of Black Rod, but was liberated on bail, himself in twenty thousand pounds, with two sureties of ten thousand each. No further proceeding in the matter was taken during this session.

A motion was also made for the impeachment of Sir Elijah Impey, the late Chief Justice of India, who had been dismissed from his high office in Lord Shelburne's administration, and whose complicity in many of the criminal transactions charged on Hastings was sufficiently evident. But the courage and promptitude with which Impey met the danger, and the advantage which a practised lawyer possessed over unskilled opponents, enabled him to crush the prosecution in the bud. Many persons, persuaded of the guilt both of the Governor and the Judge, thought the latter the worse of the two; inasmuch as tyranny and oppression perpetrated under the forms and with the sanction of law are more terrible than the undisguised violence of arbitrary power. One writer, far removed from contemporary passion and prejudice, the latest and greatest authority on this period of Indian history, has not hesitated to declare, that 'no other such judge has dishonoured the English ermine since Jeffries.'* That the Chief Justice stretched the law in support of the Governor, and his policy, there can be little doubt. That he accepted a stipend from the Governor, partly in consideration of this service, is also probable; but it must not be forgotten, that this bribe, as it has been termed, was ostensibly accepted in compensation for claims to which Impey had certainly some pretensions, but which derogated from the power hitherto exercised by the Governor and his council. The trial and condemnation of Nuncomar for forgery were in accordance with the law of England, which obtained at Calcutta no less than in London, and

Impeachment of Impey.

---

* MACAULAY's *Essay on Warren Hastings.*

though it may be doubted whether the extreme penalty should have been enforced in the case of an offence which was very different in India to what it was in England, it does not follow, because the execution of the Brahmin was useful to Hastings, that 'Impey, sitting as a judge, put a man unjustly to death in order to serve a political purpose.'* To compare such a judge, culpable as he was, with Jeffries, who perpetrated a series of judicial murders, with a ferocity which the French revolutionary tribunal of the Reign of Terror did not equal, is surely an exaggeration. Impey produced testimonials in his favour from some of the first lawyers in the country; and though testimonials are of little value in proof of positive merit, it is not to be supposed that such men as Blackstone, Dunning, and De Grey would write complimentary letters to a man who had disgraced the robe of justice. The House of Commons were of that opinion; they discriminated between the case of Impey and the case of Hastings; and acting as a grand inquest, they found that there was not sufficient to put Impey on his trial.

The trial of Hastings commenced on the 13th of February, in the following year. Westminster Hall was fitted up for the great state pageant; and amidst the crowd, which completely filled the area of that vast chamber and the galleries erected round it, was included almost every person of distinction then in England. The Queen and the three elder Princesses were present. The Ambassadors' box was filled with the representatives of the European powers. A gallery was appropriated to persons of eminence not members of either House of Parliament. Female beauty added largely to the grace and lustre of the scene. When the splendid assembly was collected, a door was thrown open, and the heralds appeared, marshalling the peers of the realm to their places.

* MACAULAY.

Foremost of this illustrious body appeared, according to usage, the junior baron, England's latest hero, Elliot, Lord Heathfield of Gibraltar, and the long line was closed with the greatest, if not the most ancient, representative of the feudal peerage, the hereditary Earl Marshal of England, Charles Howard, Duke of Norfolk. The grand procession terminated with the Princes of the blood. The Lord Chancellor, as President of this High Court of Parliament, took his seat on a throne. Opposite to him on one side was the manager's box, and on the other, the space assigned to the prisoner and his counsel.

The proceedings were opened by the Chancellor, whose voice and mien were peculiarly adapted to the imposing duty which he had to perform. The prisoner was ordered to fall upon his knees, while he was formally put upon his trial.

Opening of proceedings against Hastings.

The preliminary proceedings occupied two days. Burke then opened the first charge, in a speech which was continued for four days. Nearly the first half of this great oration consisted of a rapid but brilliant review of the History of British India, up to the period of Hastings' administration. The inculpatory part of the harangue was prefaced with a discourse on arbitrary power, in which the orator strove to persuade his hearers by references to the Koran, the institutes of Tamerlane, the Gentoo Law, and other authorities, that the people of the East had been accustomed to good government, and that they had had no experience of despotic power, until it was introduced by the English Governor. The third day's speech was filled with loose and general charges of bribery and peculation; but the greatest impression was made upon the audience by horrible details of the atrocities perpetrated by Deby Sing, one of the native lieutenants

Burke's oration.

appointed by Hastings, to administer the affairs of certain provinces distant from the central seat of Government. No attempt was made to connect Hastings with this abuse of power; on the contrary, it appeared that when intelligence was received at Calcutta, of disturbances in the provinces ruled by Deby Sing, an English Commissioner was sent by the Council, with the concurrence of Hastings, to make full inquiry on the spot; and, on the report of this Commissioner, Deby Sing was summoned to Calcutta to answer for his conduct. The inquiry was protracted; and all that can be gathered from this transaction, as detailed by Burke, was that the House of Lords was bound to find Hastings guilty of a high crime and misdemeanour, because the Council at Calcutta, in which he had only a single voice, thought fit to hear Deby Sing in his defence, and to hesitate before they implicitly adopted every statement which the British Commissioner, in a report filling three volumes, had adopted, on evidence tainted with Oriental perjury and exaggeration. The manager concluded his speech with a summary of the charges:—1. The abolition, for private purposes, of the six Provincial Councils. 2. The illegal delegation of power. 3. The establishment of a Committee of instruments and tools. 4. The appointment of an infamous person to exercise the power of which the Provincial Councils had been deprived. 5. Taking bribes from Gunga Govind Sing. 6. Neglecting the services for which he had been bribed. 7. Robbing the people of whom he took bribes. 8. Fraudulently alienating the fortunes of widows. 9. Appointment of Deby Sing as guardian of the minor Raja. 10. Appointment of Deby Sing as manager of three provinces, and with having *thereby* wasted the country, destroyed the landed interest, cruelly harassed the peasants, burnt their houses, seized their crops, tortured and degraded their persons, and destroyed the honour of the whole female race of that country.

It is not necessary, nor even practicable, that the articles of a State impeachment should be framed with the rigorous precision of a bill of indictment; but justice requires that a distinct and substantive charge should be made before the accused person is put to his answer. Of the ten charges which Burke thus strung together, the fifth only fulfilled this condition. The first and second might be reduced to a tangible form. The third and fourth were too general. The sixth was assuredly the strangest accusation ever brought against a delinquent in a court of justice. It distinctly charged the prisoner with having broken an iniquitous contract; and for this he was to be held responsible to the supreme justice of the nation. The seventh was of a similar character. The eighth and ninth were mere loose scandal. The tenth enunciated the extraordinary doctrine, that a ruler was to be held personally responsible for every abuse of power of which his lieutenant might be guilty.

Nature of State impeachments.

After Burke had concluded his opening speech, a proposal was made on the part of the managers that the charges should be heard and disposed of separately. A proceeding more at variance with the course of justice, more unfair and oppressive to the accused, could hardly have been devised. The counsel for Hastings, of whom Law, afterwards the Chief Justice Ellenborough, was the leader, forcibly urged the hardship of subjecting a prisoner to a series of trials, for the purpose of establishing what must result in a single charge. Loughborough, to his shame as a lawyer, taking a party view of the trial, vindicated this course of proceeding; but the Chancellor exposed the scandalous injustice of the proposal, in such strong and pointed terms, that it was rejected by a large majority. Thurlow also referred, in language of just severity, to the violent and extravagant style in which Burke had opened the prosecution. He said, that as the manager had disclaimed any intention to exaggerate the crimes of the accused, he should be held to strict proof of the allegations he had made. If the crimes charged upon the prisoner were proved, no punishment which the House could inflict would be adequate to his guilt; but this was an additional reason why care should be taken that the prisoner was not harassed by an unusual mode of proceeding. The decision of the House disconcerted the plans of the prosecution, rendering it intolerably tedious, confused, and impracticable. After a short interval, Fox proceeded to open the Benares charge. The evidence upon this article of the impeachment having been concluded, the trial was adjourned for a month, during the absence of the Judges upon their circuits. The Begum charge followed, and afforded the occasion for another great display of oratory by Sheridan. Indeed, if it had not been for these repeated exhibitions of the highest powers of eloquence, it is difficult to understand how the great delinquent who stood at the bar could have escaped conviction on some of the charges preferred against him. The acceptance of a bribe from Cheyte Sing, and the torture of the Begums for the purpose of extortion, were charges clearly established; but the public mind was so excited by the amazing feats of oratory exhibited in Westminster Hall, that the dry details of evidence were little regarded, and the whole proceeding came to be looked upon as the display of a school of oratory, rather than a grave judicial inquiry.

The Hall was crowded in every part during the delivery of the speeches; but few remained to hear the proof; and the managers were left to squabble with the counsel for the prisoner, day after day, on points of evidence, in the presence of some dozen Lords, a score of members of the Lower House, and a hundred or so of listless spectators. As the trial proceeded, the real state of public opinion on the subject began to be manifested. Stockdale, the publisher, was prosecuted by order of the House of Commons for a libel, consisting of a pamphlet by a respectable clergyman, named Logan, in which the impeachment and its authors were censured with much severity. Stockdale was defended by Erskine; and his trial, which took place at the end of the year, resulted in an acquittal. The House itself, before the trial had proceeded many weeks, entertained a motion, in spite of the earnest opposition of the managers, for an account of the expenses, and plainly showed the disapprobation of the mode in which the prosecution was conducted, if not of the prosecution itself. In the following session, the House passed a vote of censure on Burke for having asserted in his speech, on opening the sixth charge, that Hastings had 'murdered Nuncomar by the hands of Sir Elijah Impey.' The Lords subsequently pronounced a decision which had the effect of excluding altogether that part of the impeachment which related to the case of Nuncomar. Another great blow was afterwards given to the impeachment by the refusal of the court to admit evidence as to the cruelties alleged to have been perpetrated by Deby Sing, the narrative of which by Burke had produced so deep an impression on his audience. And, finally, Burke himself, after the trial had lasted three years, proposed to abandon sixteen of the charges. Thus, the trial dragged on with little or no other result than brilliant displays of eloquence by the most accomplished rhetoricians of the age.*

* The speeches on the trial of Hastings have been published verbatim, from the MSS. in the British Museum, under the authority of the Treasury

CHAPTER XXX.

THE SLAVE TRADE — KING'S ILLNESS — DEBATES ON THE REGENCY — CLAIMS OF THE HEIR-APPARENT — RECOVERY OF THE KING — CONDUCT OF THE PRINCES — FIRMNESS AND PRUDENCE OF PITT — PITT'S COLLEAGUES — PROCEEDINGS IN IRELAND — THURLOW — DIVISIONS IN THE ROYAL FAMILY — WILBERFORCE — STAMPS ON NEWSPAPERS — ADDINGTON CHOSEN SPEAKER.

The Slave Trade. The session of 1788 is rendered memorable by the agitation in Parliament of a question which, though it never partook of a party character, for many years excited a greater amount of public interest than any matter of political importance which was discussed during the same period. The practice of kidnapping and importing negroes from Africa to the continent and islands of America, had been, from time to time, represented by writers of every description, not merely as an outrage on humanity, but as one commonly attended with circumstances of peculiar cruelty and oppression. It was said that men, women, and children—creatures bearing at least the form of human nature—had been torn from their homes, thrust into floating dungeons more horrible than any which the imagination of romancers had painted, frequently tortured, sometimes wantonly slaughtered, and habitually subjected to treatment more grievous than is endured by the lowest order of the creation. Such tales, sometimes put forward as facts, sometimes presented in the form of fiction, appealed at once to every feeling and principle by

which the minds of the people of this country are
wont to be influenced. Religion was scandalised by
the impious presumption of man in asserting the
right of property in his fellow-creature: morality
was outraged by the same idea; the free spirit of
Englishmen revolted against slavery; and the common feelings of humanity were shocked by the systematic cruelty with which this odious traffic was
conducted. At length, some zealous persons formed
themselves into an association, with the ulterior
object of abolishing slavery altogether throughout
the British dominions, and with the immediate
purpose of mitigating its evils. Granville Sharp,
Clarkson, Macaulay, and Wilberforce are names
which will be ever mentioned with honour in connection with this effort on behalf of Christian philanthropy. The abolition of the trade in slaves was,
therefore, demanded in the first instance. Many
persons were far from being convinced that the condition of slavery was indefensible on grounds of
religion or morality, and were still less prepared
for a hasty measure of emancipation, which must
seriously injure, if not ruin, some of our most
valuable colonies. Evidence collected by enthusiastics in support of their cause is accepted with
reserve by sober reason; but exaggeration itself was
baffled in depicting the horrors of the Middle Passage. Transports were built especially for this service; and the principle upon which these vessels
were constructed was such an economy of space as
was barely consistent with the possibility of keeping
the cargo alive during a voyage of average duration.
Many of the negroes perished, nevertheless, during
the passage. The sickliest were thrown overboard.
If the voyage was protracted, or the weather was
unfavourable, the cargo was lightened without scruple; a few negroes, more or less, were of little
account in a trade which yielded unusually large

profits. It is not to be supposed, that merchants of the highest class engaged largely in ventures of this description; but it is certain they were not confined to traders of doubtful character or desperate fortune. Many houses of good commercial credit chartered vessels for the slave trade, and if any doubt could exist as to the mode in which the trade was ordinarily conducted, there is not wanting precise proof of the fact. The statements made by pamphleteers, and by persons tendering themselves for examination before Parliamentary Committees, may be taken with allowance; but the evidence given in a court of justice, by witnesses interested in showing that they took sufficient care of the property committed to their charge, is in the nature of an admission. In 1783, an action on a policy of insurance on the value of certain slaves was tried in the Court of King's Bench. The question was, whether the loss of the slaves had been caused 'by perils of the sea,' against which the defendant had insured. The facts as they appeared on the trial were these: The ship 'Zong,' with four hundred and forty-two slaves, was bound from the Coast of Guinea to Jamaica. It was incidentally proved, that sixty of the slaves died during the passage from over-crowding; but in respect of these, it was not contended that the underwriter was liable. The master having, by some accident or miscalculation, missed Jamaica, found himself short of water, and under the apprehension of scarcity, but before the crew and cargo had been put on short allowance, he threw ninety-six of the sickliest slaves overboard. On the second day after he had thus lightened his cargo, there was a fall of rain, which gave him a supply of water for eleven days. Nevertheless, he subsequently drowned twenty-six more of the slaves. Ten wretched creatures threw themselves into the sea. The ship arrived at her port of discharge before the water was exhausted.

Thus one hundred and thirty-two human beings were wilfully murdered. But a City jury were of opinion, that they were chattels lost by perils of the seas, and found for the plaintiff, with thirty pounds damages for each slave cast overboard. The Court granted a new trial, on the ground that it did not sufficiently appear that there was any such necessity for destroying the second batch of twenty-six slaves, as could be said to constitute a loss by perils of the seas; but it seems never to have occurred to the Judge at Nisi Prius, nor the Court in Banco, to order criminal proceedings against the captain and the crew, for their wholesale homicides.*

It had been proposed, that Wilberforce, who was rising to Parliamentary eminence, and was supposed to have the ear of Pitt, should bring this vital question before the House of Commons; but Wilberforce was languishing at Bath under a disease which his physicians had pronounced mortal; and Pitt, in the absence of his friend, introduced the subject with a formal motion, that the slave trade should be taken into consideration early in the following session, when, if Mr. Wilberforce should continue incapacitated to conduct the inquiry, he would himself undertake it. The Minister, however, refrained from committing himself to any decided opinion on the subject. Fox, on the other side, free from official responsibility, declared at once for the total prohibition of the trade. Pitt's motion was agreed to without a division.

Wilberforce.

Pending the more solemn inquiry to which the House was thus pledged, a Bill was brought in by Sir William Dolben, for regulating the conveyance of slaves from Africa. But even this modified measure was not allowed to

Examination of delegates.

---

* Gregson and others v. Gilbert.—Douglas's *Reports*, and Park *on Marine Insurances*, eighth edition, vol. i. p. 138.

pass without opposition from those who were interested in the abominable traffic. The merchants of London and Liverpool prayed to be heard by counsel; and their prayer, according to the practice of Parliament at that time, was granted almost as of course. A partial investigation had already taken place, by order of the Government, before a Committee of the Privy Council. Delegates from the parties interested in the slave trade had appeared before this Committee, and asserted with confidence that the charges brought against the trade were either absolutely false, or gross distortions of the truth; that so far from instigating wars among the savage chiefs of Africa, for the purpose of procuring slaves, they were the benefactors of the negro race, by rescuing them from the cruelty and oppression of their native rulers; that the transport of these creatures across the seas was effected with every consideration for their health and comfort; that they danced and made merry on deck; and that the mortality did not exceed an average of five or six per cent. These representations were not unfavourably received by the Privy Council; a body of men who, from their education and habits, would be inclined to regard with incredulity, if not aversion, the tales which were adapted to, and were eagerly devoured by, the unthinking multitude. The weight of unimpeachable testimony, however, with which the impudent assertions of the slave dealers was met, overbore the prejudices of the Committee; and though they abstained from making a decisive report, the inclination of their opinion was evidently to the side of reason and humanity.

The slave dealers, therefore, when they went before the House of Commons with the same tale by which they sought to amuse the Privy Council, met with a very different reception. Whitbread, the Chairman of the Commons' Com-

Whitbread.

mittee, to which Dolben's Bill was referred, cross-examined the witnesses sent to support their case by the merchants of London and Liverpool with the zeal indeed of a partisan, but with the skill and ability also of a man of business, well informed in the details and true character of the trade which was the subject of inquiry. It was proved from the mouths of these delegates, that the ample accommodation provided in the slave ships was a space of five feet and a half by one foot and four inches for each man; that the space between decks varied from four to five feet eight inches; that this space was fitted with shelves, upon which living bodies were packed in the same manner as upon deck; that the people were chained together by their hands and feet, and secured by ring-bolts to the decks and shelves; that the daily allowance of each man was a pint of water and two feeds of horse-beans; that the miserable captives were confined between decks all the time that the ship remained on the coast, which varied from six weeks to as many months; that they remained below for sixteen hours a day; that they were compelled to exercise themselves by jumping about in their irons under the application of the lash; and this was what the witnesses for the slave dealers represented as dancing. All these facts were clearly established. Nevertheless, so difficult is it to disturb established usages, especially when any interest is involved in them, that a Bill, which contained only a few simple provisions of a sanatory character, was criticised with as much jealousy as if it was a wanton interference with vested interests, and a mischievous obstruction to the freedom of commerce; nor would the Lords consent to pass it without clauses of compensation to the ship-owners and merchants for the additional charges to which they would be subjected by the intended regulations.

Parliament was prorogued on the 11th of July. In the previous month, the King's health had become seriously deranged; and, by the advice of his physicians, he relaxed his ordinary application to public business, and, after the prorogation, sought relief for his malady, which was a disorder of the biliary system, by drinking the Cheltenham waters. The novelty of the scene—for so simple were his habits, that on no former occasion since his accession had the King been at so great a distance from his capital—at first had a beneficial effect. The comparative retirement, the beauty of the country, and the respectful demonstrations of sympathy and attachment to his person, which he found among all ranks of the people, could not but be agreeable to a mind susceptible of such impressions. No permanent benefit, however, resulted from this visit; and after a few weeks, the King returned to London, his malady increased, and the symptoms were alarming. The aberrations of his intellect, which had been disordered from the commencement of his illness, became more frequent and palpable. In October he was worse, and early in November it was known that His Majesty had ceased to be capable of transacting business, and that his life was in imminent danger.

Parliament was prorogued to the 20th of November; and, though it had not been intended to proceed to despatch of business until after Christmas, yet the exigency which had arisen, as well as the absence of any power to extend the prorogation, rendered it necessary that the Houses should assemble on the prorogation-day.

The greatest excitement prevailed. A demise of the Crown was immediately expected; and even should the King's life be spared, it was understood that the physicians had pronounced his insanity hopeless. The Prince of Wales had taken

up his abode at Windsor, and assumed the control of
the King's person. The Opposition were assured of
an immediate return to power under the new reign,
whether that of King or Regent. Fox, who was
travelling on the Continent, was sent for, and arrived,
in post haste, four days after the meeting of Parliament.
Pitt and Dundas were making arrangements
for their return to the bar. But though the meeting
of Parliament on the prorogation-day was inevitable,
it was impossible to proceed to the despatch of business.
Formal proof of the King's incapacity was
requisite before the ordinary mode of inaugurating
the business of the session could be dispensed with;
and respect for His Majesty dictated the propriety of
a short adjournment. Accordingly, an adjournment
for a fortnight was proposed by Ministers in both
Houses, and agreed to without observation; and the
Commons ordered a call of the House for the adjournment
day. On the 4th of December, when
Parliament reassembled, it was determined by both
Houses to appoint select committees to examine the
King's physicians. The Commons Committee reported
on the 10th of December the evidence of the
medical witnesses, who declared the King to be incapable
of meeting Parliament, or attending to public
business; but expressed, at the same time, a confident
hope of His Majesty's recovery. The minister, therefore,
in a short and guarded speech, moved, 'That a
Committee be appointed to examine and report precedents
of such proceedings as may have been had
in case of the personal exercise of the royal authority
being prevented or interrupted by infancy, sickness,
infirmity, or otherwise, with a view to provide for
the same.' After this motion, a brief but most important
debate took place. When Pitt sat down,
Fox immediately rose. He said the motion could
result in nothing but a loss of time, since no precedent
could be found bearing upon the case. The

circumstances to be provided for did not depend upon their deliberations as a House of Parliament. There was then a person in the kingdom, different from any other person, that precedents could refer to;—an heir-apparent of full age and capacity to exercise the royal power. In his opinion, the Prince of Wales had as clear, as express a *right* to assume the reins of Government, and exercise the power of sovereignty, during the continuance of the illness and incapacity with which it had pleased God to afflict His Majesty, as in the case of His Majesty's having undergone a natural and perfect demise. Fox went on to say, that if His Royal Highness did not at once assume his rightful functions, it was from respect to those principles which had placed his family on the throne, and which taught him to seek the sanction of Parliament to his claim. But this deference had its limits; and it was not reasonable that he should be expected to wait during a pretended search for precedents which did not exist. Fox, however, did not oppose the motion, as he should have done if he had felt any confidence in the position which he asserted.

Pitt was prompt in availing himself of the advantage which his great rival, now apparently on the eve of triumph, had afforded him. With an air of authority which seemed to defy question, he stood up, and, in the most emphatic language, denounced the doctrine of the Whig leader as utterly at variance with the laws and history of the country, and little less than treason to the constitution. He met the claim of right preferred on behalf of the heir-apparent with a positive contradiction, and denied that under the circumstances the Prince of Wales had more right to assume the Government than any other person in the kingdom. Whatever may have been the pretensions of His Royal Highness, it was the province of Parliament, and of Parliament alone, to make provision for the government of the country, whenever any interruption of the royal authority took place. He said that the doctrine of Mr. Fox was incompatible with the rights of the Legislature, and went to deprive it of any deliberate power under the circumstances which had arisen. This was an argument of the gravest weight for the inquiry which he proposed, since it was of the utmost moment in such an exigency that the rights of Parliament should be ascertained as well for their own guidance as for the information of the country.

To those who understood the question in its constitutional bearing, the argument of Pitt was irresistible; to those who were little versed in such matters—the great majority of his audience—the reckless assertion of Fox seemed an indecent and impatient attempt to grasp at power, worthy of the hero of the Coalition, and the author of the India Bill. Fox himself saw that he had gone too far; but his attempt at retreat was as unskilful, as his advance had been rash. I admit, he said in effect, that *Parliament* would have a right to deal with the question, or to alter the succession to the throne, or to change the laws and constitution of the kingdom; but I deny that we are a Parliament. But, it might have been answered, neither was the body which abolished the Commonwealth and restored the Monarchy; nor that which declared the throne to be vacant, and filled it with two persons, one of whom had no right whatever, and another whose right was secondary and contingent. It made no difference, so far as the argument was affected, whether the throne was actually vacant, or whether, as in the present case, the functions of the Sovereign were suspended by the act of God. Fox's explanation of the law which he had deliberately laid down was at variance with the most conspicuous precedents, and impeached the validity of acts upon which the rights and

liberties of the country were for the most part founded.
If any ordinary member of the House had propounded
such notions as these, he would have been laughed
at for his ignorance and presumption. If a Tory, he
would have been told that he had been educated in
the school of Filmer and Sacheverell. But these
were the words, not of an empty prater, not of a
pre-revolutionary Tory, but of a great statesman, the
chief of the party of 1688. And it is to be observed,
that this strange doctrine was founded on another
position, which, to say the least, was extremely questionable, namely, that Parliament was disabled by
the incapacity of the Crown. But the point was more
a theoretical than a practical one. If the integrity
of Parliament was destroyed, it still subsisted as a
Convention; and in that capacity, it could deal with
this, as it had dealt with still weightier exigencies.
Fox objected to the motion for a committee to search
for precedents (in accordance with the practice)
because no precedent existed. But if no precedent
existed, it was surely more in accordance with the
law and constitution of England that a precedent
should be created by Parliament, or by the Lords and
Commons, if they were not to be called a Parliament,
rather than by an authority unknown to the constitution, and which had never been heard of in the
history of this country.

Only one person could be found to support Fox
on this occasion; and that was a person
Burke's attack on Pitt. for whom anything extravagant and offensive had a fatal charm. Burke stood forward, not
indeed to contend for the doctrine of right in such
absolute and unqualified terms as Fox had employed,
for he knew that these were untenable. He rather
took the turn of vindicating the Prince's pretensions
as a question of comparison; and, if he had done so
with judgment and temper, he would have obtained
the concurrence of all reasonable men. It was so

manifestly just and convenient that the heir-apparent should, in the absence or disability of the Sovereign, exercise his power, that nothing less than such a personal disqualification as would justify postponing him in the succession, would justify a preference of any other regent. But, instead of pointing out this distinction, Burke, after his fashion, must needs provoke the derision of the House, by taking Pitt to task for not arguing the question with temper and moderation, and for setting himself up as a competitor with the Prince! Irritated by the cries of 'Order,' and the expressions of disapprobation with which this indecent and unwarranted remark was received, Burke reiterated the charge, and went off in a storm of wild declamation on the preposterous idea which he had taken up. A few contemptuous words from Pitt closed this singular debate, which certainly was not calculated to reconcile the country to a change in the administration of public affairs.

Two days after, the debate was renewed on bringing up the report of the Committee to search for precedents. Fox, having been *Fox's attempt at explanation.* by that time convinced of the grievous error into which he had fallen, took occasion to explain away much of what he had said on the question of right, and to deny what he could not explain away. Lord Camden had in the meantime declared, in his place in Parliament, that there was nothing in the Common Law to warrant the doctrine which Fox had set up; that no lawyer ever mooted such a doctrine; that he had never met with it in any writer; and he censured, with due severity, the rashness which had given utterance to a notion so novel and dangerous. Fox now declared, that the claim which he had preferred on behalf of the Prince went no farther than a naked right, and that he never intended to maintain that this right could be reduced into possession without the consent of Parliament. Neither did he say, that the Prince was entitled to assume power while Parliament was sitting. He was content to adopt a statement of the point, with which many persons were satisfied; namely, that the Prince had such a claim as Parliament could not disallow without a dereliction of its duty. He could see no distinction between such an irresistible claim and an inherent right. But whatever doubt might exist as to the Prince's right to exercise royal authority under the present circumstances of the country, Fox still maintained there could be none as to the propriety of investing him with the sole administration of the Government, and with the unlimited exercise of all the royal functions, powers, and prerogatives. And he declared, that, much as he valued unanimity upon such a point, yet he would take the sense of the House if any proposal should be made to place any material restrictions on His Royal Highness's power as regent.

Blunder of Fox.

The explanation which Fox offered was not, as Pitt took care to point out, consistent with the language which he had formerly used with regard to the Prince's forbearance to *assert his claim*, and, indeed, savoured more of the astuteness of the shifting lawyer* who was supposed to have led him into this error, than of the ingenuousness which distinguished the Whig leader. A greater blunder never was committed by a public man. The pretensions of the heir-apparent to exercise the powers of the Sovereign during his incapacity were so obvious and so paramount, that any attempt to pass them by would certainly have recoiled upon any minister, however powerful. Fox had no right to assume that these pretensions would not be respected; nor did it belong to him, invested with no official responsibility, to propose, in the first instance, a

---

* Lord Loughborough.—See Fox's *Correspondence*, vol. ii.

candidate for the first office in the State. Such a precipitate proposal seemed rather to suggest the possibility of competition, than to consult the dignity of the exalted personage referred to. Whether the unconstitutional character of the claim is considered, or the indecent haste with which it was preferred, or the quarter from which it came, or the plain motive* by which the whole proceeding was actuated, a more unlucky mode of inaugurating the return of the Whigs to power could hardly have been conceived.

The real question was not whether the Prince should be regent—for on that point there could be no doubt—but whether he should be regent on the terms demanded by Fox, or with restrictions. If the claim of right could have been established, this question of course could not have arisen; and it was this consideration which gave rise to the doctrine propounded by Loughborough and Fox. Pitt, whose firmness, consistency, and clearness of purpose, shone conspicuously throughout this trying period, and the more so from being contrasted with the intemperance and indecent eagerness of the Opposition, in answer to Fox, stated, without hesitation or reserve, his views on the subject of the regency. He said that, as a matter of discretion, and on the ground of expediency, it was highly desirable, that whatever part of the regal power it was necessary should be exercised at all should be vested in a single person, and that person the Prince of Wales; and that he should exercise the 'authority so limited' unfettered by any permanent council, and with the free choice of his political servants.

<small>[margin: Real question to be considered.]</small>

---

* Fox, writing to a friend on the 15th of December, says, 'I think it certain that in about a fortnight we shall come in.'— *Correspondence*, vol. ii. p. 299. The ministers calculated on being dismissed immediately on the passing of the Regency Bill.— *Courts and Cabinets of George the Third*, vol. ii. p. 41.

The minister added, that whatever powers were necessary for carrying on the public business with vigour and despatch, and for providing for the safety and interests of the country, ought to be given; but, on the other hand, any powers not necessary for these purposes, and capable of being by possibility employed in any way which might tend to embarrass the exercise of the King's lawful authority when resumed, ought to be withheld. Fox made a conciliatory reply, and the matter might have passed away but for the interposition of Sheridan, who, at the close of the debate, concentrated in a few words, and exaggerated all that was offensive in the several speeches of Fox and Burke on this painful subject. In the course of a violent declamation against the resolution which Pitt had intimated his intention of proposing at a future day to negative the claim of right as regarded the regency, Sheridan, in a menacing tone, warned the minister to beware of provoking *the Prince to assert his right.* Loud and indignant shouts of 'Hear! hear!' burst from the ministerial side of the House; and such an excitement prevailed as had not for many years been experienced within those walls.* The severity with which this audacious language was rebuked by Pitt, and his solemn exhortation to the House to do their duty in spite of threats from any authority, however high, were hardly wanting to complete the confusion with which the Opposition were covered.

On the 16th, the House being resolved into a committee to consider the state of the nation, Mr. Pitt moved three resolutions, the first, declaratory of the King's disability; the second, affirmatory of the right and duty of both Houses to provide for the exercise of the royal authority; the

Pitt's resolutions.

* Grenville to Lord Rockingham.—*Courts and Cabinets,* vol. ii. p. 56.

third being a corollary from the other two. The second and material resolution offered so direct a challenge to the new doctrine of indefeasible right, that the Opposition, after the length they had gone, could not evade it. They did not think it prudent, however, to meet the propositions by a direct negative; but resorted to one of those evasive amendments by which the main question is disposed of without being decided. The ordinary mode of effecting this object is by moving what is called the previous question; which is, in fact, what it imports, a preliminary question whether the main question shall be put. But as this particular mode of proceeding cannot, by the forms of the House, be adopted in Committee, a course somewhat analogous was adopted, by the motion that the Chairman report progress, the effect of which would have been substantially, though not technically, the defeat of the proposition. This motion was made by Lord North in a speech which, like almost all the speeches of that most able man, showed that it was possible to be argumentative and forcible, without being violent and abusive. The Opposition entertained a sanguine hope of carrying this motion. It was not necessary that the right of Parliament to provide for the exigency which had arisen should be affirmatively stated; and it was calculated that many would be unwilling to vote for a theory, the assertion of which was ungracious and offensive to the personage whose claims were practically admitted to be beyond dispute, and who would probably continue to exercise sovereign power until his vicarious authority merged in hereditary right. But the persons who felt the weight of these considerations were equally unwilling to be parties to a doctrine which was not only unconstitutional, but seemed to require that they should transfer their allegiance from a living monarch, who might be in a

[margin: Modes of Parliamentary delay.]

condition any day to resume his authority, to a prince whose tenure of power must necessarily be precarious. The time-servers, who were afraid of offending the son by adhering to the father, or of offending the father by going over to the son, it was thought, would seek refuge from their dilemma in Lord North's proposition. But the waverers of every description were scared by the tone and language of the Opposition leader, and proximate minister of the Regency. Fox's native vehemence overbore his newly adopted discretion; and he supported the evasive motion of his coadjutor by an argument which reiterated, in all its breadth, the obnoxious dogma of positive right which he had modified, if not abandoned, the previous day. Not satisfied with this, he concluded one of his most powerful speeches with an invective against Pitt, who, he said, would have proposed no limitation on the power of the Regent, unless he had been certain that there would be a change of Ministry. Pitt retorted by pronouncing the attack made upon him unfounded, arrogant, and presumptuous. An observation of Fox, that his rival, conscious of not having deserved the favour of the Prince, was envious of his successors, and desirous to obstruct their credit, drew down upon his royal patron, as well as himself, a severe but merited rebuke. As to my being conscious, said Pitt, that I do not deserve the favour of the Prince, I can only say that I know but one way in which I, or any man, could deserve it, by having uniformly endeavoured in a public situation to do my duty to the King, his father, and to the country at large. If, in thus endeavouring to deserve the confidence of the Prince, it should appear that I, in fact, have lost it, however painful and mortifying that circumstance may be to me, and from whatever cause it may proceed, I may indeed regret it, but

I will boldly say it is impossible I should ever repent it. The whole speech is described as one of his happiest efforts, and it produced an impression such as had seldom been witnessed since the days of his father. It had a sensible effect on the division. Lord North's amendment was negatived by a majority of sixty-four, a surprising result, considering that a change of Ministry and a new order of things were generally believed to be inevitable and imminent; and considering, also, that means were used without scruple to secure a different result. The Duke of York, a weak young prince, entirely devoted to his brother's interests, was brought down to the House of Lords, in which he had lately taken his seat, to deprecate the sense of Parliament being taken on a question of right. The Prince of Wales himself wrote to Lord Lonsdale, requesting, as a personal favour, that his nominees might be instructed to vote against the ministerial resolutions—a request which was dutifully obeyed.[*] A canvass was actively prosecuted among members of both Houses and their connections. People were emphatically assured that the reign of George the Third was virtually at an end, and those who sought preferment received friendly warnings to consider the present crisis as the turning point of their fortunes. These representations were not without their effect, and the division list showed numerous deserters from the Court. But the debate and the majority for Ministers on the 16th of December put a stop to the panic. Many of those who had committed themselves became alarmed, the waverers fell back into the ranks; and the day after the division, Pitt's position was commanding as ever.

The day before the debate in the Commons, a dis-

---

[*] Lord Grenville to Lord Rockingham.—*Courts and Cabinets*, vol. ii. p. 64.

cussion on the question of the Regency had taken place in the House of Lords. On this occasion, the Duke of York made the speech to which reference has been made. The Duke of Gloucester, the King's brother, spoke in the same sense, though he had no connection with the Prince's party. These demonstrations could not fail to have their weight; and it was fully thought they would prove decisive of the questions in the Commons on the following evening. The Duke of York was the avowed mouthpiece of his brother;* and the Duke of Gloucester was supposed to represent the sentiments of the Royal Family. On the other side, the Chancellor made a speech which produced a great impression. On the first alarm of the King's illness, this man, who affected on all occasions a rough uncourtly bluntness, excelled the most vigilant courtier in his promptitude to cultivate the favour of the Prince and the Whigs. When the character of the King's malady was declared by the physicians, the Chancellor made haste to negotiate with Sheridan and the other confidential advisers of the Prince the terms on which he would support the pretensions of His Royal Highness to the Regency; and it is stated as a fact, that this negotiation was concluded in a room at Windsor, at the very time when a Cabinet Council was being held in another part of the Palace to deliberate on the grave and anxious questions to which the unforeseen interruption of the royal authority had given rise.† The agreement was, that, in the event of a regency, Thurlow should continue to hold the Great Seal in consideration of his support to the Prince's party;

---

* Prince's Memorial to the King (drawn up by Sir Gilbert Elliott).—Fox's *Correspondence*, vol. ii. p. 300.

† LORD JOHN RUSSELL's *Life of Fox*, vol. ii.—LORD CAMP-BELL's *Lives of the Chancellors.*—*Locker* MSS.—Lord Grenville, also, in his letters, repeatedly alludes to Thurlow's intrigues with the Prince's party.—*Courts and Cabinets*, vol. ii.

and this compact Fox, on his return from the Continent, was reluctantly compelled to ratify.*

But in a few days the prospect of affairs was changed. Thurlow had acted on the opinion of Warren, the physician originally consulted, and who confidently declared that the King could not recover. But Warren became suspected of a disposition to flatter the Prince's hopes; and Willis, who was subsequently called in, pronounced a different opinion, and as confidently predicted that the King's early and complete recovery was probable, if not certain. His Majesty's symptoms improved under the treatment of Willis; and the Chancellor began to think he had been hasty. Accordingly, on the 11th of December, when Lord Camden attacked the claim of right which had been put forward by Fox, the Chancellor made a moderate, trimming speech, which showed the painful doubt and hesitation under which he laboured as to the best course to pursue for his own interest. But on the 15th his mind was made up. On that day he stood up in his place in Parliament, and, with many tears, admonished his amazed audiences, that their first duty was to preserve the rights of their King *entire*, so that, when God should permit him to recover, he might not find his situation worse than it had been before his infirmity. He then dwelt on his own grief, and the debt of gratitude which he owed to his afflicted Sovereign; concluding with these well-remembered words, 'When I forget my King, may God forget me!'†

Hopes of the King's recovery.

---

* His letter to Loughborough (to whom he had promised the chancellorship in the event of his return to power) expresses great annoyance at the arrangement. 'I have swallowed a bitter pill. . . . I do not remember ever feeling so uneasy about any political thing I ever did in my life.'—*Correspondence.*

† The witty remarks of Wilkes and Burke, who stood near him when he uttered these tremendous words, are well known. I have seen another version of this celebrated peroration. According to Sir J. B. Burgess, who was present, when the Chancellor came to the words 'May God'—he suddenly stopped in his career;

On the report of the resolutions carried by Pitt in Committee, there was a debate which lasted for two days, originating in an amendment, moved by Mr. Dempster, to the second resolution. The right of Parliament to make provision for the exercise of royal authority during its temporary interruption having been confirmed, the proposal of the Opposition was, that the Prince should be addressed to assume the Government. The debate yielded no novelty in argument on either side, and was chiefly remarkable for one of those outbursts of spleen, folly, intemperance, and bad taste, interspersed with striking phrases and passages of brilliant oratory, which Burke so frequently poured forth. His fury was on this occasion directed against Thurlow, who, by his recent speech, had finally severed his fortunes from the heir-apparent. It was proposed by the Ministry, that the Great Seal should be affixed to the Regency Bill as a substitute for the royal assent. This operation Burke described as setting up a phantom of sovereignty, 'a man with black brows and a large wig, a puppet, an idol, an idiot, a *thing* to which he disclaimed allegiance.' The House, tired and disgusted with this raving, at length showed the usual signs of impatience and disapprobation; upon which he called them a pack of hounds, and at length sat down, leaving a doubt on the minds of many of his hearers whether he was not as fit a subject for restraint and discipline as the unhappy personage whose affliction he commonly alluded to in the most coarse and inhuman terms. The division showed an increased majority for Ministers, being seventy-three, in a house less full than that which voted on the previous occasion. The resolutions were then

---

a word, the most familiar to his lips, having naturally arisen, but after a pause, he substituted 'forget,' and so created a household word when he was about to utter an ordinary imprecation.— *Locker* MSS.

communicated to the other House, which, upon a division, agreed to them by a majority of thirty-three. The Houses having adjourned over the Christmas week, a farther delay took place in consequence of the death of the Speaker, on the day the Commons reassembled. Grenville was elected to the chair by a majority of seventy-one over Sir Gilbert Elliott, the candidate put forward by the Opposition;* and the day following, being the 6th of January, a crowded House was assembled, on the understanding that Pitt was to declare the restrictions on the regency. But the Opposition contended, that, before determining a point of such importance, the House should be possessed of information as to the present state of His Majesty's health. This objection was urged by Fox with temper and decency, and supported by Burke in a speech which displayed the opposite qualities. Pitt immediately fell in with the suggestion, which was certainly plausible, and moved for a committee to examine the physicians and report the state of His Majesty's health. To this motion, Sheridan proposed, as an amendment, to leave out the limitations as to conducting the inquiry by an examination merely of the King's medical attendants; but the result showed the increasing strength of the Government, their majority being increased to eighty.

Grenville elected Speaker.

The restrictions which Ministers proposed to place on the power of the Regent were submitted to the Prince by Pitt on the 30th of December. The royal authority was to be exercised by His Royal Highness in the name and on

Proposed restrictions on the Regent.

---

* The numbers were 221 to 141. The Opposition hailed this event as a new source of embarrassment to the ministers. The Duke of York went about exulting, that now the immediate appointment of a Regent was inevitable, as the new Speaker could not be confirmed without the royal authority. — *Locker MSS.* But the decision and promptitude of Pitt easily disposed of this minor difficulty.

behalf of His Majesty; the care of the King's person, the management of the household, with the appointment of its officers and servants, being reserved to the Queen. The Regent was not to dispose of the King's real or personal property, nor grant any office in reversion, nor for any other term than during His Majesty's pleasure, nor any pension, nor any office except one which must be granted for life, nor create any peer. These stringent conditions were proposed, on the assumption that His Majesty's illness might not be of long duration. 'Should it unfortunately be protracted'—so concluded the Minister's letter— 'Parliament might reconsider these provisions.' The Prince's reply, a masterpiece of composition, was drawn up by Burke. Considering that the person called upon to exercise the sovereign power was the immediate heir to the Crown, and a prince of mature age, it must be admitted, that the restraints imposed upon him were somewhat strict, and afforded strong grounds for remonstrance, if not complaint. The preparation of a paper, which should convey any such remonstrance or complaint in a style not unbecoming the exalted rank and peculiar position of the personage who signed it, was a task which seemed to demand the soundest judgment and discrimination. Yet this task was successfully accomplished by a man who had never opened his mouth in Parliament on the subject of the regency, without shocking and revolting his hearers by an exhibition of violence and folly. The style of the paper was chaste; the arguments against the scheme proposed by the Minister were stated with simplicity and force; and the tone of the document throughout was maintained with dignity and temper.

The examination of the physicians before the Committee occupied a week, and was conducted in a manner which, on one side at least, showed little regard for decency or humanity. The two parties which divided the Legislature

Names of physicians appointed.

were represented in the sick chamber of the sovereign. Dr. Warren, a physician of the highest reputation, who had been in attendance on the King from the first appearance of the malady, maintained his unfavourable opinion of the case. The other doctors in regular attendance on His Majesty, Sir George Baker, Sir Lucas Pepys, Drs. Heberden and Reynolds, concurred with Warren. On the other side was Dr. Willis, who had, for nearly thirty years, been manager of a private asylum for lunatics, and whose treatment had been eminently successful. Willis was called in on the 4th of December, and without hesitation declared that His Majesty's recovery was more than probable, and might be confidently expected in a few weeks.

From that time Willis had the entire confidence of the Queen and Pitt. The authority of Warren was upheld by the Prince's party, while that of Willis was always quoted by the King's friends. *Confidence of the Queen and Pitt in Dr. Willis.* At the second examination before the Commons Committee in January, Warren declared that the opinion which he had given a month before was unchanged; that there was no improvement in His Majesty's condition, and that if there was any difference, it was for the worse. Willis, on the contrary, maintained that the disorder had materially abated, that the chances of recovery had greatly increased since he had been last examined, and that he hardly entertained a doubt of His Majesty's complete restoration. This evidence, so unwelcome to Sheridan, Burke, and the other friends of the Prince who sat on the Committee, was subjected to a severity of cross-examination such as the most jealous advocate in a court of justice could not have excelled. Willis was required to justify every word of every statement which he had made with respect to His Majesty's health, and to explain every particular of the treatment he had adopted. He was censured for having allowed the King to read the play of Lear; for having allowed him to read at all; for permitting him to have interviews with the Queen and the Princesses; for allowing him to use a razor. The cross questions, and more especially the manner in which they were put, disclosed too plainly the motive and feeling by which they were prompted, and had no other effect than to engage the sympathy of the public still more strongly on the side of the King, the Queen, and the Ministers.

On the 16th of January, Pitt moved five resolutions, embodying the restrictions on the regency contained in his letter to the Prince. It required all the authority and credit which he possessed to carry this measure. Parliament had with difficulty been brought to a vote, regarding which the Prince, about to mount the throne, had expressly declared his displeasure; and now the Houses were required to confer the royal authority on the heir-apparent diminished by such restrictions as seemed to imply a distrust of the individual, and were certainly incompatible with the efficient exercise of the royal prerogative. The Prince was not permitted to deal with the property of the Crown; he was denied the right of making peers, as if he were unworthy to unlock the fountain of honour; the household, comprising some of the great offices of state, was to be placed beyond his control. When this scheme of a regency was first propounded, His Royal Highness declared he would not consent to it; but when he understood that the unbending minister had determined, in case of his refusal, to offer the regency to the Queen, and, in the event of Her Majesty's declining the burden, to delegate the royal authority to a council, the Prince was advised to yield; but it was made known, that his first act as Regent would be the dismissal of the Ministers who had put such an indignity upon him.

In the speech with which he introduced the resolutions, Pitt made use of an insinuation which had been rashly hazarded in the Committee upstairs, and circulated by the Opposition press, that the Queen and Dr. Willis were in collusion, for the purpose of misrepresenting the state of the King's health, with the view to defeat the just claims of the Prince to the full and free exercise of the royal authority. This was one of the most notable of the series of blunders which the too zealous and interested friends of His Royal Highness had committed throughout these proceedings. During the twenty-eight years that Her Majesty had shared the throne, her conduct had been irreproachable. She had neither taste nor talent for political intrigue, and seemed to have no idea of her station beyond the observance of a dull decorum in her court and household. The King seldom alluded to public affairs in the presence of his consort or his family; and Charlotte rarely evinced any interest in matters beyond the precincts of her court and household. When the King's illness cast responsibility upon her, it was as unwelcome as it was unwonted. She hardly ventured to take any step, and her whole anxiety was lest the King should disapprove of any part of her conduct, if he should at any time be in a condition to resume his authority.* The conduct of her sons, indeed, particularly of the Prince of Wales, was so gross, so utterly wanting in common feeling and decency, that she did not hesitate to treat them with marked displeasure. It was no less her duty than the natural dictate of her heart in this trying emergency, to be guided by those counsellors who were trusted by the King, and who were still the responsible advisers of the Crown. It was not to be expected, that Her Majesty should set aside Pitt and

---

* *Locker* MSS. LADY HARCOURT's *Diary*.

Thurlow to consult Fox and Sheridan; and it was
with the entire approval of Pitt, and the sullen
acquiescence of Thurlow (who could never cordially
support what Pitt, or, indeed, anybody else approved),
that the management of the King's health was principally entrusted to Dr. Willis. There was no pretence, as the Prince well knew, for the insinuation,
that Willis was a creature of the Queen. Mrs. Harcourt, the wife of one of the equerries (General,
afterwards Earl Harcourt), had drawn up a paper,*
in which she stated her knowledge of the qualifications of Willis, from his successful treatment of her
mother, who had been afflicted with mental disease.
This paper, on the 28th of November, having been
laid before the Prince, the Duke of York, the Chancellor and Pitt, it was determined that Willis should
be sent for; and the confidence with which he soon
inspired the Queen was the necessary consequence of
the superior skill and courage which he showed in
the care of his patient.

It was under these circumstances, that the mother
of the Prince was attacked by an insinuation, which His Royal Highness knew to
be false and unfounded. Pitt's indignant and scorn-
ful refutation of this charge, or insinuated charge,
could not fail to produce its effect, and to reconcile
his hearers to restraints on the authority of a Regent
so little likely to make a good use of power. After
a lengthened debate, in which Sheridan took the
leading part on behalf of the Prince, four of the five
resolutions were carried after two divisions, in which
the majority for Ministers was maintained. On the
19th, a final struggle took place on the fifth resolution, which related to the household. The Opposition had, at one time, entertained a sanguine hope
of defeating this part of the scheme; and doubts had

* *Locker* MSS. LADY HARCOURT's *Diary*.

been expressed, whether Parliament could be induced to go the length of separating the patronage of the Crown in such a manner as to create a Queen's party, in opposition to the government of the regent. But such was now the ascendency of Pitt, that a moderate amendment proposed by Lord North, that the control of the household should be withdrawn from the Executive only 'for a limited time,' was negatived by two hundred and twenty to one hundred and sixty-four. The resolutions having been voted by the Lords, though not without an animated debate, a division, and a protest of the minority, signed by the Dukes of York and Cumberland, they were laid before the Prince in an Address from both Houses. His Royal Highness returned an answer consenting to accept the regency on the terms proposed, presuming that the resolutions were founded on the hope, in which he ardently participated, that His Majesty's disorder might not be of long duration. The next step was to confirm these proceedings by an act of the Legislature; but, as it was considered necessary for this purpose that Parliament should be opened by a commission under the Great Seal, letters patent were directed to be issued, empowering certain commissioners therein named to observe as nearly as possible the usual formalities. The names of the Princes of the blood were inserted in the commission, but subsequently withdrawn by their desire. This formal proceeding was adopted on the authority of a precedent in the reign of Henry the Sixth, which was followed in 1754, when Lord Chancellor Hardwick, during the illness of George the Second, affixed the Great Seal to a Commission for opening a session of Parliament. Some doubts were expressed in both Houses as to the sufficiency of the precedents, but the authority of Lord Camden, who proposed the measure, outweighed these objections.

The Regency Bill was introduced on the 5th of

February, and was read a second time on the following day without a division. The Opposition, having exhausted all their efforts to obtain better terms for the Prince, were, for the most part, content that the Bill should pass, and that they might come into power without unnecessary delay. Fox, who had returned from the Continent in a bad state of health, and had struggled for some time against his disorder, which occasioned serious apprehension to his friends, absented himself from the House during the farther progress of the Bill. Sheridan moderated his tone, and went so far as to deny that he had ever gone the length of asserting the Prince's indefeasible right. Lord North, who was not a candidate for office under the approaching dispensation, contented himself with some practical comments on the Bill as it passed through its stages. Burke alone pursued the Bill with unmitigated hostility; but his violence and exaggeration only caused pain to his friends, and drew from the supporters of the Government expressions of anger and disgust. He described the Bill as intended to degrade the Prince of Wales, and to outlaw, excommunicate, and attaint the whole house of Brunswick. When the House laughed at this raving, Burke broke into a fury, and charged the Ministers with acting *treasons* for which the justice of the country would one day overtake them. Here he was stopped by loud cries of 'Order,' amidst which Pitt rose, and observed, that, though he seldom thought it worth while to interrupt the right honourable gentleman, and call him to order, or indeed, to make him any answer, yet when he so far violated common decency, as to describe in such terms as he had employed, a Bill founded on principles which the House had sanctioned by distinct resolutions, it was necessary that the House should interpose its authority. But, so far was Burke from being checked by this rebuke,

Second reading carried without a division.

or by the manifest repugnance with which his loose
invectives, his pointless sarcasms, and strained, in-
appropriate metaphors, were habitually received,
that, on the next occasion when the Bill was in Committee, he so far cast off every restraint of decency
and humanity, as to speak of the afflicted monarch
'as having been hurled from his throne, and plunged
into a condition that drew down upon him the pity
of the meanest peasant in his kingdom.' A cry was
raised throughout the House to take down these
words; and Burke, staggered by the storm of indignation, attempted to explain, but the agitation
hardly subsided before the close of the debate.

The Bill was passed through the Commons with
increased majorities, and carried to the Lords on the 12th of February. It was Bill passed in the Commons.
read a second time, and had passed through several
stages in committee, when the Lord Chancellor, on
the 17th of February, announced that so great an
improvement had taken place in the King's health
as to render it extremely probable that it would not
be necessary to proceed with the Bill. Upon this
intimation, the House adjourned to the 24th, and
the consideration of the Bill was not resumed.

The King's disorder took a favourable turn on the
6th of February. His pulse, which, in the height of
the malady, had varied from one hundred and twenty
to one hundred and thirty, and had seldom been
below ninety, beat steadily on this day from seventy-
two to eighty-two; and Dr. Willis expressed a confident expectation that His Majesty would be well in
a week. This expectation was substantially verified;
but had it not been for the rapid progress with which
the Regency Bill was advancing to its final stage,
Willis would have deferred the announcement until
His Majesty's recovery was so far confirmed as to
enable him to resume his authority without fear of a
relapse. As it was, Warren still refused not only to

pronounce the King convalescent, but even to admit that any material amendment had taken place. The other doctors, either sharing Warren's jealousy of Willis, or swayed by the authority of the senior physician, maintained a cautious reserve. Willis, therefore, took upon himself the sole responsibility of informing the Chancellor that the King's state was such that the Regency Bill ought not to be proceeded with. Thurlow, after his rough fashion, said he did not believe it, and refused to act on any such information. But the courageous doctor was not to be browbeat. He declared, that if his deliberate opinion was disregarded, he would publish it to the world; and threatened the astonished Chancellor with impeachment, if he dared to act on the assumption of his Sovereign's continued incapacity.* Thurlow, upon this, consented to see the King, and judge for himself. An interview of two hours satisfied him, that the representation which had been made to him was correct; and on the following day Willis attended the Cabinet at which it was determined to abandon the Bill. On the 23rd of the month, the King wrote to Mr. Pitt, announcing his convalescence; and on the 26th the last bulletin of the physicians was issued. It was signed by Sir George Baker, Sir Lucas Pepys, and Dr. Willis, and apprised the public of the 'entire cessation of His Majesty's illness.'

Dr. Willis did not hesitate to declare, that if he had been consulted in the first instance, the King's illness would, in all probability, have been of very short duration. And this opinion appears to have been well founded. Mental disease was, at that time, a branch of art little understood; and the specific treatment of lunatics was worthy only of

Dr. Willis's opinion.

---

* Lady Harcourt's *Diary*. This fact was afterwards confirmed by Dr. Robert Willis, who told Mr. Locker that his father actually *bullied* the Chancellor before he could make him stir in the matter.—*Locker* MSS.

the barbarous age of medicine. The unhappy patient, upon whom this, the most terrible visitation of Heaven, had fallen, was no longer dealt with as a human being. His body was immediately enclosed in a machine, which left it no liberty of motion. He was sometimes chained to a staple. He was frequently beaten and starved; and, at the best, he was kept in subjection by menacing and violent language. The history of the King's illness showed that the most exalted station did not wholly exempt the sufferer from this stupid and inhuman usage. The King's disorder manifested itself principally in unceasing talk,* but no disposition to violence was exhibited. Yet he was subjected constantly to the severe discipline of the strait waistcoat; he was secluded from the Queen and his family; he was denied the use of a knife and fork, of scissors, or any instrument with which he might inflict bodily injury. Such petty vexatious treatment could not fail to aggravate a disorder, the leading symptom of which was nervous irritability, caused by over application, extreme abstemiousness, and domestic anxiety. It would have been well if the errors of the physicians had been confined to ignorance. But their negligence was still more reprehensible. While the poor maniac was deprived of those tender offices, which his wife and daughters might have rendered, he was abandoned to the care of low mercenaries; and so little discrimination was observed in the choice of his attendants, that the charge of his person devolved chiefly on a German page, named Ernst, who was utterly unworthy to be trusted with the care of the humblest of his fellow-creatures. This man, who had been raised by the patronage of His Majesty, repaid the kindness of his royal master with the most brutal ingratitude. He went so far as to strike the

* He talked on one occasion for nineteen hours without intermission.—*Diary, Locker MSS.*

helpless King; and on one occasion, when His
Majesty wished to protract his exercise in the gardens
at Kew, Ernst seized him in his arms, carried him
into a chamber, and throwing him violently on a sofa,
exclaimed in an insolent manner to the attendants:
'There is your King for you.' *

<small>Treatment of the King at Kew.</small>
These outrages were perpetrated in the seclusion
of the Palace at Kew, to which the King
had been removed in the month of October,
at the instance of the Prince of Wales.
His Majesty had been persuaded to leave Windsor,
to which he was much attached, by the promise that
he should see his children at Kew. He entered the
carriage cheerfully; but on passing through the iron
gates of the little park, he put his hands before his
face, and burst into tears. Recovering his composure, however, he talked to the equerries who
accompanied him in the carriage in his ordinary
hurried manner, pointing out the objects in the
road, and anticipating the pleasure, long denied him,
of seeing his wife and daughters. But on his arrival
at Kew, he found himself a prisoner. Proceeding
towards the apartments he usually occupied, he was
stopped, and conducted into a large room, where he
found the pages who were to be his keepers waiting
to receive him. The equerries, among whom was his
faithful and valued servant, General Harcourt, according to the orders they had received, withdrew.
The physicians also, who had accompanied the royal
patient from Windsor, having consigned him to the
charge of the pages, also thought proper to retire,
and actually returned to London the same night.
The King then impatiently demanded to see his
family; and the promise under which he had been
induced to leave his Palace of Windsor was, in cruel

---

* The King, who, after his recovery, remembered and related almost everything that happened to him during his aberration, mentioned this fact to Lady Harcourt.—*Diary, Locker MSS.*

mockery, fulfilled. The Princesses were brought before the window; the King, on seeing them, rushed forward to lift the sash, but it was screwed down. A paroxysm was the immediate consequence of this cruel restraint; the Princesses were hastily removed, and the King was dragged from the window, entreating to be allowed to speak to his children.*

It is not surprising that the King made no progress towards recovery under treatment such as this, which continued until the first week in December, when, happily, Dr. Willis was called in.

The King's abhorrence of his physicians, under whose sanction he had been subjected to such cruel indignities and vexatious restraints, did not dispose him to a favourable reception of a new medical adviser, whom he considered only as another added to the number of his persecutors. When Willis was introduced, the King displayed, in a remarkable manner, the quickness which lunatics often exhibit. He reproached the doctor with having given up the sacred calling to which he had been ordained for a lucrative profession. Willis replied, that our Saviour cured demoniacs. 'Yes,' said the King, 'but he did not get seven hundred pounds a year for it.' The mild yet firm manner of the wise and humane physician, into whose hands His Majesty had at last happily fallen, soon obtained its usual influence over the irritable patient. At a second interview, the poor King opened his heart to the new doctor, and poured forth all its grievances; among the most prominent of which were, the seclusion of his wife and daughters, the refusal of a razor, of a knife and fork, and the insolence of the pages. The doctor soothed his agitation upon all these points. The King was particularly indignant at being denied the use of a razor, lest he should cut his throat. 'I

Reception of Dr. Willis.

---

* LADY HARCOURT's *Diary*; *Locker* MSS.

am sure,' said Willis, 'your Majesty is too good a Christian, and that you have too much sense of what you owe to your people to commit such an act;' and immediately presented him with a razor,* which the King quietly applied to its proper purpose, under no other restraint than the doctor's eye. The other offensive and unnecessary restrictions were relaxed, and ultimately removed. When the King demanded the use of a knife and fork, Willis readily assented, adding, that, with His Majesty's leave, he would have the honour of dining with him. In like manner, the Queen and the Princesses, whom he had not seen since the 5th of the preceding month, were brought into his presence.† The King seized Her Majesty's hand, kissed it, and held it in his during the whole interview, which lasted half an hour. The little Princess Amelia, who, from her infancy, had been his favourite child, sat upon his lap. The care of His Majesty's person was no longer entrusted to the uncontrolled discretion of the pages, and the brutal Ernst was dismissed altogether.

I have selected these few particulars from the sad detail of suffering and privation to which the afflicted monarch had been wantonly subjected, before the Willises, father and son, introduced a more careful and enlightened system of treatment. Yet it was happy for the sufferer that he was conscious of no emotion more keen than that which the ignorance of physicians, or the insolence of menials, could inflict. The delinquencies of those who owed him the first debt of duty and reverence were concealed from his view. The Prince of Wales had been so long

---

* Warren, in his capacity of first physician, took upon himself to reprimand Willis for venturing on such an act without the sanction of the other physicians. Willis, according to Warren's evidence, admitted that he shuddered at what he had done; but Willis denied any recollection of having used such an expression, or of having been conscious of any tremor on the occasion.— *Lords' Journals*.

† 13th December.

estranged from his father, that nothing beyond an outward regard to decency could fairly be expected from him. But the Duke of York was differently placed. He had not before him the immediate prospect of succession to a throne; he had no pretence for saying or feeling that his youthful errors had been harshly rebuked, and that no allowance had been made for the temptations to which he was exposed. Frederick was ever the favoured son of George the Third, from whom he had experienced signal marks of affection and indulgence. But no sooner was this fond father prostrated by an affliction, which drew towards him the sympathy and compassion of all his people, except the heir-apparent, his political associates and sycophants, than this beloved son deserted to the party which treated his sufferings with mockery and hate. It is not without disgust that we read of the indignities to which the helpless monarch was subjected by a vile menial; but human nature itself revolts from the parricidal outrages with which these brothers treated the infirmity of their parent. It is not necessary to dwell in detail on the odious conduct of these men. One or two well authenticated facts will suffice. The Prince of Wales, who had a talent for mimicry, and indeed possessed the social qualities suited to the witty and profligate men and women with whom he lived, was in the habit of amusing his companions by *taking off*, as the phrase was, the gestures and actions of his insane father. That which he did himself he suffered his friends to do; and the standing topic in the Prince's circle was ridicule of the King and Queen.* The Duke of York

* At Brookes's, a cant phrase at the whist tables was: 'I play the lunatic (the King).' Jack Payne, the Prince's secretary and confidential man, one day uttered some ribaldry about the Queen in the presence of the Duchess of Gordon: 'You little, insignificant, good-for-nothing, upstart, pert, chattering puppy,' said her grace, 'how dare you name your royal master's royal mother in that style!'—LADY HARCOURT's *Diary; Locker MSS.*

vied with his brother in defamation of his parents; but he was wholly destitute of the lively talent which sometimes carries off the grosser parts of the most ribald discourse; and the brutality of the stupid sot disgusted even the most profligate of his associates.

Party spirit had never been known to run so high as during the King's illness. Private society was infected by it; and the partisans of the Prince could not meet the King's friends at the same table. The confident assertions of Dr. Warren, that the King was a confirmed lunatic,* materially influenced the conduct of the Princes, and determined the policy of the Opposition. Warren had committed himself to this opinion in the first instance; and within a few days of the King's recovery he quarrelled with Sir Lucas Pepys in the Prince's presence for expressing a doubt upon the subject. On the other hand, Dr. Willis had been equally confident in maintaining that the King's recovery was merely a question of time; and did not hesitate to say, that if his patient had been in a private station, a few weeks would have sufficed to re-establish his health.

<small>Violent party spirit.</small>

While factions were thus raging over the prostrate monarch, the people were of one mind in their royal attachment to the Crown. George the Third, without going out of his way to court the favour of his people, was the most popular King since Charles the Second; and, like Charles, his popularity was in a great measure owing to dislike and distrust of his successor. The futile attempt of a poor silly woman in 1786 to wound the King by thrusting a knife at him as he was entering the theatre drew forth a de-

---

* See a letter from General Grant to Lord Cornwallis, 18th March, 1789. CORNWALLIS' *Correspondence*, vol. i. p. 445, and WRAXALL's *Posthumous Memoirs*. Lady Harcourt's *Diary*, and the papers in Mr. Locker's Collection, bear abundant evidence to the same effect.

monstration of loyalty such as this country had not exhibited since the days of the cavaliers. The attachment to his person manifested by the country people when he visited Cheltenham is said to have accelerated his malady, by the excitement which it produced. During his illness, the Court physicians received letters daily, urging them, as they valued their lives, to care for His Majesty's health. Sir George Baker, the physician in ordinary, was stopped in his carriage by the populace, demanding an account of the King's health; and when he gave an unfavourable report, he was assailed with cries of anger and reproach.* The rejoicings and thanksgivings on his recovery were loud and universal throughout the kingdom.

The firmness and judgment displayed by Pitt through these three anxious months were more remarkable even than the signal exhibition of the same qualities during the crisis of 1784. His successful struggle with the Coalition was a feat of political courage and conduct, which has never been surpassed; but the circumstances of 1788-9 were far more complicated and critical than those which accompany a party conflict, however desperate. The task which Pitt undertook was one of unparalleled difficulty. He stood forward at once to defend the rights of the Crown, no longer in a condition to defend itself, and to vindicate the supreme authority of Parliament, assailed by those who had always assumed to be its champions. He had to encounter not merely the rage of a party eager for place, and burning for revenge, but the avowed displeasure of a Prince, who, in all human probability, would soon have the fortunes of statesmen and politicians at his disposal. Would those devoted followers who had yielded him a blind obedience while his courage and capacity were backed by the whole weight of the

Difficulties of Pitt's position.

---

* MADAME D'ARBLAY's *Diary*, vol. iv. p. 336.

Crown adhere to their fidelity when that support was withdrawn, and when he ventured to stand in the way of the Prince who had already one foot on the steps of the throne? Some, indeed, had already deserted him; others, who were faltering, remained for the moment, fascinated by his undaunted resolution and imperturbable fortitude. Yet it is hardly possible that he could have maintained his position, had his opponents availed themselves of the advantages they possessed. But in 1789, as in 1784, Pitt prevailed as much through the short-sighted insolence of his foes, as by his own consummate skill and prudence. Had the undoubted pretensions of the Prince of Wales been put forward with firmness and moderation, they would have been irresistible; and it is probable that any attempt to place restrictions on his power, such as those which Pitt made Parliament adopt, would have utterly failed. The prejudice caused by the abstract question of right, so gratuitously and perversely started by the Opposition, enabled Pitt to propose a restricted Regency Bill; and the delays interposed by the Opposition to the completion of the arrangement by which the Whigs were to return to power, prevented that arrangement taking effect. If the Regency Bill had been passed with the despatch which a due regard to the grave exigency occasioned by an interruption to the royal authority seemed to demand, the Prince of Wales must have assumed the government soon after Christmas, and Fox would have been minister. A few weeks of power under such circumstances might have entirely altered the relations of political parties. The whole body of time-servers would have passed over to the Prince's party, and many others would have entered into engagements from which they would have found it difficult to recede. It seemed hardly possible that Pitt should bear up against the accumulated difficulties which surrounded him. Unlike any of the statesmen who had struggled for power since the Revolution, he had not the support of any leading political connection. His kinsmen, the Grenvilles, were no longer the powerful family which they were thirty years before, when the strong will of the head of the house could bend the pride of Chatham, and when one of his cadets was at the head of the Government. Earl Temple, lately created Marquis of Buckingham, was one of the most wayward and impracticable of men; he had all the ill-temper of his family, without any of their firmness and aptitude for affairs. William Grenville, the Speaker, who, in after years, revived the credit and authority of his house, was as yet young and little known in public life. The Cabinet included but one man of mark besides Pitt, with a spirit as proud as his own—the able and sagacious Thurlow. But the First Minister and the Chancellor were as much opposed to each other as if they had sat on different sides of the table. While Pitt supported the impeachment of Hastings, the Chancellor declared his readiness to affix the Great Seal to a patent of nobility which should recognise the great services of the Indian ruler. On the question of the slave trade, Thurlow was openly opposed to the Chief Minister. On smaller matters, their differences were not less bitter. Pitt had advanced his Attorney-General and personal friend Arden to the office of Master of the Rolls, in spite of the determined protest of the Chancellor, who claimed this appointment as part of the patronage of the Great Seal, and openly derided the pretensions of Arden to such an office. Jealousy of Pitt's predominance had rendered Thurlow always a turbulent and impracticable member of the Cabinet; but his undoubted ability and vigour, joined with a reputation for honesty, which a blunt and sarcastic manner obtained for the most corrupt and selfish of public men, rendered the Chancellor too formidable to be overborne; and he could venture, not only to thwart his colleagues in council, but even to deride and frustrate their policy in his place in Parliament, with an insolence which the avowed Opposition could hardly equal. When the King was pronounced incapable of administering public affairs, Thurlow was the first to desert him and to go over to the Prince. When the King's malady assumed a more favourable aspect, and some difficulty arose as to the fulfilment of the bargain he had made with the Opposition, he returned to his colleagues, calling God to witness his unshaken loyalty; and even to the last, while His Majesty's recovery was still doubtful, the Chancellor, with an assurance which, in any other man, would have been amazing, loudly proclaimed that the conduct of the Prince of Wales had, throughout this trying time, been admirable and exemplary.*

The other colleagues of Pitt were either trembling for their political fortunes, or were incapable of affording him any substantial support. Dundas alone remained firm to his patron; but the shrewd Scotch lawyer, though a useful subordinate, had no pretensions to the political and social weight which the emergency demanded. In such a situation, many a minister would have persuaded himself that he consulted the public interest as well as his own, by opening a correspondence with the heir-apparent and his friends. There can be no doubt that any such overture would have been eagerly received, and that Pitt might have obtained any terms not wholly incompatible with the just pretensions of the Whigs to a share of power. But the courageous son of Chatham maintained the same unbending spirit which he had displayed in 1786, when he was supported by the whole weight of the Crown, by the whole tribe of courtiers, and by a rapidly increasing majority of the nation, against a

marginal note: Dundas.

* LADY HARCOURT's *Diary*; *Locker* MSS.

desperate majority of the Commons. Like that statesman, whose arrogance of power his father had denounced, Pitt was determined to be *sole* minister or none. And, anticipating his retreat from power, he constructed a plan of administration which would have paralysed the arm of his successor. Fox was charged with having devised a scheme, which, under the name of a Bill for the Government of India, was really intended to secure to himself and his friends the government of England. But the Regency Bill of Pitt may, in this respect, be fairly compared with the India Bill of Fox. The latter created a source of patronage independent of the Crown, and which would probably continue under the control of the party then in power; the former severed the patronage of the Crown, and assigned one portion of it, the offices of the household, to the Queen, who would probably place it at the disposal of the minister about to pass into Opposition. Fox would have had enough to contend with, in succeeding to an office from which a Minister in the height of his reputation had been displaced by an arbitrary act of vicarious prerogative; but if he should have had to encounter the organised opposition of the Lords of the Bedchamber, whose votes had turned him out in 1783, it is probable that his career would have been of short duration. The transference of the appointments to the household from the Regent to the Queen, was a snatch at power not more audacious than the famous Indian Council of Seven; but Pitt, with a character unsullied, and with the credit to which he was justly entitled for his able and successful conduct of public affairs, could exalt his reputation by an act which, if attempted under similar circumstances by his great rival, would have covered him with confusion.

Before quitting this subject, it is necessary to advert to the proceedings of the Irish Parliament, in consequence of the King's illness.

This was the first occasion on which the experiment

of an independent legislature in the sister island was brought to a decisive test; and the result was such as might have been expected. In whatever way the royal authority should be delegated to a lieutenant during the incapacity of the sovereign, it was obviously indispensable that there should be a concurrence on either side of the Channel in the arrangements to be made. A Regent exercising the power of the Crown with limitation in England, and without limitation in Ireland, would be a reduction of the theory of a double parliament to the practical absurdity to which it evidently tended. And this was the conclusion actually attained. The Lord-Lieutenant in his speech, on opening the session of 1789, informed the parliament of the King's incapacity; but having communicated the information in terms which seemed to imply that their proceedings should be shaped according to the course pursued by the English parliament, the Irish Commons immediately took umbrage. 'Ireland,' said Grattan, 'waits not a lesson from Britain, nor a model whereby to frame her proceedings.' The Government proposed, that the House should go into committee for the purpose of considering the Regency on a day which would be subsequent to the decisive vote of the English Legislature; but the House refused to postpone the committee, and they withheld supplies until the committee had sat. When the committee was constituted, the Ministry were not permitted even to bring in a Regency Bill, but a resolution offering the government of Ireland, unconditionally and without limitation, to the Prince of Wales, was voted without a division. The Lords concurred in this vote; and the Irish Viceroy, after much doubt and perplexity, determined on refusing to transmit this resolution to the English Government. The Houses thereupon appointed a deputation to carry their resolutions to England; and six persons of the highest rank and influence in the country consented to go upon this ridiculous errand. When these noblemen and gentlemen arrived in London, they found the Regency Bill abandoned in consequence of the King's recovery. Nevertheless, they proceeded to the discharge of their commission, by presenting the address to the Prince of Wales; and, consequently, His Royal Highness was reduced to the necessity of thanking them for the merely formal part of their address, which contained expressions of loyalty to the Sovereign, and of postponing to a future day his answer to the essential portion, referring to his assumption of the sovereignty of Ireland. The King's recovery prevented a collision between the English Government and the Irish Parliament, which was proceeding, after having passed votes of censure on Lord Buckingham, to pass resolutions declaring his Commission as Lord-Lieutenant to be terminated, and of transferring his authority to Lords Justices. Many of the Irish placemen calculating on the virtual demise of the Crown, and the fall of the great minister of whom they had hitherto been the servile followers, joined in this revolt; and had entered into an association to 'stand by each other' (so ran their phrase), should the Government attempt to dismiss them from their offices and pensions. These people, when they heard of the unexpected turn which affairs had taken in London, made haste to deprecate the vengeance of the justly-incensed Minister. Two or three of the ringleaders were dismissed; but the abject submission of the rest of the placemen and sinecurists was contemptuously accepted. The proceedings of the Irish Parliament only excited ridicule in London; but they were significant of the fate which befell that factious and impracticable body after a few years."

* *Courts and Cabinets of George the Third*, vol. ii. p. 124.

The restoration of the King's health was sufficiently ascertained on the day to which the Lords had adjourned, to justify the discharge of the order for proceeding with the Regency Bill. His Majesty's recovery, however, was far from complete; and it was not without anxiety that the Willises watched the effects upon his mind of the disclosures which must be made to him. The Chancellor was the first minister who saw the King; his visit was on the 20th of February, and lasted two hours. He found the King as clear and collected as his ordinary manner, which was confused and hurried, would permit him to be; but Thurlow avoided every topic of an irritating character, and confined himself chiefly to answering the questions which were put to him. The King had conceived a prejudice against Pitt; he fancied that Pitt had been a party to the deceit which had been practised on him, when he was induced to quit Windsor for Kew, by the promise of being allowed to see the Queen on his arrival. He fancied, also, that his minister had been unnecessarily hasty in bringing forward the Regency Bill. Dr. Willis, however, removed these impressions. In a long conversation which he held with the King, on the 23rd of the month, he entered fully into the narrative of public events during the last three months. The King bore this communication, in many respects so painful and exciting, with firmness and composure. He expressed great satisfaction at being relieved from the impression which he had received, unfavourable to the loyalty and fidelity of his minister. The same evening, His Majesty addressed a letter to Pitt, announcing his recovery, and desiring Pitt's attendance at Kew on the following day.

The King also received his sons for the first time since his recovery on the afternoon of the day on which Dr. Willis had related the eventful history of the interregnum. The Princes were such prominent figures in that history, that it was impossible altogether to disguise the part they had taken. The King prepared himself for the interview with the dignity and self-command which he could assume on befitting occasions. When the Princes were announced, the King paused for a moment to suppress his emotion, observing to Colonel Digby, the equerry, that the House of Brunswick never shed tears.* Nature, however, asserted her influence, and tears flowed on both sides when the King clasped his sons in his arms, and embraced them with the unreserved affection of a parent. The conversation, however, was general, no allusion being made to His Majesty's illness or to political affairs, and the interview lasted only half an hour.

On the 10th of March the King formally resumed the reins of Government by opening Parliament. He did not appear in person, but a speech was delivered by Commission in the usual manner. Addresses were unanimously voted by both Houses. London was illuminated; and the spontaneous demonstrations of joy from all ranks of the people sufficiently testified the popularity of the King and his Government. Public business, which had been interrupted by the debates on the Regency Bill, at once returned to its accustomed channel; and the Commons were soon engaged in animated debates on the Estimates and the Budget.

The King's recovery was celebrated by a solemn thanksgiving in St. Paul's Cathedral on the 23rd of April. Their Majesties, with the royal family, attended by the Lords and Commons, went in state; and as they passed through the crowded streets, the acclamations which greeted them from every side were to be regarded not merely as expressing loyalty and attachment to the person of

General Thanksgiving.

---

* LADY HARCOURT'S *Diary*, MSS.

the Sovereign, but, in some measure, as an adverse feeling towards the individual who had so nearly succeeded to his place. An attempt was made by the friends of the Prince of Wales to get up a demonstration in his favour; but its partial success had the effect of provoking a more enthusiastic and general ebullition of loyalty as the procession advanced through the more populous quarters of the metropolis. The partisans of the heir-apparent had predicted that the King's mind, so recently and imperfectly restored, would give way under the excitement of this scene; and His Majesty's friends were not without apprehension on this score; but the event was contrary to the hopes and fears on either side. The King, whose ordinary manner was hurried and perplexed, showed great firmness and composure during the affecting ceremony. Once only tears started to his eyes, but he immediately recovered his self-command; and while the Queen and the Princesses were weeping beside him, he succeeded in suppressing any outward sign of emotion. The Prince of Wales, on the other hand, made no attempt to suppress his chagrin, and could not behave with common temper or decency. The Duke of York imitated the example of his brother; and the petulance of these Princes was exposed not only before their own countrymen of every class, but before strangers, and the representatives of foreign powers.

The King's condition, however, was not yet that of assured sanity. The hurry of his spirits continued, while the unsoundness of his mind was exhibited in a new and offensive form. His Majesty became, or fancied himself to be enamoured of a lady of high rank, and of an age equal to his own. He talked incessantly of his passion for this lady to the members of the household, and even to the pages in attendance; while, at the same time, his behaviour to the Queen was marked with tender-

Singular delusion of the King.

ness, and even devotion. The object of this passion, a woman of sense and virtue, was much distressed by a preference so unwelcome and ridiculous. Every effort was made to estrange the King from a fancy unbecoming his years, and at variance with the whole tenour of his life. The lady removed from Court; and four days before Parliament was opened, Dr. Willis, with the Chancellor's concurrence, informed the King that he could not be pronounced capable of conducting public affairs while he continued under this delusion. Nevertheless, this painful symptom of a mind still affected by disease continued for some weeks, causing great anxiety to the Court and the ministers. At length, the lady herself, with great spirit and firmness, undertook to bring His Majesty to a sense of his delusion; in a long interview, she convinced him that his passion was hopeless, if not ridiculous; and, after some days of despondency, the delusion happily disappeared.*

The divisions in the royal family, consequent on the late events, were less easily repaired. The King had formed so just an estimate of the character of his eldest son, that the Prince's conduct seems to have given him neither pain nor surprise; but the ingratitude of the Duke of York, for whom he had a tender affection, wounded him deeply.† The Queen, so far as her cold and cautious nature permitted, had usually shown a preference for the Prince of Wales; but his recent conduct had inspired Her Majesty with a deep and just resentment. Instead of that support on which she would naturally desire to place her chief reliance in

<small>*Disagreements in the royal family.*</small>

---

* Lady Harcourt's *Diary*.—*Locker* MSS.

† 'It kills me—it goes to my soul—I know not how to bear it,' were his expressions when alluding to this subject. He repeatedly declared, that if the Regency Bill had passed, he should have regarded it as a statute of lunacy, and that nothing should have induced him to resume power.—*Locker* MSS.

the trying circumstances of her situation, the Queen had found in her son the chief of her opponents. The measures which she approved, as well for the management of the King's person as for the administration of public affairs, were alike thwarted and derided by the heir-apparent and his friends. The physicians who thought favourably of His Majesty's case, and were, therefore, more particularly consulted by the Queen, were treated as enemies to the Prince's interest. Dr. Warren, who maintained that the King was a confirmed lunatic, was openly and vehemently supported by the heir-apparent; while Dr. Willis, who predicted the King's recovery in a few weeks, was stigmatised by the Prince and his followers as an empiric and a creature of the Queen's. If the first Prince of the blood had been a dutiful son and a loyal subject, his treatment of his sisters would have been sufficient to stamp his character with the brand of cowardice and treachery. It seems that one of the contemplated measures of the Regency was the union of the Princesses with subjects; not with the view certainly of consulting the happiness of those exalted ladies, but with that of countenancing and confirming the Regent's marriage with a private gentlewoman. The Princesses, however—those at least who were of an age to have an opinion on the subject—did not very readily fall in with this plan. His Royal Highness revenged himself by slandering their characters.*
An incident, which occurred in the spring of this year, painfully exhibited the estrangement of the

---

* At a public ball soon after the King's recovery, at which the royal family were present, the Prince cast significant and contemptuous glances at the person of the Princess Royal, meaning to insinuate a calumny for which there was not the slightest foundation. The innocent lady was unhappily sensible of the insult, and mentioned it to Lady Harcourt, who relates the fact in her Diary. The Prince had selected three noblemen who were to marry the three elder Princesses.—LADY HARCOURT's *Diary; Locker* MSS.

royal family. The Duke of York having used an offensive expression with reference to the conduct of Colonel Lennox in some private affair, the colonel, after the usage among gentlemen in those days, demanded explanation or satisfaction. The Duke refusing the former, condescended to grant the latter alternative, and received, without returning, his adversary's fire. His Royal Highness, so far as he was concerned, could not without infamy have sheltered himself behind his rank; but the case was different as regarded Colonel Lennox. That gentleman was an officer of the King's Guards, and might well have doubted whether he was forced by the laws of honour to attempt the life of the King's son and heir-presumptive. Their Majesties at least might have been excused, if they had shown some displeasure towards a man who had been guilty of such conduct; but Colonel Lennox was received at Court immediately afterwards as usual; and, it was even said that the Queen treated him with marked approbation. Time, however, assuaged these griefs. The Duke of York recovered in a great measure, if not wholly, the affection of his father; and the Prince of Wales, to whom the Queen was always supposed to have shown a preference, was ultimately restored to Her Majesty's favour.

The Administration, which had approached so near to the term of its existence, was now reinstated in all its former power. The business of the session, though it resulted in no legislation of importance, was not without interest. Wilberforce, having recovered his health, now came forward as the champion of that great cause, which, while it spread his fame throughout the civilised world, redounded still more to the honour and glory of his country. He gave notice of a motion to consider the slave trade, with a view to its entire abolition. On the 12th of May, Wilberforce introduced

Wilberforce's speech on slavery.

the subject in a speech which made a deep impression
on the House and on the country, and which Burke
went so far as to compare to the finest efforts of
Demosthenes. Nevertheless, an attack on vested
interests of great magnitude, and on a lucrative trade,
provoked an angry opposition. The debates in the
Commons raged with a fury unknown to modern
times. The House, in accordance with a vicious
practice which then obtained, admitted evidence at
their bar on every Bill which affected the interests of
any class. The consequence was, that counsel made
long speeches to which nobody listened, and that witnesses made statements which it was not thought
worth while to subject to the ordinary tests of proof.
No definite result, therefore, was arrived at during
this session; and indeed many years elapsed before
such a result was attained; but the question was now
fairly launched on that career, more or less lengthened,
but always long, which every capital question in this
country has to run before it receives the impress of
the Legislature.

The other business of the session was not of memorable importance. Two provisions in the
financial arrangements of the year may,
however, be noticed as significant of the character of
the times, and the progress of public opinion. With
a view to extend the wise and beneficial measures for
the extension of legitimate, and the discouragement
of contraband trade, the Chancellor of the Exchequer
proposed to transfer the article of tobacco from the
Customs to the Excise. Time was, when a proposal
to extend the Excise Laws, involving, as they did, an
encroachment on the right of trial by jury, as well as
an odious system of inquisitorial visit, would have
shaken the Administration. But now attempts on
the part of the City Corporation, and of some other
public bodies, in connection with the manufacturers
of tobacco, to provoke an opposition to the proposal,

met with little or no encouragement. The people, who had formerly regarded an exciseman as, next to a soldier, most dangerous to their liberties, now looked upon him with indifference. Fox, indeed, in an outbreak of spleen, declared that the people were so changed that they had become, as it were, enamoured of the tax-gatherers, especially the excisemen, and that they accepted with eagerness and gratification the most wanton exercise of power. There was another tax in the budget of the minister which attracted hardly any notice, but which fifty years later would have raised an opposition such as no minister in latter days could withstand. This was an addition of a halfpenny to the stamp duty on newspapers, together with an increase of the advertisement duty. Yet so feeble was the power of the press, that no voice was raised in Parliament against this impost. The newsmen, indeed—a very different class from the capitalists now engaged in the business of retailing newspapers— petitioned against a part of the proposed tax, which prohibited the hiring of daily journals; but their humble protest was silenced by an adverse majority of three to one in the thinnest House of the session. The half-contemptuous terms in which Pitt referred to the commodity from which he proposed to derive a small addition to the revenue showed how little he appreciated the growth of those potent organs of public opinion, which, in a few years, were destined to control, if not to dictate, the policy of the minister. He knew not, he said, whether he was to call newspapers a luxury or an article of commerce, or, as some were extravagant enough to think, a mischief; he, however, was disposed to treat them with all possible respect, as most gentlemen would think it perhaps prudent to do. Referring to the increased number of newspapers, especially of late, when they had sprung up, one almost every month, he thought that these additional duties would be very well borne by them.

During the session, Lord Sydney having resigned the seals of Secretary of State, Grenville, the Speaker, was appointed his successor.

<small>Grenville succeeds Lord Sydney.</small>

Some difficulty was experienced in finding, at least on the ministerial side of the House, a person possessed of the peculiar qualities suited to the Chair. Since Onslow had retired at the commencement of the reign, after a rule of thirty-four years, the Chair had been filled by a succession of inferior Speakers. The consequence had been a marked deterioration in the character and conduct of the House. He was no ordinary man who could moderate the debates of an assembly, in which the strife of faction was more fierce than in any period of our history; in which Walpole, and Windham, and Yonge, and Pulteney, and Pitt, were leading orators. But though political conflict was carried on in the days of Speaker Onslow without quarter, and with a cruelty unknown to an age of comparatively civilised warfare, the haughtiest combatant and the most angry tumult yielded to the authority of the Chair. The successors of Onslow, after in vain employing expostulation and entreaty to quell disorder, continually resorted to threats of *naming* the ringleaders. But the great Speaker seldom had recourse to a proceeding which is only resorted to in the last extremity; and when he did announce the necessity of NAMING a contumacious or unruly member, he rarely had occasion to carry the awful menace into execution. Sir John Cust, the immediate successor of Onslow, was a weak man, who suffered his authority to be openly set at naught. Sir Fletcher Norton, who followed Cust, was coarse and insolent without firmness or dignity, and was constantly engaged in unseemly disputes with members who resisted his authority. Cornwall, who had recently filled the chair, was so little distinguished, that

when he died, not even a complimentary word was
bestowed on his memory, although he had filled the
office nearly nine years. Grenville, though he had
presided only during a part of a single session, had
satisfied the House that something more than knowledge and abilities were required for the Chair. Under
a weak and irresolute Speaker, the House must be in
a state of anarchy; though on the other hand, a dic-
tatorial style can never prevail with a fastidious and
high-spirited assembly. Grenville's manner was cold,
arrogant, and disagreeable; his knowledge of the law
and forms of parliament was imperfect; and the
House was little disposed to show deference to a
young man of thirty, merely because he inherited a
great parliamentary name, upon which he seemed to
presume to a degree hardly warranted by the ability,
which he unquestionably possessed.

After much hesitation, Pitt determined to place his
friend Addington in the chair. This was
certainly a bold step, and was justified only *Addington's antecedents.*
by the absence of any competitor with pretensions of
a decided character. Addington was the son of a
physician of some provincial repute, who had been
called into consultation on the late King's illness.
But Dr. Addington's son, instead of being Speaker at
thirty-two, and Prime Minister at forty-three, might
have passed his parliamentary life on the back benches
of the House of Commons, but for a happy accident.
His father had been Lord Chatham's physician; and
this circumstance led to the introduction of young
Addington as the early associate of William Pitt;
and, though no great friendship appears at any time
to have existed between them, yet this early onnec-
tion undoubtedly suggested Addington as a person
who, in the absence of any member better qualified,
might be eligible to the Chair of the House of Commons. This fortunate young man had been only five
years in Parliament, and during that period had done

nothing to distinguish himself from the crowd of followers whom the great popularity of his distinguished friend had brought into public life. With the exception of a good person, and an agreeable manner, Addington's qualifications were of a negative character. If he had not been eager to present himself to the House, it probably argued in favour of his good sense. If he had taken no prominent part in any public question, he had avoided collision with any interest or prejudice. Addington had been selected soon after he came into Parliament to second the Address; and a speech on seconding the Address is successful, if it is not ambitious, and if it touches on topics of controversy without provoking a reply. Such a success had been achieved by Addington. On one other occasion only had he been tempted to break the golden silence, which is so little appreciated by aspirants to a parliamentary position. If it could not be contended that Addington had shown eminent qualifications for the Chair, no man could make any objection to him. Sir Gilbert Elliott was again put forward by the Opposition, but Addington was elected by a majority somewhat larger than Grenville had obtained a few months before.

The session was protracted to an unusual period, Parliament not being prorogued until the 1st of August.

CHAPTER XXXI.

FRENCH REVOLUTION—AFFAIR OF NOOTKA SOUND—THE TEST ACT—A NEW PARLIAMENT—ABATEMENT OF IMPEACHMENT BY DISSOLUTION—THE SLAVE TRADE—THE RUSSIAN ARMAMENT—SEPARATION OF BURKE FROM THE WHIG PARTY—PROGRESS OF THE FRENCH REVOLUTION—RIOTS AT BIRMINGHAM.

SINCE the Treaty of Paris, England had been enabled to maintain peace; but though there might be no reason to apprehend a disturbance of friendly relations with foreign powers, the state of Europe during the years 1786-7-8 was far removed from tranquillity. Russia had begun to unfold those gigantic schemes of aggrandisement which modern statesmen have regarded as menacing the independence and civilisation of the Continent with a new irruption from the Northern hive. A new spoliation of Poland, which should annex to the vast dominions of the Czarina the fairest portion of the ancient territory of the Republic, was about to be perpetrated. The seizure of Bessarabia, Wallachia, and Moldavia, was in immediate contemplation. But the ambition of the Court of Petersburg was not bounded by the Danube. The restoration of the Lower Empire had long possessed the mind of Catherine; and one of her sons had been destined, at the font, to rule in the city of Constantine. The Crimea had already been appropriated; and a bloody war, which, on the side of the Christian power, was carried on in the savage spirit of a war of extermination, was raging between Russia and the Porte. Austria, under the rule of Joseph, the unworthy son

Russian policy.

of Maria Theresa, had become the ally and tool of
Russia. The independence of the Baltic powers was
in like manner menaced. Sweden had been insulted;
but her sovereign, Gustavus, had taken up arms with
a vigour and promptitude becoming the successor of
Charles the Twelfth. Denmark had been coerced
by Russia into an offensive alliance against her
neighbour, but was afterwards detached by the interference of the British minister at Copenhagen.

While Russia was making advances which seemed
to portend schemes of universal dominion,
France, though powerless for active aggression, was diligent in the prosecution of diplomatic intrigues against the interests of this country.
She succeeded in preventing a treaty of commerce
which Pitt had proposed to negotiate with the Court
of Petersburg. French agents were likewise busily
engaged in Holland, encouraging the democratic
party, which was animated by a bitter hostility to
this country, and ready to provoke a war with England if they could obtain the ascendant in the councils of the States. The intrigues of the French were
closely watched by Sir James Harris (afterwards Lord
Malmesbury), the English ambassador at the Hague;
and so critical were the circumstances, that a rupture
between the Courts of London and Versailles was
imminent during the negotiations for the great treaty
of commerce and amity which was afterwards effected.* The French intrigue, however, was brought
to a premature crisis by an outrage which the democratic party offered to the Princess of Orange.
Without any assignable reason, a body of soldiers,
acting by the local authority, stopped her carriage,
seized her person, and detained her prisoner. The
States of Holland avowed this proceeding, calculating

* Pitt to Lord Cornwallis, *Memoirs*.

that the insult put upon the consort of the Stadtholder would not be resented by that unworthy representative of the House of Orange. But the Princess was sister to the King of Prussia; and the successor of Frederick the Great demanded full and immediate reparation for the indignity put upon his blood. The insolent burghers still thinking that the King would not proceed to extremities, and counting on the support of France, refused compliance and made military preparations. But the policy of the French Court was entirely exploded by the violent and precipitate conduct of their Dutch allies; they were in no condition to engage in a war with Prussia, and probably with England. They advised the States of Holland to make the concession demanded by the Government of Berlin; and, upon their hesitation, the French ambassador was withdrawn from the Hague. The Prussian army, under the Duke of Brunswick, was advanced to the frontier of the Netherlands; and the Government of the States was required to give an answer to the King of Prussia within four days. The deputies returned a vaunting defiance, and the Prussian troops crossed the frontier. Their progress was almost uninterrupted. The democratic levies retreated; the towns opened their gates; the people, so far from rising in support of the patriots, hailed the invading army as their deliverers from an odious yoke. The Orange colours, which the ruling faction had peremptorily prohibited, dazzled the eye in every direction; and the Stadtholder, with his courageous consort, entered the Hague in triumph. The city of Amsterdam, behind the walls of which the discomfited faction attempted to make a stand, surrendered after a short resistance; and thus, after a campaign of three weeks, the authority of the House of Orange was restored, the democratic party was dispersed, and the government of the

United Provinces was replaced on it's ancient foundations. The States General then concluded treaties of alliance with the Courts of London and Berlin.

While France, intent upon a policy which should tend to the embarrassment and humiliation of England, was aiding a popular revolution in America, and encouraging a democratic resistance to establish authority in the United Provinces, the doctrines she had espoused had reacted with fatal effect upon her own institutions. Some of the greatest writers that ever influenced public opinion in any country flourished in Fance during the thirty years which preceded the fall of the monarchy. Voltaire, Rousseau, D'Alembert, Condorcet, Diderot, all wrote within this period; and the great ends to which they devoted their surpassing abilities were the subversion of those truths on which the eternal interests of mankind are founded, and of the principles on which civil government had hitherto proceeded. The whole intelligence of France, led by all that was distinguished in the most polite and brilliant society in the world, surrendered itself to the guidance of these illustrious teachers. It was proclaimed from the saloons of Paris, that Revelation was a falsehood; and that all the received maxims of civil policy were obsolete. Reason was the only guide of reasonable beings; and a republic after the pattern of antiquity was the only form of government suitable to an enlightened people. These doctrines, thoughtlessly ventilated as the sport of wit and wantonness, were taken up in a practical and earnest spirit by the millions throughout the country, labouring, as they were, under the oppression of religious and political institutions equally wicked and corrupt. The Revolution in the New World inflamed the imagination of the French people, and gave an impulse to the new opinions. The old monarchy was falling to pieces from corruption and decay. Vain efforts had been made to prop up the falling structure; and at length it fell with an awful crash, to the amazement and terror of mankind.

This tremendous event is to be dated from the 17th of June 1789. On that memorable day, the third estate of the States General, having absorbed the two other estates, declared itself the National Assembly, and assumed the supreme and undivided legislative authority. The abolition of the privileges of the nobility, the iniquitous and oppressive character of which justified resistance, was decreed by acclamation. The property of the Church was afterwards confiscated; and religion itself, though formally tolerated, was practically suppressed. A Declaration of the Rights of Man, wholly inconsistent with all received maxims of government, was promulgated by the National Assembly. The monarchy was thus virtually extinguished; the King was soon after detained a prisoner at the palace of the Louvre, to which His Majesty and the royal family had been dragged from Versailles with every circumstance of outrage and indignity. *The French National Assembly.*

The French Revolution was regarded with deep interest but with various feelings, in this country. The two nations had been hitherto accustomed to regard each other as rivals, and almost natural enemies; but the sudden and successful effort of the French people to throw off the yoke of despotism appealed to the sympathies of Englishmen, and recalled the glorious memory of similar struggles in which they had been engaged, and of the liberties which they had, in like manner, conquered. It was to be expected, therefore, that, in its earlier stages, the French Revolution should have excited a great amount of honest enthusiasm throughout these islands. This feeling was abated by the atrocious crimes which marked the bloody progress of democracy. The more ardent lovers of freedom were willing to *Opinions in England.*

palliate the cruel and tyrannical conduct of the popular party in France; and there were some who showed that they would not be unwilling, if they had the opportunity, to follow the examples of the Jacobin Club, and to emulate the excesses of the Parisian populace. But the bulk of the people were never infected by French principles.

When Parliament assembled after Christmas, the recent events in France necessarily became the subject of discussion in the House of Commons. The vote on the army estimates afforded the first opportunity for a debate on French affairs. The Government had thought fit to propose some augmentation of the forces; and as the standing army still excited some constitutional jealousy, the increased vote, at a time when the speech from the throne announced the continued existence of friendly relations with the European Powers, became the subject of animadversion. The leader of the Opposition seized this opportunity of expressing his admiration of the French Revolution, through the medium of a doctrine more subversive of freedom, and indeed of all civil government, than any opinion which had ever been uttered within the walls of the House of Commons. The example of a neighbouring nation, said Fox, had proved that the fear of standing armies was unfounded; since it was now shown, that by becoming a soldier, a man did not cease to be a citizen. Such a statement, made without any qualification, went to the root of the principle on which military discipline is based, and constituted the army the supreme judge and arbiter in all civil commotions. All the objections that have been urged by theoretical writers and popular orators against permanent military establishments, sink into insignificance when compared with the appalling magnitude of the danger attendant on an armed force which is to arbitrate in disputes or conflicts between the people and their rulers. The argument against a standing army is, in theory, at least, sound and intelligible; it is founded on the assumption of a soldier's implicit obedience to his officer; but Mr. Fox's language implied, that in questions of civil war or commotion, the soldier's obedience was reserved. If that were so, far better would it be to abandon the military defence of the country than to trust its defence to an army who should virtually be acknowledged as masters of the commonwealth. Occasions may arise when the soldier is justified in preferring his original duty as a citizen to the obligations of military allegiance; but such occasions are so rare, that no code, either of municipal or martial law, has ever held them in contemplation. Fox's panegyric on the army was suggested by the conduct of the French guards, a favoured corps, which had been seduced from their duty by the gross arts of the popular party, at a time when their helpless Sovereign was threatened with violence from a blood-thirsty and lawless multitude. Colonel Phipps, an officer in the English guards, repudiated with just indignation this scandalous and insulting compliment offered to his profession; but as the language of Fox was uttered in a thin House, no further notice was taken of it at this time; and it might have been passed over as a hasty ebullition in debate, had not the subject of the French Revolution been revived on the report of the votes for the army service.

It was known that Burke regarded the late proceedings in France in an unfavourable light; and as the opinions of this eminent *Burke's protest.* person were seldom tempered by moderation, everybody who knew him was prepared to bear unqualified praise or censure of events so momentous. On the 9th of February, Burke went down to the House of Commons, prepared with a solemn protest against the sympathy which the chief of his party had de-

clared for the French Revolution, and especially
against those loose and dangerous doctrines on the
obligations of military allegiance which Fox had
ventilated on the previous evening. The speech was
in his finest manner; not one of those strange com-
positions of fustian, vulgarity and nonsense which
had so often of late excited the derision of his audience, and grieved the few who can only regard with
pain the aberrations of genius; but grand, wise,
eloquent, affecting, worthy of the incomparable orator who had delivered the speeches on American Taxation, on Economical Reform, and on the wrongs of
India. It was long since anything uttered by Burke
had made any impression either in the House or on
the public. It was generally believed, that the genius
which had produced the 'Thoughts on the Causes of
the Present Discontents,' and the description of the
Carnatic, was on the decline, and that no sustained
effort of a similar kind could be expected in future.
But the speech of the 9th of February was the first
of a series of speeches and writings which were never
surpassed, and could only be equalled by the finest of
his own oratorical and literary achievements. The
effect produced upon the public mind by Burke's
speeches and essays on the French Revolution was
unparalleled. The horrors of that event were portrayed in their most revolting form. The cruelty,
the rapine, the anarchy, which attend the progress
of unbridled democracy, and the military despotism
which closes its career, were traced with the master's
hand. It is not probable that these islands could
have been extensively or permanently infected by
French principles; the English people had cause to
complain of defects in the constitution, and abuses
in the administration; but there was no ground of
comparison between the political and social condition
of England, and the political and social condition of
France, before the meeting of the States General in

1789. Nevertheless, the example of France had the effect of stimulating the demands for reform in the Government of this country, to an extent which was calculated to excite uneasiness, if not alarm. The genius of Burke checked the dangerous precipitation of these demands, rebuked the evil spirits which are ever ready to foment civil commotion, reassured the fainting hearts of those who had begun to despair of the fortunes of the commonwealth, and rallied round the altar and the throne, all who wished well to the united cause of religion and order.

Fox, whose mind had little depth or capacity, possibly thought that the French Revolution was an event which would immediately advance the liberty and happiness of the people; still more likely was he to regard it as a means which might indirectly be made available to turn out the Ministry, and bring himself and his friends into power. Burke's speech on the 9th of February seems to have suggested to the Whig leader some doubts whether he had not been hasty in committing himself to French principles; for he took occasion to qualify the rash opinion which he had expressed on the former day, with reference to the conduct and duty of the military profession. He said, that, in his allusion to the French army, he had gone no further than the general principle by which that army showed itself indisposed to be an instrument in the servitude of their fellow citizens, but did not enter into the particulars of their conduct. If Mr. Fox had merely enunciated an abstract opinion, that standing armies were not bound to make themselves instrumental to the servitude of their fellow citizens, every Englishman must have given his assent to such a doctrine; but his remarks were pointed to the conduct of the French Guards, who had deserted their duty without just cause, tempted only by the gross allurements held out to them by the revolutionary

Retractation of Fox.

party. It was evident, however, from the tone in
which he replied to Burke, that Fox was desirous to
avoid a breach with his old friend and coadjutor, and
that he was checked in the unbounded approbation
which he had been willing to bestow on the newly
developed principles of liberty in France; and the
debate might have closed satisfactorily, had not
Sheridan exasperated the incipient differences into a
bitter quarrel, by a violent speech in favour of the
French Revolution, and in praise of all its actors and
all their proceedings. Such sentiments might have
been expected from such a quarter. A man of desperate fortune, profligate habits, damaged character,
and great abilities, would not be unwilling to play
the part of Mirabeau, if an opportunity offered, or
could be made. Burke rose once more to denounce
the language of his former colleague, and to declare,
that thenceforth his path in political life lay in an
opposite direction to that of Sheridan. This interesting and momentous debate was summed up by Pitt
in a prudent and temperate speech, dictated by the
desire, so becoming a person in his position, to avoid
the discussion of French politics in the spirit of a
partisan. He did not hesitate, however, to draw the
distinction, so important to be observed, between
liberty harmonising with law and order, such as had
been ascertained for a century past under English
institutions, with a freedom which consisted only in
the ascendency and dictation of a tyrannical populace.

The House exhibited a novel and significant appearance during this debate. Burke's speeches were
received with great applause on the ministerial side;
but though the Opposition did not cheer, it was
manifest that their silence was not altogether the
silence of dissent. Sheridan's harangue on the other
side was received with ominous coldness by the
benches to which he usually looked to for applause.
On those benches sat men of high rank and great

estate, who loved liberty but not equality, and who were not disposed to offer up their rights and privileges as sacrifices on the altar of their country. The Whigs had no desire to see the Crown degraded, the peerage absorbed, or the Church abolished; and the language of Sheridan and Fox caused many of the Opposition to lend a willing ear to the eloquent warning of Burke. On the other hand, there were among that party, which had always stood by the great principles of civil and religious liberty, many eminent persons who thought that the French Revolution was justifiable, and should not be hastily condemned on account of the excesses which had discredited some of its proceedings. An attempt was made to accommodate the differences which threatened to break up the party; a meeting took place at the house of the Duke of Portland, comprising the principal members of the Opposition; but, after a conference which lasted five hours, the divergence of opinion was so great as to prove wholly irreconcilable. Burke was immovable in his hostility to the French reformers; and Sheridan was equally uncompromising in his support of the revolutionists. Fox adhered to the opinions he had already expressed; the consequence was, that many persons of note, who had hitherto acted with the Whig party, seceded from that connection.

The attention of Parliament and the country was for a time diverted from French affairs by a rupture with Spain. In the preceding summer, a Spanish vessel of war had made a descent upon a small trading settlement, which some Englishmen had formed on an unoccupied spot at the extremity of a neutral water on the north-west coast of America, then known by the name of Nootka Sound, but since called St. George's Sound. The Spaniards, claiming this place as part of the territory of the Catholic King, seized an English merchantman which lay in the Sound, and put the crew in irons. Other British merchant ships were subsequently captured by the Spanish cruiser, and all the property of the settlers was confiscated.

There was not the slightest pretence for those proceedings. No Spaniard had ever before visited the spot; and the English adventurers were the first Europeans who had landed there. They had settled some years before with the knowledge and sanction of their own Government; and they had acquired a title to the small territory which they occupied by treaty with the native chiefs. Several months elapsed before any authentic intelligence of this outrage reached England. When the facts were fully ascertained, a demand of ample reparation was of course made by the English Government. The Spanish ambassadors offered to restore the ships which had been seized, on the ground that the owners had been ignorant of exclusive pretensions of the Crown of Spain to the north-west coast of America. These terms were peremptorily rejected, and the British resident at the Court of Madrid was instructed to demand a full indemnity, and an unqualified recognition of the right of the British flag, to cover the navigation and commerce of British subjects, and to protect their settlements in countries which had not been appropriated by other European powers. The Spanish Court, after their fashion, protracted negotiations, and, in the meantime, made military preparations. The British Government were equally on the alert; the King sent a message to Parliament, and a vote of credit for one million was taken. The Spanish Government held out for some time, calculating on the support of France; and not without hope of effecting an offensive alliance with Russia or Austria. But, whatever part the Northern powers might have taken in the actual event of war, they were not disposed to embark in a Spanish quarrel. France, indeed, made an insidious offer of mediation, which probably meant the dictation of terms unfavourable to this country. The British Cabinet declined the proposal, and sent positive instructions to Fitzherbert, the minister at Madrid. Nevertheless, the negotiations were protracted for several months, during which the Cabinet of Madrid vacillated one way or the other, as they relied more or less on the support of the other powers. At length they yielded upon every point. The British adventurers were fully indemnified. The disputed territory was restored; the right of free navigation and commerce was conceded; the claims of Spain on the American coast were defined and settled; and those disputes relating to points involving considerations of no intrinsic importance to either party were brought to a conclusion without disturbing the peace of Europe. The treaty was not concluded until some months after the prorogation of Parliament. The proceedings of the session, unconnected with foreign affairs, were not of sufficient importance to require a detailed record. The claim of the Dissenters to a repeal of the Test Act, which had for several successive sessions been brought forward by a private member of no great station or authority, was this year revived, at the request of the Dissenters, under the auspices of Fox. In the preceding year, the motion had been defeated by so small a majority,* that hopes were entertained of a successful result on this occasion. It seemed absurd to attach importance to the retention, upon the statute book, of laws which had long become obsolete; and the operation of which had been suspended by a series of indemnity acts, since the year 1731. When the question of the repeal was brought before the House of Commons, in 1787, Pitt had consulted the bishops, but the whole bench, with the

* 122 to 102.

exception of Shipley and Watson, were against the proposal; and Pitt, though with evident reluctance, refused to give up this faded relic of an intolerant age. The motion was rejected by a majority of seventy-eight. Two years after, the majority had dwindled to twenty; but in 1790, while the number of those who were favourable to the removal of the disqualifications affecting Protestant Dissenters remained nearly stationary, the majority, on the other side, had increased to an overwhelming amount.* This result was significant, not certainly of a relapse to old sectarian bigotry, but as an indirect expression of the sense of the House of Commons, with reference to the events in France. Many of the non-conformist ministers had lately pointed, in terms of exultation, to the downfall of ecclesiastical establishments in the neighbouring State; and the claim of the Dissenters for relief from civil disability was consequently met as the first step towards the ulterior design of dismembering the constitution of the country. A cry of ' *The Church in danger!* ' once raised, is not easily allayed; and it was not until after the lapse of thirty-eight years, that the next attempt was made to repeal the Test and Corporation Acts. Circumstances were then propitious to such a proposal. The Legislature was on the eve of conceding the far more questionable point of Catholic Emancipation; and the epoch of parliamentary corruption was hastening to its close. Yet, even then, the Government which had just acceded to power, thought it worth while to resist the final repeal of laws, which had been annually suspended for eighty-five years past, and to sustain an adverse vote in the House of Commons on such a question! The very same Government, in the following year, proposed and carried the unconditional repeal of Roman Catholic disabilities.

* The division in 1790 was 299 against 105.

But if the time was inopportune for so small a measure of relief as that which the Dissenters asked, a more unfortunate season for renewing the question of Parliamentary Reform could hardly have been chosen. Neither of the party leaders ventured to stir a topic so inflammable at such a critical period. But Flood, the Irish orator, who had been connected with this question, not very much to his credit, in the sister island, conceived he had a vocation to take up the great question which Mr. Pitt had thought it prudent, for the present, to lay aside. He introduced the subject in a highly wrought oration, not exactly suited to the taste of the English House of Commons. The benches, which were filled by curiosity, were soon emptied by weariness and disappointment. Mr. Flood's plan was to increase the House by the addition of a hundred members, to be chosen by a county household suffrage. This notable proposal was, however, treated with decency, and underwent the formality of a debate. The motion was disposed of by the adjournment of the House.

Question of Parliamentary Reform.

The prorogation was followed by a dissolution of the Parliament which had entered the sixth year of its existence, and would consequently have expired by efflux of time in the following year. This event having, therefore, been foreseen, was looked forward to by the party out of power with the sanguine hope that it would improve their position. But the impulse which the movement in France had at first given to the progress of liberal opinions in this country had been suddenly checked by the frightful rapidity of the Revolution; and the people of England were more disposed to rally round the throne and their old institutions than follow an example of reform which was fast leading to anarchy and confusion. According to ordinary experience of the course of public opinion, a reflux of the impetuous tide, which had borne the new minister to the height

Parliament dissolved.

of power at the former elections, might have been
expected. But the prudent administration of affairs
during the past six years, and the advancing prosperity
of the country, had confirmed and extended the public
confidence in Pitt. Many supporters of the former
Ministry had, as usual, passed over to the successful
side; and many consistent Whigs, adverse to the
principles of the French Revolution, had viewed with
alarm the alacrity which the leaders of the party had
shown, in giving their adhesion to those principles.
Few, indeed, who were not personally interested in a
change of Ministry, thought this a convenient time
for disturbing the King's Government. The result
of the general election was, therefore, an increase of
the ministerial majority. Several prominent members
of the Whig party lost their seats. A remarkable
example of the decay of popularity which has no solid
foundation was the failure of John Wilkes to procure
his return for Middlesex. The Parliamentary career
of this once noted person was thus brought to a close.
Wilkes, though his talents and accomplishments were
far above those of an ordinary demagogue, never obtained the ear of the House. His parliamentary
efforts were chiefly directed to the removal from the
Journals of the celebrated resolution of the 17th
February, 1769, which declared his incapacity to sit
in Parliament. For successive years, he raised an
annual motion on this subject, which was invariably
opposed on both sides of the House. At length, in
1784, the House, weary of this antiquated dispute,
which had lost all interest, yielded the point without
further struggle, and the obnoxious entry was ex-
punged. When he found that sedition was out of
date, Wilkes affected the character of a staunch friend
to law and order; and, with amusing effrontery,
denied that he had ever been a *Wilkite*. There was,
indeed, much truth in this assertion; for at the very
time when his professions of patriotism were most

loud, he used to take pleasure in scandalising political puritans by the cynic impudence with which he avowed his contempt for such professions. The profligacy of his life and conversation were remarkable, even in a dissolute age. The badness of his character, no doubt, was an obstacle to his success in the House of Commons, but will not account for his utter failure. His character was not much worse than that of Fox, and hardly so bad as Sheridan's; but his talents, though eminently suited to influence a mob, and to shine in private society, were not adapted to that fastidious assembly, which has proved the grave of so many reputations founded on the platform and the hustings.

The new Parliament assembled in the autumn, and an attempt was made to get rid of the trial of Warren Hastings, of which both Houses were weary, and somewhat ashamed, by the pretence that the impeachment had abated in consequence of the dissolution. Erskine contended that the point was one for the Lords in their judicial capacity to determine, and that the Commons, as prosecutors, had no power to move further in the business until the law was laid down by the proper authority. It cannot be denied, that this view of the question was plausible, and, according to strict legal analogy, sound. On the other hand, the Speaker, founding himself on the precedents, advised the House that the impeachment was in full force. The precedents, however, were of no great value. The Lords had resolved, on the report of a Committee of Privileges in 1673, that their functions as a Court of Appeal were not determined by a dissolution of Parliament; but this did not settle the question as to the extraordinary proceeding by way of impeachment. The distinct question arose in the next Parliament, the trials of the Earl of Danby and the five Popish lords having been interrupted by a dissolution. The Committee of Privileges resolved, that impeachments stood on the same footings as appeals and writs of error; consequently they did not abate. But the decision of the Protestant Parliament of 1679 was reversed by the packed Parliament assembled under the influence of James the Second in 1685. It might be argued, that the latter decision was not entitled to much weight; but it was equally open to observation, that the resolution of 1679 was biassed by the strong prejudice against the popish lords. The question, therefore, in 1791 might be said to stand very much on its own merits; and as no political passion interposed in the particular case, to sway the judgment of Parliament, a decision, founded on high legal and constitutional grounds, might be fairly arrived at. The opinion in Westminster Hall was in favour of the abatement. The great legal authorities in the Commons, the Master of the Rolls, the Attorney-General, and Sir John Scott, were of that opinion. The Lord Chancellor and the Lord Chief Justice in the Upper House argued against Lord Loughborough, the only law lord who opposed the doctrine of abatement. But the majority in both Houses took the more enlarged view of the question. The lawyers argued, that an impeachment was more in the nature of an inchoate parliamentary proceeding, such as a bill or motion, than a legal process; and as a bill of attainder would lapse by a dissolution, so should an impeachment. But this argument proved too much, for a bill was terminated by a prorogation; but the impeachment of Hastings had continued over several prorogations, yet its validity had never been disputed on that account. But, though it was resolved that the impeachment should proceed, the debates on the subject extended over so large a portion of the session, that little or no progress in the trial was made during this year. The trial had, in fact, dwindled to a merely formal proceeding, from which all life and spirit had departed. It was necessary to arrive at a result, about which there was no longer any doubt, by slow and tedious stages, which interested nobody, though they were oppressive and indeed ruinous to the accused, who might have to wait for years, as, in fact, he did wait, until the verdict of acquittal, long since agreed upon, should be formally pronounced.

Other questions of great importance were agitated with vigour by the new Parliament. The *Religious liberty.* cause of religious liberty, after an interval of twelve years, was advanced a further, though not a very long stage, by the repeal of a variety of disabling statutes, affecting persons professing the Roman Catholic faith. The benefit of this relief was, however, limited to persons who should abjure the power of the Pope to absolve them from their allegiance, a qualification which was objected to by Fox, on the ground that the exaction of religious tests was contrary to the broad principle of toleration. But opinion was not yet sufficiently liberal, especially as regarded the claims of this class of religionists, for such a concession. The Romanists themselves asked for no more than was offered them by the Bill, and especially disclaimed any idea of seeking admission to civil offices of power and trust. The Bill, which did little more than abolish laws which had long been obsolete, gave rise to some curious discussions on religious freedom, but passed both Houses without any serious opposition.

Another measure, of far more practical importance, was Fox's Bill for enabling juries to give a general verdict in cases of libel. For *Right of juries to decide as to libels.* many years the press had struggled in vain against the doctrine laid down in Westminster Hall, that the province of the jury was confined to the fact of publication, and the application of the writing as pointed by the inuendoes; but that the character of the publication, whether libellous or otherwise, was exclusively a question for the Court. Lord Camden, and some other lawyers, took the popular view of the question; but Lord Mansfield, with the great majority of the judges, supported by the current of authority since the Revolution, maintained the separate functions of the court and jury. The point had been frequently raised in the State trials; and upon a motion for a new trial, on the ground of misdirection, in the great case of the Dean of St. Asaph in 1784, the argument had been stated, with an ability seldom equalled in Westminster Hall, by Erskine, the counsel for the defendant. Lord Mansfield, on that occasion, laid down the law in a judgment of equal ability with the argument at the bar; and from that time the doctrine of the King's Bench was considered settled law.

An attempt had been made twenty years before, under the auspices of Chatham, to settle this question by a Bill substantially the same as that which Fox now introduced. That Bill miscarried in the Commons, in consequence of a disagreement between the First Minister and the Chancellor of the Exchequer; but had it reached the Upper House, it is not likely that the Bill would have passed into a law in the face of the opposition, which it would certainly have encountered, of Lord Mansfield, at that time in the vigour of his authority. But the great Chief Justice no longer dictated law in Westminster Hall; and his successor, Kenyon, an uncouth special pleader, was not listened to in that assembly which the graceful eloquence of Mansfield had swayed for thirty years. The Bill for placing the liberty of the press under the protection of trial by jury, brought in by the Whig chief, appropriately supported by Erskine, and assented to by the son of Chatham, passed the House of Commons almost without a dissenting voice: in the Lords it met with a favourable reception; but Thurlow, in mere waywardness, made a difficulty, and succeeded in postponing the Bill for the session. In the following year, however, it passed into law.

The discussion on the slave trade was revived during this session, and so much progress had the question made by means of agita- *Wilberforce's motion.* tion out of doors, that the ardent friends of humanity, who, when the matter was first brought before Parliament three years before, thought it prudent to disclaim any intention of seeking more than the prohibition of the trade in slaves, now avowed their ultimate object to be the abolition of slavery throughout the British dominions. Wilberforce, however, on this occasion limited himself to a Bill 'to prevent the further importation of African negroes into the British colonies.' The arguments in support of the motion were obvious—the injustice, the immorality, the impiety, the cruelty of the traffic. All these considerations were enforced with great power and many striking examples, by some of the ablest men on either side of the House. Both Pitt and Fox supported the motion; but the strength of vested interests, and the indisposition to sudden change, so far prevailed, that the motion was negatived by a majority of seventy-five.

In this session, the prosperous and triumphant minister sustained a reverse on the first important question of foreign policy on *Case of Oczakow.* which the House of Commons had been called upon to pronounce an opinion since his accession to power. The designs of Russia on the Danubian provinces and on Constantinople have been mentioned. In pursuance of the policy which aimed at the conquest and annexation of Turkey, the Empress in 1788 had taken military possession of the fortress of Oczakow, which commanded the road to Constantinople. This formidable aggression seems to have hardly attracted the attention of the English Government, until an urgent representation was made by Prussia of the danger which threatened the balance of Europe from the aggrandisement of the Russian Empire. Pitt was at length so impressed by a danger, which has long been established as one of the first magnitude in the estimation of modern statesmen, that he determined to check the ambition of the Court of St. Petersburg. Accordingly, in March of this year, he brought down a message from the Crown for a vote of credit. This novel view of foreign policy was most strenuously opposed; for it had ever been the maxim of the Whigs to cultivate friendly relations with the great Northern Power.* Circumstances, however, had changed. The avowed intention† of the Empress to take possession of Constantinople, and the progress she had made in carrying that intention into effect, in open defiance of the earnest remonstrances of the British Government,‡ was supposed to justify a military demonstration on the part of this nation. But Pitt, in this instance, seems hardly to have acted with his usual prudence. A military menace to a great power like Russia, in the full career of conquest and with vast resources, was likely to irritate, but certain not to deter. War with Russia seemed to be hardly in contemplation; and a war undertaken without alliance, except the doubtful alliance of Prussia, for an object which concerned all Europe, would have been, at the best, but an ill-considered enterprise. The Russian armament was, in fact, a mistake, and disclosed the weak point in the statesman who had conducted the domestic affairs of

---

* 'Alliances with the Northern Powers ever have been, and ever will be, the system of every enlightened Englishman.'—Fox to Harris, April 11, 1783.—*Malmesbury Correspondence*, vol. ii. p. 40.

† Adolphus's *History*, vol. v. p. 20.

‡ *Ibid.*

the country with such signal prudence and success.
The Opposition made a vigorous attack on this policy,
which was defended with unwonted hesitation on the
part of the Government. The country, for the first
time during the last six years, showed tokens of disapprobation; the majorities in the House of Commons
were diminished on every successive vote relating to
this question; and at length, the Ministry, finding
their policy was not understood, and that there was
no probability of obtaining that support which could
alone enable them to interpose with success in an
affair of such magnitude, were content to abandon
the projected armament altogether. The Duke of
Leeds, who held the office of Secretary of State for
Foreign Affairs, quitted the Ministry in consequence
of this decision. He was succeeded by Lord Grenville,
the late Speaker, who had lately been advanced to
the peerage. In the autumn of this year, the Empress of Russia, wishing to prosecute her longcherished designs on Poland, concluded a peace with
the Porte; and thus, for the present, the schemes
which threatened a disturbance of the balance of
power in this part of Europe were suspended.

This session, in which so many topics of the
greatest interest and importance were discussed, was remarkable also for the formal *Breaking-up of the Whig party.*
separation of Burke from the Whig party, and the
consequent disruption of the party itself on the vital
question of the French Revolution. In one of the
debates on the Russian armament, Fox had taken
occasion to pronounce an elaborate eulogy on the
French constitution,* describing it as 'altogether the
most stupendous and glorious edifice of liberty which

---

* Lord John Russell notes the fact, that this eulogy was pronounced some months before the Constitution was called into existence.—*Life of Fox*, vol. ii p. 251. In the debate on the recommitment of the Quebec Bill, Fox corrected this mistake, but made the matter worse, by saying that his panegyric applied not to the Constitution but to the *Revolution*.

had been erected on the foundation of human integrity in any time or country.' The Whig leader had, in addition to this, taken every opportunity which the license of debate afforded, to allude, in terms of approbation, to the proceedings in France. Burke, on the other hand, had entered on the great literary and oratorical warfare against French principles and proceedings, which produced a more powerful effect on public opinion in this country than any speeches or writings before or since. The *Thoughts on the French Revolution* had been published in the last autumn, and was in the hands of every man who took an interest in the prodigious events which convulsed the neighbouring country, and agitated civilised Europe. The wide popularity which this book obtained, incensed the democratic party, and dashed the hopes of a section of the Opposition, who, willing to return to power on any terms, had endeavoured to convert the French Revolution to their purpose. Burke, therefore, as the champion of religion and order, was to be borne down by obloquy and clamour. The press, the platform, and even the pulpits of non-conforming congregations, were made use of for the propagation of revolutionary doctrine, and defamation of Burke. In the House of Commons, Sheridan took the lead in this unworthy warfare; and Fox, carried away by the vehemence of his nature, habitually used language which exaggerated his real opinions. At length, the collision, which had been long expected, took place between the two eminent men who had for so many years stood in the front of the great Whig party.

Early in the session, a Bill was introduced by the Government, for the division of the province of Canada, and for the establishment of a local legislature in each division. This measure was in itself remarkable, as recognising, for the first time, the wise and generous principle of independent

Canada Bill

colonial institutions, which has since been fully developed in every dependency of the British Crown, capable of local self-government. The line of demarcation, marked by the difference of religion and race, was traced in the division of the province into Upper and Lower Canada. The former was inhabited chiefly by English and American settlers, belonging mainly to different denominations of the reformed faith; Lower Canada being occupied almost exclusively by the old French emigrants, members of the Roman Catholic Church. The main institutions of the mother country were laid down as the political basis of the Canadian States: Socage tenure of land; an allotment of land in the Upper Colony for a Church establishment; the *habeas corpus* and freedom of taxation. Provision even was made for the foundation of hereditary chambers, by titles of honour which should descend like peerages in this country. The creation of an aristocracy by Act of Parliament was, however, soon found to be impracticable; and this part of the scheme has never been carried into operation. The creation of an ecclesiastical establishment, by the appropriation of a part of the territory of Upper Canada in mortmain was hardly adapted to modern ideas, or to the exigencies of a rude and scattered population; the clergy reserves, therefore, were strongly objected to by the Canadian people, and were a cause of strife between the colony and the Imperial Government, until they were finally abandoned to colonial legislation by the Act of 1853. On the whole, however, the Quebec Bill was a plan worthy of the minister who conceived it, and constitutes one of his titles to the enduring reputation of a statesman.

The Bill passed through its earlier stages without opposition, and almost without discussion; Opposition of but on the report, Fox, for the sake of re- Fox. peating and enforcing the French creed of freedom

which he had adopted with the zeal of a proselyte,
moved the recommittal of the Bill. He complained
that the Bill had not been framed on the new model
of liberty; that the proposed assemblies of the provinces would not sufficiently provide for the representation of the people; that the duration of the
provincial parliaments should be annual or triennial;
and that the qualification of the electors was too high.
He inveighed against the introduction of titles of
honour and hereditary rank: antiquated distinctions
which might be tolerated in old countries where they
had long existed, but were unsuited to communities
constituted on modern principles. He sneered at
Burke's famous lament over the fall of chivalry,* and
deprecated the revival in Canada of those odious
artificial distinctions which had been exploded in the
country from which that colony derived its origin.

Quebec Bill. Burke was not present at the delivery of this speech, which, though ostensibly on the Quebec Bill, was really levelled at the writings and speeches of the great Conservative orator. On the recommittal of the Bill, Burke determined to reply to the attack which had been made

Fox's visit to Burke. upon him in his absence. On the day when the Bill was to come on, before the House met, Fox, who had lately shunned the society of Burke, visited his old friend, and a long and earnest conversation took place between these two great men before they separated for ever. Fox, whose warmth of heart was his redeeming virtue, could not contemplate without emotion the dissolution of a friendship which had been uninterrupted during the vicissitudes of twenty years. He endeavoured therefore to dissuade his old colleague from taking this opportunity of broaching the subject of the French Revolution, a request which was

---

* *Reflections on the Revolution in France*, vol. iii. p. 111, 4to. edit.

hardly reasonable, after the course he had himself taken. Burke refused to comply, and gave Fox the outline of the speech he intended to make. The friends walked down to the House together for the last time; but this being the last day before the adjournment for the Easter recess, they found the question had been postponed.

On the 6th of May, the Bill was recommitted; and no sooner had the chairman taken his place at the table than Burke rose, and plunged at once into the subject of the French Revolution. *Burke's violent speech on the Quebec Bill.* For a time he shaped his remarks with such a reference to the question before the committee, as kept him tolerably within the line of order; but he soon forgot Canada, and launched into an invective against the doctrines of the Rights of Man. From thence he passed to a description of the indignities offered to the King and royal family of France by the Parisian populace; a topic which had no bearing whatever on colonial affairs. He was therefore called to order. This was the commencement of a scene of confusion and excitement, the like of which has probably never since been witnessed in the House of Commons. Mr. Baker, who spoke to order, was content to object to the irrelevancy of the line of argument upon which Burke had entered, and called upon the chairman to state the question; but Fox, who, notwithstanding his much vaunted good nature, was throughout his parliamentary career singularly intolerant, acrimonious, provoking and personal in debate, interposed in a manner calculated to disturb the equanimity of any man, and certain to irritate Burke beyond control. He affected to defend the course which Burke was taking; 'this,' said he, with bitter irony, 'was a day of license, on which any gentleman might get up, and abuse any Government he pleased. To be sure, the French Revolution had no more to do with the question before the committee than the Government of Turkey, or the laws of Confucius; but what of that?' Stung by the taunt, Burke retorted in anger, and compared his position with that of Cazales, the great Conservative orator of the National Assembly, whose voice was always drowned by the clamour of the friends of liberty. Notwithstanding repeated interruptions from members who rose to order, Burke still persevered, but was at length met by loud calls for the Chair from the Opposition, answered by equally loud shouts of 'Hear!' from the ministerial side. An angry debate ensued, in which Fox, Grey and Pitt, took part. At length, Lord Sheffield, acting on a suggestion thrown out by Pitt, moved 'That dissertations on the French Constitution, and to read a narrative of the transactions in France, are not regular or orderly on the question, and that the clauses of the Quebec Bill be read a second time.' This amendment, however, was calculated to defeat the object of the mover. A dexterous and practised debater could easily avail himself of such a question as this to introduce the very topic which it was intended to exclude. Pitt, in speaking to the motion, observed, that it was important to discriminate between a point of discretion and a point of order, and though he could have wished that a more fitting opportunity had been taken to discuss the late proceedings in France, he could not say that an allusion to the constitutions of other countries was altogether foreign to the question of a new constitution for Canada. Fox, whose impetuosity was only less impatient of restraint than that of Burke, in his turn broke over the bounds of order, and dashed off in defence of the French Revolution. To make the inconsistency and irregularity of the whole proceeding complete, he did this in seconding Lord Sheffield's motion for confining the debate to the subject before the committee. He maintained,

that the rights of man were the foundation of every
sound political system, and that he had first learned
this doctrine from Burke himself. He rejoiced that
France had founded her new constitution on this
principle, on which the British constitution was
founded. He charged Burke with deserting his
principles, and quoting a fine expression of his own
with reference to the American war, with drawing
an indictment against a whole people.

When Fox sat down, Burke rose slowly from his
seat. For some years past he had lost the *Burke's reply to*
ear of the House. His want of taste and *Fox.*
temper had revolted an assembly singularly patient
of dulness and folly, but intolerant of offences against
good manners. His conduct on the Regency Bill
had sunk him so low, that it seemed hardly possible
he should ever recover any influence either in the
House or in the country. His violence against
Hastings had shocked every person who respected
the English virtues of justice and fair play. His
opposition to the French Commercial Treaty, so utterly at variance with the sound doctrines of political
economy which he had enunciated a few years before,
seemed to indicate a decay of his faculties, rather
than a change of his opinion. But the Indian speeches
were sufficient to refute this idea, and proved that,
with a fitting topic and adequate preparation, his
oratorical power and grasp of intellect were unimpaired. On these special occasions, the great
rhetorician could still command an audience; but
in the height of his reputation, when it was known
that Burke was to make a great speech, his rising
had never been looked for with more eager expectation
than was manifested on this ' 6th of May, which was
to commemorate the division of the Whig party into
two sections; the one embracing the new doctrines
of French democracy; the other adhering to the old
English principles of constitutional liberty.'

Burke spoke for some minutes in a subdued tone, as resolved that no intemperance of language should injure the cause which he had most at heart. He said, though he had been frequently called to order, he had listened, without interrupting it, to a speech, the most disorderly perhaps that had ever been delivered within those walls. He complained that a personal attack had been made upon him by one of his oldest friends; that his language and conduct had been misrepresented; that not only his public acts, words and writings had been arraigned, but that even *confidential conversation* had been divulged, for the purpose of convicting him of inconsistency. After a short excursion on French affairs, he returned to the difference between himself and Fox. He reviewed the subjects on which they had disagreed, during the twenty-five years of their political connection and private friendship. Of these, Parliamentary Reform, the Dissenters' question, and the Royal Marriage Act were the chief; but differences on such matters had never for a moment interrupted their friendship. It was indiscreet, he said, at any period, and especially at an advanced time of life, to provoke enmity, or to risk the loss of friendship; but if his fidelity to the British constitution placed him in such a dilemma, he would risk all, and his last words should be, 'Fly from the French constitution.' At this point, Fox interrupted, with an eager whisper, 'There was no loss of friends.' 'Yes,' said Burke, in a loud voice, 'there *is* a loss of friends. I know the penalty of my conduct. I have done my duty at the price of my friend—our friendship is at an end.' He then, as though he were himself taking leave of the scene, solemnly adjured the two great rivals in that House, whether they moved in opposite spheres, or walked like brethren, hand in hand, to guard the British constitution.

Fox immediately rose, but so great was his emotion, that he could not utter a word; nor was it until tears had come to his relief, that he was enabled to proceed. He complained in broken accents, that a friendship of more than twenty years should be terminated by a difference of opinion on a political question. They had differed on other matters without disturbing their friendship; why not on this? He complained that Burke had held him up as professing republican principles, and had applied ignominious terms to his conduct; but when Burke denied this, Fox, willing to grasp at the slightest overture of returning kindness, declared that such expressions were obliterated from his mind for ever; and alluding to Burke's complaint of the frequent interruptions he had received, affirmed that he had done everything in his power to discountenance such conduct. *Fox's complaint against Burke.*

Burke, in his reply, plainly intimated that all hope of a reconciliation was at an end. His feelings were too much involved with his opinions on this all-important question, to admit the intercourse of private friendship with a man who upheld revolution and anarchy, in their most hideous aspects. He spoke without passion; but reiterated his former sentiments with a solemn and fervid earnestness, which made a deep impression on the House. Pitt concluded this remarkable debate, with some high compliments to Burke, who was thenceforth to be considered a supporter of the Administration. *Severance of Burke from Fox's party.*

The subject was renewed a few days after at the next sitting of the committee on the Quebec Bill. On that occasion, Fox showed a marked desire to qualify, and even retract many of the extravagant sentiments which he had uttered with reference to the French Revolution. He pronounced a laboured panegyric on the aristocracy, *Fox inclined to retract.*

which he described as the balance of the Constitution; maintaining the mean between monarchy on the one side, and democracy on the other. His former speeches on the subject of the French Revolution were, both in sentiment and expression, such probably as no demagogue in the present day would venture to address to the House of Commons; this speech was of a kind which a high Tory would hardly now give utterance to in a debate on a Reform Bill. The truth was, that many of his followers in both Houses had intimated their disapproval of the democratic opinions lately ventilated by the Whig chief, and were desirous of preventing the breach, which the secession of Burke on a question of such moment was likely to produce in the Whig party. Fox, himself, found that he had gone too far; hence his subdued tone on the 11th of May. But it was too late; the breach had been made, and was irreparable; not only had the old Whig statesman been attacked in Parliament; but the revolutionary press, a portion of which was under the control of the Opposition leaders, had opened upon him, as their most formidable foe, the battery of slander, menace and scurrility. Burke, therefore, was not to be propitiated by a few phrases, such as might have fallen of yore from the lips of George Grenville, or of John, Duke of Bedford. On the contrary, he was rather disposed to repel any overture from his old allies, as an attempt at compromise, which would deprive him of the power effectually to resist that irruption of democracy, which threatened to destroy the ancient institutions of the land. Deep resentment had taken possession of his soul. The hootings and interruptions in the House; the sharp-pointed attacks of Fox, Sheridan, and other members of the Opposition; the clamour and mendacity of the declaimers, pamphleteers and newswriters out of doors; of all these he bitterly complained, as the result of a conspiracy to ruin his reputation, and cover his age with infamy. He defended his consistency, and said that he now supported the monarchy, not because it was better than aristocracy or democracy, but because it was assailed and put in peril. He was told, that if he would repent, he might be received again by the party which had discarded him. 'But,' said the proud old man, 'though I have been disgraced in my age, I am content to stand alone; I seek not the friendship of the right honourable gentlemen, or that of any man on either side of the House.'

The session was brought to a close on the 10th of June; but the great controversy which had agitated the House of Commons was not wholly abandoned to the meaner spirits of the platform and the press. Burke himself took advantage of a formal announcement that had been made in the principal journal of the Opposition,* that he had been repudiated by the party, to publish a sort of supplement to his work on the French Revolution, under the title of 'An Appeal from the New to the Old Whigs.' The principal work had excited an amount of enthusiasm such as hardly any publication before or since has created. The sale, at a price, which was never lowered, reached thirty thousand in a few weeks. The replies were numerous; but none of them are remembered except the 'Rights of Man,' by Thomas Paine, and the 'Vindiciæ Gallicæ,' by Macintosh. The former writer had gained reputation in America during the War of Independence, by the vigour of his attacks on the British Government and on monarchical institutions. The famous Declaration of In-

---

* 'The great and firm body of the Whigs of England, true to their principles, have decided on the dispute between Mr. Fox and Mr. Burke; and the former is declared to have maintained the pure doctrines by which they are bound together, and upon which they have invariably acted. The consequence is that Mr. Burke retires from Parliament.'—*Morning Chronicle*, May 12, 1791.

dependence, on which the Constitution of the United States is founded, was drawn up from the writings of Paine. The author of the 'Rights of Man' undertook to show that both monarchy and aristocracy were incompatible with those rights; that religion was open to the same objection; and he held up the French constitution as a model of government which realised the theory of political truth and justice. The book was written in a plain and forcible, though a coarse and unlettered style. The tone, the arguments and illustrations were admirably calculated to hit the taste of the vulgar, the envious and half-educated. By this class of persons, therefore, the author was received as an apostle; but it does not appear that he made many converts. On the contrary, his work, assailing as it did every established institution with unbounded ribaldry and insolence, reacted in favour of religion and order. The writings of Paine have probably done as much as the writings of Burke to bring republican doctrines into disrepute, and to confirm well-disposed people in their attachment to the old institutions of this country. The work of Macintosh was one of a very different character, as Macintosh was a very different man from Paine. The 'Vindiciæ Gallicæ,' though it defended the principles, and excused the errors and even the crimes of the Revolution, was nevertheless a book which a man of taste and candour might read without disgust. The author was an obscure student of law, but he wrote in the spirit of a scholar and a gentleman; Burke sought the acquaintance of his able and candid opponent. A friendship soon sprang up between these generous disputants; and, in after years, when Sir James Macintosh was recognised as one of the wisest and best of the Whig party, he revered the memory of the illustrious adversary whom he alone, of all the writers of the day, had assailed with success.

The democratic party were not content with recommending their doctrines by the agency of the press. They sought to take advantage of an opportunity so favourable, to precipitate a revolution in this country, and to found a republic on the ruins of the altar and the throne. For this purpose, associations were organised in connection, and in direct correspondence, with the political clubs at Paris. The Revolution Society, an old connection principally of Dissenters, formed to commemorate the principles and the transactions of 1688, had, in 1789, been abused to the purposes of the modern revolutionists, by some of the earliest admirers of French liberty in this country. The Revolution Society, which had of late years fallen into decay, held its anniversary meeting at the London Tavern, on the 4th of November, in the first year of the French Revolution. Earl Stanhope, a peer remarkable for his eccentricities, took the chair, and an address of congratulation to the National Assembly of France on the triumph of liberty and justice over arbitrary power, was voted by the society. In the morning, Dr. Price, the well-known and able Presbyterian minister, who had gained so much reputation by his scheme for the payment of the national debt, and who had moved the address to the National Assembly, delivered a political sermon to his congregation in the Old Jewry. This strange discourse promulgated constitutional doctrine as unsound as the financial dogmas which had made the name of the preacher famous. Other friends of freedom had been content to recommend the adoption of the French code of liberty as a new and brilliant discovery in political science; but Dr. Price undertook to prove that it was nothing more than a development of the principle established by our revolution a century before. By that revolution, according to Dr. Price, it was intended to establish the right of the people to choose

Revolution society.

their rulers, to retain them only during good behaviour, and to change the government at their pleasure. Whatever may be urged in support of these positions, it is certain that they derived no authority from the statesmen of 1688, who were studious to avoid speculative and abstract questions of government. This was demonstrated by Burke in his great work with an amplitude of argument and illustration. But the Revolution Society was not sufficient even for the purposes of the Opposition. Another association, called the Friends of the People, was formed under the direction of Mr. Grey and other leading Whigs, for the express purpose of promoting the cause of Parliamentary Reform. Fox, who had learned, from the example of France, the effect of these clubs in superseding Parliament, and diverting public opinion into a channel over which the House of Commons would have no control, expressed his disapprobation of them;* but he had not sufficient firmness to resist a movement to which his friends had already committed themselves. Other clubs, affiliated to the clubs in Paris, were established in London and the principal towns in Great Britain. The proceedings of an association, called the Unitarian Society, consisting of persons belonging to the denomination of Dissenters which its title imported, led to disastrous consequences. Dr. Priestley, a teacher of the Unitarian persuasion, a pious and learned man, though of extreme political opinions, had lately employed himself in propagating the revolutionary doctrines at Birmingham, where he resided. He seized the occasion of the death of Dr. Price, who first set the example, which had been extensively followed, of making the dissenting pulpit available for the dissemination of the new political faith, to preach a funeral sermon, holding up the American and French

* Lord J. Russell's *Life of Fox*, vol. ii. p. 281.

republics as models for imitation in this country. The people of Birmingham, who were, for the most part, still attached to the old-fashioned principles of Church and King, resented an attack upon the fundamental institutions of the country, which they considered alike indecent and unwarrantable. A bitter animosity, such as religious differences frequently create, had long raged between the adherents of the Establishment and the dissenting body in Birmingham; the latter were in possession of most of the municipal offices, and Churchmen were practically disqualified from any participation in the local government. The agitation for the repeal of the Test Act in the preceding year had, consequently, caused greater excitement at Birmingham than in any other part of the country; and the open union of dissent with democracy, as adopted by Dr. Priestley, both in his sermons and in his writings, but more especially in the latter, irritated and alarmed the public feeling in that town to a degree which indicated the probability of an outbreak upon any further provocation. This provocation was unhappily supplied by an indiscreet announcement on the part of the Unitarian Society, of their intention to celebrate the anniversary of the destruction of the Bastille, which was held to be the inauguration of the French Revolution, by a public festival in the town of Birmingham. The meeting was preceded by inflammatory handbills, distributed, as the projectors asserted, not by themselves, but by their opponents, for the purpose of discrediting their intentions. It was in vain, however, that the promoters of the meeting disavowed all connection with the offensive handbills; a strong feeling against the Dissenters was manifested through the town, and the principal persons concerned in the arrangement of the dinner were disposed, under the circumstances, to relinquish their purpose. But the counsels of the rash and violent, as usual in such matters, prevailed; and though many of the respectable persons who had been engaged in the preliminary proceedings, and among them Priestley himself, refused to attend the celebration, a diminished number of about eighty persons assembled on the appointed day, the 14th of July. A great crowd gathered outside the building, and assailed the guests as they arrived with hootings, execrations, and shouts of 'Church and King!' The crowd increasing in number and excitement, the dinner-party was abruptly terminated, and the company separated at an early hour. The populace having demolished the windows of the hotel, dispersed, intent on mischief and plunder. A Dissenting meeting-house was set on fire; another was pulled down. One portion of the mob proceeded to the house of Dr. Priestley in the suburb, and set it on fire, the family having barely time to make their escape. The library, philosophical apparatus and manuscripts, containing the labours of a life devoted for the most part to scientific investigations, were utterly destroyed. The houses of several other obnoxious persons were, in like manner, burned or battered down. The riots continued, without effectual interruption from the civil power, from Thursday until Sunday night, when the exhausted rabble were suppressed by a small military force. The damage done during these three days was only measured by the physical capacity of the mob. Not only were numerous houses in the town plundered and destroyed; but several country houses of wealthy individuals were wholly or partially demolished. It was said, that the movements of the mob were directed by persons of superior station; that they were incited by the clergy, and even that the magistracy were unwilling to interfere; but no proof of these allegations was offered either in a court of justice, or before the parliamentary committee which enquired into these disgraceful transactions. The rabble of a large town are always ready to take advantage of any excuse for riot and plunder. The disturbances no doubt originated in political and religious dissension; but the riots of Birmingham in 1791 had as much to do with the cause of Church and King, as the riots in 1780 had to do with the maintenance of the Protestant faith.

Twelve persons only suffered the penalties of the law for these outrages. Three were executed; one was pardoned after sentence; the others were punished according to the degrees of guilt proved against them. The rioters who perished in the flames they had raised, and who died of intoxication, were far more numerous than the convicted offenders. The persons whose property had been injured or destroyed, recovered damages from their respective hundreds, to the aggregate amount of about twenty-seven thousand pounds. But no compensation could repair the losses of Dr. Priestley, and Mr. Hatton, the mathematician. Such, however, was the exasperated state of party feeling, that the misfortunes of these respectable persons were regarded more with exultation than sympathy by those who were opposed to their religious and political opinions. Dr. Priestley appealed to the public both by speeches and writings; but his complaints attracted little notice, and he soon after retired to the more congenial region of the American United States.

CHAPTER XXXII.

ANTICIPATION OF PROLONGED PEACE—THE 'FRIENDS OF THE PEOPLE'—PROCLAMATION AGAINST SEDITIOUS PUBLICATIONS—THE SLAVE QUESTION—INVASION OF FRANCE BY THE GERMAN POWERS—ITS EFFECTS ON THE REVOLUTION—SCHISM IN THE WHIG PARTY—THE MILITIA CALLED OUT—THE ALIEN BILL—RUPTURE WITH FRANCE—DECLARATION OF WAR.

THE session of 1792 was opened under circumstances of extraordinary prosperity and promise.

Surplus revenue. A surplus revenue, little short of a million, bore testimony at the same time to the increasing wealth of the country, and to the prudence with which its financial affairs had been administered; while so confident was the Government in the maintenance of peace, that in the Speech from the throne, they announced a reduction in the military establishments, and a corresponding remission of taxation.

The Opposition, unable to controvert the facts contained in the royal Speech, and agreeing with the Government that the state of Europe warranted a return to a peace establishment, directed their censures chiefly against the abortive preparation of the previous year. It was not often that Pitt had afforded his opponents a fair opportunity of assailing him; the Russian armament was, indeed, the only considerable blunder he had committed during the six years of his administration. The policy of resisting the settlement of Russia on the banks of the Bosphorus has been long recognised by every Court in Europe, as essential to the balance of power; but in the last century it was considered that the expulsion of the Turks from Christendom

Movements of the Opposition.

was a consideration of far greater moment than the restraint of the semi-barbarous monarchy, which already spread over nearly half the Continent. Pitt's resistance to the grand scheme of conquest, projected by the Russian potentate would seem to show that he was the only statesman of the day who foresaw the drift and consequence of the policy of St. Petersburg; but he should have seen, also, that it was hopeless to resist a plan well matured, and urged with great force of will, unless he could obtain the concurrence of the other great Powers, and enlist the public opinion of this country in his support. A small vote of credit, and the equipment of a few ships of war, were hardly a sufficient demonstration to arrest a huge military despotism in its career of conquest, and to set an example which the great Powers of Europe might safely follow. It must be admitted that this inadequate attempt was justly censured. Catherine desisted from the consummation of her purpose, not because she was deterred by the disapprobation of Great Britain, but in order to complete another scheme of spoliation, upon which she had long been bent—the final extinction of the liberties of Poland. It was in vain, however, that the Opposition exposed the want of calculation, with which the Government had entered on this project, and the undignified precipitation with which it had been abandoned. The argument was on their side; but the matter was at an end, and already half forgotten, amid the excitement of more stirring scenes abroad and at home. The confidence of Parliament and the country in the most successful minister of modern times was not to be shaken by a single error. The majorities in the House of Commons recovered the balance[*] which had been for a moment lowered by

[*] On a motion by Mr. Whitbread, condemnatory of Ministers for their conduct in the affair of Russia and Turkey, the division was 244 to 216.

the Russian armament; and the people took little heed of the censorious eloquence of Fox and Sheridan on an affair which had passed into history.

The Budget. The financial arrangements of the year were based on the assumption, which none disputed, of uninterrupted peace. A moiety of the available surplus was, therefore, applied to the liquidation of the standing debt, and the other moiety to the diminution of the public burdens. In fifteen years, said Mr. Pitt, the period prescribed for the accumulation of the sinking fund would cease; and there never was a time, when, from the situation of Europe, we might more reasonably calculate on fifteen years of peace. But his expectation of peace was as ill founded as his expectation of paying off the national debt by means of his sinking fund. Within a year after these words were uttered, under the auspices of the minister who hazarded such a confident prediction, England had entered on the longest, the greatest, the most costly, and the most doubtful war she had ever undertaken. It was not until an advanced period of the session, that the discussion relating to the affairs of France, and their bearing on the domestic policy and constitution of this country, was revived. A notice by Mr. Grey, acting as the organ of the association styled the 'Friends of the People,' of his intention to bring forward the question of Parliamentary Reform, gave rise to a conversation in which Pitt, Fox, and Burke took significant parts. The minister wisely thought that the reform of our representative system should not be undertaken at a time when it would be connected with new and foreign theories, which had been adopted wholly or in part by some of the leading advocates of reform. Fox, on the other hand, took credit for his adherence to the cause of reform, and taunted his adversary with inconsistency,—as if consistency in public affairs was a virtue, not to be qualified by any consideration of circumstance or opportunity. But almost in the same breath in which this taunt was uttered, the Opposition leader plainly intimated, that the time was not convenient for the agitation of such a question. He said he had not joined the Society of the 'Friends of the People,' for though he saw the grievances, he did not see the remedy; and he expressed his disapproval of the course which Mr. Grey had been advised to take. The appalling progress of the French Revolution, not to say the sense of the party which he led, had materially abated the ardour with which Fox had hailed the earlier stages of an event apparently of such glorious promise to the friends of freedom. Burke, no longer provoked by extravagant eulogies on the French constitution, also spoke in a more subdued tone. His speech was principally in condemnation of the societies which had been formed in this country, in connection with the political clubs of Paris, and upon this point there was no material difference of opinion between himself and Fox. Sheridan, Erskine, and others, defended the associations of which they were members; but the more judicious friends of free institutions and parliamentary government, viewed with alarm the erection of a new and irresponsible organisation, which could have no other object or tendency, than to control the action of Parliament, and usurp the legitimate expression of public opinion.

Encouraged by these manifestations of adherence to the cause of order and free institutions, the Government ventured on a bold measure. They issued a proclamation, reciting that seditious writings had been circulated for the purpose of bringing the laws and institutions of the country into contempt; and that correspondence had been opened with persons in foreign countries to forward these criminal purposes. The people were

Seditious publications.

warned against such attempts; magistrates were required to discover the authors and publishers of such seditious writings; and the different officers charged with the execution of the laws were commanded to suppress and prevent riots and disorders, and to give information to the Secretary of State.

Conduct of the French minister. The draught of the proclamation was communicated to the principal members of the Opposition before it was promulgated; and through this channel, probably, a copy reached the hands of Chauvelin, the French Minister Plenipotentiary, who had been lately accredited to London in the name of His Christian Majesty. Upon this information, the Frenchman took a proceeding unprecedented in diplomatic transactions. He addressed a note to Lord Grenville, the Foreign Secretary, remonstrating against the publication of the document as injurious to his country, and requesting the Minister to communicate his note to both Houses of Parliament. Whether this extraordinary paper was dictated by ignorance or insolence, or a combination of both, may be doubtful; but Grenville returned the only answer which it was capable of receiving. He said, that his duty was to lay any note from a foreign minister before the King, and to take His Majesty's commands; that the deliberations of Parliament with reference to questions of domestic policy were matters with which diplomatic correspondence had no connection, and upon which he could enter into no discussion with the representatives of foreign Courts. Notwithstanding this rebuke, the offensive demand was repeated, though in terms of civility and with professions of goodwill.

Address to the Crown. A loyal Address to the Crown, with reference to the proclamation, was moved in the Commons by the Master of the Rolls, and seconded by Mr. Powys, who had until lately taken a leading part with the Opposition. The debate was conducted with much bitterness. Grey moved an amendment to the address, condemning the policy of the proclamation, and denying its necessity. He angrily reproached the Minister with an intention to foment discord among the party opposed to him, and arraigned his whole public life as a series of inconsistencies, hollow promises, delusion, and apostacy. So violent was Grey, that he was repeatedly called to order by a House far more tolerant of personality than the Parliament of the present day. The rest of the debate turned very much on the writings of Paine, whose revolutionary doctrines, enforced by a vigorous and popular style, had attained a wider circulation than the works of ordinary libellers. The writings of Paine in former years, when he was an American colonist, had been mainly conducive to the Declaration of Independence, and had greatly aggravated the breach between the colonies and Great Britain. His more recent residence in Paris, and his intimate alliance with the leaders of the French Revolution, altogether rendered him one of the most formidable of the demagogues who have, from time to time, disturbed the country. Fox thought it prudent to disavow all connection with this man, and to express reprobation of his theories. Grey's amendment was negatived without a division.

The Address in the Lords afforded a fitting opportunity to the Prince of Wales to present himself before that assembly for the first time. *The Prince's speech.* His speech was such as became his high position; he declared his unqualified adherence to the laws and constitution of the country, and deprecated in the strongest terms the wild ideas and seditious publications against which the proclamation was directed. This declaration was received with applause. It was satisfactory to be assured, that the principles which Fox and Sheridan had espoused were not such as the heir-apparent could sanction.

The slave question, which had now taken its place as a question of the first magnitude, was revived this session. The friends of the negro, animated by enthusiasm in the cause they had undertaken, kept the subject before the public by every means which zeal and energy could devise. So effectual were their exertions, that upwards of three hundred thousand persons were induced to deny themselves the use of sugar, because it was the produce of slave labour. More than five hundred petitions, many of them numerously signed, and by persons of all classes, were presented to parliament, praying for a total abolition of the slave trade; and on the 2nd of April, Wilberforce made a motion to that effect in the House of Commons. It is needless to recapitulate the facts and arguments which were adduced on either side. The advocates of abolition were justly charged with exaggeration and credulity; the opponents were, in like manner, open to the imputation of denying facts which were capable of proof. But the real question was little affected by the matters most hotly disputed. Whether the slaves were criminals condemned by the laws of their country, and doomed to transportation and loss of liberty, according to the extravagant assertion of the persons engaged or interested in the trade; or whether they were unoffending natives torn from their homes, as the abolitionists maintained to be invariably the case, were controversies not material to the argument. The real question was, whether a civilised and Christian country could defend a traffic of this character under any circumstances. Pitt put this argument with great force and perspicuity. But, on such a subject, arguments addressed to the senses and the imagination were far more effective in moving the gross mass of public opinion, than arguments which appealed only to the understanding. Accordingly Mr. Wilberforce and

Mr. Clarkson produced a far greater effect on the people of this country by highly-wrought pictures of the cruelties inflicted on the negroes and the horrors of the middle passage, than Pitt and Fox produced on the House of Commons by demonstrating, that the traffic in human beings was indefensible on any ground of natural right or municipal law. The arguments of the abolitionists went far beyond the specific proposition; if they had any validity, they proved that slavery itself, as well as the slave trade, should be abolished. This was admitted by all candid disputants; but the abolitionists disclaimed any intention of taking away the property of the planter. Even the most zealous friend of the black man professed to contemplate no more than his gradual emancipation. An immediate liberation of the slaves would not only have ruined the planters, but in all probability have caused a servile war. But the powerful interests involved in slave labour succeeded for many years in defeating the combined efforts of reason and sentiment—powerful agents, either of them, and seldom found in alliance. The slave trade was not declared illegal until the year 1807; and the emancipation of the negroes throughout the dominions and dependencies of the Crown was not completed until 1833.

A motion by Fox, made at the instance of the Unitarian Dissenters, not for the redress of any specific grievance, but rather with a view, which the non-conformist body had lately manifested, of provoking a renewal of the old quarrel with the Establishment, gave rise to some animated debate. Burke, who reognised the hand of Priestley in this motion, broke forth in a violent invective against that respectable philosopher and narrow-minded politician, who appeared to his heated vision only as the Birmingham incendiary. He treated the motion as an attack on the Church; and

Motion to repeal the Test Acts.

he connected the attack on the Church with the systematic invasion on all the institutions of the country by the party in connection with the French revolutionists. The ostensible object proposed by Fox was the repeal of certain obsolete statutes, which no one wished to revive; but the Dissenters were at this time in bad repute with the House, and the motion was rejected by a large majority.*

A still more unsuccessful attempt was made by the Opposition to connect the Birmingham riots with misconduct of the magistracy, arising from political bias; and to charge the Government with a wilful failure of duty in neglecting to prosecute the offenders, and in screening those who were convicted. The answer of Dundas, the Secretary for the Home Department, was conclusive on these points, completely exonerating the Government, and the administration of justice, from the rash imputations cast upon them. The motion obtained only forty-six supporters in a House of two hundred and thirty-five members.

During the year 1792, the Revolution in France advanced rapidly to its crisis. The Assembly had become almost as powerless as the Crown; and the government of the country had passed into the hands of the municipalities and clubs of Paris. These again were under the control of a few daring and bloodthirsty anarchists, who intimidated both the Legislative and the Executive by means of the populace. On the 20th of June, an armed rabble, secretly instigated by the infamous Orleans, who had assumed the name of Egalité, and led by a butcher and a prostitute, burst into the Assembly. The multitude, after remaining two hours in the hall, shouting, singing, dancing, and menacing the terrified legislators, departed for the palace of the Tuile-

* 142 to 68.

ries. The guards, unable to resist, suffered the obscene rabble to make their way to the royal apartments. The King was loaded with insult. He was compelled to drink the health of the people, and the red cap of liberty was placed upon his head. The Queen, being the especial object of popular hatred, was prevented by her attendants from taking her place by the side of the King; and the Princess Elizabeth, who was mistaken for Her Majesty, had nearly fallen a victim to the murderous fury of the mob.

The regal authority being thus annihilated, and the lives of the royal family threatened, a secret negotiation was opened with the Emperor and the King of Prussia, by an agent of Louis. The result was a resolution by the Courts of Vienna and Berlin to march an allied army into France.

Negotiations with Austria and Prussia.

A manifesto had been prepared by Mallet du Pan, the agent referred to, justifying the invasion in guarded terms, as directed not against the French people, but only against that portion of them who usurped the government, and coerced the King. But the Allies, rejecting these modified terms, issued a proclamation so insolent and sanguinary, as to leave the French people no alternative but to prepare for defence against the foreign foe. It would have been hardly possible, perhaps, for an invader to frame any justification of an act which should disguise its real character; Mallet du Pan would therefore have failed, no less than the Duke of Brunswick, in persuading the French people to welcome the armies of Austria and Prussia as their deliverers from domestic tyranny; but a proclamation which threatened proscription and martial law at once suspended civil dissensions, and united the whole nation against the common enemy. It was in vain that Louis endeavoured to disconnect himself from this rash proceeding; in vain did he seek publicly to discredit the authenticity of the proclamation, and, by urging the vigorous prosecution of a defensive war, to allay the indignation which had been excited against him as a traitor to his country. A new Revolution, more dreadful than the former, was the immediate consequence of the threatened invasion. There was an insurrection at Paris; the populace rushed once more to the Tuileries; the guards, with all the attendants, were massacred; the King and royal family sought refuge in an apartment within the walls of the National Assembly; from thence they were conveyed to the Luxembourg, and finally to the prison of the Temple —their last abode on earth.

A proclamation, such as that which the commander of the allied armies had been advised to promulgate, should have been followed up by prompt and vigorous proceedings; but the Allies lingered for several weeks; nor was it until late in August that they crossed the French frontier. The fortified towns of Longwy and Verdun successively surrendered after a short resistance; and it was announced at Paris, that the Prussians were marching through the Ardennes, by way of Chalons, on that city.

Dilatory proceedings of the Allies.

This intelligence excited the people to frenzy. The Reign of Terror had commenced. The foreign ambassadors had withdrawn after the deposition and imprisonment of the King. The Assembly was impotent; the municipal authorities were suspended; and six Jacobin leaders shared, with the populace, despotic power. A special tribunal was erected for the murder of obnoxious persons under the forms of law; but even this summary process was too slow to appease the ravenous appetite for blood. Numbers of persons of all classes and from all parts of France, accused or suspected of ill will to the Revolution, were collected, at the lowest

The Jacobins.

computation, to the amount of five thousand, in the prisons of Paris. The populace rose upon the prisons, burst them open, and massacred, with every circumstance of barbarous cruelty, the whole of the unhappy, and, for the most part, guiltless inmates. The National Assembly was superseded by a new body, called the National Convention, which proved more ignorant, more violent, more unprincipled, and more servile than its predecessors. One of the first acts of the Convention was to abolish royalty; titles of honour and marks of distinction were at the same time put an end to, as being incompatible with that perfect equality which, according to these fanatics, was the true condition of civilised society.

The delay of the invading army enabled the French to draw together a force for the defence of the capital. Had the Prussians pushed on, they would have found the city almost defenceless. In the few days that were spared to him, the French general Dumourier augmented his army from twenty thousand to seventy thousand, and occupied the passes of the forest of Argonne, through which alone the invaders could reach the capital. The first encounter was calculated to encourage the overweening confidence of the Prussian commander. The advanced guard of the French, amounting to ten thousand men, fled from the charge of fifteen hundred Prussian hussars; and, in their panic, spread reports, which reached Paris, that Dumourier was a traitor, and that his army was disbanded. Within a week, however, this disaster was fully repaired, and the fortune of the war had taken a different and a decisive turn. General Kellerman, commanding an army of twenty thousand men on the Rhine, came up by forced marches to the relief of Dumourier, and defeated the Prussians in a general action at Valmy, on the 20th of September. The immediate result was a negotiation, in which the Prussians made a feeble attempt to treat for the restoration of Louis, which had been so haughtily demanded in the proclamation of the Allies. The answer of Dumourier was the production of a despatch just received from Paris, announcing the abolition of monarchy. After some further efforts to obtain terms, which should enable them to abandon their rash and ill-conducted enterprise without disgrace and ridicule, the Prussians were reduced, by the firmness of their adversaries, to stipulate for an unmolested retreat into their own territory. This was conceded; Verdun and Longwy were evacuated, and the Prussian army retired from the soil of France with more expedition than they had invaded it.

These events were regarded with a deep interest throughout Great Britain. The friends of order and liberty, of religion and property, in other words, the great majority of the nation, ranged themselves on the side of Government, and were resolved to defend the constitution in Church and State. On the other hand, a few zealots, combining with avowed democrats and the herd of evil spirits, always ready to take advantage of civil commotion, openly embraced the principles and defended the proceedings of the French Revolution. Two associations, the London Corresponding Society and the Constitutional Society, were founded for the express purpose of propagating the new doctrines. These societies established branches in most of the large towns. They adopted the forms and imitated the language of the French Assembly. The members styled each other 'citizens,' after the newest fashion of Parisian democracy; and as these clubs were in acknowledged sympathy and concert with the ruling party in France, there was reason to believe, not only that their movements were directed by that party, but that funds were supplied to them from the same source. The Society of the Friends of the

People, consisting of the leading members of the Whig party, and which had been established solely for the purpose of promoting a reform in the representation, took care to separate itself from the revolutionary clubs. An address, or manifesto, promulgated by the Constitutional Society, having been communicated by Major Cartwright, the chairman of that body, to the Friends of the People, Lord John Russell, in replying on behalf of the latter, took the occasion to disclaim the extreme opinions enunciated in that address, and to define the more limited views entertained by the body of which he was the organ. But in agitated times like these, public opinion ranges itself on the one side or on the other, and can find no resting-place in a middle term, such as that which a few fastidious noblemen and gentlemen might seek to recommend.

The Government meanwhile had observed the proceedings of the democratic party, with the intention of checking their career by an appeal to the law. *Paine's Rights of Man.* The publication of the second part of the 'Rights of Man,' by Paine, afforded the desired opportunity. This treatise, written with great ability by one of the revolutionary leaders, and adopted as an authentic exposition of the views and objects of the democratic reformers, was selected as a subject for prosecution by the law officers of the Crown. A criminal information was filed against Paine, the avowed author of the book; his defence was provided for out of the funds of the Constitutional Association. His counsel was Erskine, and the cause was the first tried under the new Libel Act, which had lately been passed, principally through the exertions of that incomparable advocate. The case, however, was sufficiently clear on the record; but if any doubt could exist as to the character of the publication, it would have been removed by an insolent letter, which the writer, who had been elected a member of the National Convention, addressed to the Attorney-General from Paris. In this epistle, Paine, boasting his security in a foreign land, treated the proceedings which had been taken against him with derision and defiance, menaced the Attorney-General, and insulted the King. It was in vain that Erskine employed all his ingenuity and eloquence in defence of such a cause and such a client. The jury would not hear the reply of the counsel for the Crown, nor even allow the judge to sum up, but immediately after Erskine had concluded his address returned a verdict of guilty.

<small>Measures taken against sedition.</small> This verdict, operating as a sentence of banishment against the man who might be considered the leader of the revolutionary party in this country, far from deterring, exasperated his followers. Seditious speeches and publications of increased virulence abounded more than ever; and it became evident, that the persons, who were intent on subverting the institutions of the country, and establishing, or attempting to establish, a democratic republic on the ruins, had engaged in organizing a wide-spread conspiracy for those purposes. The Government, therefore, deemed it necessary to take decisive measures. By a proclamation issued on the 1st of December, the militia was embodied.

<small>The militia embodied.</small> The Tower of London was fortified; and other measures were taken for the defence of the country against foreign aggression, as well as domestic treason. And, in conformity with the Act, which required parliament to be assembled within fourteen days in the event of the Crown calling out the militia, the Houses were summoned for the 13th of December instead of the 3rd of January, to which day they had been prorogued.

<small>Thurlow's overbearing conduct.</small> During the recess, a change of some importance had been made in the Ministry. The Great Seal was at length taken from

Thurlow, who had held it since 1778, with the exception of the short period of the Coalition Ministry. Impracticable, insubordinate, overbearing, insolent, and treacherous, Thurlow was nevertheless a man of considerable powers, well able to sustain his part in either House of Parliament, and in the presence of men who have had no superiors in debate. He was a sound lawyer, and though he had no pretension to profound and extensive acquirements, he is entitled, on the whole, to be ranked among the most eminent who have presided in that great tribunal, which lawyers and statesman have, for centuries, adorned.

Thurlow had long tempted the fate which at length overtook him. Under each successive administration, he had indulged the same wayward and overbearing temper; proposing nothing in council, objecting to every proposal, and, if the humour seized him, opposing and deriding, in his place in Parliament, those measures of administration which it was his duty often to conduct, and always to support. His conduct, during the King's illness, undeceived those who thought that so much roughness and insolence must, of necessity, represent an honesty and independence more robust than the virtues of ordinary men. One of the few occasions on which Pitt is known to have been provoked beyond the power of self control, was when Thurlow made his tremendous profession of loyalty,* after he had satisfied himself that the King would recover, and, consequently, that it was no longer necessary to keep terms with the Prince. Since 1788, Pitt had not admitted the Chancellor to his confidence; and his reason for making Grenville a peer was, that he might have a colleague, whom he could trust to take charge of the Government business in the House of Lords. The Chancellor,

* Pitt was on the steps of the throne, and, after Thurlow's celebrated imprecation, rushed out of the House, exclaiming several times, 'Oh, what a rascal!'— *Locker MSS.*

nevertheless, relying on the favour of the King, and his own personal influence, continued to oppose the measures of the Administration, and to censure on many occasions the policy of his chief. At length this course of proceeding reached its limit, and Pitt informed the King, that either he or the Chancellor must retire from His Majesty's service. This alternative was decisive; and Thurlow was desired to resign the Great Seal.

During the summer and autumn, various attempts had been made to effect a junction between the Government and the Whigs. The King made no objection to such an arrangement; and Pitt appears to have been willing to come to terms with the leaders of the Opposition. His administration was so powerful, that it required no additional strength; and it was not to be expected, that he should make overtures to his adversaries, at a time when their counsels were divided, and when many of them, including some of the most distinguished, were ready to give him unconditional support. On the other hand, however, the state of the country, and the aspect of foreign affairs, were such as to make it desirable that there should be a suspension of party conflict. Accordingly, a communication was opened with the Whigs through the medium of Dundas. It was proposed that a certain number of offices, both in and out of the Cabinet, should be placed at the disposal of the Opposition; but the unreasonable arrogance of that party brought the negotiation, if it ever went so far as a negotiation, to a hopeless point. The Whig leaders, the Duke of Portland, Lord Fitzwilliam, and Fox himself, considered it an essential preliminary that Pitt should resign, and that some great Lord should be placed nominally at the head of the Government.* Such a

Failure of attempts to conciliate the Whigs.

* Lord John Russell, in his *Life of Fox*, speaks of this as an absurd suggestion of Lord Fitzwilliam; but Lord Malmesbury,

proposition as this might have been just and reasonable in 1784, when Pitt at the age of five and twenty had taken upon himself the first place in administration, under circumstances, which, apart from the presumption of the act, were of somewhat doubtful propriety; but in 1792, a demand on the part of a broken and discomfited Opposition, that a minister, who, with signal credit and success, had conducted the affairs of the empire for eight years, should resign his office, was, to the last degree, arrogant and preposterous. And if an arrangement, which has the effect of placing the post of First Minister in commission, can be, at any time, otherwise than fanciful and mischievous, it was assuredly most inexpedient at a juncture when the authority of an experienced and trusted statesman at the head of affairs was needed as much as ever it had been. But even if this absurd obstacle had not been raised, it is not likely that the proposed coalition could have been effected. Fox had committed himself so far by the rash opinions he had uttered and maintained, with all the vehemence of his temperament, in reference to the French Revolution, that he was considered, even by his own party,* disqualified for the only office which he could

---

* who made a minute record of the transaction, and was a party to it, expressly states that the Duke of Portland, who was the acknowledged head of the party, as well as Lord Fitzwilliam, insisted, as they had done in 1784, on Pitt's resignation. Fox said to Malmesbury, in reference to the proposed junction, 'it was so damned right a thing that it must be done.' He, however, still held out on the impossibility of acting *under* Pitt. — *Malmesbury Correspondence*, vol. ii. p. 466. Again, in an interview which Lord Malmesbury had with Fox, at St. Ann's Hill, on July 30, 'Fox made Pitt's quitting the Treasury a *sine qua non*, and was so opinionative and fixed about it, that it was impossible even to reason with him on the subject.'—p. 472. Dean Pellew, who would be equally well informed on the other side, asserts, in his *Life of Lord Sidmouth*, that Fox stipulated that Pitt should resign the premiership.

⸺ Lord Malmesbury relates that at a dinner of the Opposition, at Burlington House, shortly after the proclamation for calling out the militia, Fox denied the necessity for the measure, maintained that there were no *unusual*

well have taken—that of Foreign Secretary. Sheridan, who could not have been omitted from an arrangement which included Fox, was still more deeply compromised with the Revolutionary party. These eminent men, had they joined the Administration, must have submitted to the policy, with regard to French principles, which Burke had set up, and which Pitt approved. The leaders of the Coalition could hardly have ventured on such an act, without abandoning any character for stability and consistency which they might still retain. All the sacrifices which usually accompany the union of parties, would have been on the side of the Whigs. The minister would give up nothing; his opponents would give up everything. Pitt, therefore, was more willing that his adversaries should come over to him, than they were to take such a step. The Whig leaders felt that they could not join the Government, while Pitt retained his position as its chief, without an absolute surrender and unconditional adhesion. The project, therefore, of a union between the great parties was abandoned as impracticable.

In the summer of this year, died Francis, Earl of Guildford, better known in the history of this country as Lord North. His character, as a minister, has already been reviewed in these pages. With abilities of a superior order, with integrity and disinterestedness, which, though never ostentatiously displayed, always guided his conduct, Lord North managed the affairs of the empire, as if he had been the weakest and most corrupt minister that ever held the reins of power. All the high and noble qualities which he possessed, were perverted by a fatal facility of temper, which made him the passive tool of an ignorant and bigoted, though well-meaning master.

symptoms of discontent, and denounced the proceeding as a trick. But none of the company assented to these observations.—*Malmesbury Correspondence*, vol. ii. p. 474.

Yet there was nothing of servility in the nature of the man. He yielded to the pressure of an obstinate and pertinacious will; though earnestly desirous to retreat from a position which he felt to be one of danger to the country, and discredit to himself. A mistaken sense of honour and loyalty held him to his post. The generosity and placability of his temper, the tenderness of his heart, the simplicity of his manners, his gaiety and wit, kept round him a host of friends, long after he had lost the power of gratifying them. No public man provoked more fierce political foes than Lord North, but of personal enemies he had none.

The death of Lord Guildford afforded the King an opportunity of conferring a just reward upon Pitt. The office of Warden of the Cinque Ports, worth three thousand pounds a year, was one for which His Majesty declined to receive any recommendation, as he had determined to bestow it on the minister who had served him with so much fidelity and distinction. If Pitt had, up to this time, been deprived of office by any political vicissitude, he would have been left destitute of income; an appointment, therefore, which placed him in a condition of pecuniary independence, was one to which he could prefer a fair claim, after having given up for the public service a profession in which he would probably have attained the highest eminence.

Pitt made Warden of the Cinque Ports.

Although the imprisonment of the King of France necessarily suspended diplomatic intercourse between the Court of St. James's and the French Government, we learn from the private correspondence of Lord Grenville,* the Foreign Secretary, that Ministers entertained no immediate apprehension of war; even the irruption of the French army into Belgium, and

* *Courts and Cabinets of George the Third.*

the occupation of Brussels, do not appear to have materially shaken their hope of maintaining peace; but the famous decree of the 19th of November, by which the French Convention invited all nations to follow the example of France, and promised them the aid of her armies in throwing off their allegiance, at length determined the action of the British Government. Within a few days after this decree had reached London, the proclamations, calling out the militia and summoning Parliament, appeared in the Gazette. So sudden was the decision of the Cabinet, that the order for proroguing the Parliament to the usual time of meeting after Christmas had been made only two days before the promulgation of the French decree.

The Speech from the throne intimated the probability of a rupture with France, though it expressed some faint hope that peace might still be maintained. The incendiary policy of the French Government, its tendency to violate the rights of neutral States, and its aggressive attitude towards the States General, the allies of the British Crown, were pointed out as inconsistent with the faith of treaties and the law of nations. Parliament was accordingly informed of an augmentation of the naval and military establishments, which would render it impossible at present to proceed in the reduction of the National Debt, or the further alleviation of the public burdens. This ominous announcement necessarily produced a great excitement and a violent conflict of opinion throughout the country. In the Lords, the language of the speech was censured, though in guarded and doubtful terms; and an amendment to the Address, proposed by the Marquis of Lansdowne,* who now separated himself from Pitt, and joined his old opponent, Fox, was negatived

---

* Lord Shelburne had been lately created Marquis of Lansdowne.

without a division. In the Commons, a more determined ground was taken by that section of the Opposition which adhered to the principles of the French Revolution. Fox put forth all his strength in denouncing the spirit which pervaded the Speech from the throne. He broadly asserted that there was not one allegation in the Speech which was not false—not one insinuation which was not unfounded. He declared, moreover, his conviction that the Ministers themselves did not believe their assertions to be true. He utterly denied the existence of any insurrectionary spirit in the country; and referred to some disturbances which had taken place, as arising from a demand of the working people for an increase of wages, and wholly devoid of a political character. The pretence under which the militia had been called out he denounced as a fraud; and he treated with contempt the violent and revolutionary demonstrations of certain societies in this country, which had been made the pretext for the alarm which the Government had raised. He maintained, that the best mode of allaying discontent was to remedy the grievances under which the people laboured, to repeal the Test and Corporation Acts, and other penal laws, and to amend the representation. He concluded by moving an amendment, censuring the adoption of measures which the law required only in cases of actual insurrection within the realm, and pledging the House to immediate enquiry into the circumstances which justified assembling Parliament in a manner so unusual, and so calculated to raise alarm.

Pitt was not present to answer this general attack on the Government, his seat being vacant by his acceptance of the Cinque Ports; *Windham.* but his absence at this moment was the less to be regretted, since the member who rose immediately after Fox, for the purpose of opposing his amend-

ment, and answering his speech, was one of the most
distinguished members of the Whig party. This
was William Windham, whose name was then, and
is, to this day, associated with the idea of a perfect
English gentleman. Independent, brave and generous, courteous and kind, the amiable qualities of the
member for Norfolk were accompanied by fine talents
and oratorical powers, which enabled him to hold
the first rank in an assembly with such associates as
Pitt and Fox, Burke and Sheridan. Neither could
Windham be called one of those timid and aristocratic
Whigs who had been scared from their principles by
the first burst of the French Revolution; on the
contrary, he supported the great principles of civil
liberty, until they were perverted and disgraced by
a sanguinary and tyrannical democracy. Long after
the sagacity and forecast of Burke had penetrated
the surface of the Revolution, and warned his country
of the consequence, Windham continued his generous
confidence in the good intention of the French democrats, though he deplored the errors into which
enthusiasm had hurried them. But no false pride
or pusillanimous adherence to consistency withheld
him for a moment from taking the opposite part, when
he perceived the real tendency and aim of events in
France. He now stood up to avow the change his
opinions had undergone. Like Burke, he announced
his separation from those with whom he had hitherto
been connected by political sympathy and personal
friendship. He disagreed with almost every sentiment which Fox had uttered. He affirmed, from
his own knowledge, the existence of a conspiracy
between persons in this country and France for the
subversion of the British Government; and that the
agents of this conspiracy, acting under the obligation
of an oath, were to be found in every town, in every
village, and almost in every house. He exposed in
forcible language the intolerable policy of the ruling

party in France, who, under the pretence of aiding other nations in the conquest of their freedom, really sought to invade the independence of every country in Europe.

Attempts were made by the followers of Fox and Sheridan to intimidate Windham by clamour, in the same manner as Burke had been assailed. But these attempts were easily put down by the high-spirited gentleman against whom they were aimed. Windham's speech, though immediately following one of the most powerful and striking efforts of oratorical power that had ever been exhibited in the House of Commons, produced a great impression; nor did the debate, though ably sustained by Grey, Dundas, Sheridan, Burke, and Erskine, recover from the effect produced by an expression of opinion so emphatic and decided, from a member so high in character, station, and ability, as the member for Norfolk. The division was decisive; only fifty votes were recorded for Fox's amendment, while the Address was carried by two hundred and ninety. On the report of the Address, Fox, irritated by defeat and the defection of his friends, made a violent speech, in which, after alluding with bitter exultation to the triumph of the French army over the allies, and taunting the Government with the disaffected state of Ireland as a serious obstacle to any effective military enterprise, he recommended that friendly negotiations should be opened with the rulers of France. The following day, Fox reduced this proposal into the form of an Address to the Crown, that a minister might be sent to Paris to treat with the persons who had assumed provisionally the functions of the executive government. The motion, after a long debate, was negatived without a division.

A few days, however, produced a marked change in the tone of the leader of the Opposition. On the 15th of December, he asserted that the war in which

Attempts to intimidate Windham.

we were about to be plunged was caused by a matter of mere form and ceremony—referring in this manner to the cessation of diplomatic intercourse with France in consequence of the deposition and imprisonment of the French monarch, to whom our ambassador was accredited. On the 20th of the month, the Government proposed to increase the number of seamen by nine thousand. In the interval, intelligence had reached England that the French Convention were about to proceed to extremities against the King, and that his life would certainly be taken. Both Fox and Sheridan expressed their entire approbation of the proposed armament; Fox admitted, that the state of the Continent and the progress of the French arms rendered such a measure absolutely necessary. He spoke with abhorrence of the contemplated murder of Louis; and though he still wished for negotiation, the negotiation he desired was one that should be supported by arms. Sheridan spoke still more strongly in the same sense, urging that every exertion should be made to render the war, should we be forced into it, one of a decisive character.

Pitt, who had now resumed his seat, was prompt in committing the Opposition to their support of the warlike policy which the Government had adopted. He added, that the declarations from all sides of the House, according with the unanimous sentiments of the people, must make every nation in Europe feel, that this was not a safe moment to force the British empire into war.

At the same time Lord Grenville, the Secretary of State for Foreign Affairs, introduced a Bill in the Lords, for the purpose of enabling the Government to register and control the movements of foreigners in this country, and to remove them if necessary from the British Islands. The Alien Bill was opposed by the Marquis of Lans-

downe. He moved an Address to the Crown for an
embassy to France, with a view as well of averting
the impending fate of Louis, as of obtaining some
provision for the destitute French Royalists, who in
great numbers had sought refuge in this country.
This proposal, though dictated by motives of humanity,
was unhappily impracticable. Since the deposition
and imprisonment of the King of France in
August, the British Government had held no diplomatic
intercourse with the French nation; there
was, indeed, no Government at Paris to which a
British minister could have been accredited; for it
was not until the 27th of December, that Chauvelin,
who continued to reside in London after Earl Gower
had been withdrawn from Paris, described himself
in an official note to the Secretary of State as Minister
Plenipotentiary of the French Republic. Lord
Lansdowne's motion was made on the 21st of December,
a time when, neither in fact nor in law, was
there any authority at Paris to which the Government
could address itself. To remonstrate with murderers
intent on the immediate consummation of their
crime, would have been a merely futile proceeding;
the indignant protest of Europe against this wanton
deed of blood had already resounded in the ears of
the ferocious demagogues who ruled in the French
capital; and it was plain that nothing short of force
would deter them from their fell design. Lord
Lansdowne's proposal was not supported; but the
Bill, in the last stage of its progress through the
Upper House, was opposed, on the ground that it
was virtually a suspension of the Habeas Corpus
Act, and ought not, therefore, to pass without evidence
of its necessity. This view was maintained by
the new successor to the title of Guildford, and enforced
by Lord Lansdowne, who still contended that
the Bill was unnecessary, and originated in groundless
alarm. The debate was chiefly remarkable for

the speech of Lord Loughborough, who not only defended the Bill, but vindicated the whole policy of the Government, with regard to the affairs of France.* The vacancy on the woolsack was perhaps not altogether unconnected with this opportune support of His Majesty's Government. Loughborough received the Great Seal about a month after his speech on the Alien Bill.

The Bill was debated with more keenness in the Commons. The Conservative Whigs selected this as a fitting opportunity to announce their secession from their former political friends, and their adhesion to the Government. Lord Titchfield, representing the House of Bentinck, Sir Gilbert Elliot, Windham, Powys, and others, supported Ministers in the repressive and precautionary measures which they considered necessary. Fox, and the majority of the Whig party, on the other hand, though approving of measures for the defence

---

* It had been arranged that the Duke of Portland should take this opportunity of declaring his adhesion to the Government, by speaking in the same sense as Loughborough; but, like his predecessor, the Marquis of Rockingham, the Duke was deficient in Parliamentary nerve and ability.—*Malmesbury Correspondence*, vol. ii.

The change which the opinions of other eminent men underwent about this time is remarkable. Romilly, in a letter, dated 15th May, 1792, 'The conduct of the present Assembly has not been able to shake my conviction, that it (the Revolution) is the most glorious event, and the happiest for mankind, that has ever taken place since human affairs were recorded.' On the 10th of September, he writes, 'How could we ever be so deceived in the character of the French nation as to think them capable of liberty! Wretches who, after all their professions and boasts about liberty and patriotism, and courage and dying, and after taking oath after oath, at the very moment when their country is invaded, and while an enemy is marching through it unresisted, employ whole days in murdering women and priests and prisoners, and then (who are worse than these) the cold instigators of these murders, who, while blood is streaming round them on every side, permit this carnage to go on, and reason about it and defend it; nay, even applaud it, and talk about the example they are setting to all nations.'—*Correspondence*, vol. ii. p. 3.

of the country, denied the existence of any emergency which could justify either the proclamation of the 1st of December, or any interference with foreigners visiting or resident in these islands. The debate on the second reading of the Alien Bill referred mainly to explanations of the points on which the recent schism in the Whig party had turned; but Burke, by an error of taste more than usually unfortunate, threw an air of ridicule over these interesting and important statements. It had been asserted during the discussion, that the Bill could affect only a few less than a score of individuals, and, therefore, that it was unworthy of Parliament to suspend the law of hospitality on a consideration so trifling. In reply to this argument, Burke maintained with much reason, that great mischief might be done by a few energetic individuals, acting in concert for a common object. He said that orders for three thousand daggers had recently been sent to Birmingham, and drawing forth a weapon of this description, cast it on the floor, exclaiming, 'This is what you are to *gain* by an alliance with France!' Nothing short of complete success could have redeemed from disgrace and contempt such an experiment on the House of Commons. The feelings of the audience must have been wrought to the highest pitch; the acting must have been perfect, to carry off this transcendent flight of oratory. But the House was not in a humour for rhapsody. The severance of old political connections, which, on this evening, had been performed, was rather regarded as a painful necessity than a matter of exultation on the one side, or of anger on the other. The prospect of a European war, at a time when the country was entering on a career of domestic improvement and commercial prosperity, was not agreeable to either party. The House was grave and thoughtful. When, therefore, Burke stood up, and, after fumbling in his coat pocket, flung a dagger on the floor, declaring that he voted for the bill, to prevent the introduction of French principles and French weapons, the House was too much amazed to laugh; and Burke, confused and mortified, brought his speech to an abrupt conclusion.*

The Bill was discussed with more animation on the report; but the debate, like every other which had a reference to French affairs, took a wide range, extending from the policy of the English Government to the original principles of civil liberty. The Bill passed through its several stages without a division. Three supplementary Acts were passed without much observation. The first prohibited the circulation of French assignats; by the second, the Government took power to prevent the exportation of arms, ammunition, and naval stores; the third was an act of indemnity, confirming an order in Council, prohibiting the exportation of grain and flour to France.

Non-recognition of Chauvelin.

Chauvelin, though no longer recognised in a diplomatic capacity, after the incarceration of the French King, and the abolition of monarchy in France, still lingered in London, and had kept up an irregular correspondence with Lord Grenville, during the summer and autumn. The Frenchman, indeed, attempted to invest these communications with a diplomatic character, by assuming the style of Plenipotentiary from the executive Council; but the English minister, while he declined

---

* This dagger had been sent to a manufacturer at Birmingham, with an order to make a large quantity after the pattern. Instead of executing the order, the manufacturer communicated the fact to the Secretary of State, and left the dagger with Sir J. B. Burgess, the Under Secretary. Burke happening to call at the Foreign Office on his way to the House, Burgess told him the circumstance, and showed him the dagger, which Burke borrowed for the purpose of exhibiting in the House.—Twiss's *Life of Lord Eldon*, vol. i. p. 218. This story was told by the present Lord Eldon, on the authority of Sir C. Lamb, the son of Sir J. B. Burgess.

to correspond with Chauvelin officially, did not discourage his communications. Accordingly, several letters passed, and some personal interviews took place between the Secretary of State and the late Minister of the French King. This unusual proceeding, while it evinced the moderation of the English Government, and their desire to avoid a rupture with France, only exposed them to insult, without in the least degree promoting the object they had in view. The tone of the French correspondence was at first irritable and querulous; but at length it became so insolent and menacing, that there could no longer be any doubt, that the rulers of France meant to provoke a war with this country. On the 27th of December, M. Chauvelin, styling himself, for the first time, Minister Plenipotentiary of the French Republic, addressed a letter to Lord Grenville, demanding, on the part of his Government, a definitive answer to the question, whether France was to consider England as a hostile Power? He then proceeded to defend the decree of the 19th of November, and the forcible opening of the Scheldt, as warranted by reason and justice. He added, that England, by attaching importance to these acts, merely proved that she was determined to fix a quarrel on France; and that a war founded on such futile pretences would not be a war by the people of England against the French nation, but a war by the English Ministry against the French Revolution. To this audacious statement, Lord Grenville replied, that the decree of the 19th of November was a plain invitation to every country to rise against its Government, and that the reception given by the French authorities to the leaders of sedition in this country gave that decree a special application to Great Britain. The opening of the Scheldt, being contrary to positive treaty, could not be justified by any vague assertions of reason and

<small>Grenville's reply to Chauvelin.</small>

justice, which France might think proper to set up; and that if she was desirous of maintaining peace with Great Britain, she must renounce her views of aggression, and confine herself within her own territory, without insulting other Governments, without disturbing their tranquillity, without violating their rights. He repelled, with just resentment, the insufferable appeal which the French envoy had ventured to make from the Government to the people of this country, to which he professed to be accredited. Such an appeal was, indeed, tantamount to a declaration of war, and could, under no circumstances, be tolerated, consistently with the maintenance of diplomatic intercourse or the comity of nations.

Lord Grenville's reply to Chauvelin's note or letter of the 27th of December was laid before the French Convention, and became the subject of an elaborate report from a committee. This paper was a coarse inflammatory libel, worthy of the Assembly from which it emanated, and the hand of Brissot, by which it was drawn up. On Brissot's report, the Convention passed a decree, that Great Britain should be required to abandon the Alien Act; to repeal the recent enactment prohibiting the exportation of grain; and to explain the meaning of her recent armaments; unless these demands were complied with, it was plainly intimated that the Republic would declare war. Nevertheless, some further communications took place between the French agent at London and the English Minister; but the execution of Louis on the 21st of January brought this too protracted correspondence to a close. Chauvelin was simultaneously ordered to leave London by the British Government and the French Convention. A few days afterwards, the Convention declared war against England and the United Provinces.

On the 28th, the minister brought down a message

from the Crown, announcing that the military and naval establishments were to be placed on a war footing. The message was accompanied by the correspondence between Chauvelin and Lord Grenville, which in itself sufficiently explained and justified the necessity of such a proceeding.

Message from the Crown.

On the 1st of February, when the King's message was taken into consideration by the House of Commons, Mr. Pitt opened the business by a review of the policy of France, with regard to other countries, since the party of the Revolution had become predominant — the occupation of the Netherlands, with the avowed purpose of dispossessing Austria of those provinces; the forcible opening of the Scheldt by ships of war, in violation of treaties to which France was party; the decree of the 19th of November, which 'advertised for treason and rebellion;' and, finally, the letter of Monge, the Minister of Marine, threatening to make a descent on this island with fifty thousand caps of liberty, and promising to assist the English republicans in overturning the Government of this country.

Pitt's speech.

Fox, though opposed to war, admitted, in great part, both the facts and the inferences upon which were founded the necessity of extreme measures. With reference to the decree of the 19th of November, which, if not treated as empty rodomontade, must be considered as a declaration of war against every established Government in Europe, the leader of the Opposition said, in terms, that neither a disavowal by the executive Council of France, nor a tacit repeal, by the Convention on the intimations of an unacknowledged agent, of a decree which they might renew the day after they had repealed it, would be a sufficient security.[*] He admitted also, that the an-

---

[*] *Parliamentary History*, vol. xxx. p. 305.

nexation of Belgium to France would be a just cause of alarm to this country; but he added, that a demand on our part, that France should withdraw without conditions from the territory of an enemy which had invaded her territory, was, in the highest degree, arrogant and unreasonable. The argument so stated was unanswerable; but the French rested their occupation of the Belgian provinces on a very different ground. They professed to withdraw, not when they should receive satisfaction for the wrong which had been done them by the Sovereign of that country, but when they had *established the liberties of the Belgians*. It was the revolutionary and aggressive spirit of the invasion which concerned England, and made her a party to the quarrel between Austria and France. Equally weak and imperfect was the argument of Fox, that this country had not been formally called upon by Holland, in pursuance of treaty, to vindicate the inviolability of the Scheldt. The answer was, that though the opening of that river might not be in itself a *casus belli*, yet the assumption by the French nation to set up an arbitrary standard of justice and right, by which the validity of all treaties should be determined, was a pretence subversive of the law of nations, and fatal to the independence of every other Government. The Address was voted without an amendment or a division.

The French Government, however, still professed a desire to avoid extremities. By their desire, Lord Auckland, the British Ambassador at the Hague, was empowered to meet Dumourier, the French General; and, notwithstanding the dismissal of Chauvelin, another envoy, M. Maret, was sent to London. But the proposed interview between Dumourier and Auckland was prevented by the intrigues of De Maulde, the agent of the Executive Council; and Maret, after remaining eight days in London without instructions from his Government, returned to Paris on the 6th of February.

On the 1st of February, the day on which the House of Commons took the royal message of the 28th of January into consideration, the French Convention declared war against Great Britain and the United Provinces; and on the 11th of February, this fact was communicated by His Majesty to both Houses of Parliament.

CHAPTER XXXIII.

THE WAR WITH FRANCE—MISCONDUCT OF THE ALLIES—STATE OF FRANCE—PUBLIC OPINION IN ENGLAND—PROSECUTIONS OF THE PRESS.

War with France.

THE war in which England became thus involved was unlike any former war, in which any civilised power had been hitherto engaged. It was not a war of ambition, of self-defence, or of national rivalry. The elements of those quarrels which had aforetime involved this country in 'just and necessary' warfare with her mighty rival were, indeed, still extant; but at this time, there was no struggle to retain or acquire some distant possession more burdensome than useful to either party; there was no question about the balance of power; there was no dispute, to serve as a pretext for the indulgence of military emulation. Our ancient rival was no more. That famous house of Bourbon, whose aggrandisement it had up to this period been the leading policy of English statesmen to restrain, was levelled with the dust; but in its place had uprisen a power more terrible than the French monarchy, at the height of its insolence and power. A country without a Government, denouncing all regular governments, dispersing the missionaries of anarchy throughout Europe, and inviting all nations to cashier their rulers, to level society, to confiscate property; in a word, to dissolve all the bonds by which civilised communities had hitherto been held together;—such was France—and France had declared war against England.

Disinclination of the Ministry for war.

England had simultaneously declared war against France; nor was it possible that peace could have been maintained between the two countries. The ministers of the

Crown, accused of provoking a rupture with the French democrats, were the last to admit the necessity of war. They desired only to guard this country against the contagion of French principles; they gave no encouragement to the rash aggression of the German Powers; they used their influence to prevent the States General from joining Austria and Prussia;[*] and desired to maintain a strict neutrality in the conflict between France and the Continental States. The policy of the First Minister, during a lengthened administration of unrivalled prosperity and success, had been essentially the policy of peace. Shortly before the rupture of 1793, he said that the map of Europe might be closed;[†] and the measures which he had in contemplation were, for the most part, such as were incompatible with the prosecution of a great war. But the decree of the French Convention, exhorting the people of every nation to rise against their government, and promising them material aid: the notorious efforts to give effect to the decree in this country by agents of the Convention and the Executive Council;[‡] the outrages of the

---

[*] See Lord Grenville's Letter to Lord Auckland, July 21 and November 6, 1792.

[†] *Auckland Correspondence*, 419 and 464.

[‡] The agents of Egalité were busily engaged in endeavouring to revolutionise the country; and there can be little doubt, that they were in communication with Talleyrand and Chauvelin. The order for three thousand daggers, given to a manufacturer at Birmingham, referred to by Burke in his speech on the 28th of November, was connected with a conspiracy to which the Government attached so much importance that a Cabinet was summoned. Sir J. B. Burges, the Under Secretary for the Foreign Department, who had furnished the information upon which the Government proceeded, and was present at the deliberations of the Cabinet thereupon, relates that Pitt expressed to him, after the Ministers had separated, his conviction that war was now inevitable. He desired Burges to draw up a pamphlet to prepare the public for the event. This pamphlet was corrected and added to by by Pitt, and a large impression was immediately bought up. Three days afterwards, Pitt, at the instance of Marot, received that person at a private interview; and then distinctly in-

rulers of France on religion, on law, on public decency, and on common sense; their robberies, tortures, and indiscriminate massacres, ending with the cruel murder of their too patient and inoffensive Sovereign;—all these enormities had excited throughout the British Empire feelings of grief, rage, and alarm, which no Government could have restrained within the bounds of moderation. The immediate cause of war was, however, complete in itself; and might have led to a rupture, had it been the act of Louis the Sixteenth and a regular Government. England was bound by a treaty with Holland so recent as the year 1788, to which both France and England were parties, to guarantee to Holland the exclusive navigation of the Scheldt and the Meuse. The French Government, in open violation of public law, which respects the property of neutral States, and of the express compact by which they were not less bound than the Government of Great Britain, decreed that the exclusive occupation of navigable rivers was contrary to the rights of man, and instructed their general in Flanders to employ the means at his disposal for the opening of the Dutch waters. This measure was, therefore, almost as much an act of hostility towards England as towards Holland. It could bear no other construction, and it had no other intention. It had, indeed, already become manifest that the time had arrived when England, unless prepared to submit to the last in-

formed him, that, in the event of an invasion of Holland by a French army, England would support her ally; and further, that, in the absence of explanation, the decree of the 19th of November would be considered an act of hostility. Maret promised that satisfactory assurances on both these points should be furnished by Le Brun, the French Minister.—Sir J. B. Burges to Mr. Locker, and Memorandum of Interview with Maret, in Pitt's handwriting.—*Locker MSS.* This memorandum does not differ in substance from the account given by M. Maret, and published by the French Government.

dignity, must accept the quarrel which the rulers of France were determined to fasten on her. The outrageous decree of the 19th of November, which was all but avowedly directed against this country; the act of the 15th of December, annexing the Austrian Netherlands to France, a measure which, however justifiable by the laws of war, was most dangerous to the peace and safety of these islands; and lastly the open breach of treaty to which the honour of England was pledged, formed a combination of insults which no independent nation could endure. There was, indeed, no substantial difference of opinion on the subject among Englishmen who did not hate the institutions under which they lived, or were not desirous that their country should become a province of France. Public spirit overcame party considerations; and many persons, of various ranks and conditions, who had hitherto been hostile to the Administration, thought the main object to be regarded was the support of the King's Government. The Duke of Portland, who, since the death of Lord Rockingham, had been considered the head of the Whig party, seconded Lord Grenville in moving an Address to the Crown on the message announcing war with France. The Earls Spencer and Fitzwilliam, with many other peers, followed their chief. In the Commons, the accessions to the ranks of the Government were also numerous and distinguished. Fox him- <small>Admissions</small> self admitted that the decree of November, <small>of Fox.</small> the opening of the Scheldt, and the annexation of Brabant were just grounds of complaint. In the debate of the first of February, he said: 'The plain state of the matter was, that we were bound to save Holland from war, or by war, *if called upon*; but to force the Dutch into a war at so much peril to them which they saw and dreaded, was not to fulfil, but to abuse the treaty.' This was no doubt a correct statement of the obligation which the treaty imposed, but on the very day these words were uttered, France declared war against England and *Holland*; in such an event, it was absurd to contend that England was bound to wait for a formal requisition before she interposed for the defence of her ally. Yet when the King's message came down announcing war, Fox moved an amendment to the address, purporting that defensive war only should be undertaken, and that negotiations should be renewed to obtain redress for the wrongs of which Great Britain had reason to complain.

This amendment, though moderate, received so little encouragement, that the proposer suffered it to be negatived without a division. A few days afterwards, Fox moved a series of resolutions, declaring that war was not justified by the internal affairs of France, nor by the expression of opinions or principles however pernicious; that ministers had not exhausted the resources of negotiation with respect to those differences which afforded this country just grounds of complaint; that they had not distinctly stated to the French Government the terms on which they would observe neutrality in the war which then existed; that they had neglected to interfere when the rights of Poland had been invaded; and, finally, that the British Government should enter into no engagements with foreign powers which should preclude them from making a separate peace, nor take any part in attempting to impose upon the French people a form of Government which they did not desire. His speech consisted chiefly of an invective against the German Powers for their rash invasion of France and their violence towards Poland; neither of which acts were the Ministry concerned to defend; and, accordingly, no member of the Government took part in the debate. It might have been replied, that negotiation, both regular and irregular, had been pushed to its utmost limits; and that any attempt to go further in that direction would only expose the Government to insult from people who hated England, as the only power which could chastise their insolence, and arrest their career. Burke reminded his former colleague that he had stood by without interfering when Po- *Burke's reply to Fox.* land was invaded; when her constitution was abolished, her king dethroned, and her territory divided. The state of Europe was at that time such that England might have interfered to prevent this outrage, if she had deemed it her province to interfere. But such an idea never appears to have entered the head of the minister, or of the leader of Opposition, or of any person engaged in public affairs. It was not perhaps to the credit of England, that these successive acts of rapine should have been perpetrated, without one word of protest or remonstrance on her part; but if she failed to interpose in the first instance, her good offices on behalf of Poland could have been employed with little effect, when circumstances compelled her to draw towards an alliance with the offending Powers against the common enemy of every established Government. Upon the first of Mr. Fox's resolutions, which was substantially in accordance with the opinion of Pitt,* the previous question was moved, and the House decided, by a great majority, that the question should not be put.† And even of the decreasing minority, which still adhered to the leader of Opposition, there were several reluctant votes.

---

* In a letter to the Marquis of Stafford, 13th November, 1792, quoted by EARL STANHOPE, in his *Life of Pitt*, v. ii. p. 173, and in the *Correspondence of Sir George Rose*, the following passage occurs:—' Perhaps some opening may arise which may enable us to contribute to the termination of the war between the different Powers in Europe, leaving France (which I believe is the best way) to arrange its own internal affairs as it can.'

† 270 to 44.

All the principal Powers of Europe were now in arms against France; Austria, Russia, Prussia, Great Britain, Spain, Portugal, Naples, Rome, and Sardinia, severally declared war; while the Republic had not an ally in the world. Undismayed by this combination, the Regicide Government made the most vigorous efforts. The Duke of Brunswick's insolent proclamation, which treated the French as a nation of rebels, to be scourged by foreigners into submission to their rightful rulers, did more to prepare this great people for effectual resistance to the foreign enemy than the most prudent and patriotic efforts of their statesmen and generals could have accomplished. Every Frenchman felt that the domestic calamities under which he groaned were as nothing compared with the dictation of a foreigner, and the partition of his country by the rapacious intruders. The military blunders of the allied Powers, and their ignoble abandonment of the conquests they had made, before the invaded people were prepared to offer resistance, had greatly elated the natural confidence in their own resources of a proud and warlike race.

The French had already occupied the Austrian Netherlands, and drawn large contributions from those provinces. Within a fortnight after their decluration of war against Great Britain and Holland, they had nearly overrun the territory of the States General. But they were now to experience reverses. A turn of fortune enabled the Allies to regain some important posts in Flanders; and, following up their successes, the French were, in a few weeks, deprived of all their conquests in Flanders, and forced to retreat on their own territory. These events caused great consternation at Paris. They were owing, in a great measure, to conduct on the part of the French, similar to that which they so justly re-

sented, when practised or threatened by the Allies.
The military progress of the French army in Flanders
had been a series of exactions and pillage, ending in
annexation. The Flemish people, groaning under
this oppression, and resenting the treatment to which
they had been subjected, afforded every assistance in
their power to the allied armies, and mainly facilitated the re-conquest of the country. But the
French Government, after the fashion of democracies,
laid the whole blame of the disaster on their unsuccessful general, and despatched Commissioners to
the camp to summon him before the Convention.
Dumourier, who knew that to obey such a summons
was to submit his head to the guillotine, placed the
Commissioners under arrest. This act was the prelude to a treason which he had for some time meditated. He fancied that he could play a similar part
to that which General Monk, favoured by a concurrence of circumstances, successfully performed in the
history of England. His idea was to march to Paris,
and proclaim the Restoration of the Monarchy.
With this design, he had obtained a truce from the
allied generals, and he sent the Commissioners of
the French Convention to the Prince of _{Plans of}
Coburg, as hostages for his fidelity to his _{Dumourier.}
new engagements. A more rash and hopeless enterprise could hardly be conceived. If Dumourier had
been at the head of an army which had fulfilled its
duty, and scattered the German hosts, he might have
hoped to achieve the deliverance of his country from
her domestic tyrants, as well as from the foreign foe.
But his army was beaten; all the conquests which
he had made a few months before were wrested from
him; and if he marched to Paris, he must be accompanied by the victorious legions of Austria, which
had threatened his country with the extreme of military law. It is not surprising that, under such circumstances, his attempt to seduce his army from

their allegiance, met with a cold reception. His design, instead of being kept secret until the moment of action, had long been canvassed throughout the camp; and the agents of the Convention had already taken measures to secure the fidelity of the troops. A few regiments were, nevertheless, disposed to follow their leader; but an attempt which he made to deliver up Condé to the enemy wholly failed. Dumourier himself escaped with difficulty; and when he appeared the next day, guarded by a body of Austrian dragoons, he was driven away with indignation by the French soldiers, and compelled, finally, to take refuge within the Austrian lines. Louis Philippe, the young son of Egalité, with two or three other officers, and about fifteen hundred men, accompanied his flight.

Defection of Dumourier. The defection of Dumourier caused no surprise at Paris; his hostility to the Revolutionary Government having been openly declared to the deputies, who had been sent to confer with him on his retreat from Flanders. But the signal discomfiture of this formidable treason gave new vigour to the regicides, at the moment when they were threatened by the advance of the European armies, and by the loyalist insurrection in La Vendée, and in the great city of Lyons. The truce which the Allies had made with Dumourier, to afford him time for maturing his design of marching to Paris, resulted in the loss of an opportunity, which, if judiciously used, might have brought the war to a speedy and successful termination. Had the Prince of Coburg, after the battle of Nerewinden, instead of tampering with the French general, pushed his advantage, and made a general attack on the French army, it is more than probable that he would have obtained an easy and a final victory; after which, there would have been nothing to prevent the Allies from dictating a treaty of peace at Paris.

The Convention, fully sensible of the dangers they had escaped, and of those which still threatened them, took prompt and vigorous measures. They ordered an additional levy of 300,000 men, and enforced this decree with the utmost rigour. The army was to consist of ten divisions, over each of which were placed three commissioners of their own body, with absolute control. Dampierre, an officer of tried fidelity, was appointed as the successor of Dumourier.

The allied armies had remained inactive for several weeks, when they were joined by the British contingent of ten thousand men under the Duke of York. A congress of the numerous powers at war with the French Republic was held at Antwerp, to consider the future course of proceeding. Lord Auckland and Count Staremberg, the representatives of England and Austria, took the lead at this Conference. At the instance of Dumourier, the Prince of Coburg had recently issued a proclamation in studied contrast to the famous manifesto with which the Duke of Brunswick opened the first campaign. The Austrian general now declared that the sole object of the Allies was to terminate anarchy in France, and to restore 'limited monarchy,' according to the constitution of 1791, subject to any modifications which the French people might themselves think proper to adopt; that it was his wish to see these benefits conferred on France by the agency of her own army; that the troops of the Emperor would take no part without the requisition of the French themselves; and that if any fortified post was assigned to the Imperial forces, it should be held only until a regular Government was established in France. This proclamation was, by the decision of the Congress, after the treason of Dumourier had been defeated, superseded by one of a more arbitrary character. The Imperial general now declared that the war must be

The Duke of York in Flanders.

renewed, in other words, that the allied Powers were in arms, either to restore the ancient monarchy, or to exercise any of the rights which the fortune of war might confer. The language of the several joint manifestoes promulgated by the English and Austrian ministers, and which was for the most part dictated by the English minister, was quite as arrogant and offensive as any that had yet been employed by the despotic Governments, and was of a kind hitherto unused in diplomacy. In a memorial addressed to the States General, the ministers of England and Austria recommended the Dutch Government to refuse the asylum to any members of the self-entitled National Convention, or of the pretended Executive Council, who had, directly or indirectly, taken part in the crime of regicide. 'Everything,' they proceeded to say, 'induces us to consider at hand the end of these wretches, whose madness and atrocities have filled with terror and indignation all those who respect the principles of religion, morality, and humanity.' Few persons will be disposed to think these, or any terms of abhorrence, too strong as applied to the blood-thirsty miscreants who were concerned in the murder of the King of France; but the persons designated as wretches in this State paper were in possession of the Government of France; and the use of such language, therefore, implied that the object of the war was not merely, or, even mainly, to obtain redress for the insults which had been offered to the English nation, but to invade the territory of France, with the ultimate design of expelling her rulers, and changing her form of Government. The avowal of a similar policy on the part of the French Convention, by their famous decree of the 19th of November, qualified as it was by the condition, that the revolutionary movement should originate in the country to be aided by the French arms, and before it had been followed up, so far as

England was concerned, by an overt act, had been considered by the British Government as a justification of the war. The language addressed by Lord Auckland to the States was, indeed, very different to that of Lord Grenville, in announcing to the ambassador at the Court of St. Petersburg, the grounds on which a war with France was to be justified. In that well considered paper, the Secretary of State declared, that the terms to be proposed to the French Republic, were 'the withdrawing their arms within the limit of the French territory, the abandoning their conquests, the rescinding of any acts injurious to the sovereignty or rights of any other nation, and the giving in some unequivocal manner a pledge of their intention no longer to foment troubles, or to excite disturbances against other Governments.'* The like guarded language was employed by the First Minister in the House of Commons. But the diplomatists at Antwerp, untaught by the fatal mistake of the Duke of Brunswick, at the commencement of the war, and unable to understand the difference between a counter revolution, effected by a native army, and one which was to be promoted by foreign bayonets, believed they had only to appear at Paris to be received with acclamation, by a people groaning under a detestable and ignoble thraldom, and panting for the restoration of legitimate monarchy. The royalists, who at least knew the temper of their countrymen, protested in vain against a policy so fatal to their interests.

If it was possible to carry such daring and desperate plans to a successful issue, it surely behoved the Allies to avail themselves of the military advantages they had obtained, by pushing forward. But, instead of advancing, the precious time was frittered away in idle negotiations with the French Commis-

* *Parl. Hist.* xxxiv. p. 1303.

sioners, which were at length contemptuously terminated by the orders of the Convention, several weeks after the battle of Nerewinden. The heavy mass of the Austrian army then moved forward in a lengthened line, extending more than thirty miles. Condé was invested, and the Austrian general, content with this operation, though much superior in force to the enemy, determined to take no further step until he should receive large reinforcements from Vienna. The French army was encamped before Valenciennes, a strong position which Dampierre wished to maintain until the arrival of the reinforcements of which he had urgent need. But the presumptuous insolence of the Commissioners from Paris frustrated the prudent arrangements of the General. He was peremptorily ordered to raise the siege of Condé. The result was, that the French, at every point, were compelled to retreat with great loss. Again, these devoted bands were thrust forwards on the Austrian lines, and again they were driven back, leaving behind them, among a heap of slain, the corpse of their brave commander. As if this were not enough, Lamarlière, the officer who succeeded to the command, made an attack upon St. Amand, which covered one of the extremities of the allied army; but was defeated with a loss, according to his own account, of fifteen hundred men.

It was in vain, however, that fortune favoured the slow and hesitating Austrian. He would have remained inactive, waiting for the reaction at Paris in favour of the foreign invader which he still fondly expected; but more vigorous counsels prevailed, and it was determined to attack the French in their position at Famars. After a gallant resistance, the French army was forced to retreat, and the siege of Valenciennes was consequently formed by the Allies. Both Condé and Valenciennes surrendered, after a stout resistance. Mentz, after a protracted siege, fell before another allied army, and again nothing remained to prevent the march to Paris but the infatuated supineness of the Austrian general. After the fall of Valenciennes, instead of pressing forward, the English forces, under the Duke of York, were detached to form the siege of Dunkirk; and Coburg undertook to reduce Quesnoy. Admiral Lord Hood blockaded Toulon, and promised the inhabitants the protection of his fleet, if they would proclaim the monarchy. After a short conflict, the monarchical party prevailed, and the English admiral took possession of the town and port in the name of Louis the Seventeenth.

But the operations of the Allies, successful as they were, so far from advancing the object of the war, were unfortunately attended with opposite consequences. The garrisons of Valenciennes and Mentz were liberated, on condition of not serving against the Allies for a year; but by an oversight in the articles of capitulation, these troops, amounting to more than thirty thousand men, were free to act against the Vendéans, and the Lyonese, whose insurrections had caused a diversion of the utmost importance to the war. The enemy, taking advantage of this fatal omission, immediately despatched one division of their force to the Rhine, while the other marched into La Vendée. The consequence was, that the brave Lyonese were overpowered, and subjected to all the horrors of a ruthless military execution. The Vendéans made a desperate struggle, and were promised assistance by the English Government; but before their tardy succours could arrive, the struggle was at an end. The devoted peasantry, with their leaders, were scattered and destroyed by the disciplined bands of the republic; and, in the desolation of this noble province, the hopes of the Royalists were for the time extinguished.

Reverses followed in quick succession. The selfish

and arrogant conduct of the Emperor put an end to any hope of sympathy and support which the Allies might have justly expected from the French people. The way in which the Vendéans and Lyonese were left to their fate disheartened the loyalists. Condé and Valenciennes, after their surrender, were taken possession of in the name of the Emperor, and not in the name of Louis the Seventeenth. This occupation of two great towns, part of the territory of France, made it manifest that the Imperial arms were engaged in a war of conquest and aggrandisement; and that instead of coming to the aid of a Sovereign oppressed by a cruel and unnatural rebellion, the Emperor of Austria desired to take advantage of the misfortunes of a kinsman and ally for the furtherance of his own ambition. Monsieur, the first prince of the blood, protested, on the part of his infant nephew, the captive heir of France, against these treacherous acts of spoliation, which indeed created the deepest disgust, not only among Frenchmen of every class and party, but in every just and generous mind.

The vigour and promptitude of the Republican Government contrasted strongly with the tardiness and hesitation of the Allies. Hardly had the siege of Dunkirk been formed, before the garrison was increased from three thousand to more than fifty thousand men. The generals and other officers, who had been hitherto unsuccessful, were replaced by other generals and officers, who knew that the alternative was the triumph of the French arms or the guillotine. Hitherto the allied forces had been superior in all arms; but now the enemy had collected reinforcements, and concentrated his strength. Houchard, the republican general, was peremptorily ordered to hold Dunkirk. In pursuance of these instructions, the republican general attacked and routed the covering army of the Austrians, under the command of Field Marshal Freytag. The be-

sieging army, under the Duke of York, was thus left
exposed to the whole French force, consisting of the
army in the field, and the garrison of Dunkirk. The
British commander, thinking it hopeless to maintain
his position in the presence of such a force, made a
hasty retreat, leaving behind him the battering train,
and the greater part of his artillery, magazines, and
stores. In this disastrous and disgraceful manner
ended an expedition, which, had it been completely
successful, would not have advanced the object of the
war a single step. The Duke of York was permitted
to effect his retreat without molestation; but the
rulers of France thought that their general had
deserted his duty, because he had not pursued the
British, and driven them into the sea. Houchard,
who had won the battle of Lincelles, and raised the
siege of Dunkirk, instead of being loaded with
honours and rewards, was superseded in his command,
summoned to Paris, arraigned as a traitor before the
revolutionary tribunal, condemned for favouring the
escape of the Allies, and sent to the scaffold. Toulon,
the only place of importance of which the allies had
yet obtained possession—Toulon, the great arsenal of
France, which had opened its gates to the British, and
raised the standard, not of Austria, but of Louis, was
not thought of so much account as some petty fort in
Flanders. The royalists of this great port had relied
on the powerful and efficient support of England and
Austria; but their hopes were not fulfilled. The
important posts and positions which commanded the
town were defended, not by British and German
veterans, but by scanty garrisons of Spanish and Nea-
politan troops. The insurrection at Lyons being
quelled, the victorious army of the Rhine appeared
before Toulon; they were accompanied by a powerful
artillery; and this arm was chiefly under the direction of a young officer whose terrible name then
became known for the first time. It was Napoleon

Bonaparte, who pointed the guns which battered down the defences of Toulon. While the French were carrying position after position, the allied commanders were quarrelling in the town; and when it became apparent that the place must be abandoned, it was with difficulty that the English admiral could persuade the Spaniard to concur in a measure so obvious as the destruction of the French fleet in the harbour. This object was only partially accomplished, when the advance of the enemy compelled the Allies to make a hasty retreat; leaving the inhabitants of the city, for the most part, to a fate similar to that which had befallen the devoted Lyonese.

<small>Surrender of Quesnoy.</small> Quesnoy having surrendered to the Austrians, after a short siege, the Prince of Coburg proceeded to invest the more important fortress of Maubeuge; but the republicans found it was time to make a vigorous effort, if they would prevent the whole chain of forts, which guarded the western frontier of France, from falling into the possession of the Allies. The garrison of Maubeuge, consisting of fifteen thousand men, ill provided for a siege, after several attempts to dislodge the besiegers, were at length forced to retire within their entrenchments. A large army, under Jourdan, was sent to relieve the place; and after many desperate encounters, the Republican general succeeded in cutting off the communications of the Austrian army, which was compelled to raise the siege, and re-cross the Sambre. The French then made an irruption into West Flanders, but were repulsed at all points. Both armies shortly after withdrew into winter quarters.

<small>The Prussians at Mentz.</small> But the campaign in Flanders, though conducted with a want of vigour and capacity, and attended with results far from commensurate with the means and opportunities of the Allies, was successful, and even glorious, when compared with the achievements of the German armies

on the Rhine. While the Prince of Coburg was taking French towns in the name of the Emperor, the Prussians, content with the possession of Mentz, remained inactive. They were at length aroused by a formidable effort on the part of the French to retake Mentz. After this attempt was repulsed, the Allies suffered another precious month to pass away without making any movement. At length it was determined to advance into Alsace; but hardly had this movement been made, when it appeared that the views of the Allies, instead of being directed to a common object, were intent on particular and selfish aims. Strasburg, like Lyons, Marseilles, and Toulon, was willing to open its gates to a garrison which would take possession of it in the name of Louis the Seventeenth. But the Austrians desired to restore Alsace to the Empire; while the Prussians were opposed to the aggrandisement of their rival. Between the two German Powers, Strasburg was sacrificed. Two emissaries of the Rule of Terror arrived from Paris. The Royalists at Strasburg were immediately put to death, together with every member of the municipality. Not only the town, but the whole province, was laid under contribution. Many of the unoffending inhabitants were murdered, and nearly fifty thousand persons were driven, or fled into the German provinces on the Upper Rhine. A great army was formed on the Moselle; one division of which was commanded by Hoche, and the other by Pichegru. The Allies, having thus sacrificed Strasburg, laid siege to Landau; and the Austrian General Wurmser issued a proclamation, inviting the terrified and helpless Alsatians to renounce the dominion of France, and rejoin the Empire, to which Alsace had formerly belonged, in pursuance of the Treaty of Westphalia. This proclamation had nearly caused an open rupture between the Austrians and Prussians. The immediate result was that the siege of Landau was raised. The Prussians fell back, and the allied armies no longer acted in concert. The enemy, united, and full of ardour, took prompt advantage of their dissensions; and, after a series of engagements, in which the losses on both sides were enormous, the Prussians retreated upon Mentz; the Austrians, finally abandoning Landau, evacuated the French territory; and, re-crossing the Rhine, encamped the shattered remains of their army under the guns of Mannheim and Philipsburg. At the end of the year, the great allied army of the Rhine retained possession only of their original conquest, the fortress of Mentz. The campaign was creditable to the discipline and bravery of the troops. They were engaged in numerous pitched battles, and in arduous military service of every kind; yet, had the conduct of the generals been equal to the courage and constancy of their soldiers, it is doubtful whether a different fortune would have attended the campaign. It was not by superior military skill that the Allies were worsted; the leaders of the Republican armies were seldom successful in their manœuvres. Wurmser, the Austrian General, was quite equal to the commanders whom he encountered. He was a veteran well versed in the arts of the old German school of war; and in the terrible campaign, when Napoleon led the army of Italy, Wurmser was his most respectable opponent. The Duke of Brunswick, though wanting in the higher moral qualities of decision and firmness, was an officer of skill and reputation. But while the German Sovereigns made the common cause subordinate to their own selfish objects, and were more jealous of the aggrandisement of each other than of the progress of the common foe, it was in vain that they contended against a great military people, defending their own soil, led, or driven on by desperate men, conscious of inexpiable crimes, and animated by hatred of their adversaries. Had prompt and effectual support been given to the Vendéans and the Lyonese, it is highly probable that a general insurrection would have welcomed the foreign armies, which came to deliver the French nation from the ignoble bondage in which it was held. But the fate of these generous rebels, abandoned, almost without an effort, to the vengeance of their infuriated tyrants, deterred others from following their example; while the baseness of the Austrians, in taking advantage of the helpless condition of a kinsman and ally, to despoil him of his dominions, under pretence of coming to his aid, revolted every lover of his country, and made him think that before he sought his deliverance from domestic thraldom, it behoved him to expel the foreign invader.

In accordance with this brief summary of warlike operations, it remains only to notice the further proceedings of the British Government in the prosecution of the war. *Captures in the West Indies.* They were few and unimportant. In accordance with the precedents of wars with France, and, apparently from no other motive, an expedition was sent to the West Indies. Tobago was taken after a slight resistance. St. Pierre and Miquelon, which were defended neither by fortifications nor soldiers, yielded when summoned. An attack on Martinique failed; and a more ambitious attempt on St. Domingo was partially successful; a few forts were surrendered to the English; but not meeting with the co-operation which they had been led to expect from the Royalist inhabitants, they could not obtain a firm footing in that extensive island.

In the East Indies, the Governments of Bengal and Madras took possession of the French factories. Pondicherry alone was in a condition to make any resistance; but after a short siege, the French Commandant was compelled to surrender at discretion.

End of the first campaign. Thus terminated the first year of a war in which the three greatest Powers in Europe were arrayed against France. A few minor fortresses on the frontiers of the Netherlands and a single town on the Rhine, were all the conquests which vast armies could achieve, with a lavish profusion of blood and treasure. Early in the campaign, jealousies sprung up between the two German Powers, frustrated their military plans, and ended in a premature dissolution of their alliance; while the French, distracted by domestic anarchy and treason, having entered upon the war with the energy of desperation, were already exulting in victory, and forming schemes for the chastisement of their insolent foes. England, though as yet she could boast of no brilliant, or even useful, achievement, had cherished no designs of aggrandisement; but had acted loyally in behalf of the cause for which she took up arms. It was, indeed, the desire of the British Government to adhere strictly and literally to the ground of their declaration; accordingly, the Duke of York was ordered to remain on the defensive in Holland; and his taking part in the siege of Valenciennes was without the orders of his Government, and contrary to the tenor of his instructions.* The siege of Dunkirk, the principal operation in which the British forces were particularly engaged, was undertaken rashly, and ended disastrously. Had it been completely successful, it would have been utterly useless. If the few troops which England was then prepared to send out, instead of being despatched in fruitless enterprises, had been employed in aiding the French people at those points where they had risen against their tyrants, the fate of France and Europe might have been changed.

* Sir J. D. Burrows's Notes.—*Locker MSS.*

Timely reinforcements might have saved Toulon and La Vendée; but while the flower of the English army were rotting in the trenches before Dunkirk, or lodged in the mole of Domingo, a few Hessians were considered sufficient to relieve the terrible exigency of Toulon; and the noblest people that ever rose in the cause of freedom were left to perish in their agony for want of timely succour.

On the part of the French, the war was conducted, at all points, with the utmost vigour and ability, at the time when civil government was nearly extinguished amidst the strife of faction in the capital. The Girondists, clever and accomplished, but with little knowledge of mankind, or the art of government, had dreamed of a Republic, in which eloquence, and a fantastic profession of public virtue, were to guide the fortunes of the State. But they had neither skill nor courage to moderate the wild elements of democracy which they had raised. The Jacobins, on the other hand, insisted on carrying the democratic theory to its extreme consequence; they asserted the right of the people to rule by the immediate expression of their will; and they denounced, as anti-popular and counter-revolutionary, those arts, by which men of education and rhetoricians have sought to influence public opinion, and draw all real power into their own hands. The sentimental and romantic school of politicians, so long as they were content to be carried down the torrent, flattered their vanity with the idea, that they were the guides and leaders of liberty. But when they attempted to stay the raging waters, they were overwhelmed. They sank after a faint resistance; and, instead of earning the respect and sympathy of mankind as martyrs in a great cause, their fall was rather viewed with derision, as that of pedants and coxcombs, whose shallow presumption had wrought irreparable mischief. The Revolution, which could neither be stopped nor turned aside, but must run its fearful course, was now to be hurried forward by fiercer spirits. The Jacobins, having, by the expulsion and proscription of their rivals, obtained the ascendency in the Convention, proceeded to deprive that body of all political power, by delegating the supreme executive authority to a committee of their own number. At the same time, the cognisance of political offences was withdrawn from the regular tribunals, and vested in an extraordinary court, which soon acquired a terrible notoriety, as the 'Revolutionary Tribunal.' The machinery of tyranny and murder being thus completed, liberty and law were no longer any protection to the citizen. Political offences included everything which the fear and malice of a jealous despotism could suggest. Cart-loads of victims were every day and hour dragged from the hall of the Tribunal to the place of slaughter. The Girondists, who had not effected their escape, were the first to suffer. Then followed a crowd of aristocrats, who, though for the most part, guilty of no overt act against the Republic, were, doubtless, justly accused of disaffection.

In the midst of this proscription of all that was eminent and respectable, it was to be expected that one exalted personage, who, from the commencement of the Revolution, had been regarded with malignant eyes, would meet her fate. The head of Louis had fallen in January; yet, in October, his widowed consort still lingered in her dungeon. The execution of the King, though wholly unprovoked by his personal character and conduct, was redeemed from utter atrocity by political fanaticism; but the murder of Marie Antoinette, was a wanton indulgence of a savage lust for blood. The once brilliant Queen of France was no longer a formidable enemy, if she ever had been such, to the Republic. Since the death of the King, she had been kept in close confinement, secluded from intercourse with everybody but her child and the Princess Elizabeth. At length, in the process of the torture to which she was to be subjected before death, even these two dear companions of her captivity were torn from her; and she was confined to a filthy cell in the prison of the Conciergerie. There the illustrious lady might have hoped that no length of time was to elapse before she should arrive at the final stage of her sufferings. But the Queen was doomed to nearly three months of misery and insult, before she was conducted to the welcome guillotine. A few days after the murder of Marie Antoinette, another member of the royal family was brought to the scaffold. Among the prodigies of wickedness which the Revolution had produced, Philip, Duke of Orleans, was, by common consent, foremost in the race of infamy. This prince, after a youth wasted in the foulest debauchery, had conceived the idea of converting the misfortunes of his country and his family to his own purposes, by supplanting his kinsman on the revolutionary throne of France. With this view, he had used every art and influence to irritate the causes of discontent, and to precipitate the convulsion which he might have done much to avert. He thought to gain the favour of the populace by flattering their humours, and by a servile compliance with all their demands. At length he renounced his rank and name, assuming the ridiculous appellation of Egalité. It was then thought that he had reached the lowest depth of degradation; but it remained for this recreant prince and gentleman to commit one more act of mixed atrocity and baseness, which the history of the world cannot equal. Without the criminal motive which formerly actuated him, for he could no longer hope to revive, in his own person, any form of monarchy—without even the necessity of self-preservation, for he might have fled—Philip of Orleans, while the fate of the captive king depended on the vote of the Assembly wavering between banishment and death, declared for death. The feelings of human nature were not yet wholly extinguished even in the French Convention; for when the revolting sentence was uttered by such lips, a burst of execration burst from every part of the hall. The wretched Orleans sealed his own doom on that dreadful day. For some time he was suffered to remain at large, a mark for universal horror and scorn. At length he was thrown into prison, and a few days after the murder of the Queen, was dragged out, and, after having been put through the usual form of an iniquitous trial upon charges too frivolous or indefinite to admit of answers, was hurried to the place of execution.

The frenzied career of democracy now became accelerated, and rapidly approached that utmost limit, when a reaction must take place. It was but natural, that the perpetrators of the enormities which form so large a part of the history of the French Revolution, should reject the idea of a ruling providence, and a future state of retribution. Accordingly, the existence of a Deity was denied, religion was abolished, and its ministers were interdicted from performing any of the rites or offices of the Church. Reason alone was thenceforth to be the guide of mankind, and the Reason which these votaries worshipped was aptly represented by a half-witted prostitute, who was publicly exhibited, and set up in the cathedral of Notre Dame, as the emblem of the new creed. With the view of removing every association connected with religion from the minds of men, the calendar was revolutionised. The names of the seasons, the months and days, were altered; and a new division of time, which set at defiance the law of nature itself, was declared to be the law.

But the oppression of the Rule of Terror was mostly

felt in the capital, and in the municipalities, where any sign of disaffection was immediately detected, and visited with unfailing punishment. *The rule of terror.* Yet, even in Paris and the large towns, where the Committee of Public Safety had few friends, there were, perhaps, fewer still who desired the restoration of the old Government as it existed before the demolition of the Bastille. Absolute monarchy may be endured, as it is endured throughout the greater part of civilised Europe; but, under a pure despotism, or paternal Government, though there may be distinctions of rank, and a social separation of classes, there is political equality, if not freedom; and, under many despotisms, especially those of the modern fashion, a measure of practical freedom has been enjoyed which is not always ascertained under more regulated forms of Government. But a despotism combined with a privileged order, claiming immunity from the common burdens, assuming a right to impose burdens and restrictions on other classes, and excluding the rest of the community from any participation in the honourable and profitable service of the State, constituted a system of tyranny, oppression, and injustice, which no people of spirit and intelligence could endure. Every young Frenchman born in the Third Estate, which comprised the whole nation except the Sovereign and nobility, found himself hopelessly shut out from all the higher offices of the Church, the State, and the military service. The cultivator of the soil found in every hamlet a petty tyrant in the Seigneur, who could rob him of his labour, or ruin him by burdens which he could not bear. The French people might not like the Committee of Public Safety and the Revolutionary Tribunal; but they never thought of bringing back the privileged orders, of setting up again the barriers which closed the career of life to merit and ambition, of re-establishing the *taille* and the *corvée*. And every Frenchman would have preferred the worst Government, which despotic and feudal institutions, or the crazed infatuation of his countrymen, could inflict, rather than submit to a Government dictated by a foreign potentate, or an invader of his country. The proclamation of the Duke of Brunswick and the occupation of French territory in the name of the German Emperor made domestic affairs a secondary consideration. Military glory and the integrity of the country were of the first importance; and the three-coloured flag became the emblem of national independence, as well as of civil liberty.

Conduct of the Whigs.

The energy and fire with which the French people and their Government repelled the invaders of the country, and defied the armaments of Europe, contrasted forcibly with the listlessness and hesitation of their numerous and powerful enemies. England alone showed a determination to persevere in the war. The Whig party, which had maintained an unbroken consistency of opposition to the American war through its various fortunes, which had survived the disasters of the Coalition, and which had held together during long years of hopeless opposition, was disbanded and scattered by events which under happier fortunes might have rallied and consolidated the great party of the Revolution. When

Intemperate language of Fox.

Fox, with the generous impetuosity of his nature, hailed the first outbreak of French liberty, some of his oldest friends and supporters were silent. They thought his congratulations premature, and his language too strong. In memorable phrases, the great orator pronounced the French Revolution to be the most stupendous and glorious edifice of liberty which had been erected on the foundation of human integrity in any age or country. This language was used at a time when violence and injustice of the grossest kind had been perpetrated by the popular party in France. But an English statesman, the leader of that famous party which had always been foremost in the struggle for liberty, might well declare his sympathy for the cause in which the French people were engaged without approving of the outrages on the royal family, or the sweeping demolition of the whole fabric of their ancient Government. No man who was acquainted with the state of the Government and people of France before the Revolution would have been disposed to measure nicely the excesses of the people in the first transport of their emancipation from a tyranny, perhaps, the most wearisome that ever, for any length of time, oppressed a civilised nation. The case of France was not a case for reform. It was not even a case for a mere political revolution. Organic change was demanded not only in the institutions, but in the moral and social condition of the country. The necessity could hardly have been avoided of breaking up the whole system of society, and laying it down anew. A just discrimination between the state of France and the state of England would have gone far to allay those fears of the contagion of French principles, which the speeches and writings of Burke did so much to inflame. There were faults in our institutions, but the institutions themselves were sound; our representative system, which was the most faulty, contained all the elements of a free legislature, and required only moderate reform to make it efficient, if not perfect. We had a Crown with a limited and defined prerogative; we had an aristocracy without exclusive privileges; we had an established Church with complete toleration, while every office in the State, and every occupation in the country, was open to merit and ambition. A Government like this had nothing to fear from the example of a people just broke loose from the bonds of ages and delirious with liberty. A few enthusiasts, and a few malcontents embittered by disappointment, or seeking advancement, which they could not fairly earn, might dream of a democratic republic; but the sense of the nation was favourable to institutions, under which Englishmen had enjoyed a greater amount of liberty and prosperity, than any other people in the world. Men of sober judgment saw no ground to fear that the populace of London would break into Windsor Castle and carry George the Third by force to St. James's; or that the House of Commons would be overawed by a Jacobin club, or that the Goddess of Reason would be worshipped in Westminster Abbey. But the arguments used by the most eminent assailants, and by the most eminent defenders of the French Revolution, were equally calculated to pervert public opinion in this country, and to precipitate a war which temperate counsels might have averted. Burke, who maintained that every thing the French had done since 1789 was wrong, and that they had wantonly destroyed instead of amending their old institutions, always implied, and sometimes asserted in terms, that there was no material distinction between the case of the French people in 1788 and the case of the English people a century before. But, in fact, no two cases could be more unlike. A monarchy which, for centuries, had gone on adding prerogative to prerogative; an aristocracy which enforced the feudal privileges of the middle ages with unabated rigour; a Church which tolerated no freedom of conscience, were treated on the same footing with a monarchy which had been reduced within narrow limits by the incessant assertion of popular rights; with an aristocracy which had no exclusive privileges; with a Church which was at once the offspring and the emblem of religious freedom. In 1688, the people of England had been long in possession of their liberties. Their title to freedom they traced back for nearly five hundred years. They obeyed no laws which were not made by the joint authority of king, lords, and commons in parliament assembled; they paid no taxes but those which were imposed by their own representatives. And when the king stepped beyond the limits which the constitution had prescribed, and assumed to dispense with the laws of the realm, the nation declared that he had violated the compact under which he reigned, and thereby forfeited his crown. If the people of England were justified in their act, much more were the people of France justified in rising against their Government. It was no question of a mere excess of prerogative with which they had to deal. The whole of their liberties had to be conquered. They had no Magna Charta, no Habeas Corpus, no trial by jury, no House of Commons. Finally, the existing generation of this people had been taught, by their deepest thinkers and most brilliant writers, that liberty and equality were the birthright of man; that the true models of Government were the republics of the ancient world; that the Christian religion was an absurd falsehood; that there was no religion but virtue; and that the act of Brutus was the perfection of virtue.

In such circumstances, it was hardly reasonable to expect that the French people would proceed with the moderation of the statesman who completed, in 1688, the noble edifice of liberty, in the erection of which their predecessors, for many generations, had toiled. No temperate remonstrances would have induced even the mild and indolent Louis to give up his Beds of Justice; to throw open his Bastille, and to restore to his people those free institutions, of which his ancestors, for upwards of four hundred years, had deprived them. No temperate remonstrances would have induced the privileged orders to give up their

Moderate proceedings hardly to be expected in France.

immunity from the common burdens, and their right to grind the faces of the poor.

In 1640, and in 1688, the English people conquered their freedom, under the guidance of their foremost statesmen and gentlemen, who had a common interest in the good old cause. But it would not have been a very hopeful undertaking for the people of France to attack the Crown, the church and the nobles, under the guidance of the philosophers and men of fashion, who talked infidelity and democracy in the saloons of Paris. The Third Estate, therefore, deprived of their natural leaders, the seigneurs and educated politicians, sent up to the Assembly of the States-General, provincial lawyers, curates, and local men. These representatives, imperfectly educated, but with more knowledge of books than of men, ignorant of political affairs, but animated with a keen sense of wrongs, suddenly found the whole power of the State, from the least share of which they had hitherto been excluded, transferred to their hands. The Third Estate, permitted to out-number the privileged orders in the States-General, and taking advantage of their majority, insisted that the States should sit and vote in a single Chamber. From this commencement, the Revolution proceeded with accelerated speed, and soon swept away the pedants and rhetoricians who vainly thought to control its tremendous career.

Burke, in directing the public opinion of this country against the doctrines and excesses of the French Revolutionists, put out of sight altogether the causes which had led to it; nor is there a passage in his speeches and writings on this subject, from which it can be inferred that the people of France had any justification whatever for rising against their Government. Fox, on the other hand, who undertook to defend the Revolution, instead of dwelling on the provocation which the French people had received, excused their excesses, and missed the solid ground of defence which alone was tenable. By this shallow and unskilful advocacy, the Whig leader not only strengthened the case of his opponent, but discredited the principles from which the traditions of English liberty are derived.* The cause of freedom was not to be vindicated by palliating the acts of fanatics, anarchists, and murderers, whose folly and wickedness could not fail to discredit, if not ruin, any cause with which they were associated. A temperate argument, setting forth the grievances of the people of France under their old Government, and justifying a revolution by the exigency of the case, might well have been sustained on Whig principles; but when the Whig leader defended the French Revolution, in the style of Paine, men who understood and valued true freedom thought it time to separate themselves from a leader so undiscriminating and rash. Fox, it is true, did not in terms support the people who had undertaken to propagate the doctrines of the Parisian clubs in the metropolis and the large towns, but his language and conduct were calculated to aid and encourage these emissaries of sedition. While he extolled the French constitution as the perfection of wisdom and virtue, he omitted to qualify this eulogy by any approval of the British constitution. He was, indeed, content that titles and distinctions of ranks should be preserved in countries which had adopted them; but he avowed his preference for the formulary of the Rights of Man, which declared all men free and equal. And throughout all the discus-

* 'On Friday night, Charles [Fox] told us distinctly that the sovereignty was absolutely in the people; that the monarchy was elective, otherwise the dynasty of Brunswick had no right, and that when a majority of the people thought another kind of government preferable, they undoubtedly had a right to cashier the King.'—*Lord Sheffield to Lord Auckland.*—(*Memoirs*, vol. ii. p. 499.) These may be good democratical principles; but they certainly are not Whig doctrine.

sions on this subject, Fox will be found to assent, with a cold and formal profession, to the institutions of his country, while all the force of his eloquence, and the warmth of his nature, are exhibited in sympathy with the French revolutionists.

Conduct of Pitt. While Burke and Fox were thus distracting public opinion by the vehemence with which they enforced the extreme of opposite views on this great question, there was one man of pre-eminent authority who might have interposed to moderate the violence of debate. Pitt, for a long time, referred to the domestic affairs of France with the reserve which became his position. The son of Chatham looked with no unfriendly interest on the struggles of the French people, to free themselves from corrupt despotism and feudal oppression. But he was willing that the French people should be left to work out their liberties in their own way. On that memorable night, when the rupture between Fox and Burke first agitated the House of Commons, Pitt adverted to the great question in controversy, in just and liberal terms. He touched leniently on the excesses which had already marked the rapid progress of the Revolution, and declared, that he could not regard with jealousy the approach of a neighbouring nation to those sentiments which had so long been characteristic of his countrymen. But while the great minister maintained his own equanimity, he made no effort to check the alarm, which the violence of partisans on either side equally contributed to excite. Corresponding clubs, debating societies, the tracts and *Seditious clubs.* harangues of demagogues, might safely be left to the good sense and good temper of a country whose liberties had long since been secured, and which was at that time more prosperous and better governed than at any former period of its history. The country gentlemen, however, took the alarm; every foolish paragraph was magnified into a seditious libel; social meetings were turned into conspiracies; disturbances in the streets became tumultuous assemblies.* The Home Office was inundated with letters from justices of the peace, reproaching the Government with their supineness, but seldom furnishing authentic information upon which proceedings could be instituted. A few words from Pitt might have sufficed to allay these unfounded and mischievous fears; but, instead of stopping the panic, he yielded to it. In May of the preceding year, many months before they entertained any serious apprehensions for the public peace, the Government issued a proclamation against tumultuous meetings and seditious writings; they instituted a foolish prosecution against Paine, who immediately withdrew from their jurisdiction; and from his secure retreat at Paris, treated the futile verdict against him with ridicule and scorn. It was not until within a few weeks of the declaration of war, that Pitt shared in any degree the fears, which brought over so many of his political opponents to the support of Government, and rallied round him as the champion of order, all the friends of the monarchy, the Church, and the constitution. It was the discovery of the French plot, or the supposed French plot, to revolutionise this country by an armed intervention, which first shook the firm mind of Pitt.† From that time, he determined to suppress freedom of opinion in this country,

May 21, 1792.

---

* Lord Grenville to the Marquis of Buckingham.—*Courts and Cabinets of George III.* vol. ii. p. 226.

† See ante, p. 305 note. It seems hardly credible, that the Ministry should have attached so much importance to a tale which, according to his own statement, Burgess first heard from a foreigner whom he met' in the street. After the Cabinet, which sat till four in the morning, Burgess relates that Pitt sat musing over the fire, and then turning to him, asked, 'What he thought of the state of affairs?' adding 'probably, by this time to-morrow, we may not have a hand to act or a tongue to utter.' He then said that nothing could save the country but a war.—*Locker MSS.*

by force of law; and he contemplated the early suppression of the Revolution in France, by a counter-actionary movement, with the aid of foreign arms.*

From the first, therefore, the war was regarded by all ranks of people in this country as a war against French principles, and especially against the existing Government and rulers of France. It was viewed in the same light by the French themselves, and though the military demonstration of this country was on a very small scale when compared with the armaments of Austria, yet the accession of England to the league against France was considered at Paris an event of the gravest importance; and the Convention paid Pitt the compliment of voting him an enemy to the human race. The opposition to the war could not muster much more than a score of supporters in the House of Commons. And while such men as the Duke of Portland and Windham avowed, that until some Government, with which it would be safe to treat, should be established in France, the war must go on, it was evident that England had virtually adopted the new principle set up by the despotic Powers, that the subversion of the domestic Government of an independent nation was a legitimate object of war.

The measures taken by Government for the repression of democratic opinions in this country must now be noticed. These proceedings were not dictated by the judgment which had hitherto characterised the administration. Among the liber-

---

* 'It will be a short war,' said Pitt to his friends, 'and certainly ended in one or two campaigns.' 'No,' said Burke, 'it will be a long war and a dangerous war, but it must be undertaken.'—*Life of Wilberforce*, vol. ii. p. 10. Lord Grenville also thought the conflict would be promptly decided. 'I am much mistaken in my speculation,' he writes to his brother, 15th September, 1793, 'if the business at Toulon is not decisive of the war.'—*Courts and Cabinets of George III*. vol. ii. p. 241.

ties which Englishmen most highly prize, is the liberty of giving utterance to their opinions, both by speaking and writing; and they have always regarded with jealousy any attempt to impose restrictions on this privilege. The long conflict between the Bench and the Jury-box, with regard to the right of determining the character of offences charged against the press, had recently been closed by the law, which restored, or rather transferred, to the popular branch of the court, the exclusive determination of such questions. Since the Revolution, the Government had seldom resorted to the law for the purpose of coercing the license of public opinion. During the present reign, although provocation had not been wanting, the press had been rarely prosecuted. Wilkes, and the publisher of Junius, indicted for libelling the King; and Horne Tooke, for charging the troops with murder in the American war, were the only State prosecutions which had been instituted, since the accession of His Majesty. The obscure libellers of the first half of this reign were never thought worthy of such an antagonist as the Attorney-General. They were either left unnoticed, or were left to be dealt with by hired scribblers equally obscure.

But now a change was to take place. That wholesome freedom of speech, in which the people had been so long indulged without detriment, was no longer to be permitted; and an attack was to be made on the liberty of speaking and writing, such as had not been attempted since the time of Charles the First. There may be times and seasons of trouble in the best ordered Government, when the malignant promoters of sedition and discontent should not enjoy a contemptuous impunity. With France, in the agonies of a democratic revolution, a minister of this country might well feel some anxiety on account of the glaring defects in the popular part of the British constitution; and some

Indiscriminate prosecutions.

restraint on the tongues and pens of incendiaries would be one of the measures of precaution to be considered in such circumstances. But instead of selecting, for prosecution, a few prominent offenders, about whose guilt and powers of mischief there would not be much difference of opinion, the Government made an indiscriminate attack upon all persons whom their spies and informers reported as having given utterance to any expression of discontent with the existing order of things. Not satisfied with instructing the law officers to prosecute in every case where an information could be laid, the Government sent agents into the country to collect materials for indictments at quarter sessions *—tribunals quite unfitted to deal with political libels. Of the numerous cases thus tried, it would be difficult to find one which was not more calculated to bring the Government and the institutions of the country into hatred and contempt, than the words and deeds so charged against the prisoners. A poor ignorant bill-sticker was sentenced to six months' imprisonment at the Clerkenwell sessions, for posting up an Address from the Corresponding Society relating to Reform in Parliament. At the Essex sessions, a disbanded soldier was sent to six months' solitary imprisonment for some idle words about the King and the Government. A man of some education was tried before the recorder of Newcastle for publishing a seditious libel; the publication consisted in the fact of the witness having snatched the manuscript containing the alleged libel from a friend to whom the prisoner had been induced to lend it. The jury, however, had sense enough to acquit the prisoner. Another person, not so fortunate, was sent to prison for twelve months, by the recorder of Man-

* Lord Grenville to Lord Buckingham. Nov. 14, 1792.— *Courts and Cabinets of George III.* vol. ii. p. 227.

chester, for uttering some seditious words of which nobody but the informer had taken any notice. These are examples of the proceedings adopted to vindicate the law, and to protect the institutions of the country in the provincial courts. The cases, selected for prosecution in the superior courts, were still more numerous; but, with the exception of the charges against Paine, which were rendered futile by his withdrawal from the jurisdiction, none were of a flagrant character. So far from establishing a necessity for resorting to the extraordinary powers of the law, these trials proved that seditious practices were confined to a few obscure individuals, and that, wherever the conduct of such persons attracted attention, it generally called forth expressions of resentment and disgust.

One of the earliest cases tried, and one to which the Government attached great importance, was that of John Frost. This man had been a member of a political club called 'The Society for Constitutional Information,' established during the American war, mainly for the purpose of promoting a reform in the representation of the people. The founders of this Association were some of the leaders of the Reform party; and at one time it comprised the Duke of Richmond, Fox, Sheridan, and Pitt; Mr. Wyvill of Yorkshire, Major Cartwright, and Horne Tooke. Universal suffrage was declared, on the authority of these eminent names, to be the only true basis of the representation; and an annual recurrence to the constituency was also held to be indispensable. When it was discovered that such conditions were not quite compatible with a mixed constitution, and possibly not with monarchy on any terms, some of the more distinguished members withdrew; but among their associates, who knew from the first what universal suffrage and annual parliaments meant, was Mr. Frost; and he thought

Society for Constitutional Information.

the French Revolution offered a fitting opportunity
to push the doctrines of the Society to their natural
consequences. He became, therefore, an active
member of other Associations professing the same
object as the Society for Constitutional Information,
but directed to more practical aims. Frost was an
attorney of broken fortunes and doubtful character.
He had lived lately in France, and was in correspondence with the leaders of the Convention. He was a
man of energy and address, and, in troubled times,
might have been dangerous. The Attorney-General
thought him of sufficient importance to be the subject of a criminal information; though the particular
offence with which he was charged had no reference
to his political convictions, and was, in itself, of no
grave character. He had been heard to say, at a
coffee-house, that he was for equality and no king—
language which was often idly used at that excited
period, and which might mean no more than a speculative preference for a republican form of government. The company resenting such an expression
of opinion, turned Frost out of the room; a punishment which would have seemed sufficient for the
offence. But the jury, under the direction of Lord
Kenyon, a high prerogative judge, found him guilty
of seditious words, and the Court of King's Bench
sentenced him to six months' imprisonment, to stand
in the pillory, to find security for good behaviour,
and to be struck off the roll. The only effect of this
prosecution appears to have been the elevation of
Frost to the honour and advantages of political mar-
tyrdom. Hudson, another coffee-house politician, was
indicted for using some gross language about the
King, and proposing, as a toast, 'The French Republic.' The company, however, drank the King's
health instead, and Hudson, with a companion, Pigott,
author of a scurrilous publication called 'The Jockey
Club,' were given into custody. Hudson was indicted

at the Old Bailey, convicted and sentenced to a fine of two hundred pounds, with two years' imprisonment.

A dissenting preacher, named Winterbotham, was, with more reason, punished for abusing his pulpit by teaching seditious doctrine. His defence, indeed, was a denial of the language imputed to him; but the jury, after considerable hesitation, found him guilty on two charges founded on different sermons. By an unusually harsh sentence, he was condemned to a fine of one hundred pounds and two years' imprisonment in respect of each offence. But the most indefensible prosecution of this class was that of one Briellet, a working mechanic, who was indicted for railing against kings, and vociferating for a revolution. He was condemned to a year's imprisonment, to a fine of one hundred pounds, and to find heavy security,—a sentence equivalent to the ruin of a person in that rank of life.

Prosecution of Winterbotham

There was, however, one of the State trials which surpassed all the others in absurdity, if not in oppression. Two debtors, named Duffin and Lloyd, were inmates of the Fleet Prison, at the end of the last year. Lloyd was a prisoner in execution; but Duffin was detained on mesne process, a law (long since happily abolished), by which any man could, at a moment's notice, be deprived of his liberty by the unsupported oath of another. One of these persons conceived the idea, which he communicated to the other, of writing a lampoon, in the following terms:—
'This house to let. Peaceable possession will be given by the present tenants, on or before the 1st of January, 1793, being the commencement of the first year of liberty in this country. The Republic of France having rooted out tyranny, Bastilles are no longer necessary in Europe.' A small scrap of paper, containing these words, was stuck on the chapel door, after the fashion of a churchwarden's or overseer's notice. The paper was immediately removed by a

Duffin and Lloyd's case.

turnkey, who had seen it affixed by Duffin. A moderate application of the discipline of the prison would surely have been sufficient for an act of insubordination, which was either a dismal jest, or an outbreak of spleen, not very heinous in such circumstances. But the offenders were placed under rigorous confinement in the strong-room, and the matter was reported to the Secretary of State. In the following term, an ex-officio information was filed by the Attorney-General against Duffin and Lloyd for a conspiracy to break prison, and to incite the other prisoners to commit the same offence. At the trial no evidence whatever was offered in support of the averments, which constituted the gravamen of the charge, namely, that the defendants had conspired either to break prison themselves, or to incite their fellow-prisoners to the like attempt. It was proposed to show that Lloyd was connected with a political club, but the proof entirely failed. Thus the case for the Crown rested entirely on the paper, from which the jury were to infer the intent charged in the indictment. Upon this point the following evidence was given in cross-examination by Eyles, the warder, who was the principal witness for the Crown.

Duffin.—' Did you ever hear that either Mr. Lloyd or I intended to escape from the prison?'—'No; I never heard so.'

' Or that we excited others to escape or break the prison?'—' No.'

' Did you think that we, or any of the prisoners, ever contemplated such a measure?'—'No; otherwise than as I inferred from the handbill which had been stuck up. I thought the paper might have that tendency.'

This evidence ought to have put an end to the case. It was ridiculous to say, that the paper published by the defendants themselves was evidence of a conspiracy to effect their own escape; and as it was proved that none of the other prisoners saw the paper, it could hardly have incited them to break out of prison. The absurdity of two men conspiring to break through a jail, strongly guarded, surrounded by a wall forty feet high and six feet thick, and giving notice of their conspiracy by a written placard, was too gross for argument; and, as to the second part of the charge, that the defendants had published the placard in pursuance of a conspiracy to incite their fellow-prisoners, there was no proof that anybody had been tampered with, or that the paper had been stuck up as a signal for insurrection. But these poor debtors had not the means of retaining Erskine to protect them from an attack which was prompted more by a foolish panic than by wanton tyranny. They defended themselves; and, like most persons who are so unfortunate, or so injudicious, as to undertake such a task, they urged topics which were either irrelevant or injurious to their interests. Duffin attacked the officers, and exposed the mismanagement of the prison. Lloyd, who described himself as a citizen of the United States, wearied the Court by a long dissertation on imprisonment for debt, and exasperated the judge by reminding the jury that they had a right to draw their own conclusion from the facts without any regard to the opinion of the bench. A special jury of the City of London, under the direction of Lord Kenyon, found both the defendants guilty. They were brought up for judgment in the following term; but there was a marked difference in their sentences. Lloyd was condemned to imprisonment in Newgate for three years, to stand in the pillory, and to find security for good behaviour for five years. Duffin was let off with the comparatively milder sentence of two years' imprisonment in the Counter, with security for good behaviour during two years more. Nothing appeared on the trial to warrant this distinction. Whether the

Court were of opinion that Lloyd drew up the paper, and that Duffin was no more than his agent, or that they were influenced, as is stated in a contemporary publication,* by the demeanour of the defendants at and since the trial, the whole proceeding, from first to last, was equally a disgrace to the Government, and to the administration of justice.

Proceedings against the press.

The proceedings against the press generally were conducted in a spirit which seemed to aim at the suppression of all freedom of opinion. It is always a question whether the prosecution of political libels is not the best advertisement they can receive. A work of literary merit, however faulty in doctrine, requires a confutation of a different kind from that which the Attorney-General is prepared to offer. Fine and imprisonment have never yet put down opinions which the public is willing to discuss. I do not here advert to publications addressed to ignorance and vice. These, whether they assume a political or moral disguise, are dealt with as a matter of police; and, when they acquire sufficient notoriety to become a nuisance and a scandal, are crushed by the strong hand of the law. But the systematic attack upon political writers and printers, in which the Government had engaged, was as much at variance with the spirit of our institutions, as it was unnecessary for their protection. The test of sound popular Government is the liberty of speaking and writing. No despotic rule, no hollow form of a liberal constitution, no stimulated democracy can endure the temperature of a free press. But institutions which had been the growth of centuries, and which had, by common consent, nearly, if not quite, ascertained the mean between liberty and order, were surely not so frail that they must give way before the shock of foreign opinions, unless

* *Annual Register*, 1793, p. 6 Chronicle. For report of the trial, see *State Trials* vol. xxii.

sustained by ex-officio informations, and indictments at quarter sessions. Such, however, seemed to be the apprehension of the Ministers of the Crown; unless, indeed, which was probably the truth, they weakly yielded to the panic of their supporters. However this may be, the censure which attaches to their conduct is equal in either case; and it is impossible to record, without shame and regret, that an administration, of which William Pitt was the head, could lend itself to proceeding so cruel, so wanton, and so unconstitutional as those which have been described, and as others which remain to be mentioned.

During the last century, and up to a period within living memory, it was the fashion to frequent the shops of the principal London booksellers, as the morning rooms of the principal clubs are now frequented. Men of letters, members of Parliament, and the numerous loungers of a luxurious capital, assembled there, to discuss the new publications, political topics, and the gossip of the town. It was at the shop of Davis the bookseller, that Johnson first met his biographer, Boswell; and fifty years later, at Murray's, in Albemarle Street, such men as Hallam, Byron, Rogers, and Moore were daily visitors. The London booksellers were formerly, to a greater extent, perhaps, than at present, men of education and attainments, living on terms of friendship and social equality, not only with their authors, but with many of the most accomplished persons of the day. The names of Tonson and Lintot are as familiar nearly as those of Addison and Pope. Such men as Miller and Strahan, and the two Davies's, were no less known and esteemed in succeeding generations. I might easily extend the line to the present day; so numerous is the list of publishers who have not dealt with literature merely as a sordid trade, but are entitled to be placed in

London Publishers.

the ranks of its discriminating friends and liberal patrons.

Among the booksellers, whose shop was thronged by men of wit and fashion about town, was Ridgway, of Piccadilly. His business lay chiefly in the publication of pamphlets and political works in connection with the Whig and popular party. Among the publications which lay on Ridgway's counter, were Paine's 'Rights of Man,' and his 'Address to the Addressers,' together with a rather heavy but very harmless political satire called, the 'Jockey Club.' In selling these three books, Ridgway was subjected to as many prosecutions in the King's Bench, was convicted, fined 200*l*., and sentenced to four years' imprisonment. Several other booksellers, both in London and in the country, were prosecuted for similar offences, and punished with more or less severity. One Holt, the printer of an obscure newspaper, called the 'Newark Herald,' was thought worthy of a criminal information, because, in addition to having sold Paine's book, he had printed in his newspapers an address to its readers, on the subject of parliamentary reform. Holt was fined 100*l*., and sent to Newgate for four years; but being utterly ruined by the proceedings taken against him, the poor man died in prison, long before the expiration of his sentence, of a broken heart.

The judges were not unwilling to promote the success of these prosecutions; and some of them were eager to obtain verdicts for the Crown. Kenyon, the chief justice, a sound lawyer, but, in other respects, an ignorant and narrow-minded man, tried most of the important cases, and set an example, which the judges of assize, and the chairmen of quarter sessions, did not fail to follow. In the trial of charges for sedition, temperance, caution, and discrimination are especially demanded of the judge. Treason is so distinctly defined by statute, and the nature and amount of proof required to sustain the charge are so positively prescribed, that the judge has little or no latitude; but seditious words, having no fixed rule of interpretation, remain very much in the breast of the judge; and thus the boasted field of free discussion is full of the concealed pitfalls of the law. The chief justice, who seems to have shared the terror and hatred of innovation and reforms, which prevailed at this time among the middle and higher classes, was disposed to regard as a seditious libel any hostile criticism of an established institution, or any proposal to amend its defects. With the Middlesex juries, he generally carried his point; but when he went beyond Temple Bar, the spirit of independence, which has always distinguished the City, began to assert itself. One Eaton, a bookseller, was twice put upon his trial for selling Paine's pamphlets; but in each case, the jury, notwithstanding the pressure of the Court, steadily refused to find more than the fact of publication, a verdict, which would have been sufficient in the former state of the law, when the Court assumed the right of determining the quality of the writing; but under the recent statute, which assigned to the jury the right of determining the compound question of publication and *libel,* amounted to a verdict of acquittal. Eaton was then indicted for the publication of a ribald tract, entitled 'Politics for the People; or, Hog's Wash.' In this case, the City jury settled the question by a verdict of not guilty. The verdict was not in accordance with the evidence; but it was a just rebuke of the vindictive proceedings of the Government, and especially of the unconstitutional manner in which this particular prosecution had been conducted. Excessive bail had been demanded, which, being unprepared to find, the defendant had been iniquitously detained two months in Newgate, abiding his trial.* But the most signal check which the Government encountered, at the early stage of their headlong career against the press was, in the case of Mr. Perry, the respectable proprietor of the 'Morning Chronicle,' a newspaper of the highest class, though written in the popular interest. With Mr. Perry, were joined in the indictment, the printers, Lambert and Grey, who were responsible only for the mechanical department of the paper. Yet these men were associated in the charge as if it were one of conspiracy or felony, in which all the persons engaged were equally guilty. Such was the spirit in which these prosecutions were conducted. The seditious libel which Perry and his coadjutors were charged with publishing consisted partly of an enumeration of grievances, about some of which there might be difference of opinion, and partly of a statement of facts, which no person of credit ventured to dispute. The inference drawn from these particulars was the necessity of a reform in the representation,—a measure which had been repeatedly recommended to Parliament by the highest authority, including the First Minister himself. The article, though vigorously written, contained nothing unbecoming the character of a respectable journal. The counsel for the defendants having admitted the formal proof, no evidence was tendered, and the alleged libel alone was, consequently, before the jury; yet the Chief Justice, having nothing to sum up, did not venture to pronounce the paper a seditious libel in itself, but told the jury that it ac-

---

* ADOLPHUS's *History*, vol. v. p. 531. The learned writer, than whom no advocate of his time had a more extensive experience of the administration of the criminal law, plainly intimates, though he does not express in terms, his disapprobation of these proceedings. Mr. Adolphus's testimony is the more valuable, because his bias was that of a prerogative lawyer. But his opinions, though always frankly given and ably supported, are never suffered to affect the authenticity of his narrative.

quired that character from the fact, of which there was no evidence before the court, that certain French emissaries were going about the country propagating revolutionary doctrines. This, together with a very weak argument against parliamentary reform, constituted the judge's charge; and, when it is added, that the proprietors of the 'Morning Chronicle' were defended by Erskine, it is not surprising that a Guildhall jury should have returned an acquittal.

Before quitting this subject, it is necessary to advert to some proceedings of a similar character in Scotland, which attracted much attention in this country and are still commemorated with indignation by every lover of freedom in North Britain. Among the malcontents at this period, there was unquestionably a numerous class which sought for a reform in the representation of the people as a pretext for a means for bringing about a democratic revolution. But there were many who thought then, as the great majority of the nation thought forty years later, that the disturbance of ancient abuses in the neighbouring kingdom offered an apt opportunity for reforming our democratic institutions. Bad as was the state of the English representation, that of Scotland was infinitely worse. If there were close boroughs in England, there were also open boroughs, in many of which the suffrage was widely extended. The counties exhibited, for the most part, a numerous array of freeholders at the poll. In Scotland, there were neither open boroughs, nor open constituencies of any kind. The members for the burghs were returned by self-elected corporations; and the members for the counties were nominated by the great proprietors. The greatest number of electors in any Scotch county was two hundred and forty, of which a considerable proportion was non-resident and without property qualification. At an election for the county of Bute, it is related that only one of the twenty-one electors was present, who proposed and seconded himself, and was declared by the returning officer, duly elected. So late as 1823, the aggregate number of persons entitled to vote for the forty-five members for Scotland, which included such cities as Edinburgh, Glasgow, and Aberdeen, was under three thousand.*

Movement for parliamentary reform.

That a movement in favour of parliamentary reform, originating in England, should, in such circumstances, spread to Scotland, was an inevitable consequence, if any public spirit and intelligence were to be found in that part of His Majesty's dominions. The Scotch, however, are a cautious people; they are not easily swayed by political passion. Even the Stuart insurrections, although they involved a national feeling, were supported chiefly by the Highland clans; and the Highland clans took no interest in the question of parliamentary reform. During the present reign, the Scots had experienced, almost for the first time in their history, the benefits of a mild, yet firm and regular government. Many of them had sought and found their fortunes in this country. The impulse given to their hopes by the appointment of their countryman Bute to the head of the Government at the beginning of the reign, had not subsided with his premature fall from power. The energy and pertinacity with which the Scots continued to cultivate the patronage of the Crown were visible throughout the public departments. The Scottish people, therefore, sensible of the substantial benefits which they enjoyed, were not keenly sensitive to the defects in their representative system. Long after

---

* May's *Constitutional History*, vol. i. pp. 295-298. The Scottish representation, which, up to the time of the Reform Act, was the most servile and variable, has, since that period, been as free and independent as any constituency of the United Kingdom.

England had been stirred, and Ireland had been wrought to madness by the spectacle, Scotland continued to regard, without much sympathy, the struggle for liberty in France. The agents of the London Corresponding Society, together with delegates from other political bodies, succeeded at length in organising an Association in Edinburgh, for the purpose of obtaining 'Universal Suffrage and Annual Parliaments.' These inducements, however, proved so little attractive, that sufficient funds were hardly collected to defray the working expenses. The meeting of the 'National Convention,' as this little knot of humble patriots styled themselves, was dispersed by the magistrates; and it is probable that little more would have been heard about parliamentary reform in Scotland for some time, had not the violent proceedings of the Government provoked a bitter feeling of which the Scotch character, when irritated, is peculiarly susceptible.

Among the few persons of a superior class who joined the Edinburgh Society, was Thomas Muir, formerly a member of the Faculty of Advocates. Muir was a man of strong political impressions, and despairing, it seems, of finding any field of political action among his countrymen, had gone over to Ireland, and joined a Society in Dublin called the United Irishmen. The Irish Government having held him to bail for sedition, he forfeited his recognisances and escaped to France. He was of course outlawed, and the Advocates expelled him from their body. After a few months, Muir, hearing of the movement in his own country, returned to Scotland, where he was safe from Irish process, and became an active member of the National Convention. He was prosecuted for sedition by the Scotch Government. The trial was conducted with little regard to justice or decency. The jury consisted of members of a society which had offered rewards for the apprehension of persons accused of offences similar to those with which the prisoner stood charged. Muir objected to be tried by a jury so prejudiced, but the objection was overruled. He then proved, both by cross-examination of the Crown witnesses as well as by independent testimony, that his influence had been exercised in behalf of order and moderation; that he exhorted his friends to confine their exertions to legitimate objects, and to avoid all connection with persons who harboured disloyal and revolutionary designs. It was shown that he had recommended to his associates the study of works which contained sound historical and political information; but among these he included some of Paine's political tracts, which the English Courts had pronounced seditious libels. It was, therefore, a case for conviction; but assuredly one for a moderate sentence. Muir conducted his own defence. In this case, no advocacy could have been successful against a hostile court and a servile jury; but the decent behaviour of the defendant, the argument and eloquence of his pleading, were exhibited in contrast with the intemperate zeal and folly of his judges. The Lord Justice Clerk, following the example of his brethren at Westminster, thought proper to inform the jury of his opinions on the question of parliamentary reform. Kenyon's prelections on this subject, though dull, were not indecent; but the chief of the Scotch bench raved in the language of Jeffries or Scroggs. In refuting the doctrine of universal suffrage, which, however extravagant, had been supported by respectable authority, his lordship laid it down that 'the landed interest *alone* had a right to be represented; the *rabble* had nothing but personal property, and what hold had the nation on them?' In this strain he proceeded. Other of the judges referred without disapprobation to the infamous laws of a former age, when the offence charged against the prisoner might have been brought within the penalties of treason. The prisoner was convicted and sentenced to transportation for fourteen years; his punishment being increased, as the judge informed him, because the audience at the trial had applauded his defence.* Three other members of the National Convention, Skirving, Margarot, and Gerald, emissaries of the London clubs, were tried for similar offences and received the like sentences. Fysbe Palmer, a local dissenting minister, was indicted, at the Circuit Court at Perth, for distributing seditious publications, and transported for seven years.

<small>Palmer's case.</small>

In England, where the mischievous activity of democrats and disaffected persons was notorious, and by a large party in the country regarded as sufficiently formidable to call for strong measures of repression, the sentences upon the publishers and authors of sedition never exceeded fine and imprisonment. In Scotland, there was no pretence for urging that such practices demanded exemplary punishment. The only association after the French fashion, formed in Edinburgh, consisted, for the most part, of a few obscure persons who were easily dispersed by the civic force, and who never reunited. There had been no disturbance of the public peace, nor were there in Scotland, as there were in Ireland, and possibly in parts of England, inflammable materials, which might make political incendiaries more than ordinarily dangerous. Yet it was thought necessary to inflict upon a few zealots who had infringed the law the dreadful penalties which are reserved for incorrigible felons. These proceedings were brought under the notice of Parliament early in the following session. Mr. Adam, a Scotch lawyer of eminence, who was afterwards himself a

<small>Undue severity of the Scottish courts.</small>

* *State Trials.*

judge, in an argument of great learning, undertook to show that the Scottish judges had exceeded their power in sentencing the political offenders to transportation, and urged the necessity of an appeal from the Scottish tribunals to the House of Lords. The motion was, of course, opposed, and easily defeated by the majority which blindly followed the minister; but it is painful to record the language in which Pitt denounced men who, less ably indeed, but with more sincerity, continued to support the cause of which he had not long ago been the leading advocate. 'Instead of meriting blame,' he said, adverting to the conduct of the judges in the cases of Muir and Palmer, 'they deserved the thanks of their country for having expelled from its bosom those unnatural miscreants whose aim was to effect its ruin; who, by their wicked daring attempts to subvert the constitution, had forfeited all title to its protection, and all claims to mercy.'

The Attorney-General brought in a Bill, intituled the 'Traitorous Correspondence Bill,' the object of which was to prohibit intercourse and commerce of any kind with the French people. The bill contained some usual and necessary, but other unusual and futile provisions. As to the restrictions placed on furnishing the French Government with articles known as contraband of war, no objection could be anticipated; but Fox, either carried away by the narrow spirit of party opposition, or inspired with an uncompromising zeal for free trade, which he had not exhibited when the Commercial Treaty was under discussion, thought it false economy to prevent the armourers of Birmingham from manufacturing weapons for the service of the French Republic. On the other hand, the prohibitions of investments in French securities was a reasonable measure, since it would have been hardly decent, that the English capitalist should have an

Traitorous Correspondence Bill.

interest in stocks, which would rise or sink according as the fortunes of the enemy were prosperous, or the reverse. The Bill attached the extravagant penalty of high treason to any breach of its provisions. It was vehemently opposed in every stage, but it passed without any material alteration.

Early in this year, symptoms of commercial distress became apparent. In their alarm at misfortune so unusual, people hastily ascribed it to the war. But in fact, paradoxical as it may seem, the public embarrassments were caused by the rapid development of sources of prosperity hitherto imperfectly worked, or altogether unknown. Since the American war, agriculture, commerce, and trade had made great progress; the new processes, invented by the ingenuity of the Lancashire mechanics, had given a sudden and prodigious impulse to domestic manufactures. The demand for capital consequently became urgent, and the system of paper credit, which had lately been developed, afforded new and dangerous facilities of accommodation. Banks sprang up in every part of the country, and these establishments freely issued their paper, mostly without adequate capital, and not unfrequently without any capital whatever, on speculative securities. The first check experienced in this rash career necessarily produced a convulsion. Towards the end of the preceding year, bullion became scarce; and the exchanges showed an unfavourable balance against this country. The Bank of England immediately contracted her issues. Two or three great houses failed. A general crash speedily followed. Of about three hundred and fifty country banks, more than one hundred stopped payment; and of these, fifty, at least, proved insolvent.[*] A general panic ensued, and the stability of trade and credit was in imminent danger.

[*] MACPHERSON's *Annals of Commerce*, vol. iv. p. 26 ; SMITH's *Wealth of Nations*, by M'CULLOCH, note on Money.

In these circumstances, the merchants demanded the interposition of the Government. Such interference was, on principle, manifestly open to the greatest objection. But the exceptional nature of the exigency was recognised by Pitt, with a promptitude and energy which redound greatly to his credit. The minister consented to recommend to Parliament the issue of Exchequer Bills to the extent of five millions, upon the deposit of mercantile securities. A Committee of the House of Commons sanctioned this arrangement, the result of which was a revival of commercial credit, not measured by the advances of Government security, but by the confidence so opportunely shown in the soundness and stability of the national resources. Less than four millions of the Exchequer Bills, though they were issued at a low rate of interest,* were, therefore, taken up by the traders; and of this amount, the greater part was repaid before the expiration of the period fixed by the Act. No loss whatever was sustained by the public on the whole transaction.

* Two-pence half-penny a day, equivalent to 3*l*. 18*s*. 3*d*. per cent. per annum.

CHAPTER XXXIV.

FOREIGN MERCENARIES AND VOLUNTEERS—TRIALS FOR TREASON—HARDY, THELWALL, HORNE TOOKE.

WHEN Parliament separated in June, there was some ground for the hopeful anticipation of the King's speech, with reference to the war. At that time the Duke of York had not raised the siege of Dunkirk; Lyons had not surrendered; Toulon had not been evacuated; the Austrians had not retreated. During the recess, a succession of disasters had taken place; and though nothing had yet occurred to show that England had engaged in a conflict of unprecedented magnitude and difficulty, people were beginning to murmur; and it was said that the fortunes of our arms should be guided by a leader who had some better qualification for high command than being the favourite son of their revered monarch.*

The Opposition took advantage of this partial reaction in the public mind to urge a policy of peace. But the Ministry and its supporters vehemently repelled such counsels, declaring that no terms of peace could be entertained until a permanent Government should be established in France. And as the original

* Lord Mornington, afterwards better known as Marquis Wellesley, thus writes to Speaker Addington, in November, 'What do you hear of the public temper respecting the war? I meet with much discontent and disappointment.. , . The general turn of people's minds seems to be to condemn the *conduct* of the war.' —PELLEW's *Life of Sidmouth*, vol. i. p. 112. Lord Mornington's younger brother ARTHUR was at this time an aide-de-camp at Dublin Castle.

cause of war no longer existed, the French having
withdrawn from the Dutch territory, it was difficult
to assign any other reason for continuing the war.
It was now plainly understood, therefore, if not ex-
plicitly avowed, that Great Britain was at war not
with France, but with the French Republic; and that
the object sought was the restoration of monarchy,
if not of the ancient despotism. The policy of this
country, as it was enunciated at the declaration of
hostilities in the preceding year, had a definite and
lawful aim, measured by the language of treaties,
and the obligations of public law; but now it was
identified with the doctrine of the Treaty of Pilnitz,
which asserted the right of foreign Powers to dictate
the internal polity of an independent nation. It had
become, in fact, like the Thirty Years' War, a war of
opinion; and was destined to a duration, and an
infliction of misery on the human race only inferior
to that desolating and protracted strife.

Numerous debates were raised in both houses
during the session of 1794, with reference to the
policy and conduct of the war. But the former
branch of the subject was already exhausted by previous discussions; the Ministers and their supporters
continued to dwell on the enormities of the French
Revolution, and to quote the language of the French
rulers, menacing to the independence of foreign
powers. The Opposition no longer attempted to
palliate the crimes and outrages of the revolutionary
leaders. Mr. Grey, indeed, who took a leading part
in condemning the war, declared in his place, that
he would rather live under the King of Prussia or
the Empress of Russia than under the Government
of France. But the Opposition denied that the violence and wickedness of domestic faction was any
justification of foreign war. The minister did not
controvert this position; but he maintained that it
would be futile to propose negotiation to a Govern-

ment—if Government it could be styled—which no treaty would bind, and which set at open defiance all the laws of human society.

Two questions of a constitutional nature, incident to the conduct of the war, were raised by the Opposition. Early in the session, a royal message announced that a body of Hessian troops, destined for foreign service, had been landed in the Isle of White. It was contended that this proceeding was contrary to the Bill of Rights, and Grey moved a resolution, ' that to employ foreigners in any situation of military trust, or to bring foreign troops into this kingdom, without the consent of Parliament first had and obtained, was contrary to law.' But the Bill of Rights could not be appealed to in support of this proposition. If statute law is cited, the point must be precise; and the Bill of Rights referred in terms to the introduction of foreign troops in time of *peace*, not in time of war. A great constitutional safeguard would be made absurd, if it could be maintained that a handful of mercenaries on their way from their own country to the seat of war could not be removed from their transports to the shore for temporary ease and discipline. The employment of German troops in the wars in which England had been engaged was no novelty; and it was shown, by numerous precedents, that the course taken by the Government was usual and regular. Serjeant Adair, the only Whig lawyer who took part in the debate on Grey's motion, admitted there was nothing in it, and moved the previous question, which was carried.

Another question of a cognate character followed the debates — for there were several in both Houses—on the landing of the Hessian auxiliaries. A circular was issued from the Secretary of State's office, addressed to the Lords Lieutenants of counties, recommending the formation of volunteer companies in aid of the militia, and suggesting the expediency of making pecuniary contributions in support of the scheme. The King's message, requiring Parliament to provide for the augmentation of the forces, contained no mention of the project to raise a force by voluntary contributions; yet the minister, when questioned on the subject, replied, that the design announced in the circular of the Secretary of State had not been relinquished. A resolution was, therefore, moved by Sheridan, declaring it 'dangerous and unconstitutional to solicit money from the people as a private aid, loan, benevolence, or subscription, for public purposes, without the consent of Parliament.' There could, indeed, be no pretence for suggesting that the ministerial letter invited a *benevolence* in the sense which has consigned that term to infamy and odium; nevertheless, the proposal of the Government was, in principle, open to censure. It was unconstitutional and unnecessary. To the House of Commons belongs exclusively the right and the privilege of granting supplies for the service of the Crown; and any immediate appeal to the people for extraordinary aid for any of those legitimate services is an invasion of that right and privilege. An intimation from His Majesty's Secretary of State is half a command; and if that equivocal message may go forth for the equipment of an armed force, by whatever name it may be called, within the kingdom, the safeguard which the constitution has so carefully provided against the undue exercise of monarchical power might be wholly set at nought. Parliament might one day refuse the supplies for an augmentation of the army, and the next day a royal rescript might issue to raise funds for a purpose substantially the same as that from which Parliament had thought fit to withhold its sanction. There was no excuse of urgency in the particular instance. The House of Commons was wholly for the war; it was also wholly under the control of the minister, and would have readily given him any supply which he might have thought fit to demand. The compulsory means of recruiting the militia were then in full force; and there existed no such necessity, as arose some years later, of calling upon voluntary effort to defend the country against threatened invasion.

The Government rested their defence on the precedents of 1745, 1778, and 1782. But neither of these precedents was precisely in point. In 1745, it would have been merely frivolous to regard constitutional niceties, when an armed rebellion called for every means of resistance which the country could furnish; in 1778, the Government, during the vacation, had encouraged, not by official solicitation, but by private influence, the formation of volunteer corps in aid of the force which Parliament had sanctioned for the suppression of the colonial rebellion. Even this modified proceeding did not escape the strongest animadversion. But the precedent most relied on was that of 1782, when it was said that Lord Shelburne had done the very thing against which exception was now taken by the men who were at that time his coadjutors in office. In 1782, Lord Shelburne had addressed a circular letter to the mayors and other local authorities, enclosing the heads of a plan for a volunteer force. But it contained no proposal that funds should be raised by subscription, and placed at the disposal of the Government. On the contrary, the proposal was that local battalions should be raised, and officered by gentlemen recommended by the Lord Lieutenant of the county, or the chief magistrate of the borough in which the regiment or company was raised; that the non-commissioned officers should be supplied from the regular service and paid by the Government; that arms, accoutrements, and ammunition should be found

Defence of the Government.

Raising of local battalions.

by the Government; and, finally, that in the event of invasion or rebellion, the whole corps should be liable to serve with the regular army, and in that case, be taken into Government pay. It is obvious, that this plan could not be carried into effect, but by funds which Parliament would have to provide in the ordinary way. A very different proposal from that of Secretary Dundas, who sought to raise money without the intervention of Parliament, for establishing an irregular military force. There was certainly no design on the part of the Government to initiate an unconstitutional practice. The object they had in view was right, but there was no reason why it should be attained in a wrong way. An Act was subsequently passed, authorising a volunteer force for a period limited to the duration of the war. By another Act, French refugees, resident in this country, were rendered eligible for service in the British army. This measure was also opposed as unconstitutional and impolitic; but no valid objection could be urged against the employment of these foreigners in a war in which they were personally interested. The enlistment of foreigners had been such a common practice in former wars, that it was vain to characterise it as unconstitutional. Yet this Bill was resisted in every stage of its progress, with an indiscriminating pertinacity which detracted sensibly from the force of opposition.

The course which the Government had hitherto pursued for the purpose of stopping revolutionary principles had not been marked by success. The proceedings against the printers and sellers of questionable writings, as well as against authors and propagators of sedition;—the prosecution of every ignorant and thoughtless person who, in the excitement of the times, had uttered idle words, had exasperated, rather than intimidated, the radical reformers; and had offended many who though not radical reformers, thought that opinion in

Renewed proceedings against seditious writings.

this country was entitled to some latitude and toleration. The Government, however, appeared to think otherwise, for they prepared to renew the system of prosecution with increased vigour, and to arm the law with new terrors against political delinquents. The political clubs, on the other hand, so far from being daunted, were stimulated to increased activity and louder defiance by the proceedings of the Government. The 'Corresponding Society' and the 'Constitutional Society,' which had hitherto pursued different paths, now acted together. Debating clubs were formed in every tavern; and political assemblies were held in the tea-gardens, and the fields, surrounding London. Similar associations were established in the large manufacturing towns.

The Government was well informed of these proceedings, and only watched for a favourable opportunity to suppress the societies, *Vigilance of the Government.* and inflict condign punishment on the leaders. At length a few weapons were found in the possession of one of the societies at Edinburgh; papers were seized; several of the leaders and office-bearers of the political associations were arrested, examined before the Privy Council, and committed for high treason. The minister brought down a message from the Crown, announcing these facts; and the papers were referred to a committee of secrecy, consisting exclusively of members of the Government and their supporters. The report which was presented two days afterwards made no disclosure; it contained merely a mass of papers, which had been published by the societies from time to time, during the last three or four years. The contents of these papers were already well known; many of them had been quoted in Parliament and elsewhere, as warnings of an imminent revolution; some of them had been prosecuted. Mr. Pitt, as chairman of the committee, now brought forward this array of documents as proof of the existence of a plot, well digested and matured, to set up a General Convention, which should usurp the powers of Government, supplant the Parliament, and abolish the monarchy. He therefore proposed, in accordance with the report of the committee,—that the executive should be forthwith armed with extraordinary power, and he moved for a partial suspension of the Habeas Corpus Act.

It is certain that some of the more recent proceedings of the societies were of such a character as no regular Government has ever thought fit to pass over without notice. The Corresponding Society had thirty branches, many of them enrolling more than six hundred members within the bills of mortality. The Constitutional had a separate organisation almost equally formidable. A regular communication had been established between these central bodies and numerous provincial associations, of a similar character, in the three kingdoms. The society called 'the Friends of the People,' which had been established by, and was under the management of Sheridan and Grey, and comprised many members of the Opposition, was invited to join this great political union, by appointing delegates to represent them at the projected National Convention. 'The Friends of the People' sent a civil excuse. The Whig Reformers, nevertheless, offered the most strenuous opposition to the coercive policy of the Government. They argued, that a convention was not unlawful, because there had been conventions corresponding with societies in Yorkshire to obtain a reform in the representation, and conventions of Roman Catholics in Ireland to obtain relief from civil disabilities; as if there was any comparison between the co-operation of persons to obtain a specific and legal object, and a general assemblage of delegates from all parts of the kingdom, to effect unknown changes in the laws, the government, and constitution of the realm. There was more point in the ridicule which the Opposition heaped upon a conspiracy, in which the conspirators took every means to court publicity and to promulgate their designs. It was in vain, however, that either argument or ridicule were employed to allay the terrors which French principles had inspired. A proposal to terminate the war, in which few men, from the first, had faith or hope, would have been welcomed, both by Parliament and the country; but the unparalleled power of Pitt himself would have been shaken by an attempt to make a truce with the reformers.* Yet it is no light matter to tamper with the Habeas Corpus. The great statute had been suspended on no less than nine occasions in the hundred years since the Revolution. In the precarious reign of William the Third; during the rebellions of 1715 and 1745; and on the occasion of Bishop Atterbury's plot in 1722, it was necessary, for the moment, to set aside a law which might act as a shield for treason; but could it be said that such a case of urgency was made out in 1794? There had never been a time in the history of the English people, when professions of loyalty and attachment to the constitution were more general. The laws were in full force, and had recently been administered with all but invariable success, if not, in some cases, with extreme rigour. The leaders and principal agents of sedition were well known; they had been apprehended without difficulty, and were at this moment in custody, awaiting their trial on the capital charge. There might be good ground for setting the highest powers of the law in motion; but it was difficult to understand the extreme peril to the safety of the State, which rendered it necessary to touch the most sacred guard of

* 'Arguments against the war and our alliances are heard favourably in the House of Commons, although they do not get us a vote; but sentiments of liberty and complaints of oppression are very little attended to, however well founded.'—Fox's *Correspondence*, 1794, vol. iii. p. 67.

English liberty. An Act, however, was passed, in May, suspending the writ of Habeas, in cases of treason, until the following February. Thus was the Government, during the six months when Parliament would not be sitting, empowered to arrest and shut up in prison, without bail and without trial, any person whom they might think proper to accuse of treason or treasonable practices. A power so invidious, far from strengthening the hands of Government, must certainly weaken them, unless the State is exposed to such imminent and great danger as the ordinary powers of the executive are inadequate to deal withal.

Impolitic measures.
If the Government of England had not shown such an unworthy want of confidence in the stability of her institutions; if they had not been so ready to control the freedom of the press; if they had passed over, with wise contempt, the idle bravadoes and loose talk of obscure adventurers and drunken mechanics in prisons and in taverns, they might have relied on the support and sympathy of the people in punishing the insolence of pretenders, who assumed to put aside all constituted authority, and to set themselves up as the dictators of the country. But the Ministers of the Crown took a different course; and they were now to experience the mortifying results of precipitate counsels, misplaced vigour, and ignoble concession to extravagant fears.

Country prosecutions.
During the spring and summer, the petty warfare at assizes and quarter sessions was resumed, but without the success which had generally attended the prosecutions in the preceding year. The few convictions obtained were chiefly at the quarter sessions, where juries gave verdicts in accordance with the wishes of their landlords and customers who sat upon the bench. At the assizes, where this influence was not so potent, a successful prosecution

became rare. A practice which the Government had adopted for the purpose of swelling the calender of State offences served more than anything else to frustrate their ends. A body of spies and informers had been employed to drag to light utterers of sedition, of whom nobody otherwise would have heard. These eavesdroppers insinuated themselves into every place of public resort, and hung about every knot of persons who stopped at corners of streets, or in doorways, to talk about the news from France, or of the latest plot that had come to light in this country. The informers, who expected to be rewarded in proportion to their zeal and success, got up numerous cases which broke down ignominiously at the trials. The evidence of these people, always strained, and, not unfrequently, perjured, drew frequent expressions of indignation and disgust from the audience in court, and sometimes from the jury themselves. Juries, availing themselves of the new law, refused to find general verdicts of guilty in cases of libel, in spite of the judges, who, following the example of Lord Kenyon, invariably exceeded their duty, by pronouncing judicially on the character of the publication, which the recent statute had declared to be a question of fact for the jury, and not a question of law for the court.* Among the minor cases, the most signal defeat which the Government sustained this year was in the case of Walker and six others, tried on a conspiracy to overthrow the Government, and to assist the French in an invasion of the kingdom,—a charge which was barely short of high treason. Walker was a respectable

<small>*Prosecution of Walker and others.</small>

<small>* 'The judge is only bound to tell the jury that if, from the contents of the paper and the circumstances under which it was published, it was meant to vilify the Government and constitution, and to infuse discontent into the minds of the people, it was, in point of law, a libel, without taking upon himself, as a matter of fact, to determine that such was the intent.'—Lord CAMPBELL'S *Lives of Chief Justices*, vol. iii. p. 51.</small>

inhabitant of Manchester, who had rendered himself obnoxious to suspicion, as the leader of the reformers in that important town. He had organised a branch of the Constitutional Society at Manchester, and had announced the objects of the association in an advertisement, which did not exceed the bounds of moderation; nor does it appear that either he or his fellow reformers ever avowed revolutionary designs. Nevertheless, Walker was a marked man; and the Tories of Manchester who emulated the zeal and violence of the Church and King party at Birmingham, sought to put down their adversaries by force. On the occasion of the war with France, a mob, instigated by these heated partisans, having made several attacks on Walker's house, Walker assembled some friends and armed them for his defence. Upon this fact, the charge was afterwards founded of taking up arms to wage war against the King. A spy named Dunn swore the information upon which Walker and the other persons were put upon their trial, and was the principal witness. But, fortunately, this wretch was so unskilful in his infamous profession, that the prisoners, defended by Erskine, were in no danger, even from a Church-and-King jury. Dunn prevaricated; his evidence was shown to be false in material particulars; it was even proved, that, in a transient fit of remorse, he had gone down on his knees before Walker, and confessed that he had been bribed to undertake the business. Law, the Attorney-General for the county palatine, who conducted the prosecution, gave up the case, and the witness was committed for perjury. He was afterwards convicted and sentenced to two years' imprisonment, with the pillory. It is worthy of remark, that a punishment which had seldom been considered adequate to the crime of uttering some idle words in a public-house, or selling a democratic publication over the counter of a bookseller's shop, was deemed sufficient for a villain who had attempted to swear away the liberties and fortunes, if not actually the lives, of seven of his fellow creatures.

In one capital case, the Government had been successful; and the trial, though it took place in Scotland, was conducted fairly, to a satisfactory result. Watt and Downie were arraigned for high treason, and the charge was fully proved. These men had laid a plan to surprise the castle of Edinburgh, to take possession of the city, to massacre the troops, to imprison the judges, and demand from the King certain measures; in the event of refusing which, he was to take the consequences. Watt had been a spy in the pay of the Secretary of State; but his services having been disregarded, or not sufficiently rewarded, he engaged, either from treachery or revenge, in the formation of this plot. He was condemned and executed without commiseration from any quarter. His coadjutor, Downie, was also convicted, but recommended to mercy; and the capital penalty was, in his case, commuted to transportation for life. *Case of Watt and Downie.*

In September, a Special Commission was issued for the trial of the State prisoners who had been committed by the Privy Council in May on charges of high treason. Eyre, Chief Justice of the Common Pleas, with Chief Baron Macdonald and four of the ablest and most experienced puisne judges,—Hotham, Buller, Grose, and Lawence,—constituted the Commission.* On the 6th of October, the Grand Jury found true bills against all the prisoners, namely, Hardy, Horne Tooke, Stewart Kyd, Bonney, Joyce, Richter, Baxter, and Thelwall. They also found true bills against four other persons *Horne Tooke and others.*

* Lord CAMPBELL states that Eyre was placed at the head of the Commission in preference to Kenyon, whose temper and discretion could not be trusted.—*Lives of the Chief Justices,* vol. iii. p. 52.

not in custody. One of these persons, Thomas Holcroft, immediately surrendered, and was committed to Newgate. An interval of several days took place, while the prisoners were severally furnished with copies of the indictment, with a panel of the jury, and the names of the witnesses to be called by the Crown, in accordance with the law and custom in cases of high treason. On the 25th of October, the prisoners were called upon to plead. All pleaded not guilty; and Erskine, as leading counsel for all, having desired that the prisoners should be tried separately, the Attorney-General signified his intention of proceeding in the first place with the indictment against Thomas Hardy. Accordingly, on the 28th of October, Hardy was placed at the bar charged with the crime of high treason in compassing the death of the King.

Within the memory of living men, trials for political crimes had been of rare occurrence.

<small>La Motte.
Lord George
Gordon.</small> Only two cases of high treason had been tried in London during the present reign. One was that of La Motte, a spy in the pay of France, convicted and hanged, in 1781. Another trial in the same year, was that of Lord George Gordon, who, by reviving a prejudice about which the people of this country have always been sensitive, afforded a pretext for riot and plunder to the rabble of London. But, though all persons deplored the mischief which had been done on that occasion, few desired the capital punishment of a crazy fanatic, who, so far as he could be considered a responsible agent, did not appear to have been actuated by malice. The impeachment of Hastings had excited extraordinary interest; but it was an interest which concerned the higher and educated classes rather than the multitude. The novelty and grandeur of the spectacle; the unparalleled magnitude of the charges; the astonishing display of oratory by performers who

had never been surpassed—all contributed to dazzle the senses and to fire the imagination of the vast audience. But there was no feeling of reality in the scene. When Burke described the torture of the Begums, or when Sheridan depicted the duress of Cheyte Sing, the audience were moved, as they were moved when Siddons gave the daggers to Macbeth, or when Kemble portrayed the agony of Lear. None felt an impulse to tear in pieces the venerable gentleman who sat at the bar, unshaken by the storm of eloquence which raged around him. Nobody regarded the impeachment as really intended to put the life of Warren Hastings in jeopardy. The proceedings, indeed, were so wholly unlike a trial for life, such as the public were accustomed to behold in the regular tribunals, that it was hardly possible to regard them as a stern reality. A counsel, for the prosecution in a criminal case, whether a petty larceny, or a capital charge, who should resort to rhetorical arts to procure a conviction, or who should go beyond a plain statement of the facts which he meant to prove, would infallibly draw down upon himself the heavy censure of the court, or be looked upon as a tyro who did not understand the rudiments of his profession. The great impeachment, therefore, was treated as a splendid anomaly, and after the first rage of curiosity was gratified, it was suffered to drag on its slow and lingering course without any person—hardly the parties immediately concerned—manifesting any interest in its progress or its issue.

Far different was the feeling excited by the State trials of 1749 [1794]. No personal interest, indeed, attached to any of the prisoners. They were with the exception of Horne Tooke, men in the middle and lower ranks of life, without anything to distinguish them from the swarm of envious malcontents who rise to the surface in civil commotion. But these men—obscure, half educated, of

Rash proceedings of the Government.

doubtful repute, insignificant as they were,—represented principles and sentiments, associated with the most favoured traditions of English liberty. Hardy the shoemaker, Thelwall the lecturer, Holcroft the dramatist,—were, by the rash act of the Government, raised up as the confessors of a political faith which, but for the fostering aid of persecution, would in due time have languished and been forgotten. Hardy and his fellows founded themselves on parliamentary reform, the cause to which Chatham had faithfully adhered to his last day, and of which the son of Chatham had only ceased to be the foremost champion, when he rose to be the head of the State. Upon this foundation, the prisoners had reared wild and foolish theories, which they had sought to effect by wild and lawless means. There could be no doubt that these men had offered deliberate insults to the Government, which could hardly be suffered to pass with impunity. But it was one thing to deal with a set of obscure and desperate adventurers who were willing to obtain notoriety on any terms as minor offenders, and another to elevate them to the dignity and importance of delinquents charged with the highest crime known to the law. The question raised by these prosecutions was, whether the terrible penalties of high treason were to attach to every man who held extravagant opinions on the subject of parliamentary reform, and who openly sought to enforce them by illegal methods. Was it levying war against the King and compassing his death, in accordance with the precise language of the statute, to issue a prospectus for a Convention which should assume functions incompatible with the rights of Parliament? For, putting aside minor details of questionable import, this was the sum and substance of the charge against the prisoners.

On the 28th of October, Hardy was placed at the bar. After some challenges, both on the part of the

Crown and on that of the prisoner, a jury was sworn, consisting of merchants and substantial tradesmen, who fairly represented the intelligence and opinions of the middle class of the metropolis. The Attorney-General* opened the case in a speech which lasted from ten o'clock in the forenoon to seven in the evening. The style of this great lawyer was never remarkable for vigour or perspicuity; and as he went on hour after hour, piling fact upon fact, and endeavouring to demonstrate by a cumbersome process of reasoning, that a conspiracy to compel the King to govern otherwise than by the laws, was a conspiracy to depose him from the royal state, title, power, and government, as set forth in the indictment; that such an attempt must lead to resistance—that resistance must lead to his deposition, and that his deposition must endanger his life;—the jury, overwhelmed by this heterogeneous mass of argument and detail, gaped in dreary bewilderment; and men accustomed to the practice of the courts, saw that the prisoner was already half acquitted. It was past midnight when the jaded court adjourned for a few hours' repose. Before the adjournment, however, Erskine, with exquisite dexterity, took occasion in this early stage, to prejudice the evidence for the prosecution. After the Attorney-General's speech, the remainder of the sitting had been occupied with putting in and reading the papers taken from the possession of the prisoner. Upon these voluminous documents, the case for the Crown mainly rested, and some of them were of a serious character. To obviate the impression which such evidence was calculated to produce at the outset of the trial, Erskine affected to complain that the legal advisers of the prisoner had hitherto been refused

Trial of Hardy.

---

* Sir John Scott, afterwards Lord Eldon. The Solicitor-General was Mitford, afterwards Lord Redesdale, Lord Chancellor of Ireland.

permission to see the papers put in evidence; and, as the charge of compassing the king's death was to be extracted from these papers, which it took the Attorney-General *nine hours to read*, it was but reasonable, he said, that he should have an opportunity of examining them. Erskine knew very well that neither the Crown, nor any party to a private suit, discloses the evidence beforehand to the other side. He had long known the papers on which the weight of the case chiefly rested; but the remark, for which this pretext afforded an introduction, was intended not for the Court, but for the jury; and it had its effect. *It told upon the jury.** The reading of the documentary evidence occupied the whole of the next day. The correspondence between the different societies established throughout the kingdom, and with the French Convention and the Jacobin Club;—the election of some of the French revolutionary leaders as honorary members of the Constitutional Society;—the affectation of the French term, *citizen*, all sufficiently showed that the sympathies of the prisoners were with French rather than English ideas of freedom. When pressed by such evidence, Erskine would get up and ask, how all this bore on the charge of compassing the King's death, which was the precise charge the prisoner had to meet? An atrocious piece of ribaldry in the shape of a play-bill, purporting to be the cast of a performance called 'La Guillotine; or, George's Head in a Basket; for the benefit of John Bull,' having been brought home to Baxter, one of the prisoners, Erskine tried to get rid of it as a fabrication of the spies who

---

* Many years after the trial, a gentleman who had served on the jury said to Mr. Adolphus, 'Sir, if the evidence had been much stronger than it was, I should have had great difficulty in convicting men of a crime, when it occupied the Attorney-General nine hours to tell me what it was.'—ADOLPHUS's *History*, vol. vi. p. 75.

had got up the prosecution. Several sharp altercations took place between Erskine, who bore the brunt of the battle, and the counsel for the Crown; sometimes he menaced the judge, who showed no unwillingness to push the case for the prosecution. A most important witness for the Crown was sinking fast under a terrific cross-examination, when the Chief Justice interposed to help him; but the counsel sharply rebuked this irregular interference. 'I am entitled,' said he, 'to have the benefit of this gentleman's deportment. If your lordship will indulge me—' and he waved the judge aside. 'Give him fair play,' said Eyre. 'He has had fair play,' retorted Erskine. 'I wish *we* had as fair play. But that,' he added with fine irony, 'is not for the Court.'

The bias of the judges, was, indeed, too visible during the whole series of these prosecutions. On one occasion, during Hardy's trial, Erskine being absent from court, Gibbs, who was left in charge of the case, had to cross-examine one of the principal witnesses. The man was asked if he had not been a spy, upon which the Chief Justice, without any objection from the counsel for the Crown, interposed, and would not permit the question to be answered. Soon after, the cross-examining counsel was stopped again. On this occasion, Gibbs declining to argue the point, desired the usher of the Court to send for Mr. Erskine, and sat down. A nervous pause ensued, during which the judges consulted together with manifest uneasiness. Presently Erskine came into Court, and being informed of what had taken place, maintained that his junior had been right both in principle and in practice, and appealed to Mr. Justice Buller, the greatest authority in the commission, in support of his assertion. Buller could not help ruling, however reluctantly, in Erskine's favour, and the trial proceeded without further interruption from the Bench. At length, the court having sat every day from eight in the morning till midnight, the Attorney-General announced, on the afternoon of the fifth day, that the case for the Crown was closed. Erskine applied for an adjournment until the following day, that he might be prepared to address the jury on behalf of the prisoner. There should have been no hesitation in acceding to an application so reasonable, considering the unprecedented duration of the trial, and the multifarious evidence which had been so heaped up. But the Chief Justice showed a strong disposition to deny the indulgence asked, and haggled about an hour, more or less. The jury, resenting what appeared to them a desire to bear with undue hardship on the prisoner, interposed, in support of Erskine's application, and the Court was compelled to yield.

At two o'clock in the afternoon of the following day, Erskine rose to address the jury. Up to this time he had conducted the case with consummate skill. He had missed no point; he had made no mistake. He suffered the witnesses for the Crown to tell their story without those captious interruptions and objections, from which the jury are apt to infer that the counsel is attempting to stifle evidence which he cannot fairly meet. When he objected to a question, his objection was either arguable in point of law, or was raised with the view of prejudicing the prosecution. Cross-examination, which, in ordinary hands, more frequently corroborates than shakes the adversary's case, was ever sparingly used by this great advocate; indeed, if he could be said to fall short of excellence in any branch of his art, it was in this. He made little impression, therefore, by leading an unwilling witness for the Crown, who had acted as secretary of one of the seditious societies, to admit that the prisoner was a loyal subject; that neither he nor any of his friends contemplated anything beyond a reform of Parliament; and that they only desired to attain this end by legal and orderly means. Nor was he very happy in addressing another witness, who had assumed the name of Douglas, as Mr. Spy, and asking him 'how long he had played the part of Norval?' Such tricks as these, though frequent in the lower practice of Nisi Prius and the Old Bailey, are unworthy a performer of the highest class. But when he stood up before the jury, Erskine was incomparably the greatest advocate that had ever worn the robe. Oratory loses more than half its virtue when transferred to paper; the finest speech ever delivered seems comparatively tame to those who have not *seen* it. The *action* is lost. The voice, the eye, the gesture, the character of the orator, the surrounding circumstances, the sympathy of the audience are wanting. Erskine at the bar was as careful an actor as Chatham in the senate. The flannels and the crutch of the Great Commoner were no despicable aids to his eloquence. The advocate, in like manner, neglected none of the accessories of his art. He fixed on the spot from which he was to speak; his books and papers were disposed in picturesque disorder; his dress was carefully arranged; and though these things were laughed at, and have been quoted as proofs of Erskine's inordinate vanity, they are not beneath the notice of an adept who aims at perfection. Oratory is not the most useful, and is far from being the highest intellectual gift conferred on man; yet there is none, perhaps, which an ambitious man would more readily choose, if a choice were offered him. A great conqueror has grave cares and troubles to mar the pride and the rapture of victory. A great author too often trusts to posterity for his fame; but the great orator enjoys an unalloyed triumph. He delights at once and subdues his hearers. He exercises a faculty which lifts him at the same time to fame and power. He is the champion of the oppressed, more potent and more terrible than the leader of hosts. Even liberty and laws would languish and moulder away, if they were not fostered and revived by the art of eloquence.

It was thus, on that memorable day, that Thomas Erskine stood forth in the pride and power of a consummate orator. His theme was of the noblest. He had to vindicate the ancient liberties of his countrymen. He had to contend that men ought not to be brought to the scaffold because they had only a little outrun the example recently set them by a great nobleman who was now a Cabinet Minister, and pushed to extremity principles of which the First Minister of the Crown had once been the most eminent patron. He had to strip the case against the prisoners of those invidious accessories, which the spies and sycophants of the Crown had fastened to it, for the purpose of exaggerating a plain charge of misdemeanour into the highest crime of which a citizen could be found guilty. He had to guard from the violence with which it was attempted to confuse them, those sacred boundaries between treason and minor offences against the State, which the provident fathers of English freedom had so carefully marked. How he performed this great task is known to us by the tradition of the greatest feat of oratory ever exhibited in a court of justice. The speech itself has been preserved literally as it was delivered; and in that noble composition, we find all the elements of the highest art: propositions distinctly stated; dissection and application of the evidence; arguments and authorities; all in lucid order. The spirit and elasticity of the style; the flashes of wit, passion, and pathos; the glow of eloquence diffused over the whole may suffice to convey a lively idea of the effect which such a speech must have produced upon the jury, and all who heard it. 'My whole argument,' he said, 'amounts to no more than this—that before the crime of compassing the King's death can be found by you, the jury, whose province it is to judge of its existence, *it must be believed by you to have existed in point of fact.* Before you can adjudge a fact, you must believe it—not suspect it—not imagine it—not fancy it—but *believe* it; and it is impossible to impress the human mind with such a reasonable and certain belief as is necessary to be impressed, before a Christian man can adjudge his neighbour to the smallest penalty, much less to the pains of death, without having such evidence as a reasonable mind will accept of as the infallible test of truth. And what is that evidence? Neither more nor less than that which the constitution has established in the courts for the general admission of justice; namely, that the evidence convinced the jury, beyond all reasonable doubt, that the criminal intentions constituting the crime, existed in the mind of the man upon trial, and was the mainspring of his conduct.' He never suffered the jury to lose sight of this proposition, which his every argument and comment tended to illustrate and enforce. There was abundant proof that the prisoner, or at least the society with which he was connected, and for whose acts the prisoner was responsible in point of law, had been engaged in seditious and treasonable practices. Erskine, therefore, was forced to insist, that the precise charge laid in the indictment had not been made out. The main facts, indeed, relied on by the Attorney-General, in his opening speech, had failed in the proof. The prisoners were charged with having provided arms, and instruments called night-cats, for impeding the action of cavalry in the streets. But the arms consisted only of two or three dozen pikes; and although a model of the night-cat had been exhibited at a meeting, it did not appear that any had been ordered. The charge of making war against the King, and compassing his death, with a

few rusty pikes, was easily turned into ridicule; and
the jury were willing to accept the excuse that these
suspicious weapons had been procured to defend the
association against the violence of Church-and-King
rioters. The only evidence of an overt act, towards the
accomplishment of the crime of treason was an atrocious copy of verses found in the possession of Hardy.

Erskine spoke for seven hours. His voice and
strength failed him towards the end; and his peroration was delivered in a whisper, which was as distinctly heard through the solemn stillness of the
crowded court, as any of those resounding periods
which had so frequently drawn expressions of delight
from his excited audience. It was difficult, indeed,
to maintain the decorous restraint of a court of justice during his address. The jury themselves could
not suppress their emotions. One of the boldest
arguments in the speech was this:—that if the delegates to the proposed Convention were guilty, their
constituents must be equally guilty; thus forty thousand persons would be liable to the penalties of
treason, and be left at the mercy of the Government
—'a proposition,' said Erskine, 'from which *I observed you to shrink with horror when I stated it.*'
One of the most remarkable characteristics of an
English court of justice, is the judicial demeanour
of the twelve men who are sworn to try the issue.
While the counsel on either side are arguing, declaiming, coaxing, warning, flattering, by turns;
while the witnesses are being told to turn their faces
toward the box; while the prisoner is casting anxious
furtive glances in the same direction; while the feelings of the spectators can hardly be restrained from
open expression,—the jury remain unmoved. The
bias of the judge it is seldom difficult to ascertain;
but the most acute and practised observation can
rarely penetrate the secret of the jury box. How
great, then, must have been the power of the advocate which could extort from these grave tradesmen

a thrill of horror, and what must have been the effect on all beholders of a demonstration so unusual!

When the exhausted orator at length sunk into his seat, repeated bursts of applause, which the officers of the court in vain attempted to check, interrupted the proceedings for some minutes. The populace are so susceptible of eloquence, and their sympathies are so easily excited against any assertion of authority, that their approbation can seldom be relied on as a testimony of merit, or quoted as an expression of public opinion entitled to much weight. But, on this occasion, there were plain manifestations of the old English hatred of oppression and acts of power. The audience in court were, for the most part, persons of the better sort, who had obtained admission by favour. They represented the growing sense of resentment, at the system lately pursued of suppressing all freedom of thought and opinion by the terrors of the law; and a feeling which widely prevailed that, on the result of these trials, it depended whether the trial by jury was any longer to be treated as a sure defence against tyranny and injustice. When the court adjourned half an hour after midnight, the space before the building, the approaches, and the adjoining streets, were thronged with people drawn and kept together by the fame of the great oration which had been made for English liberty. The judges could not get to their carriages. Everybody within the building was a prisoner; for it was found impossible to penetrate the dense mass of people which blockaded every avenue to the court. At length, Erskine went out and addressed a few words to the vast assemblage. He told them to place confidence in the justice of the country, that the only security for Englishmen was in the laws, and that any attempt to overawe or intimidate the court would not only be an affront to public justice, but would endanger the lives of the accused. Such an effect had these few words, that the people began immediately to disperse, and in a short time the streets were clear. Several witnesses were called for the defence, chiefly, however, to speak to the character of Hardy as a quiet peaceable man, who only desired to promote reform by lawful means. Sheridan, Francis, and Mr. Strutt of Derby, gave evidence to that effect. The Duke of Richmond was called to prove his letter to Colonel Sharman, of which so much had been heard during the trial. This letter contained the duke's celebrated creed of Annual Parliaments, Universal Suffrage, and the Abolition of the Royal Veto on the Legislation of the two Houses of Parliament. The appearance of these distinguished persons, after the rabble of spies and informers who had been paraded before the jury for four days, would have attracted much attention at an earlier period; but the public interest in the trial subsided rapidly after the speech of Erskine. The general opinion was, that Hardy must be acquitted, and all men were impatient for the verdict. Nevertheless a very able and lucid summary of the whole case by Gibbs, the junior counsel for the prisoner, was listened to with attention. Had it not, indeed, been overshadowed by the transcendent display of his leader, the junior's speech would have been considered a brilliant performance. As it was, it made his fortune at the bar, and ultimately raised him to the great post of Chief Justice of the Common Pleas. The Solicitor-General Mitford replied upon the whole case. Mitford was a Chancery lawyer of fair attainments; but without any experience of the court in which he had now to perform the duty of replying upon Erskine. He undertook to reconstruct a long and complicated case which had been built up with great care by his leader, but had been shattered to fragments by the counsel for the prisoner. He set about his task with the deliberation and patience which he was accustomed to in the Court of Chancery. The Solicitor's speech consumed ten hours. During this prodigious performance, he fainted; but his audience bore up. The trial, which commenced on the 28th of October, was brought to a close on the 5th of November by the charge of the Lord Chief Justice, which was decidedly against the prisoner, yet on the whole temperate and fair. At the conclusion of the judge's address, the jury, having requested to be furnished with a copy of the indictment, retired to their room. After an absence of three hours, they returned with a verdict of Not Guilty. Men now congratulated each other that the worst was over. The Government had received a signal check in the headlong career against the liberties of the people. The law had been nobly vindicated against the new doctrine of constructive treason; and, at all events, an Englishman might henceforth speak his mind, or combine with his countrymen to effect a political object without being in peril of his life. It was thought that the rest of the prosecutions would be abandoned, or that if a further attempt was made, Baxter, the author of the infamous bill called the Guillotine, or Thelwall, who blew off the head of the pot of porter and said he would serve the King in the like manner, might be put up. But, after hesitating for several days, the Attorney-General announced his intention to proceed with another of the indictments, and to the surprise of all men, the individual he fixed upon, as the successor of Hardy, was John Horne Tooke.

The law officers possibly argued, that though the case was weaker against Horne Tooke than against any of the others, they might have a better chance of fixing criminal responsibility upon so notable a person than upon either of the obscure and insignificant people included in the arraignment. Horne Tooke had, for many years, been the dread of judges, ministers of State, and all constituted authorities. He was that famous Parson Horne who attacked the terrible Junius, after states-

men, judges and generals had fled before him, and
drove him back defeated and howling with his
wounds. He it was who silenced Wilkes. Some
years afterwards he fastened a quarrel on the House
of Commons, which he bullied and baffled with his
usual coolness and address.* Horne Tooke, indeed,
was no ordinary man—a profound scholar, and an
accomplished man of the world, he could hardly have
failed to obtain eminence at the bar and in the
Senate, had not a perverse destiny imposed on him
the indelible orders of the Church. He applied
himself to the study of the law, but the Inns of
Court determined that a clerk in orders could not
be admitted to the profession of the law. He
obtained a seat in the House of Commons, and, for
the same reason, an Act of Parliament was passed to
disqualify him. The disappointments, for which a
man of talents and ambition could find no compensation, embittered his spirit, and determined his
character and conduct in a direction to which they
did not naturally tend. His powers of ridicule and
satire, which the restraints of professional or political
life would have kept within bounds, became the instruments by which he sought to avenge himself on
society for the wrongs he had endured. He was as
little suited for the vocation of a demagogue, as for
that of a parish priest. He might, perhaps, have
accommodated himself with outward decency to a
profession which he hated, as Swift had done before
him; or he might have found that the conscientious
discharge of the duties of his sacred calling was not
incompatible with the most brilliant reputation, as
Sidney Smith subsequently proved. But Horne
Tooke was deficient in some of the essential qualities
of a popular leader. He neither felt, nor could with
any plausibility simulate, a hatred for the upper

* Ante, vol. ii. p. 164.

classes, because his habits and tastes were those of a scholar and a gentleman. For the same reason, he could not stoop to flatter the mob. While he abused the House of Commons as a sink of corruption, he talked about the hereditary nobility being disgraced by the intrusion of that 'skip-jack, Jenkinson,' in the spirit of a Talbot, or a Howard. He denounced the Opposition, on whom many of the democrats affected to fawn, as 'a pack of scoundrels,' like the ministerial party; and declared that both parties were equally combined to cajole 'that poor man the King,' and to deceive the people of England. But he never expressed any desire that these scoundrels should be superseded by his friends of the Constitutional and Corresponding Societies. There was, in fact, nothing in common between Horne Tooke and his fellow conspirators—not even treasonable designs. A man of his intellect and temper could hardly cabal with shoemakers, lecturers, playwrights, and that nondescript class described in the indictment as 'gentlemen.' The distempered parson would, no doubt, have gone great lengths to avenge himself on the envious tribe of placemen and parasites, who had shut him out from the high places of ambition; but he had no idea of pulling down the Constitution which had been reared by the Pyms, the Hampdens, and the Somerses, for a republic to be fashioned by the Hardys, the Thelwalls, and the Holcrofts.

Such was the man—ruined by a long conflict with adverse fortune, broken with bodily infir- *Effrontery of* mities and advanced years—whose blood *Tooke.* the Government now sought at the hands of a jury of his countrymen. The prisoner himself, however, so far from being moved by his dangerous position, was never in more buoyant spirits than when he was tried for his life. His wit and humour had often before been exhibited in courts of justice; but never had they been so brilliant as on this occasion. Erskine was his counsel; but he himself undertook some of the most important duties of his advocate, cross-examining the witnesses for the Crown, objecting to evidence, and even arguing points of law.* If his life had really been in jeopardy, such a course would have been perilous and rash in the highest degree; but nobody in court, except, perhaps, the Attorney and Solicitor-General, thought there was the slightest chance of an adverse verdict. The prisoner led off the proceedings by a series of preliminary jokes, which were highly successful. When placed in the dock, he cast a glance up at the ventilators of the hall, shivered, and expressed a wish that their lordships would be so good as to get the business over quickly, as he was afraid of catching cold. When arraigned, and asked by the officer of the court, in the usual form, how he would he tried? he answered, 'I *would* be tried by God and my country—but—' and looked sarcastically round the court. Presently he made an application to be allowed a seat by his counsel; and entered upon an amusing altercation with the judge, as to whether his request should be granted as an indulgence or as a right. The result was that he consented to take his place by the side of Erskine as a matter of favour. In the midst of the merriment occasioned by these sallies, the Solicitor-General opened the case for the Crown. It was Hardy's case over again, with the omission of some

* Horne Tooke, whenever he went before a court of justice, behaved with the greatest effrontery, and affected to turn the proceedings into ridicule. In 1781, being defendant in a civil action, to which he had no defence either in fact or in law, he nevertheless appeared in court for the purpose of insulting Lord Kenyon, who tried the cause, and of delivering a violent invective against the administration of justice. Kenyon, who had neither dignity nor temper, was so completely cowed by the parson's wit and insolence, that, after a faint struggle with the defendant, he gave up the contest. It was not without difficulty, indeed, that he could satisfy the jury that they were bound to give a verdict for the plaintiff.

aggravating circumstances, such as the infamous playbill, and the treasonable copy of verses, which had been given in evidence in the former trial. With these atrocious libels it was not alleged that Horne Tooke had any connection. The law officers did not venture to produce any of the spies who had been so damaged in Hardy's case. One of the new witnesses, a man named Sharp, on cross-examination, proved enough for an acquittal. He said that the prisoner was opposed to universal suffrage, and that he only desired such a reform as would restore the constitution to the state it was in at the Revolution; that he wished to maintain King, Lords, and Commons; that he had been denounced at the Constitutional Club as an aristocrat; and that he generally absented himself from the deliberations of that body. This witness, by an involuntary repartee, for once turned the laugh against the parson. Tooke asked if he considered him a bigot; upon which Sharp, who was evidently willing to help his old acquaintance as much as possible, replied that so far from being a bigot, he did not think the prisoner had any religion at all.

After another masterly speech from Erskine, several witnesses were called for the defence. Major Cartwright, a very honest man, known for many years, in connection with the question of parliamentary reform, came to prove what was already sufficiently shown, namely, that there was a diversity of opinion among the motley members of the Constitutional Club. Some limited their views to parliamentary reform, the greater number of these, perhaps, holding by the Duke of Richmond's plan; many would have been content with a more moderate measure. Others, no doubt, had ulterior designs, and only used reform as a pretext or a means. But it was not proved, that there existed any such common concert towards treasonable

Major Cartwright.

action, as would have involved the persons who took part in the proceedings of the club in a common guilt. Fox, Sheridan, and other eminent Whigs, were called to prove, what was not very relevant, that in former years the prisoner had been favourable to moderate schemes of reform. Pitt himself was put into the box to prove, that in 1782, he and the prisoner attended a meeting at the Thatched House, to petition Parliament in favour of reform. At length, on the fifth day, the judge summed up, and the jury, in about five minutes, agreed upon a verdict of Not Guilty.

This result was anticipated by the public with as much certainty as the catastrophe of an ill-constructed play. The whole proceeding, indeed, resembled the afterpiece which follows the grand tragedy. The intense excitement of Hardy's trial, the repeated bursts of feeling; the running commentary of rage and scorn which accompanied the cross-examination of the spies; the anxiety depicted in every countenance; the rapturous acclamation which attended and followed the great speech for the prisoner;—all these were wanting at the second trial. The people who thronged the Old Bailey to see Parson Horne tried for his life, resorted to the most attractive place of amusement for the time in London. The ready wit of the prisoner, his cool assurance, his battles with the court, and with the law officers, in many of which he had the advantage or seemed to have it, delighted the audience. Even the jury sometimes joined in the laughter, which continually pealed through the court. If anything was wanting to make the scene completely ridiculous, it was supplied by the counsel for the Crown. The Attorney-General, in his reply, attempted a touch of pathos. Alluding to his character, which nobody thought of attacking, he described his good name as the only inheritance he should leave to his children; and, having tears at command, began to weep. The Solicitor mingled his tears with those of the Attorney; and while the spectators regarded with amazement the unprovoked emotion of the two old Chancery lawyers, Horne Tooke, in an audible whisper, said 'the Attorney was crying at the thought of the little inheritance he should bequeath to his children.' After the verdict had been delivered, Horne Tooke, with the irregularity and independence which had marked his conduct during the whole proceedings, made a speech to the court and jury, in which he praised and thanked them both in an approving and patronising style, which reached the height of impudence.

Nobody expected to hear any more of the State trials; but, in the following week, the Commission again sat, when four of the prisoners, Bonney, Joyce, Kyd, and Holcroft, were acquitted, no evidence being offered against them. Holcroft, who had courted prosecution by voluntarily surrendering, wanted to address the court; but the licence, which had been permitted to the privileged veteran Tooke, was not to be extended to the ambitious playwright; and Holcroft was peremptorily silenced.

These prisoners being disposed of, Thelwall was placed in the dock for trial. Thelwall was one of those vain, shallow, half-educated persons, who are always to be found in the metropolis, and in every large town. He had set up as a political lecturer, but had not a particle of the talent and address which could raise him to the position of a demagogue. It is difficult to see what purpose could be answered by the conviction of such a man, after the Government had failed in their attempt on the secretary of the great revolutionary club, and on the only individual connected with the seditious societies, whose abilities and experience rendered him formidable. The acquittal of Thelwall, which followed almost as a matter of course, was accepted by the law officers as a final defeat, and the other prisoners awaiting their trial were immediately set at liberty.

Such was the issue of these famous prosecutions. They failed in their immediate object; but like many measures of a short-sighted policy, they were attended with beneficial effects, which their promoters never foresaw. They inspired a confidence in the tribunals far more conducive to the public safety and the maintenance of existing institutions, than the blood of a hundred traitors. The people now felt secure, under the protection of the laws, from the wild assaults of a Government stricken with craven terror; from the attempts of prerogative lawyers to torture the letter of the law to their destruction, as well as from the plots of spies and informers, who infested every haunt of business and pleasure. If the accused men, or either of them, had been brought to the scaffold, the consequence would have been disastrous. Disturbances in all the great towns, a rising in Ireland, dangerous commotions in Scotland, would probably have ensued. An Irish rebellion, already planned, and which broke out under less favourable auspices, three years later, would have afforded full employment to the available military force. The gentry and yeomanry, who were loyal to a man, could probably have suppressed any outbreak in the British Isles; but the English people are peculiarly jealous of blood shed in civil commotions; they had not yet forgotten the riot in St. George's Fields, in which only some half dozen persons were shot down five-and-twenty years before; the Manchester massacre, as it was called, which took place five-and-twenty years afterwards, agitated the island from north to south, and is yet remembered after more than forty prosperous and happy years. The spirit of the Scot-

Beneficial results of the trials.

tish people, slowly moved, but stubborn and dangerous when aroused, has repeatedly been shown. Government might, and probably would, have been able to maintain its authority; but there can be no doubt that the conviction and execution of Hardy and his associates would have given a fearful impulse to the principles of the French revolution in this country.

If the Government had been advised that a clear case of treason could be proved against the members of the revolutionary societies, it would have been their duty to prosecute for the higher offence. But, if they thought there was any reasonable doubt that twelve men of plain understanding would be satisfied with the proof of a crime which is strictly defined by a single clause in a plain Act of Parliament, upon the production of a huge mass of incongruous papers, eked out by the odious and tainted evidence of spies and informers, it is equally clear that they ought not to have charged the highest crime known to the law. We are informed, on the first authority, that such doubts existed. The Attorney-General is reported to have said, shortly after the trial of Hardy, that 'the evidence was, in his opinion, so nicely balanced, that had he himself been on the jury, he did not know what verdict he should have given.'* But Lord Eldon has himself recorded the reasons which determined him to frame these indictments.† He states, that on the examination of the prisoners before the Privy Council, the judges, who were members of that body,‡ gave it as their opinion, that the parties were

* Surtees' *Sketch of the Lives of Lords Eldon and Stowell*, p. 87.
† Twiss's *Life of Lord Eldon*. From the *Anecdote Book*, vol. i. p. 282.
‡ The only Common Law Judges who are ordinarily members of the Privy Council are the chiefs of the three courts of King's Bench, Common Pleas, and Exchequer; some one or more of whom must have presided at the trial. They would have acted with more propriety in declining functions which were within the province of the law officers.

guilty of high treason. He adds, still more strangely, that the cases, as treasonable cases, were the subjects of communication to, or debates in, Parliament. In these circumstances, he did not think himself at liberty to let the offence down to a misdemeanour. He thought the whole of the evidence in his possession should be laid before the jury, and that it was more important to expose the transactions of the societies, than to obtain convictions of the prisoners. To the obvious remark, that he might have obtained all the public benefit to arise from the exposure of these transactions, with the far greater probability of a conviction by proceeding as for misdemeanour, the great lawyer replies, that he might have proved too much, and that the prisoners might have claimed to be acquitted of the minor offence, on the ground that they had been guilty of the higher! Finally, the Chief Justice himself, who presided at the trial, is stated, on the same authority, to have felt a doubt at the trial, which he had not entertained at the examination before the Privy Council, whether the charge of high treason was made out. Yet, the evidence produced at the trial was substantially the same as the evidence which had been produced before the council; certainly it could not be materially affected, in the eye of a judge, either by the cross-examinations, or by the witnesses called on behalf of the prisoners.

It only remains to be mentioned, that the verdicts were received with gladness throughout the country. At the Lord Mayor's inauguration dinner, which took place a few days after the trial, and at which the leading members of the Government, and of the Opposition, were present, the name of Erskine, the toast of the evening, was received by the citizens with enthusiastic applause.

CHAPTER XXXV.

PROGRESS OF THE WAR—ACTION OF THE FIRST OF JUNE—MARRIAGE OF THE PRINCE OF WALES—CONCLUSION OF HASTINGS' TRIAL.

In the summer of this year, several leading members of the old Whig connection, who had given a general support to the Government since the commencement of the war, adopted the course which became them, by accepting the responsibilities of political office. Lord Fitzwilliam became President of the Council. The Duke of Portland was appointed Secretary of State; Earl Spencer, Lord Privy Seal. Mr. Windham took the office of Secretary at War. Lord Loughborough had some time previously accepted the Great Seal on the resignation, or rather removal of Thurlow. These important changes in the administration appear to have given satisfaction to nobody. The Government stood so little in need of additional strength, that its regular supporters were jealous of Whig connections. Many of Pitt's personal adherents were apprehensive that his power, hitherto supreme, would be materially diminished by the admission to the Cabinet of these great allies. The Whigs themselves were of course irritated and chagrined by the formal defection of such notable persons. It is a significant proof of the alarm which pervaded the upper ranks of society, that men of great mark should have thought it necessary to dissolve those ancient bonds of party attachment which the Whigs have ever held most sacred, and to commit themselves to measures of domestic policy wholly at variance with the principles of the Revolution.

In the course of this year, while the fall of Robespierre and the Jacobin party, and the subsequent termination of the Reign of Terror, inspired hopes that the Government of France would no longer outrage common sense and humanity, the progress of the French arms during the same period was one of almost unvaried success. While the alliance of the Great Powers was on the point of dissolution from selfishness and jealousy, the French, with an energy and determination, which, considering their unparalleled difficulties were truly heroic, had assembled armies numbering nearly a million of men. The aggregate of the allied forces did not much exceed three hundred thousand. The campaign on the Dutch and Flemish frontiers of France was planned at Vienna, but had nearly been disconcerted at the outset by the refusal of the Duke of York to serve under General Clairfait. That a young Prince, who had never seen active service until he was made Commander-in-Chief of the British troops the year before, should think it beneath his dignity to receive the orders of the ablest and most experienced general in the allied armies was an unheard-of folly and presumption; but the Emperor settled the difficulty by signifying his intention to take the command in person. Thus one incompetent prince who knew little, was to be commanded by another incompetent prince who knew nothing, about war; and the success of a great enterprise was made subservient to considerations of punctilio and etiquette. The main object of the Austrian plan was, to complete the reduction of the frontier fortresses by the capture of Landrecy on the Sambre, and then to advance through the plains of Picardy on Paris;—a plan which might have been sensible the year before, when the French were attacked on all sides, and beaten at almost every point; but was hopeless when the enemy had repaired the most formidable of his losses, and had completed his military preparations on a scale unparalleled in modern history. The King of Prussia formally withdrew from the alliance;* but condescended to assume the character of a mercenary. In the spring of the year, by a treaty with the English Government, his Prussian Majesty undertook to furnish sixty-two thousand men for a year, in consideration of the sum of one million eight hundred thousand pounds, of which Holland, by a separate convention, engaged to supply somewhat less than a fourth part. The organisation of the French army was effected under the direction of Carnot, the Minister of War, a man of great ability, and the only member of the Committee of Public Safety who rendered great services to his country without being implicated in the atrocities of his infamous colleagues. The policy of terror was nevertheless applied to the administration of the army. Custine and Houchard, who had commanded the last campaign with a credit and success which would have won honours and rewards from any Government, were sent to the scaffold, because the arms of the republic had failed to achieve a complete triumph under their direction. The guillotine was added to the furniture of the camp, under the absolute control of two conventional commissioners, St. Just and Le Bas, men well fitted for such a charge. Pichegru, the officer, now selected to lead the hosts of France, went forth to assume his command with the knife of the executioner suspended over his head. His orders were to expel the invaders from the soil and strongholds of the republic, and to reconquer Belgium. The first step towards the fulfilment of this commission was the recovery of the three great frontier towns, Condé, Valenciennes, and Quesnoy. The siege of Quesnoy was immediately

* A Declaration of the King of Prussia to the German Empire, on his secession from the Continental Confederacy, 13th March.—*Annual Register*, 1794. *State Papers*, 379.

formed; and Pichegru, informed of or anticipating the plans of the Allies, disposed a large force in front of Cambray, to intercept the operations of the grand central division of the allied army upon Landrecy. The campaign was not regularly opened until the arrival of the Emperor, which did not take place until the second week in April. His Imperial and Royal Majesty entered Brussels with a magnificent retinue, and was received with the usual demonstrations. After five days spent in public receptions, proclamations, and congratulations, on the victories which awaited him, the Emperor left Brussels, and set out for the army. On the 16th of April, the army was reviewed before Valenciennes, and on the 17th a great action was fought in which the allies obtained a success, sufficient to enable them to press the siege of Landrecy.

The Emperor, soon after this engagement, returned to Brussels, to undergo the ceremony of inauguration as Duke of Brabant. In leaving the capital of his Flemish provinces, which, in a few short weeks, was to welcome the representative of a new Sovereign, His Majesty had a narrow escape from falling into the hands of the Republican army, the vanguard of which had been pushed forward so far as to cut off his communication with the lines of the Allies. A gallant charge by a handful of British soldiers, drove back the enemy with considerable loss, and rescued His Majesty from a danger which he would not have encountered, had he not thought his performances at vain and idle pageants of more importance at that critical time, than remaining in his place at the head-quarters of the army. Pichegru, a few days after, sustained a signal repulse from the British, in an attempt to raise the siege of Landrecy; but by a rapid and daring movement, he improved his defeat, and seized the important post of Moncron. The results were, that Clairfait was forced to fall back on Tournay; Courtray and Menin surrendered to the French; and thus the right flanks of the Allies were exposed. Landrecy, which, about the same time, fell into the hands of the Allies, was but a poor compensation for the reverses in West Flanders. The Duke of York, at the urgent instance of the Emperor, marched to the relief of Clairfait; but, in the meantime, the Austrian general, being hard pressed, was compelled to fall back upon a position, which would enable him for a time to cover Bruges, Ghent, and Ostend. The English had also to sustain a vigorous attack near Tournay; but the enemy were defeated with the loss of four thousand men. It now became necessary to risk a general action to save Flanders, by cutting off that division of the French army which had outflanked the Allies. By bad management and want of concert, this movement, which had been contrived by Colonel Mack, the chief military adviser of the Emperor, was wholly defeated. The English were the greatest sufferers, chiefly through the rashness of the Duke of York, who, having detached two battalions which covered his right wing, the enemy promptly seized the advantage thus offered them. The British fought with their usual bravery; but no bravery will compensate for an utter want of military skill. The French took fifteen hundred prisoners, and sixty pieces of cannon. A thousand English soldiers lay dead on the field, and the Duke himself escaped with difficulty.

Four days after, Pichegru having collected a great force, amounting, it has been stated, to one hundred thousand men, made a grand attack *Check of Pichegru.* upon the allied army, exhausted by the recent conflict, and deprived, as he supposed, of the greater portion of their artillery. The battle raged from five in the morning until nine at night, and was at length determined by the bayonet; it was then that the French, for the first time during the war, experienced this formidable arm, which, in the hands of the British infantry of the line, is almost invincible. In consequence of this check, Pichegru fell back upon Lisle. Enraged at a repulse which proved the superiority of the British troops, the French executive, on the flimsy pretence of a supposed attempt to assassinate Robespierre, instigated by the British Government, procured a decree from the Convention, that *no English or Hanoverian prisoners should be made.* In reply to this atrocious edict, the Duke of York issued a general order, enjoining forbearance to the troops under his command. Most of the French generals, from whose breasts the principles of military honour and humanity had not been effaced by the spirit of a fell democracy, refused to become assassins; and many of the troops themselves murmured at a duty, which brave soldiers could not perform without disgrace. The decree was carried into execution in a few instances only; and the French Convention took little by their act, beyond adding another title to the execration of mankind.

The Allies gained no military advantage by the action of Pont Achin on the 22nd of May. The Emperor, alarmed at the danger which threatened his Flemish provinces, issued a proclamation, in which he acknowledged that he was no longer able to provide for their protection, unless they would recruit his army forthwith by a general levy throughout the Austrian Netherlands. With this demand the Belgians had not the means, if they had the inclination, to comply. A colourable conscription was made, but with no substantial results; and the great towns made preparations to welcome the armies of the Republic, which were soon to be their masters. The Emperor was quite disheartened by these demonstrations. Without any further attempt to protect the distant dominions of his house, of which he had only a few weeks before solemnly assumed the sovereignty, and without any regard to the common cause in which he was engaged, Francis precipitately abandoned the army, and retired to Vienna. He left some orders and proclamations behind him, to which nobody thought it worth while to pay any attention.

On the 5th of June, Pichegru invested Ypres, which Clairfait made two attempts to retain, but without success. The place surrendered on the 17th; Clairfait retreated to Ghent; Walmoden abandoned Bruges; and the Duke of York, forced to quit his position at Tournay, encamped near Oudenarde. It was now determined by the Prince of Coburg, who resumed the chief command after the departure of the Emperor, to risk the fate of Belgium on a general action, which was fought at Fleurus on the 26th of June. The Austrians, after a desperate struggle, were defeated at all points by the French army of the Sambre under Jourdan. Charleroi, having surrendered to the French the day before the decisive engagement, and the Duke of York being forced to retreat, any further attempt to save the Netherlands was hopeless. Ostend and Mons, Ghent, Tournay, and Oudenarde, were successively evacuated; and the French were established at Brussels. When it was too late, the English army was reinforced by seven thousand men under the Earl of Moira. These succours arrived at Ostend on the fatal day at Fleurus, and Lord Moira effected a junction with the Duke of York a day or two after the enemy had entered Ostend.

It now only remained for the French to recapture the fortresses on their own frontier, which had been taken from them in the last campaign. The covering army of the Prince of Coburg having been withdrawn for the action at Fleurus, a French force was detached under General Scherer, to effect the reduction of these places. Landrecy, on the capture of which, the Allies had founded their base of operations for the campaign, fell without a struggle. Quesnoy, the weakest of the chain of fortresses on the northern frontier, made a gallant resistance; notwithstanding the garrison had been threatened with the sword, if they failed to surrender within twenty-four hours after summons. Valenciennes and Condé, though each capable of sustaining a long siege, either from treachery or cowardice, opened their gates to the enemy.

The victorious armies of the Republic were thus prepared for the conquest of Holland. They found the Netherlands prepared for successful invasion. The Prince of Orange made an appeal to the patriotism of his countrymen; but the republicans preferred the ascendency of their faction to the liberties of their country. The Dutch were no longer that heroic people which had been content to restore their country to the sea, rather than its soil should be trod by the legions of France. A proposal to open the dikes was resisted by a popular demonstration at Amsterdam; and it was declared that the city would rise against the Prince of Orange and the English, if they attempted to occupy it for the purpose of preventing the entrance of the French. It is not necessary to pursue the ignominious details of the subjugation of Holland. After a series of unavailing efforts on the part of the Allies, and much valuable blood shed in an ungrateful cause, the English troops finally withdrew from the Low Countries in the early part of the ensuing year.

Dutch population in favour of the French.

The other military operations of the year, in which England was engaged, do not require prolonged notice. The Corsicans, under the guidance of their veteran chief, Paoli, who had resided for many years in this country, sought the aid of England to throw off the French yoke, and

Corsica. Paoli.

offered in return allegiance of his countrymen to the British Crown. The island itself was worthless as a permanent possession, and of little value as a military position to a country which had the command of Gibraltar; but a small force was despatched, and, after a series of petty operations, Corsica was occupied by British troops, and proclaimed a part of the British dominions.

An expedition on a greater scale was sent to the West Indies. Martinique, St. Lucie, and Guadaloupe were easily taken; but the large island of St. Domingo, relieved by a timely arrival of succours from France, offered a formidable resistance. The English, who anticipated an easy conquest, unexpectedly found themselves opposed by a French force far superior in numbers to themselves, by the disaffection of the inhabitants, and by an enemy more formidable than either, the deadly pestilence of the climate. The British, after holding out during the summer and a part of the autumn, were at length compelled to make their final stand in the town of Bassetterre, the only part of the island of which they retained possession. There they remained for more than a month, exposed to a destructive fire, awaiting reinforcements from England. But when the reinforcements arrived, they were, as usual, too late, and inadequate even if they had been in time. *British expedition to the West Indies.*

The campaign on the Rhine was undertaken by the Allies under auspices ill calculated to inspire confidence, or even hope. The King of Prussia, not content with abandoning the cause, had done everything in his power to thwart and defeat the operations of the Allies. He positively refused his assent to, and by his authority prevented the execution of, the important measure proposed by the Emperor, and sanctioned by the Diet, of arming the Rhenish provinces. He required that the sup- *Campaign on the Rhine.*

plies of his army should be furnished at the cost of
the Germanic States, and that, from a given date,
the whole of their pay and equipment should be
provided from the same source. These exorbitant
demands not being immediately complied with,
Frederic William ordered his troops to quit their
advanced position, and fall back upon Cologne.
Many of the States, alarmed at the movement, were
willing to yield to his rapacity, whereupon the Prussian
monarch rose in his demands, and insisted on
being paid the expenses of the siege of Mentz, in the
preceding year. At length he consented to receive,
for his temporary services, the British subsidy already
mentioned. It was, in fact, necessary to comply
with this extortion, unless the Allies were content
to abandon the defence of the Rhine.

In consequence of these negotiations, the season
was far advanced before the German armies
were ready to take the field. On the 22nd
of May, the Austrians crossed the Rhine,
and attacked the French in their intrenchments
without success. On the same day, the Prussians
defeated a division of the Republican army, and
advanced their head-quarters to Deux-Ponts. Content
with this achievement, the German armies
remained inactive for several weeks, when the French,
having obtained reinforcements, attacked the whole
line of the German posts. After a succession of
engagements, attended with various fortunes, the
energy of the Republicans, rather than any superiority
of military skill, obtained the advantage. The
Prussians were compelled to evacuate Deux-Ponts,
and fall back on Mentz; the Austrians were forced
once more to retreat across the Rhine. The French
having by this time virtually achieved the re-conquest
of Belgium, the armies of the Rhine and the Moselle,
detachments of which had been engaged on the
northern frontier, effected a junction, and pushed

forward to expel the Austrians and Prussians from the soil of France. In this operation they were completely successful; before the end of the year, the Allies were in full retreat, and the Republicans in their turn had become the invaders of Germany. They occupied the Electorate of Treves, and they captured the important fort of Manheim. Mentz also was placed under a close blockade. Such was the result of the campaign on the Rhine. All hope of making that river either the boundary of French ambition, or a base from which the Republic could still be attacked, had for the present vanished. The Emperor was content to think himself secure at Vienna. The King of Prussia, more jealous of the aggrandisement of Austria than careful for the common cause of kings and established governments, was prepared to make a separate peace with France, which should secure his own interests. The petty states of Germany, dismayed at the selfishness and incapacity of the two great potentates of the empire, knew not where to look for help, and already regarded their position as desperate.

At sea, England maintained her ancient reputation. The French had made great exertions to fit out a fleet, and twenty-six ships of the line were assembled in the port of Brest. This squadron was destined for a particular service, of greater immediate importance even than a victory over the British. The city of Paris had long been subject to periods of scarcity; under the monarchical government, the clamour for bread, like every other clamour, had been suppressed by the strong arm of power; but since the Revolution, the populace naturally expected the Government, which they had set up, to provide for their wants. Under the immediate pressure of hunger, they had sometimes taken the law into their own hands, and plundered the bakers' shops; but this expedient would not bear

England successful at sea.

too frequent repetition. The Government had therefore imported large supplies from America and the West Indies; and it was to ensure the safe passage of this precious freight from molestation by the English cruisers, that the best ships of the Republic were sent to sea. The English Channel Fleet, under Lord Howe, consisted of thirty-two sail of the line. Six sail having been detached to convey the outward-bound East India merchantmen, and one ship having been separated from her comrades, the British Admiral had twenty-five ships of the line under his immediate orders. The Brest fleet of twenty-six sail of the line, more heavily armed than the British, had put to sea. A fog prevented the hostile navies, equally eager for action, from coming in contact for some days. On the 29th of May, a partial engagement took place; but the fleets separated without any decisive result. After cruising and manœuvring in thick weather for two days, the fog dispersed on the morning of the 1st of June; and the English Admiral found himself to windward of the enemy. The numbers of the opposing ships being so nearly equal, almost every ship on each side was separately engaged, although the regular line of battle was maintained. Howe's object was to execute the celebrated manœuvre of breaking the enemy's line, which after an hour's hard fighting, was accomplished with complete success. This manœuvre being invariably decisive of the action, it only remained for the British Admiral to secure his prizes. Of these, six were taken into port, a seventh having sunk on her passage. One French ship went down during the engagement, with nearly all her crew. Eighteen sail of the line, though much crippled, made their escape to the French coast.

This victory was extolled in England as one of the most glorious achievements of the British arms. It was, no doubt, in the highest degree creditable to the ability of the Admiral, and to the seamanship of the fleet. The ships on each side, their rating and armament, were so nearly equal, that the difference can hardly be considered as of much account. The slight disadvantage, on the part of the English fleet, was more than compensated by the superior quality of the officers and men. Most of the French officers were taken from the merchant service, and had little or no experience in men-of-war. The crews were in great part landsmen, many of them country people, hastily pressed into the service; the proportion of seamen trained in the discipline of the service being very small. The Admiral himself, Villaret Joyeuse, had been only recently promoted from a subordinate rank. The action of the 1st of June, was, therefore, inferior to Rodney's action, which it resembled, and after the model of which it appears to have been fought; and was insignificant when compared to the subsequent achievements of Nelson and St. Vincent. The victory itself was fruitless. The American convoy which it was of so much importance to intercept, arrived in safety at Brest, twelve days after the battle.

Notwithstanding the public joy at the glorious day of June, an impatience for peace became manifest throughout every class of society. *Pressure of taxation.* The pressure of taxation began to be felt, the war having already added more than twenty millions to the permanent debt. The prospect of putting down French democracy by force of arms had faded, even from the heated visions of country gentlemen. The grand alliance of the European Powers, which was to be content with nothing less than the restoration of the French monarchy, was already on the point of dissolution; and the shameless hypocrisy of the pretences on which it was founded were exposed to the derision of all men, when the eagles of Austria, not the lilies of France, were displayed on the citadels of

Condé and Valenciennes. A war to restore Christian and civilised Government in France found numerous supporters; but a war to subject France to the fate of Poland, was a war in which the English nation could take no part. The German Powers, unable to agree on the division of the spoil, even if they got possession of it, were prepared to make terms with the Republic; and it was extremely doubtful whether either Austria or Prussia would take the field in the ensuing spring. Holland, in whose defence this country had taken up arms, was no longer willing to take the necessary measures for her own defence. The Northern States of the Union had already formed an alliance with the French Republic, and formally notified their secession at the Hague. The city of Amsterdam, the capital of the Union, was only restrained from taking the same course by the presence of an army. The English, far from being welcomed as saviours, were execrated by the Dutch, as the only obstacle to the conclusion of a treaty with France; and this appeared to be the sense of a large majority of the people of the United Provinces.

The reason which had been hitherto urged with much force against peace with France, that no Government existed with which it was possible to negotiate a treaty, was much weakened, if not entirely removed. Since the death of Robespierre and his colleagues, the reign of Terror had ceased; the Jacobin Club had been suppressed; the seventy-three Girondists who had been expelled from the Convention were restored to their places; the freedom of religious worship was decreed; and finally, to the satisfaction of all men, the ministers and agents of Terror were brought to punishment. Carrier, Fouquier Tinville, and Le Bon were sent to the guillotine. Others, who deserved the same fate, such as Collot d'Herbois and Barrère, were sentenced to transportation. The unmeaning jingle of words which Pitt had put into the mouths of his friends and followers—'Indemnity for the past, and security for the future,'—was no longer quoted except among rustics, as the motto for a future peace. Some of the minister's most staunch adherents were prepared to oppose him on the question of the war.

Parliament was nevertheless opened on the 30th of December with a royal speech in which his Majesty was made to declare his 'firm conviction of the necessity of persisting in a vigorous prosecution of the war;' and to intimate that this conviction rested on the fact, that the resources of the enemy were nearly exhausted. An amendment to the Address was moved by Wilberforce, recommending that an attempt should be made to restore peace. The mover of the amendment, though a man of character and ability, and the personal friend of Pitt, was perhaps less fitted than any member of his position in the House to give effect to such a motion. Wilberforce was chiefly guided by religious fervour in his treatment of public questions. He urged the claims of the African negro to the rights of man more from a pious abhorrence of slavery, than from an abstract or indomitable passion for civil liberty. He had opposed the war from scruples as to the lawfulness of shedding blood. But as this was not the ground upon which the argument for peace could be most advantageously placed, the motion might have fared better, if it had been put in a more popular and practical form. Windham opposed the amendment in a violent and warlike speech, in the course of which he censured the results of the State trials, employing an unhappy phrase which was justly resented and long remembered. He called the accused persons 'acquitted felons'—an expression as insulting to the juries who tried them, as to the prisoners themselves. The speech of the Secretary-at-War did not much ad-

[margin: Determination to continue the war.]

vance the cause which he had been put up to defend. He was followed in the debate by Tory gentlemen, who strongly supported the amendment, and undertook to refute the arguments by which the minister had contended for the prolongation of the war.

Pitt was sorely vexed. Long accustomed to implicit obedience from his followers, he suddenly found his policy assailed, not by some revolted place-seeker, or shallow declaimer, but by men of independence and position, whom he could not treat with contempt. He sat, in the hope that somebody behind the Treasury Bench would stand up in his defence. But the back benches were silent. The Opposition, content with the course which the debate was taking, were silent too. At length Pitt was compelled to rise, not to discharge his ordinary duty of replying to Fox or Sheridan, but for the unwonted, and perhaps more difficult task of answering the Bankeses and the Duncombes. He could not and cared not to dissemble his annoyance; and, for the first time during the many years that he had been the principal mark of opposition, his temper gave way. He began his speech with great warmth, vehemently demanding whether those gentlemen who now deserted the war, supposed that we could obtain a peace which would set our commerce free, enable us to lay up our armaments, and repeal the traitorous Correspondence Act? He did not deny the *possibility* of a peace with a republican Government in France, though he doubted whether any peace could be lasting, until monarchy was restored in that country. He then turned upon Wilberforce, and asked in his most imperious tones, what sort of a peace he wanted? Did he want to inflict upon this country a gratuitous loss of honour, and reduce it to an unnecessary despair? Were we to abandon the Austrian Netherlands to the French? Would the honourable gentleman venture to say that? It was said the ground of war was removed when the

Dutch negotiated for peace. 'So far from it,' he exclaimed, with a boldness of assertion which reminded some of the old members of a former William Pitt, 'so far from it, that, even if Holland concluded a treaty with the French, it would be necessary that we should continue in arms to secure the observance of it.' But the main argument on which he relied, and in which he seems to have had entire faith, was the inability of the French to maintain a protracted war, by reason of their financial difficulties. He laid it down as an invariable principle, that all modern warfare was carried on by money; and he had only, therefore, to demonstrate that France was in a state of bankruptcy, and that she had now arrived at her last resources. Under the system of terror, the French Government had been enabled to resort to the extremity of the maximum. The Reign of Terror had ceased, never to be revived; the law of the maximum was already obsolete; the paper currency was at a discount of seventy-five per cent., and, therefore, the revolutionary wars were approaching their termination. Peace, at such a moment, would enable the enemy to recover from his depression, and to devise new modes of providing for a future war. The speech, in its greater part, presented a remarkable contrast to the stately and measured harangues which the great minister usually delivered; and resembled more the style and manner of Chatham, when he tempted, and at the same time defied opposition. When Pitt sat down, still ruffled and disdainful, Fox, elated at the course the debate had taken, immediately rose, and put forth all his strength for the reply. He rallied Windham for lamenting the decay of zeal for a war which had proved so disastrous. That zeal had been inspired by a contempt for the enemy, and a confidence in the ability of the Administration, which had proved alike unfounded. Never since the irruption of the Goths and Vandals had such reverses been experienced on the one hand, and such acquisitions made on the other. He addressed himself with great power to the two-fold grounds on which the minister had contended for proceeding with the war. He showed the utter fallacy of an argument based on a calculation of ways and means, which, though a necessary rule of action for an established Government in ordinary times, was wholly inapplicable to a people fighting for their existence, and guided by counsels of unscrupulous energy. The other proposition, he said, that no proposal for peace should be made until a Government was established in France, which should command the confidence of His Majesty's ministers, or, in other words, until monarchy was restored, was, in itself, so extravagant and presumptuous, and opened a prospect of war so desolating and indefinite, that it could not be contemplated without dismay. The address was voted by a majority of more than three to one; but the minority was far larger than on any division since the commencement of the war, and included some of the sturdiest supporters of the Ministry. Many reluctantly contributed to swell the majority. In the Upper House, an amendment to the Address was likewise moved, but was supported chiefly by the Whig lords.

Proceedings of the Opposition. The Opposition, very properly, took an early opportunity of bringing to a direct issue the important question raised by the Ministry, whether the existence of a particular form of Government in France should be a condition precedent to a negotiation for peace. The negative of this proposition was moved by Grey; but Pitt, though he now went so far as to say, that he did not insist on the restoration of the old monarchy, or of any specific form of Government, as a preliminary to negotiation, yet still maintained, that since the commencement of the war, no Government had existed in France capable of giving security for the observance of a treaty, and, therefore, he refused to treat with the present Government. The favourite phrase, 'indemnity for the past, and security for the future,' which his flatterers and followers had never been weary of repeating last year, was no longer heard. Pitt, himself, gave up half of it as no longer tenable. 'Reparation and security,' he said, 'were the objects of the war; but we should be content with security.' He concluded by moving, as an amendment to Grey's resolution, 'Confidence in His Majesty's intention to effect a pacification on just and honourable grounds, with any Government in France, which should appear capable of maintaining the accustomed relations of peace and amity with other countries.'

Language such as this—so arrogant and offensive—could hardly fail to be resented by the whole French nation, and to aggravate the breach between the two countries. Wilberforce preferred words which professed to be a compromise between Grey and Pitt, but were substantially of the same import as those of the mover. The division showed a considerable increase of the minority on the amendment to the Address. Late in the session, Wilberforce again urged the policy of peace, and, on this occasion, the tone of the minister was sensibly lowered. He said, that he soon expected to be enabled to enter on a negotiation, and, as this expectation was not founded on any change which had taken place in the French Government, one of the grounds on which he had, a few weeks before, declared it impossible to treat, was happily abandoned. But he still clung to the shallow and fallacious idea, that the French must yield for want of means to carry on the war. Pitt, however, had by this time recovered his temper; he had acquired some knowledge of the public feeling on the subject since the last debate. He did not even venture to

Intemperate language of Pitt.

ask his supporters for a direct vote on Wilberforce's motion; he merely moved the order of the day, which would enable the House to avoid pronouncing any opinion. Even this modified course was marked by a sensible decrease of the majority which usually supported the minister.

Eighteen millions were borrowed for the military service of the year; in addition to this, Parliament was required to guarantee the interest on the loan of four millions, which was negotiated in the English market by the Emperor of Austria.

Loan to Austria.

The Speech from the throne had announced the approaching marriage of the Prince of Wales; and some interest was manifested by the public in an event, which it was hoped might have the same beneficial effect on the heir to the throne, that matrimony is proverbially supposed to exercise on men of pleasure. The prince had attained his thirty-third year, and could no longer plead youth as an apology for his excesses. His Royal Highness had, indeed, lately lived very much in seclusion with the woman to whom he was already married in the face of the church. He was not yet weary of his wife; and, therefore, he had no desire to avail himself of the law which enabled him to repudiate his engagement. No idea of his duty to the nation in this respect ever seems to have entered his mind. But he was, as usual, much troubled by debts and want of money. He had formerly obtained relief by denying his marriage in point of fact; and he was now offered relief on the sole condition of contracting a marriage in point of law. The terms were hard, but he consented. The bride selected for him was a cousin, a princess of the House of Brunswick. The choice had been made by the King; and so eager was His Majesty to conclude the business, that he dispatched an experienced

Affairs of the Prince of Wales.

diplomatist, not with discretionary powers, but with positive instructions to negotiate the marriage with a young lady whom neither father nor son had seen. No blame, however, can fairly attach to the King for the part which he took in this unhappy business. The union of two persons who had never before seen each other, and whom none of the high contracting parties had seen, was in accordance with the unnatural etiquette of royal marriages. The King himself had been so married, and the union had turned out reasonably well. Perhaps there was some precipitation in pushing on the treaty; but there is no ground for supposing that the king had ever heard any report unfavourable to the character or disposition of his intended daughter-in-law.

Notwithstanding the definite nature of his instructions, Lord Malmesbury was quite inexcusable, in suffering the matter to proceed without addressing some private remonstrance, or at least, a representation of the real state of the case to the King, or to the person principally interested. He must soon have seen enough to satisfy himself, that the Princess Caroline was not only unfit, but could not be qualified, for the exalted station to which she was destined. The experienced diplomatist was not long in discovering, that the future Queen of England was utterly deficient in tact; that she was 'missish' in character and habits, and slovenly in her person. A further acquaintance proved that she was incapable of comprehending the dignity and propriety of conduct suitable to her rank. What chance of happiness was afforded by an alliance with a lady, who was dismayed, when told of the hope expressed by her father-in-law, that she was domestic in her tastes and habits? What apprehension of public scandal must have been suggested by her alarm at hearing of the penalties which awaited a Princess of Wales who should be

Unwise conduct of Lord Malmesbury.

guilty of criminal levity! And what must have been the language or demeanour which could induce her courtly monitor to advert to such a topic! But, even supposing greater dangers might have been averted, could Lord Malmesbury believe, that a well-bred Englishman could tolerate a woman who required to be admonished, among other things, of the expediency of a more frequent change of body linen? Surely, Lord Malmesbury might have exceeded the letter of his instructions, under such circumstances, and given a hint, at least to his employers, of those observations which he has since revealed to the world. The ignoble safety which is secured by a careful adherence to the letter, is despised by great minds; and should be risked by every man who finds himself in a position of responsibility. If Lord Malmesbury had confidentially advised the Prince of the character and disposition of his intended bride, instead of misinforming him upon these points, the nation might have been spared a disgraceful page in its history, and the unhappy lady herself might have escaped a life of misery and shame.

The reception with which Caroline of Brunswick was greeted by the Prince, could only be paralleled by one odious precedent in English history. But the conduct of Henry the Eighth towards Ann of Cleves, abating one brutal phrase which does not appear to have been vented in her presence, was measured and polite, compared with that of the 'first gentleman in Europe' to his betrothed bride. No sooner had he approached her, than, as if to subdue the qualms of irrepressible disgust, he desired Lord Malmesbury, *with an oath*, to bring him *a glass of brandy*. The Princess expressed surprise, but was not discomfited. 'On the first day at dinner,' says the same authentic chronicler already quoted, 'the Princess's behaviour was flippant, rattling, affecting raillery and wit, and throwing out coarse vulgar hints about Lady —, who was present, and though mute, "le diable n'en perdait rien." The Prince was evidently disgusted, and this unfortunate dinner fixed his dislike.'* It is not surprising that a few days terminated the cohabitation of this ill-assorted pair. The bride objected to have the husband's mistress placed about her person. This was resented; and it was only by the interposition of the King, that the insolent harlot was removed from a position so offensive to decency, as well as to the feelings of the wife.

No sooner had the Princess of Wales recovered from child-birth, than a formal separation took place. From that time until the sad close of her eventful career, the conduct of the neglected wife was watched with malignant vigilance; and every tangible imprudence which she committed was distorted by treachery, and moulded into shape by the pliant arts of sycophants and lawyers. Deprived of her natural protector — a stranger in the land—unfixed in principle, deficient in judgment, delicacy, and tact—the unhappy Princess afforded ample opportunity to the unscrupulous emissaries of her lord. What began in folly ended in vice; and though there is not sufficient reason to believe that she had departed from the path of virtue before she came to England, or even during her residence here, her subsequent conduct ultimately

Separation of the Prince and Princess.

---

* *Malmesbury Correspondence.*—'April 8. The marriage day. Princess looked dignified and composed; but the Prince agitated to the greatest degree; he was like a man in despair, half crazy. He held so fast by the Queen's hand, she could not remove it. When the Archbishop called on those to come forward who knew any impediment, his manner of doing it shook the Prince, and made me shudder. The Duke of Gloster assured me the Prince was quite drunk; and that after dinner he went out and drank twelve glasses of Maraschino.'—COUNTESS HARCOURT's *Diary, Locker MSS.*

justified the most uncharitable opinion of her enemies.

A few days after the Prince's marriage, the minister brought down a message relating to the future establishment of His Royal Highness, and communicating the unpleasant information that the state of the Prince's affairs required some special provision with regard to his future income. The fact was, that the Prince's debts were nearly seven hundred thousand pounds, a sum equivalent to an average annual expenditure of one hundred thousand pounds in excess of his income, since the period* when Parliament had paid his debts, on the express promise that his expenditure should in future be confined within the limits of his ample revenues.† This disclosure coming at a moment when it was more than ever important to exhibit royalty in a dignified and respectable light, was peculiarly unfortunate. Few persons among those who were acquainted with the audacious falsehoods by which His Royal Highness silenced Rolle and the country gentlemen, in 1787, put any confidence in the promises by which, in conjunction with the falsehoods, he then obtained the means of relief from his immediate exigencies; but few persons beyond those who were honoured with the Prince's confidence, believed it possible, that, upon the payment of his debts by the nation, he would immediately begin to spend nearly three times the amount of his income. Yet such was the tale which, with a manifest sense of shame and vexation, the First Minister had to tell the House of Commons. Never before, indeed, had the Crown applied to the House to make provision for the royal family, in such terms as those which George the Third was made to employ on this humiliating occasion. He announced, with 'the deepest regret,' and without a

---

* 1787.
† His annual income being £73,000 including the revenues of the Duchy of Cornwall.

phrase of extenuation, the necessity of making arrangements to relieve the Prince from incumbrances to a large amount. The King admitted that his son could not expect any grant of public money for such a purpose, and that the only mode in which relief could be granted, would be by the appropriation of such part of the Prince's future income as Parliament might think fit for the liquidation of his debts, and by the imposition of such securities as would guard against the possibility of his being again involved in so painful and embarrassing a situation.

The House listened to this extraordinary communication with the respectful silence with which a royal message is received; but after it had been read from the chair, a murmur of surprise and indignation arose from all sides; and when Pitt made the usual motion, that the message should be referred to a committee of the whole House, a country gentleman started up and moved that the King's message of the 21st May, 1787, relating to the debts of the Prince of Wales, should be read by the clerk. This being done, the same member moved for a call of the House on the day when the subject was to be considered. Pitt resisted this as unusual and unnecessary; but the temper of the House was such that he found it necessary to give way. He even tried, against his nature, to assume a conciliatory tone; but the House would not be conciliated; and the excitement was such as had hardly been equalled by any of the debates on the French Revolution, or the war. The general feeling of indignation first found an utterance from the lips of Grey, the most rising, and the most respected member of the party of which the Prince had been long the reputed head. But Grey had ceased to be numbered among the Prince's friends, since that day when he had declined to serve his Royal Highness by

treachery and prevarication.* He now stood forth to
denounce the selfishness and meanness which sought
to add to the burdens of the people at a time when
every class was suffering, and when the poor were
reduced to the extremity of privation. He exposed
the flimsy pretext under which it was intended to
obtain a vote of money for the payment of the Prince's
debts, and desired to know, in plain truth, what
burdens they were called upon to bear for his Royal
Highness? Several members followed, and demanded
an enquiry into the circumstances which had lead to
a breach of the solemn promise of 1787, when the
Prince's debts had been paid. None of the Prince's
friends said a word in his defence. Fox and Sheridan,
not certainly rigid moralists, and neither of
them wanting in courage or generosity, maintained
a significant silence. Pitt, who had not, perhaps,
been either unprepared or unwilling to hear some
severe remarks on the Prince's conduct, became
alarmed at the course which the debate was taking.
Without attempting to palliate what had been done,
he deprecated in the most earnest manner the investigation
which was proposed. He implored the
House to recollect, before it gave way to heat and
resentment, that in the issue of the discussion was
involved the credit of the hereditary monarchy, and,
consequently, the safety of the country. He proposed
that day fortnight for the consideration of the
subject in the Committee of Supply, and it was
ordered that the House should be called over on that
day.

Pitt's proposal to relieve the Prince. The plan which Pitt ultimately proposed for the
relief of the Prince's embarrassments was a
tacit admission that no confidence whatever
was to be placed either in His Royal Highness's
promises, or the stability of any good resolutions
he might form. The Prince's income was to be

* See ante, p. 163.

increased to one hundred and twenty-five thousand a
year. The revenues of the Duchy of Cornwall were
to be sequestrated and formed into a sinking fund
which, at the end of twenty-seven years, would ex-
tinguish the principal debt. Twenty-five thousand
pounds a year were to be set aside for the payment of
interest. All this was plain matter of business; but
the plan, by which it was proposed to guard against
the growth of future claims upon the patience of the
country, was nothing less than the enactment of a
special law of contract for the particular case. The
officers and servants of his Royal Highness were to be
liable for the contracts which they should enter into
on his behalf; and the legal remedy, for the recovery
of any debt due by the Prince, should cease after the
expiration of three months from the time when the
debt accrued. Pitt had named a distant day for the
Committee of Supply in the hope that the house would
cool. But the heat had only grown more intense,
and had spread beyond the Prince of Wales to the
King, the royal family, and even to monarchy itself.
The leaders of Opposition could no longer refrain
from offering their opinion. Fox said that he took a
view of the matter which would be acceptable to none
of the parties concerned. He thought the Prince
had rashly undertaken in 1787 to make no further
application to Parliament; but having made the
promise, he was bound in honour to keep it. He
was willing, however, to grant the increased income,
provision being made either by a sinking fund or by
the sale of the duchy lands, for the liquidation of the
debt. He censured the King and the Ministers for
having suffered the matter to come before Parliament.
He contended that the debts ought to have been
defrayed out of the civil list; and deprecated the
invidious proposal to make special provision by Act
of Parliament against the future liabilities of the
Prince of Wales. He would support such an en-

nctment, if it was made to apply to the Royal Family in general, as a permanent law. Sheridan and other members, some of whom were connected neither with the Prince, nor with the Opposition, followed in the same sense. An amendment moved by Grey, to reduce the proposed additional annuity by twenty-five thousand pounds, was rejected by a majority of only two to one, which, considering the state of the House at that period, might be regarded as a strong expression of its real opinion in favour of the amendment. A great struggle was made to refuse any parliamentary recognition of the debts, and to provide only for the additional establishment which the Prince's marriage might be supposed to render necessary. Grey and Sheridan took this view, but Fox supported the proposal of the Government, that sixty-five thousand pounds of the additional income, together with the revenues of the Duchy, should be applied to the payment of debts, leaving a clear sixty thousand a year as available income. A commission was appointed for the administration of the funds so appropriated; and the stringent provisions against future debts, which Pitt had proposed, and which nothing but the incorrigible conduct of the heir-apparent could justify, were likewise adopted.*
The discussion of these various details was continued until the close of the session; and the irritation attending them was not abated by the whispers which were circulated before the Bill had left the Commons. It was said that the royal bridegroom having gained

---

* With reference to this subject, Fox writes to Lord Holland: 'The Prince's business turned out as I foretold you. Pitt adopted my plan, for which, though I believe the King and the Prince are a good deal displeased at him, they are not more pleased with me. However, I could not do otherwise than I have done, and I am sure it is the best plan for the Prince's real interests, and the only one which can operate to soften in any degree the general odium against him.' — Fox's *Correspondence*, June 14, 1795.

the end of his marriage, had already cast aside his wife, and returned to his paramour. This was the commencement of a chapter of scandal and infamy, of which the existing generation did not see the close.

In this session, Warren Hastings was acquitted upon all the articles of impeachment exhibited by the Commons. If a jury were justified in refusing to find a man guilty of a charge, which it took nine hours to state,* much more difficult was it to convict a man of a charge which it took eight years to prove. The whole trial, if trial it is to be called, was a preposterous caricature—a monstrous thing, whose proportions could not be measured by any known rule of justice. A prosecution which was opened by a succession of orations, embellished with all the arts of rhetoric, exaggerating every fact, and replete with inflammatory comments, was so great a perversion of all rule and practice, that, from the first, it was impossible to regard the proceeding as one which really involved penal consequences. As the trial proceeded, it was plain to all men that there could be no practical result, and the great speeches having been delivered, all public interest in the matter was exhausted. The case for the prosecution having been brought to a close, in the fifth year of the trial, the counsel for the prisoner, Law,† a King's Bench barrister of promise, gravely rose to address the Court for the defence. Law had conducted his case throughout with great skill and judgment. Not attempting to emulate the high flown eloquence of the managers, he opposed to their sounding periods, their metaphors, their invectives, their perorations, the impenetrable shield of legal learning, of common sense, and professional practice. The managers, although themselves assisted by counsel, conducted

* Ante, p. 276; Hardy's trial.
† Afterwards Lord Ellenborough, C.J.

the examination of the witnesses, for the most part, with an utter disregard to the rules of evidence; and whenever the counsel for the prisoner attempted to restrain the evidence within legal bounds, Burke flew into a passion, asked them how they dared interrupt the Commons of England, called them pettifoggers, and accused them of attempting to suppress the truth. Sometimes, however, the law lords interposed; and on one occasion, after the counsel, the Chancellor, and several peers, had in vain attempted to moderate the violence of Burke, the primate stood up and declared the conduct of the manager to be intolerable. 'If Robespierre and Marat,' said his Grace, 'were in the managers' box, they could not say anything more inhuman, and more against all sentiments of honour and morality, than what we have been often used to since this trial has commenced.' Another time, when the defendant complained of the hardship to which he was exposed by the great length of the trial, Burke replied, that the trial was protracted by the defendant's counsel, who would persist in making objections to evidence. The proceedings in Westminster Hall were diversified by debates on legal points in the House of Commons, in which the guilt and innocence of the defendant were incidentally canvassed by the partisans on both sides. Burke went so far as to say that Major Scott, who systematically defended Hastings, and was supposed to have owed his seat to the Indian interest, ought to be expelled the House.

The best case that ever was launched would infallibly have been ruined by such management as this. The people of England, who have always been remarkable for their deference to the law, and their jealousy of the due administration of justice, would have risen with indignation had they understood that the strange scene which might be occasionally witnessed during the session of Parliament was in reality

a solemn trial which involved the liberty and fortune
of a fellow subject. But this was what nobody believed.
Hastings was eventually acquitted of charges
so loose and vague, that the same result must have
followed a trial before a regular tribunal. But though
acquitted, the accused suffered penalties hardly inferior
to those which could have been inflicted had
he been prosecuted to conviction. He suffered a
partial imprisonment of eight years, and he was in
effect fined seventy thousand pounds. The cost of
his defence, indeed, including incidental charges, far
exceeded that amount. The whole of his private
fortune had been absorbed by the expenses of the
trial, and he left the Bar of the House of Lords without
a shilling in the world.

Such was the trial by impeachment; in theory,
the highest act of justice which can be performed by
a free people; but an act so strange and cumbrous
in its process, so transcendent in its character, that
it has been little understood by a people who chiefly
regard promptitude, precision, and fairness, in the
administration of the criminal law. The history of
impeachment in this country, until the case of
Hastings had furnished no instance in which that
remedy was resorted to or attempted, except to
gratify the revenge or the animosity of political
faction; and the case of Hastings showed that the
trial by impeachment was wholly unfitted for an
issue which involved a substantial and determinate
charge. In future, whenever it is intended to inflict
punishment on a public malefactor, some allegation
will, if possible, be reduced into a definite
form and referred to the ordinary tribunals. The
charges of bribery and extortion, into which this huge
indictment ultimately resolved itself, might have
been tried before a court of criminal jurisdiction, and
Hastings would have been acquitted within a week.
The Rohilla charge—the one charge which could not

have been tried by a judge and jury—the charge
which involved delinquency of the gravest character
—which was clear and specific—and to which it is
difficult to conjecture what answer could have been
given—was the one charge which the Commons declined to urge.

Long before the impeachment was brought to a
close, public opinion by an intuitive action of common
sense had pronounced an acquittal. The proceedings,
which had opened with such imposing grandeur,
soon dwindled into a dreary and irksome formality.
The eloquence, which had shaken Westminster Hall,
the terrible tales of cruelty, perfidy, and extortion,
which had caused men to shudder and women to be
carried fainting from the court, had been subjected
to the test of evidence. Then it was found that a
multiplicity of petty facts was insufficient to sustain
these enormous charges; the charges themselves soon
shrunk away and appeared frivolous and vexatious;
and the indignation, which had been invoked against
the accused, was turned upon the accusers. Englishmen, accustomed to see prisoners tried for their lives,
and to serve as jurymen before the judges of the land,
heard the managers for the Commons contend that
they were not bound by the rules of the courts below, and assert a license of proceeding against the
accused party only to be compared to the license
which obtained in the Revolutionary tribunal at Paris.
They heard leading questions addressed to the witnesses for the impeachment; and the very answers
put into their mouths, while the witnesses for the
defence were, under the pretext of cross-examination,
insulted and abused in a manner which the roughest
practitioner at the Old Bailey would not have ventured
to adopt. At length, when the trial was nearly over,
the Marquis Cornwallis, who had succeeded Hastings
in the Government of India, returned home. No
further testimony perhaps was needed. Indeed, the

evidence on both sides was closed—but the opinion of so great and respectable an authority, as to the estimation in which Mr. Hastings was held in India, could not be excluded. The Marquis stated, that during the seven years of his administration in India, he had been personally acquainted with the provinces which were the scenes of the alleged outrages and crimes; that the charges against the prisoner, which were matters of notoriety, were not, in a single instance, corroborated by the natives; and that the late Governor-General, so far from having brought discredit upon the English name, had conferred a far greater amount of happiness, protection, and security, upon the people under his rule, than they had ever enjoyed under the dominion of their native princes. The story of the Begums he declared to be a gross perversion of the truth; and he denied that the princesses of Oude, who were notoriously hostile to the British Government, had ever been subjected to extortion of any kind. He asserted, in fine, that the name of Hastings was respected and esteemed throughout the whole of British India.

The wealth which he was presumed to have amassed by bribery and plunder, pointed many an eloquent invective against Hastings from the managers' box. The topic was a plausible one. Clive, who had left his father's parsonage for the desk of a factory at Fort George, returned to England in a few years, to invest his millions in the purchase of manors, palaces, and boroughs. The Governor-General of India had not fewer opportunities of enriching himself than the fortunate military adventurer. But Hastings, after ruling vast provinces with despotic sway for twelve years, returned to his native country with a private fortune of sixty-five thousand pounds; and would have been content, had the malice of his enemies permitted him, to enjoy this modest competence in dignified retirement.

Bribery and plunder attributed to Clive.

The liberality, or rather the gratitude, of the great Company did not suffer the most eminent of their servants to linger out his days in the penury to which the justice of his country had consigned him. The costs of his trial were defrayed, and an annuity of four thousand pounds was granted to him for a term of years equivalent to his life. It was intended that he should have been raised to the peerage; the design was frustrated by the scruples of the Court; but he was subsequently made a Privy Councillor.

Hastings, after his trial, withdrew to Daylesford, *Retirement of Hastings.* the ancient seat of his family in Worcestershire, where he passed the remainder of his life, which was protracted to an advanced age. In 1813, when he was in his eighty-first year, the ancient Governor-General was summoned to the bar of the House of Commons, to give evidence on the Bill for the renewal of the East India Company's Charter. When the old man was announced, the whole House rose and uncovered,—a mark of respect which is never paid but to the most rare and exalted merit. In 1815, on the occasion of the visit of the Allied Sovereigns, Hastings received an honorary degree from the University of Oxford, and was received by the students with plaudits far warmer than those which greeted the crowned heads. After his death, in 1818, the East India Company erected a statue to the memory of their great servant in the Town Hall of Calcutta.

Before the impeachment had completed its final stage, a Committee of the Commons was appointed to search the Lords' Journal, and report on the progress of the trial. The report drawn up by Burke, comprised a general review of the proceedings, with many unfair and indecent strictures, not only on the conduct of the defence, but even on the judicial decisions of the Great Court itself. The publication of this document, in the form of a pamphlet, afforded an opportunity to Lord Thurlow to stigmatise it, in his place, in terms not more severe than just, as a libel which ought not to go unpunished. But all interest in the subject had long expired; and the lords did not think it necessary to vindicate their conduct, which only one person in the kingdom was disposed to impugn. Burke made a long reply to Thurlow the next day, but nobody listened to him. In the last week of the session, when most of the members had left town, Pitt, according to precedent, moved a formal vote of thanks to the managers. Even this was opposed, on the ground of the violent and intemperate manner with which the impeachment had been conducted. A few languid remarks were made by some of the managers, and the motion was carried by a small majority of the thinnest House that had divided during the session.

With the impeachment of Warren Hastings, the public life of its great author was brought to a close. On the day following the vote of thanks, a new writ was moved for the borough of Malton, in the room of the Right Honourable Edmund Burke, without a word of preface or comment.

END OF THE THIRD VOLUME.

ONE-VOLUME EDITIONS OF MR. G. J. WHYTE MELVILLE'S NOVELS.

New Edition, price 5s. complete in One Volume, crown 8vo. with Frontispiece engraved on Steel by H. ADLARD, copied by permission from GÉRÔME's Picture—

Ave Cæsar Imperator! morituri te salutant!

THE GLADIATORS:

A Tale of Rome and Judea.

By J. G. WHYTE MELVILLE.

OPINIONS OF THE PRESS.

'The Author's greatest skill is shown in the selection of his characters. The school or Family of Gladiators in the centre round which the plot mainly revolves; and with them Mr. MELVILLE is thoroughly at home. The distinctness with which he has set these people before us amounts to a positive service to classical literature. Their habits, tastes, and personal appearance, their peculiar position in society, the mingled respect and contempt excited by them, their ready instrumentality to any deed of political violence, are set forth with a clearness which invests with a living reality an important and peculiar class of persons who have hitherto been to most readers of Roman history little more than a name. The terrible sports of the amphitheatre are depicted with a vividness which owes some of its power to the personal interest we have been made to feel in the actors.... A book, prepared with so much care, dealing with such great events, and abounding in brilliant scenes and striking situations, well deserves a careful perusal.'
GUARDIAN.

'A strong interest is infused into the *Gladiators* by the glimpses it gives us of the Infant Christian Church.... The result is a book which clothes the dry bones of history with forms of beauty and strength, and animates them with the various movements and passions of humanity.'
DAILY NEWS.

'The novel is clever, it is even brilliant, it is written with a warm and vigorous eloquence, and the reader is carried on from scene to scene, and crisis to crisis, amused, interested, excited. If he takes up the book, he will read on to the end of the third volume and the destruction of the Temple.'
The TIMES.

'Mr. WHYTE MELVILLE's touch is vigorous and sharp, his power of exciting dramatic interest as conspicuous in the *Gladiators* as in his domestic novels, his power of bringing before us in picturesque delineation the world of old Rome, with all it had of repulsion and attraction, not surpassed by either of the distinguished predecessors with whom we have compared him.'
FRASER's MAGAZINE.

New and Cheaper One-Volume Editions of Works by the same Author.

DIGBY GRAND, an Autobiography, 5s.
KATE COVENTRY, an Autobiography, 5s.
GENERAL BOUNCE, or the Lady and the Locusts, 5s.
The INTERPRETER, a Tale of the War, 5s.
HOLMBY HOUSE, a Tale of Old Northamptonshire, 5s.
GOOD for NOTHING, or All Down Hill, 6s.
The QUEEN'S MARIES, a Romance of Holyrood, 6s.

London: LONGMANS, GREEN, and CO. Paternoster Row.

WORKS BY LORD MACAULAY.

SPEECHES of Lord MACAULAY (as the Right Hon.
T. B. MACAULAY, M.P.) corrected by HIMSELF.
LIBRARY EDITION, revised, 1 vol. 8vo. 12s.
PEOPLE'S EDITION, in course of publication, in 2 Monthly Parts, price One Shilling each, forming One Volume, crown 8vo.

MISCELLANEOUS WRITINGS of Lord MACAULAY, viz. Contributions to Knight's *Quarterly Magazine*, Articles from the *Edinburgh Review* not included in his *Critical and Historical Essays*, Biographies from the *Encyclopædia Britannica*, Miscellaneous Poems and Inscriptions.
LIBRARY EDITION, with Portrait, 2 vols. 8vo. 21s.
PEOPLE'S EDITION, complete in One Volume, crown 8vo. price 4s. 6d. cloth; to be had also in 4 Parts, price One Shilling each.

LORD MACAULAY'S LAYS of ANCIENT ROME, with IVRY and the ARMADA. Revised Edition with a Vignette from a Design by G. SCHARF, F.S.A..... 16mo. 4s. 6d. cloth; mor. by RIVIERE, 10s. 6d.

LAYS of ANCIENT ROME. By the Right Hon. Lord MACAULAY. With Woodcut Illustrations, original and from the Antique, by GEORGE SCHARF, F.S.A. Fcp. 4to. 21s.; morocco, by RIVIERE, 42s.

LIST of Fourteen of LORD MACAULAY'S ESSAYS, which may be had separately, in 16mo. In the TRAVELLER'S LIBRARY:

Warren Hastings .... 1s.	Lord Byron; and the Comic Dramatists
Lord Clive .... 1s.	of the Restoration .... 1s.
William Pitt; and the Earl of Chatham 1s.	Frederick the Great .... 1s.
Ranke's History of the Popes; and Gladstone on Church and State .... 1s.	Hallam's Constitutional History of England .... 1s.
Life and Writings of Addison; and Horace Walpole .... 1s.	Croker's Edition of Boswell's Life of Johnson .... 1s.
Lord Bacon .... 1s.	

LORD MACAULAY'S CRITICAL and HISTORICAL ESSAYS contributed to the *Edinburgh Review*. People's Edition, complete in 2 vols. crown 8vo. price 8s. cloth; or in 7 Parts, price One Shilling each.

LORD MACAULAY'S CRITICAL and HISTORICAL ESSAYS contributed to the *Edinburgh Review*. Cabinet Edition, in Volumes for the Pocket. .... 3 vols. fcp. 8vo. price 21s.

LORD MACAULAY'S CRITICAL and HISTORICAL ESSAYS. Traveller's Edition, complete in One Volume, with Portrait and Vignette................... Square crown 8vo. 21s. cloth; calf. by RIVIERE, 30s.

CRITICAL and HISTORICAL ESSAYS contributed to the *Edinburgh Review*. By the Right Hon. Lord MACAULAY. Library Edition, being the Twelfth .... 3 vols. 8vo. 36s.

THE HISTORY of ENGLAND from the Accession of James the Second. By the Right Hon. Lord MACAULAY.
LIBRARY EDITION, with Portrait and brief Memoir, 5 vols. 8vo. £4 cloth; or £5 15s. 6d. bound in tree-calf by RIVIERE.
CABINET EDITION, with Portrait and brief Memoir, 8 vols. post 8vo. 48s. cloth; or £4 4s. bound in tree-calf by RIVIERE.
PEOPLE'S EDITION, with brief Memoir, 4 vols. crown 8vo. 16s. cloth; or Four Volumes in Two, price £1 4s. bound in tree-calf by RIVIERE; to be had also in Fourteen Parts, price One Shilling each.

LORD MACAULAY'S SPEECHES (as the Right Hon. T. B. MACAULAY, M.P.) on PARLIAMENTARY REFORM in 1831 and 1832. Reprinted in the TRAVELLER'S LIBRARY .... 16mo. 1s.

London: LONGMANS, GREEN, and CO. Paternoster Row.